Man Through the Ages

Boris Ryb

Kievan Rus

Progress Publishers

Moscow

Translated from the Russian by *Sergei Sossinsky*
Designed by *Vadim Novikov*

Борис Рыбаков
КИЕВСКАЯ РУСЬ

На английском языке

© Издательство «Молодая гвардия», 1984

English translation of the revised Russian text © Progress Publishers
1989

Printed in the Union of Soviet Socialist Republics

Р $\frac{0503020100-467}{014(01)-89}$ 27—89

ISBN 5—01—001154—9

CONTENTS

Preface 5

THE BEGINNINGS OF RUS 9

"Whence Comes the Russian Land?" 9
    Origin and the Earlier History of the Slavs 19
    The Origins of Rus 35
The Rise of the State of Rus 42
Early Rus (9th to mid-10th centuries) 81
    Polyudye 81
    The Sale of Polyudye 100
The State Grows Stronger 119

THE GOLDEN AGE OF KIEVAN RUS 153

Vladimir the Red Sun 153
Yaroslav the Wise and His Sons 168
    The Feudal Castle of the 11th-12th Centuries . . . 181
    Popular Masses. Smerds and Craftsmen 191
    The Uprising of 1068 in Kiev 199
Quarrels and Unity (Late 11th and Early 12th Centuries) . . 207
    Princes "of Woe" and the Kievan Uprising of 1113 . . . 207
    Vladimir Monomakh, Prince of the Boyars *(1053-1113-1125)* 219

THE RISE OF INDEPENDENT PRINCIPALITIES . . . 243

Sovereign Feudal Lands 243
    Sources 259
South-Russian Principalities in the 12th and Early 13th
    Centuries 262
    Kievan Principality 262
    Chernigov and Seversky Principalities 273
    Galich-Volyn Lands 282

North-Russian Principalities in the 12th and Early 13th Centuries	295
Polotsk Principality	295
Smolensk Principality	298
Novgorod the Great	302
Vladimir-Suzdal Principality	319
THE CULTURE OF RUS IN THE 9TH-13TH CENTURIES	335
Chronological Table	384

Preface

Kievan Rus* of the 9th-12th centuries was, first of all, the birthplace of the body politic of the Russians, the Ukrainians and the Byelorussians and, second, a major power in Medieval Europe playing an important historical role in the fate of peoples and states in the West, the Orient and the Far North.

From a relatively small alliance of Slav tribes inhabiting the middle reaches of the Dnepr (the origins of that alliance go back to the times of Herodotus) Rus developed into an enormous power uniting all East Slavic tribes, certain Lithuanian and Lettish tribes on the Baltic and numerous Finno-Ugric tribes in northeastern Europe.

The rise of the Russian state did not entail the driving back or elimination of the forest tribes encountered by the Kiev princes' warriors during their expeditions to collect tribute: Lithuanians and Karelians, Mordvinians and Letts, Estonians and Chuvashes are all equal members of the Soviet Union, and all of them had been involved in the momentous process of initial feudalisation in the system of Kievan Rus.

The young state of Rus emerging in the early 9th century became known very soon in all parts of the Old World: English, Norwegian and French kings sought to establish matrimonial relations with the Grand Princes of Kiev; the Byzantine Empire was Rus' long-standing trade contractor, and in the Orient Russian merchants sailed the length of the Khorezm (Caspian) Sea and reached Baghdad and Balkh (modern Afghanistan) travelling with camel caravans.

---

* The original name of what eventually came to be known as Russia.— *Ed.*

Swedish adventure-seekers, the Varangians, sought to make their way into Rus and join Russian overseas expeditions or enter the service of a Kiev prince.

In his immortal historical work *The Tale of Bygone Years* the Russian chronicler Nestor displayed extensive knowledge of the world in his time from Britain in the West to China in the East, mentioning Indian Brahmans and distant Indonesia "on the edge of the world".

The people of Kievan Rus quickly attained mastery of Byzantine and West European culture, and Russian towns were co-founders of a European-wide Romanesque artistic style.

The boundless Russian state had matured by the mid-12th century to a point when about fifteen independent principalities were formed, each equal in size to a major West European kingdom. The process may be compared to the evolution of a large family in which the sons have grown up and become ready for an independent life at a certain point. Kiev remained nominally the "mother of Russian towns", as it was called by the chroniclers, but, on a par with it, capital cities arose, such as Chernigov, Vladimir-Volynsky, Galich, Novgorod, Smolensk, Vladimir-Suzdal, Rostov, Polotsk, Ryazan, and Turov.

The crafts developed in the towns, artistic and literary schools were founded, excellent buildings were erected with such skill that, after existing for 700-800 years and having withstood the test of time, they entered our Soviet age as specimens of ancient architecture with a romantic tinge of olden times.

The Russian lands were at the same level as the advanced European countries by the beginning of the 13th century, and only their conquest by the Golden Horde and long-term foreign oppression relegated Russia to the background and held its development back for two or three centuries.

Our ancestors had already realised the importance and necessity of studying Kievan Rus as the first state which united dozens of tribes and ethnic groups and raised them from primitive life to a highly organised feudal power: *The Tale of Bygone Years* written by Nestor in the early 12th century was copied by scribes for over 500 years. The literate part of tsarist Russia studied, and knew very well, the history of dynasties of princes, wars waged by princes, the activities of bishops and patriarchs, tsarist laws and rulings. But did the illiterate people know about the existence a thousand years earlier of a certain Kievan Rus?

Exiled by the tsarist government in 1860 to the North, P. N. Rybnikov made a discovery of world import equal to the discovery of the Icelandic sagas or the Finno-Karelian *Kalevala*: he found that the memories of living people still retained poetic tales about the deeds and exploits of people in Kievan Rus in the far northern outskirts of Russia near Archangel, along the Northern Dvina and on the coast of the Arctic Ocean. The illiterate story-tellers carefully passed from one generation to the next the *bylinas*, solemn as hymns in form, about Prince Vladimir the Red Sun, about the struggle against the Pechenegs and Polovtsi, about Dobrynya Nikitich and a peasant's son Ilya of Murom, about the courageous defence of their country, the valour and the magnanimity of the Russian *bogatyrs* (knights). The peasants and fishermen in the times of Dostoyevsky and Lev Tolstoy living far from Kiev and the South Russian steppes heard about the flourishing state of the 10th-11th centuries, its intricate and intense life when virgin lands were ploughed, travellers sailed overseas to foreign lands, straight roads were laid through primeval forests, and straight from the feasting hall people left to wage a life-and-death struggle against an enemy that appeared unexpectedly like the legendary Zmei Gorynych of Russian folk tales.

The memory of the common folk that has passed down to our day in the oral tradition, the *bylinas*, about the most important events of Kievan Rus prompts us to study the glorious epic past of our country to the full extent and variety of the historical sources available to us.

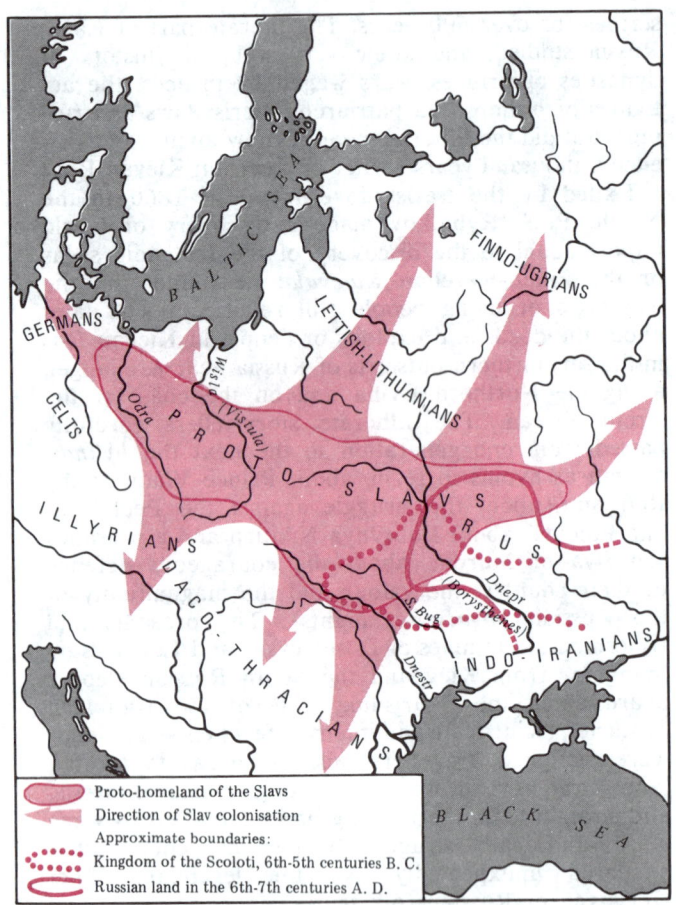

Ancient Destinies of the Slavs

THE BEGINNINGS OF RUS

"Whence Comes the Russian Land?"

Kievan Rus of the 9th-12th centuries was an enormous feudal state stretching from the Baltic to the Black Sea and from the Western Bug to the Volga River. It was known to the entire contemporary world: the kings of England, France, Hungary and Sweden established bonds of kinship with the princes of Kiev; the Byzantine Emperor Constantine Porphyrogenitus wrote a treatise *About the Rus Who Come to Constantinople from Russia*; geographers in the countries of the Arab Caliphate questioned captains and caravan-bashaws about distant Kiev and wrote down valuable facts about the Rus country, roads leading to it and its towns in their books about world geography.

The Age of Kievan Rus was a turning point almost for all the peoples in Eastern Europe. For many centuries class society was geographically restricted to a narrow strip along the Black Sea where Greek poleis—Olviopol, Khersones, Bosporus, Tanais, Phanagoria and others—were founded after the expedition of the argonauts described in the myths. To the north of this strip lay the boundless steppes and endless forests populated by hundreds of different tribes still living at the stage of barbarian primitive society. No wonder Cicero said that the towns of the ancient world were only a decorative hem on the barbarian robe. To carry the metaphor further, the times of Kievan Rus, which took shape a thousand years after Cicero, saw barbarian Europe cast off its old clothes and don a new apparel in which the hem of civilisation was much broader.

Kievan Rus was preceded by thousands of years of slow life led by isolated Slav, Finno-Ugric, Lettish and Lithuanian tribes gradually and imperceptibly improving their economy and social structure on the vast forest steppes and forests of Eastern Europe.

In the 12th century Kievan Rus achieved a level in its development enabling it, with time, to found about fifteen independent sovereign feudal states similar to the West European kingdoms. The largest among the former included the Vladimir, Ryazan, Kiev, Chernigov, Smolensk, Galician-Volynian, Polotsk principalities and the feudal republics of Novgorod and Pskov. Even a mere listing of these new states of the 12th-14th centuries revives in our memory brilliant pages from the history of Russian culture: the Kiev chronicle and *The Lay of Igor's Host*, the Vladimir and Suzdal white stone architecture with carved ornamentation, the Novgorod birchbark scrolls and the treasures of the St Sofia. Batu Khan's invasion and the Horde's yoke destroyed the vitality of early Russian culture and undermined the unity of the ancient Russian people, but successes achieved in the Age of Kievan Rus enabled the country to preserve the sound foundations of culture and overcome the consequences of the conquest.

The historical importance of Kievan Rus is attested to by the fact that the chronicle of the life of the Kievan state written by several generations of chroniclers and completed by the famous Nestor was copied in Russian towns during five centuries! In the gruelling times of foreign oppression, *The Tale of Bygone Years* was not only a recollection of former might and power but also an example of state unity and patriotic resistance along the thousand-kilometre boundary against the warring steppe tribes.

At the end of the 15th century, when dozens of Russian principalities were overcoming feudal division and uniting round Moscow, the Grand Prince of Moscow Ivan III introduced the ceremony of enthronement and ordered the making of the Cap of Monomakh, the new crown of the Russian tsardom intended to revive the memory of Kievan Rus, the highest point of that state in the reign of the Kiev Prince Vladimir Vsevolodich, the grandson of the Byzantine Emperor Constantine Monomakh. Half a century later the Tsar of All Russia Ivan the Terrible recalled the historical ties with Kievan Rus once again: the tsar's throne in the Cathedral of the Assumption in Moscow was placed under a carved tent for which the architect had made a bas-relief showing the deeds of Vladimir Monomakh. But apparently the chief proof of the vital bond with Kievan Rus was provided by the Russian epic folk tales, the *bylinas*.

In the mid-19th century, in the remote north of the Archangel province researchers discovered reciters of old epic hymns who knew through the oral tradition both Vladimir Svyatoslavich (980-1015) and Vladimir Monomakh (1113-1125) whom they brought together in the generalised epic image of the Gentle Prince Volodimir the Red Sun of Kiev. The *bogatyr bylinas* know the princes who defended the people from the Pecheneg and the Polovtsi raids and "spared no efforts for the sake of the Russian land". Many other princes lauded by the court chroniclers were not retained in the popular memory. The *bylinas* do not mention the name of Svyatoslav who was reprehended by the Kievans for "seeking foreign lands while scorning his own"; do not describe Yaroslav the Wise, instigator of internal strife who hired the ferocious Varangians to fight his own father; Yuri Dolgoruky who stormed Kiev in his fight against his nephews and the other princes who ignored common Russian interests in the heat of bloody internal quarrels. The author of the first Marxist study of Kievan Rus, historian B. D. Grekov, aptly called the *bylinas* an oral textbook of the country's history. This textbook not only describes the past but also selects the most important, progressive events and sings praise to the heroes symbolising the building of the state and Russia's defence from the foreign enemy.

Thousands of kilometres from Kiev peasants of tsarist Russia knew about Kievan Rus and passed down from one generation to another the solemn hymn-like *bylinas* about Ilya of Murom, Dobrynya Nikitich and events in Russia a thousand years before.

Academic study of Kievan Rus was not distinguished by such integrity and logic as was the popular memory of those distant times. 17th- and 18th-century historians sought to link the history of the Slavs with the destinies of other peoples who once inhabited the southern part of Eastern Europe, but they did not have sufficient data to outline the history of the Scythians, Sarmatians and other peoples mentioned in passing by authors available to the first historiographers. As to the origin of the Slavs, historians had to do with medieval ideas derived from the Bible: all peoples originated from the seventy-two languages which appeared when, angry at the people, God destroyed the Tower of Babel and divided the people building it into different nations.

During the *Bironovshchina**, when it was quite difficult to defend anything Russian, the idea that the Slavs had borrowed their statehood from North German tribes emerged among scholars invited from the German lands to St Petersburg. The Slavs were described as living like beasts (an expression of the chronicler) in the 9th and 10th centuries, and the northern robber bands of Varangians-Normans who entered the service of various rulers and terrorised Northern Europe were presented as the builders and founders of the state. Thus, there appeared in the writings of Siegfried Bayer, Gerhard Müller and August Schlözer the idea of Normanism frequently called the Normanist theory, although the sum total of Normanist assumptions in the course of two centuries is insufficient not only to call Normanism a theory but even a hypothesis, because it offers no analysis of sources or review of all known facts. As an explanation of the origin of the Russian state Normanism emerged on the basis of a frankly a priori approach and bias, referring to individual facts taken out of historical perspective and ignoring everything that contradicted the a priori idea. More than a hundred years ago Stepan Gedeonov published his monumental work *The Varangians and Rus* which showed the complete inconsistency and bias of the Normanist theory, but Normanism continued to exist and flourish with the connivance of the Russian intelligentsia fond of self-abasement. The opponents of Normanism were fully identified with the Slavo-

---

* *Bironovshchina* — a reactionary regime associated with the name of Count Ernst Johann Biron, a favourite of Empress Anna (1730-1740).— *Ed.*

philes* so that all the latter's mistakes and naive understanding of reality were attributed to the former.

In Bismarck's Germany Normanism was the only trend acknowledged as truly scientific. During the 20th century Normanism increasingly revealed its political implications, being used as an anti-Russian and subsequently also anti-Marxist doctrine. A significant fact: at the international congress of historians in Stockholm (the capital of the former Varangian land) in 1960 the leader of the Normanists, Adolf Stender-Petersen, said in his speech that Normanism as a scientific construction had died, because all its arguments had been disproved and rejected. But instead of undertaking an objective study of the prehistory of Kievan Rus, the Danish scholar urged historians to create a neo-Normanism.

Normanism's basic assumptions emerged at a time when science in Germany and Russia was in its infancy and historians had a very vague idea of the complex age-long process of the rise of the state. The scholars knew nothing about the system of the Slav economy or the long evolution of social relations. "Export" of statehood from another country by means of two or three bellicose groups seemed at the time a natural way for the state to emerge.

Let us consider a few contradictions between the facts and the constructions of the Normanists.

1. In speaking of the founding of Kievan Rus by the Normans-Varangians, a parallel is usually drawn with the setting up by the Normans of kingdoms along the seashore in North France, Lombardy, and Sicily. The Normans (Swedes, Danes and Norwegians) were excellent seafarers and did conquer the coastal population, but one glance at a map of Europe is sufficient to realise the complete difference in the situation in the oceanic and Mediterranean lands and on the Great Russian Plain.

The northern navies took advantage of the element of surprise in attacking from the sea and of the result-

---

* A trend in Russian social thinking in the mid-19th century; its advocates favoured a development road for Russia which differed fundamentally from the West European way.— *Ed.*

ing temporary numerical superiority over the inhabitants of the coastal towns.

In the East, however, to reach the Slav lands, the Varangians had to enter the Gulf of Finland where the fleets could be easily spotted from the shore (confirmed by the chronicle for 1240) and then travel five hundred kilometres along rivers and lakes against the current of the Neva, Volkhov and Lovat. There was no question of a surprise attack.

Along the entire route, the Norman ships could be shot at by the local inhabitants from both banks. At the end of the route, the seafarers were faced by the dual obstacle of the Baltic-Ladoga and Baltic-Black Sea watersheds. The ships had to be dragged over dry land, using logs, up to the ridge of the watershed, over a distance of 30 to 40 kilometres. The victorious seafarers at this point became helpless and unprotected. Only having dragged their ships to Smolensk did they reach a direct route to Kiev (500 more kilometres away), but here, on the Dnepr, they were also easily identified and vulnerable to attack.

The Varangians appeared in Eastern Europe when the Kievan state had already arisen, and for their trading expeditions to the East, they used a roundabout way via the Msta, Sheksna and Upper Volga River, skirting the domains of Kievan Rus from the northeast. Stores of coins and burial-mounds of the Varangians are known along this roundabout route.

2. The area actually reached by the groups of Varangians-Swedes in the Slav and Finnish lands is limited to three northern lakes: Chudskoye, Ilmen and Beloozero.

The clashes with the local population had varying outcomes: at times the Varangian newcomers from over the seas managed to make the Slavs and the Chud pay tribute, on other occasions the local tribes expelled the Varangians, refusing to pay tribute. Only once during the Middle Ages did the leader of a Varangian force together with North Slavs succeed in seizing power in Kiev. That leader, Oleg, proclaimed to be the founder and builder of the Rus state (his warriors came to be called Rus only after they came to Kiev), is known for certain to us only from the expedition against Byzantium in 907 and the supplementary treaty of 911. Besides the Varangians, warriors of nine Slav and two Finno-Ugric (Mari and Estonian) tribes took part in the successful expedition.

Oleg's behaviour after obtaining the indemnity from the Greeks was strange to say the least and hardly becoming the builder of a great power — he simply disappeared from the Russian scene: immediately following the expedition "Oleg went to Novgorod and from there to Ladoga. Others say that he travelled beyond the seas and a snake bit him in the leg and he died from the bite." Two hundred years later Oleg's grave was supposed to be near Kiev or in Ladoga. This alleged founder of the state left no descendents in Russia.

3. The Varangians were used in Russia in the 10th and 11th centuries as mercenaries. Prince Igor in 942 "sent beyond the sea for the Varangians inviting them to make war against the Greeks". Svyatoslav and his son Vladimir hired Varangians. When the hirelings presented Vladimir with especially impudent demands in 980, the prince sent them away from Russia, warning the Byzantine Emperor: do not keep Varangians in your city, so they don't engage in mischief as it was here; disperse them, and don't let a single one come here (to Rus).

The Varangians were hired to commit the most base murders: they stabbed Prince Yaropolk in the town of Roden; Varangians killed Prince Gleb. It was against the mischief-making of the hired Varangians in Novgorod that the Russkaya Pravda* was aimed; it put the Varangian wrongdoer in an unequal position with the injured local person of Novgorod: the court took the local person's testimony at face value, while the foreigner had to confirm his words by bringing two witnesses.

4. Should the Varangians be acknowledged as the founders of a state for Slavs "living like beasts", it would be extremely difficult to explain why the state language of Rus was Russian and not Swedish. The

---

* A code of ancient Russian feudal law.— *Ed.*

treaties with Byzantium in the 10th century were signed by an embassy of the Kievan Prince, and although the embassy also included Varangians in the Russian service, the text was written in two languages—Greek and Russian—without a trace of Swedish terms. Moreover, Swedish medieval documents denoted the levying of tribute by a word borrowed by the Varangians from Russian — *polyudye* (poluta),* which undoubtedly attests to the fact that the levying of tribute, an action characteristic of the early state, existed among the Slavs before it did among the Varangians.

Now, as to Slavs living like beasts, chronicler Nestor who lived in the time of Monomakh was referring not to his contemporaries, but to the Slavs of a considerably earlier time (before the Khazar invasion in the 7th century), and described not all the Slavs but only the forest tribes which did retain many primitive elements in their way of life. The chronicler opposed these forestmen to the "wise and sharp-witted Polyanians" who were the real founders of their state.

5. Considering the biassed arguments of the Normanists, it should be kept in mind that the bias appeared in our own sources going back to Nestor's *The Tale of Bygone Years*.

As the excellent connoisseur of Russian chronicles A. A. Shakhmatov** proved in his time, Nestor's historical work (circa 1113) underwent two revisions, and both were done by persons hostile to Nestor. In order to correctly understand the spirit of the revisions, we must gain an idea of the situation in Kiev at the turn of the 12th century.

Grand Prince Vsevolod, the youngest son of Yaroslav the Wise, died in 1093. In the last years of his reign, Rus was in effect ruled by the son of the ailing Vsevolod, Vladimir Monomakh. A fine military leader, wise ruler and educated writer, Monomakh hoped to retain the Kiev throne in his hands after his father's death, but the Kiev *boyars*, displeased that Vladimir relied on his

---

* *Polyudye*—rounds made by a prince to collect tribute among the population.— *Ed.*

** A. A. Shakhmatov (1864-1920), Russian philologist and member of St Petersburg Academy of Sciences.— *Ed.*

own entourage and warriors, invited a member of the older branch of Yaroslav's children, Prince Svyatopolk Izyaslavich. There began a twenty-year-long rivalry between two cousins—Svyatopolk and Vladimir. Nestor was Svyatopolk's court chronicler and wrote in the Kiev-Pechersky Monastery.

When Svyatopolk died in 1113 the Kiev *boyars*, at the height of a popular uprising, invited (contrary to dynastic seniority) Vladimir Monomakh to the Grand Throne of Kiev. Once elected as Grand Prince of Kiev, Monomakh decided to deal with Nestor's state chronicle; it was removed from the Pechersky Monastery and taken to Vladimir Monomakh's court monastery, the Vydubitsky Cloister where Father-Superior Sylvester undertook to revise it, leaving his entry in the chronicle under the year 1116.

Apparently the revision did not satisfy Monomakh, and he assigned his oldest son Mstislav, as Shakhmatov justly believed, to apply the finishing touches to the history of Rus, a task that was completed in approximately 1118.

The revision of Nestor's work was carried out along two lines: first, the relatively contemporary part of the chronicle describing Svyatopolk's deed and the events of the latest decades was edited in the spirit of Monomakh, and second, the historical introduction to the chronicle was significantly altered. Nestor lived in Kiev and based his study on questions having to do with the Slav south (Kiev and the area along the Dnepr inhabited by the Polyanian Russians), going back to the 5th-6th centuries A. D. His last and most resolute editor was Prince Mstislav, grandson of the King of England and son-in-law of the Swedish King, brought up from his younger years by the Novgorod *boyars* (and married the second time to a Novgorod *boyar*'s daughter). The epic legends on the invitation of princes, applied to the history of various northern kingdoms, were a familiar subject for Mstislav. He regarded Novgorod and the Varangian North as a natural environment and the Kiev *boyars* who refused to accept his father for twenty years as a hostile force.

Revising Russian history in his own way, Prince Mstislav artificially pushed Novgorod to the forefront, relegating Kiev to the background, unjustifiably transferred the emergence of the Russian state far to the north and introduced Varangian conquerors and organisers into the narrative. In the legend about the voluntary appeal for help to the Varangians by the Slav and Finnish tribes in the North (at a time when tribes fought each other), one cannot help seeing a reflection of the events of 1113 when Mstislav's father Vladimir Monomakh was invited from another land to Kiev during an uprising and insurgency.

The Normanist editor distorted much of Nestor's text and introduced many crude insertions in dissonance with the original text. This resulted in genealogical confusion, and Prince Igor the Old (whom the author of the mid-11th century regarded as the founder of the Kiev dynasty) became Rurik's son brought to Kiev as a babe, although his alleged father had never actually been in that town. It was in this way that there appeared in the chronicle a suspicious list of Slav tribes Oleg allegedly conquered, a list with highly suspect chronology. It was thus that appeared the absurd identification of the Varangians with Rus, the sole meaning of which was that if the Varangians were found in the capital of Rus, Kiev, if they entered the Russian service, they were regarded as Rus, included among the people of the Russian power.

At the present time historical science can no longer be content with isolated phrases snatched from the sources and their arbitrary and biassed interpretation. It needs an extensive system based, first, on a careful analysis of all kinds of sources, and second, on a historical synthesis of all the data obtained; third, an incomparably larger chronological scope of study is required. While a primitive understanding of the rise of the state as a result of the determination of the warrior estate was in keeping with the dated part of the chronicle (which began the history of Rus with the 850s and 860s), Marxist-Leninist science requires knowledge of a thousand-year-long process of the maturing of the primitive communal system and its natural transition to class (slave-owning or feudal) relations regardless of the existence or absence of robber raids from outside.

Origin and the Earlier History of the Slavs

In their general form Normanist assumptions boil down to two theses: first, the Slav state was set up, in their opinion, not by Slavs but by European Varangians and second, the Slav state emerged not in the Kiev partly wooded steppe area in the South but in the Novgorod marshlands and unfertile lands in the North.

The fact that the first thesis is erroneous is proved above all by an analysis of written sources dating back to the 11th and 12th centuries and revelation of the bias along which *The Tale of Bygone Years* was edited (see A. A. Shakhmatov). In addition, the validity of the pro-Varangian trend may be checked by referring to the sum of materials relating to the long-term process of Slav primitive development leading to the rise of Kievan Rus.

The second thesis on the more progressive development of the North as compared to the South may easily be checked by the same objective materials on the evolution of the economy and social relations, rates of social development in different ecological conditions, and finally, specific links between different parts of the extensive Slav world with other peoples and states in ancient times.

Both checks require, to an equal extent, knowledge of the territory occupied by the Slav tribes in pre-state times, how and when the sphere of Slav settlement changed. Having established the above, we can refer to extensive archaeological materials outlining the general features, the local differences and level of the most advanced areas where the first Slav states would naturally emerge (and actually did).

In other words, the first question without solving which we cannot set about analysing the development of primitive society into class society is the question of the origin of the Slavs in its geographical and territorial aspects: where the "original Slavs" lived, what peoples were their neighbours, what the natural conditions were, along what lines the further settlement of the Slav tribes occurred and in what new conditions the Slav colonists found themselves?

The Slav peoples belong to the ancient Indo-European entity which included German, Baltic (Lithuanian-Lettish), Romance, Greek, Celtic, Iranian, Indian (Aryan) and other peoples even in ancient times spread over an enormous area from the Atlantic Ocean to the Indian Ocean and from the Arctic Ocean to the Mediterranean Sea. Four to five thousand years ago the Indo-Europeans still did not occupy all of Europe and had not yet settled Hindustan; the northeastern part of the Balkan Peninsula and Asia Minor were the approximate geometrical centre of the initial Indo-European massif. The tribes from which the proto-Slavs emerged by means of gradual consolidation lived almost at the edge of the Indo-European area north of the mountain barrier separating South Europe from North Europe, stretching from the Alps eastward and ending in the east with the Carpathians.

When we refer to the origin of a people, we come upon a whole number of assumptions, legends and hypotheses. Far removed in time, the slow process proceeded almost imperceptibly for us. Nevertheless, certain questions must be asked: first, did the people emerge as a result of one tribe from a relatively small area multiplying and settling other lands or through the convergence of related neighbouring tribes? The second question is: what general (in this case — general European) events could have stimulated the separation of a number of tribes from the overall Indo-European massif and their consolidation on a large scale?

The answer to the first question should be that the spontaneous integration of more or less related tribes was the chief force behind the process. But of course there was also natural growth, filiation of tribes, and colonisation of new areas. Filiation of tribes made the ethnic massif more compact, filled in the gaps between the former "mother" tribes and, of course, contributed to the strengthening of that massif, and it was not one tribe multiplying that created a people.

As to general European events, the situation was as follows: at the turn of the second millennium B. C., livestock grazing developed, and property and social inequality emerged in the northern half of Europe (from the Rhine to the Dnepr). Cattle becomes the symbol of wealth (in old Russian *skotnitsa*—a derivative from *skot*, cattle—means treasury), and the relative ease with which herds could be seized led to wars and inequality between tribes and their chieftains. Primitive equality was disrupted.

The discovery of copper and bronze led to trade between tribes enhancing the inner processes of differentiation. In archaeological terms this age was marked by a culture of spherical amphorae differing abruptly from earlier, more primitive cultures. The struggle for herds and pastures which began to be waged everywhere led to tribes of herdsmen (culture of cord pottery) settling widely not only in Central but also in Eastern Europe up to the middle reaches of the Volga River.

All this was occurring with tribes which were the ancestors of the Balts, Slavs and Germans. Settlement was carried out by separate independently acting tribes. The fact is attested to by the extraordinary motley livestock terminology in Eastern Europe.

At the time of settlement—the first half of the 2nd millennium—there was no Slav, German or Balt community; all the tribes mingled and changed neighbours in the process of slow movement.

The settlement process ended approximately in the 15th century B. C. The entire zone of European deciduous forests and partly wooded steppe was occupied by these Indo-European tribes which had formerly lived in different places. A new, settled way of life began, and land cultivation gradually came to the forefront in the economy. In the new geographical situation the new neighbours began to establish relations, bring tribal dialects closer together and create related languages on large areas for the first time: in the western part the language was called Germanic, in the middle part it was Slavonic and in the northeast Lettish-Lithuanian. The names of peoples appeared later and were not linked to this age of related tribes being consolidated around three different centres: western (Germanic), eastern (Balt) and middle (Slav).

The first place in the scientific discovery of the

Greek copperware of the age of Herodotus (5th century B. C.). Found in a sunken boat at the village of Peschanoye in Cherkassy Region

earliest destinies of the Slavs belongs to linguistics. Linguists have found that, first, the proto-Slav tribes emerged from among their neighbouring related Indo-European tribes about 4,000 to 3,500 years ago, at the beginning or in the middle of the 2nd millennium B. C. Second, according to language-based data, linguists have determined that the Germanics, Baltics, Iranians, Daco-Thracians, Illyrians, Italics and Celts were the Slavs' neighbours among Indo-European peoples. The third assumption of the linguists is particularly important: judging from the names of elements of the landscape common to all Slav peoples, the proto-Slavs lived in the zone of deciduous forests and

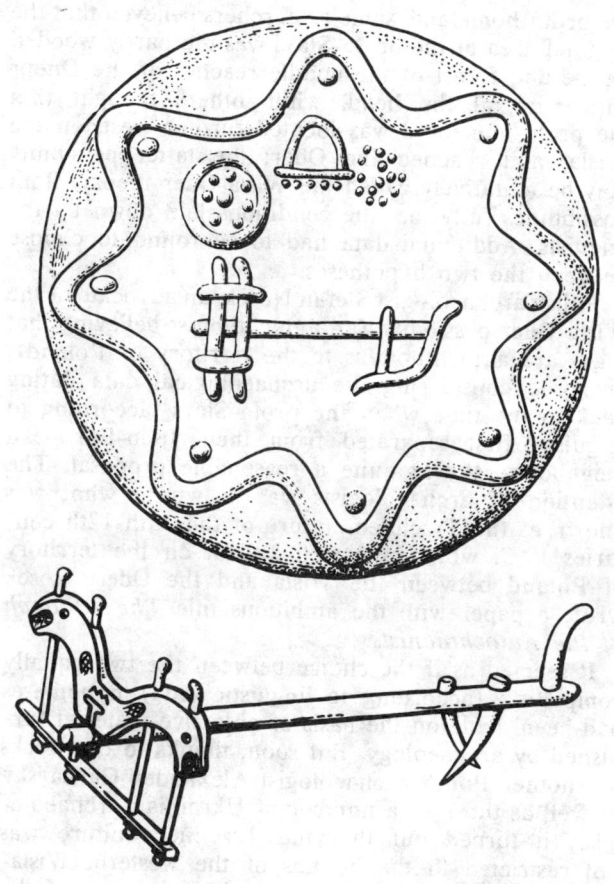

Archaic cult depiction of a plough on New Year's bread (above). Design of an Ukrainian plough (below). Drawings made according to ethnographic data

partly wooded steppe where there were clearings, lakes, swamps but no sea; where there were hills, gulleys and watersheds but no high mountains. However, the natural zones conforming to these linguistic definitions are larger than the supposed lands where the proto-Slavs lived in Europe; the proto-Slavs occupied only part of the area reflected in their ancient dialects.

Scientists now had two possibilities in determining

the proto-homeland: some researchers believed that the original area of the proto-Slavs was the partly wooded steppe and forest of the middle reaches of the Dnepr with Kiev at the head, while others thought that the proto-homeland was located further west, on the Wisla, and reached the Oder; the latter possibility may be tentatively called the Wisla-Oder theory. Both possibilities fully met the conditions laid down by the linguists. Additional data had to be found to choose between the two hypotheses.

Polish archaeologist Stefan Nosek, an advocate of the Wisla-Oder possibility (an autochthonist believing that Slavs are autochthonous to the territory of Poland), proposed considering the archaeological data dating back to the time when the proto-Slavs, according to linguists, first separated from their Indo-European neighbours. It was quite a reasonable proposal. The attention of archaeologists was drawn to what was known as the Trzciniec culture of the 15th-12th centuries B. C. which was well known on the territory of Poland between the Wisla and the Oder. Nosek wrote a paper with the ambitious title *The Triumph of the Autochthonists*.

It seemed as if the choice between the two equally compelling (according to linguistic data) hypotheses had been made on the basis of objective material furnished by archaeology. But soon, thanks to the works of another Polish archaeologist Alexander Gardavsky as well as those of a number of Ukrainian archaeologists, it turned out that the Trzciniec culture was not restricted to the bounds of the western, Wisla-Oder, hypothesis, but spread to the area east of the Wisla, reaching the Dnepr and partly extending to its left bank. Thus, the considering of archaeological material, sufficiently well studied as it was, settled the question in favour of the combining of both hypotheses.

The proto-homeland of the Slavs at the height of the Bronze Age was most probably located in a broad belt of land in Central and Eastern Europe. That belt stretched for about 400 kilometres from north to south and about 1,500 kilometres from west to east and was situated as follows: its western part was restricted in the south by the European mountains (Sudetes, Tatras, Carpathians) and almost reached the Baltic Sea in the north. The eastern half of the proto-Slav lands was bounded from the north by the Pripet and from the south by the upper reaches of the Dnestr and Southern Bug and the valley of the Ros River. The eastern boundary is less clear: the Trzciniec culture here included the middle reaches of the Dnepr and the lower reaches of the Desna and Seym.

The Slavs lived in small villages situated in two orders. The economy was founded on four branches: land cultivation, livestock breeding, fishing and hunting. The tools of labour—axes, knives, and sickles — were still made of stone. Bronze was used mostly for decorations and, among household implements, only for chisels needed in wooden building work.

The burial ritual was linked to the idea of reincarnation: the bodies of the dead were put in an embryonic position as if in preparation for rebirth. Social distinctions cannot be traced.

The richest area (it is sometimes singled out as a special Komarovo culture) were the lands near the Carpathians where there were deposits of salt, which was valued highly in the primitive age. Archaeological sites of the Trzciniec-Komarovo culture form several clusters which, perhaps, were the lands of allied neighbouring Slav tribes.

Slav alliances of tribes are known to us from Nestor; the tribes he mentions in his *Tale*, as Soviet researchers (P. N. Tretyakov) have shown, are not primary tribes but alliances of several anonymous tribes: Polyanians, Radimichians, Wislanie and others.

In the course of the 1st and 2nd millennia B. C. the ethnic map of Europe changed not only in connection with colonisation by Slavs or Celts, who moved from the west to the southeast, but also in view of the appearance of new centres of attraction. With respect to the massif of Slav tribes (before the colonisation to the northeast), the rise of two centres of attraction must be taken into account: one coincided with the basic territory of the former culture of spherical amphorae and involved part of the Slav, part of the Germanic, and part of the Celtic tribes, the other was situated outside the Slav proto-homeland, in the Scythian Black Sea area and included in the sphere of its influence only the southeastern part of the Slavs living in the fertile partly wooded steppe.

The new South-Baltic (in geographical position) community of various tribes is reflected archaeologically in what is known as the Lausits culture. Its core consisted of West Slav tribes (the territory of present-day Poland), but it also included the neighbouring Celts who were apparently the leaders in this large combination of tribes, and a certain part of the Germanic tribes along the Elbe.

It is quite possible that this community was at the time called *Veneti* or *Venedae*, which at first referred to a conglomerate of tribes speaking different languages and living dynamic common historical life, but subsequently (at the turn of the 1st millennium A. D.), when the Celtic and Germanic outlying tribes of the Lausits culture came into closer contact with their principal relatives, the name Veneti-Venedae was retained for the West Slav tribes. The ancient authors (Pliny, Tacitus) called the Slav tribes *Venedians*.

Let us take a closer look at what was happening in the eastern part of the Slav world. Even before the Scythians-Iranians appeared in the steppes of Eastern Europe, the local Slav population developed progressively here, at the edge of the steppe, in the partly wooded steppe zone convenient for land cultivation, defended from the inhabitants of the steppe by islands of forest, on the former territory of the Trzciniec proto-Slav culture. It was at the turn of the 1st millennium B. C. that ploughing appeared, abruptly promoting the economy and making it possible to export grain systematically to Greece through the Black Sea port of Olviopol in the 6th-5th centuries B. C.

What is called the Chernyi Les culture on the boundary between the Bronze and the Iron Age archaeologically conformed to the Middle Dnepr Slavs in the epoch of this upsurge. The Slav nature of that culture is proved indisputably in the works of the prominent

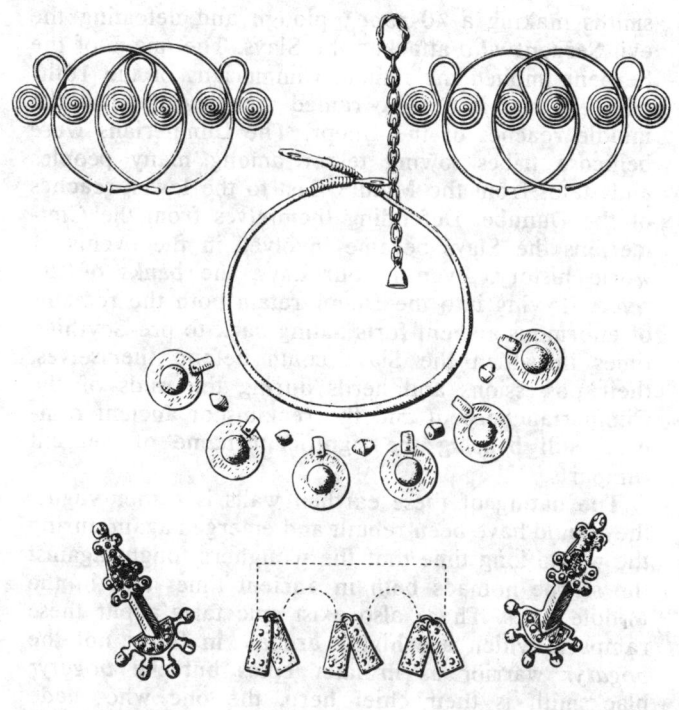

6th-century women's decorations found near the town of Sudzhi

Soviet linguist O. N. Trubachev: his map of archaic Slav names of rivers coincides in all its details with the area of the Chernyi Les culture.

The discovery of iron was the second, and most important, element of progress. Whereas in the Bronze Age tribes lacking copper and tin deposits were forced to bring the metal from afar, with the discovery of iron they grew extremely rich, since the swamp and lake ore used at the time was available in all the Slav lands with their numerous swamps, rivers and lakes. In effect, the Slavs passed into the Iron Age from the Stone Age.

It was a major turning point which was reflected in the ancient Slav epic about the *bogatyr* blacksmiths making a 40-*pood** plough and defeating the evil Serpent who attacked the Slavs. The image of the Serpent implied the nomad Cimmerians of the 10th-8th centuries B. C. who raided the Slav areas in the middle reaches of the Dnepr. The Cimmerians were bellicose tribes sowing terror among many peoples and states from the Middle East to the lower reaches of the Danube. Defending themselves from the Cimmerians the Slavs became involved in the events of world history. Even in our days, the banks of the rivers flowing into the Dnepr retain both the remains of enormous ancient forts dating back to pre-Scythian times in which the Slavs could defend themselves, their possessions and herds during the raids of the Cimmerian Serpent and the remains of ancient ramparts still bearing the significant name of Serpent ramparts.

The dating of these earthen walls is rather vague: they could have been rebuilt and emerged again during the whole long time that the ploughers fought against the steppe nomads both in ancient times and in the Middle Ages. There also exist epic tales about these ramparts which are highly archaic in form: not the *bogatyr* warrior as in later epics but the *bogatyr* blacksmith is their chief hero, the one who made the 40-pood plough and taught people to plough the land.

The legendary blacksmith did not smite the Serpent dead with his sword as the medieval *bogatyr* did but caught him in his pincers, harnessed him to the magical plough and made enormous furrows known as Serpent ramparts which reach "as far as Kiev".

The beginning of the 1st millennium B. C. should be regarded as the time when the Slav tribes along the middle reaches of the Dnepr started their historical existence, defended their independence, built the earliest forts, first encountered the hostile steppe Cimmerian horsemen and emerged with honour from these defensive battles. No wonder we can date back to this time the creation of primary forms of the Slav heroic

---

* *Pood* — measure of weight, 16 kilograms.— *Ed.*

epic which lived to the early 20th century (the last detailed recordings were made by Ukrainian folklore experts in 1927-1929).

By the time the Scythians appeared in the South Russian steppe in the 7th century B. C. the Slavs of the middle reaches of the Dnepr had gone a long way historically, which was reflected both in archaeological data and in myths, the heroic epics. The myths passed down in Russian, Byelorussian and Ukrainian folk tales (first written down by the Father of History, Herodotus, in the 5th century B. C.) tell about three kingdoms of which one was the Golden Kingdom, about the Sun Tsar (recall Vladimir the Red Sun) after whom all the people inhabiting these kingdoms were called.

What Herodotus tells us about Scythia is extremely important. That attentive author and traveller identified Scythia with an enormous, largely tentative area in Eastern Europe which he defined as a square the sides of which were equal to twenty days' travel (about 700 by 700 kilometres); the southern side of the square rested on the Black Sea.

The area was inhabited by various tribes speaking different languages, carrying on different economic activities and not submitting to one king or leading tribe. The Scythians proper after whom the tentative square was named were described by Herodotus as steppe livestock breeders roaming the area in carts, alien to land cultivation and without permanent settlements. They were opposed by the crop growers of the partly wooded steppe in the middle reaches of the Dnepr River who exported grain to Olviopol and every spring celebrated the holiday of the sacred plough the God of the Sky had given people. With respect to these Dnepr Borysthenes Herodotus makes the precious remark that the Greeks attributed them to the Scythians by mistake, while they called themselves *Scoloti*.

Three Scoloti kingdoms in the middle reaches of the Dnepr and the neighbouring partly wooded steppe (all of them were within the bounds of the ancient Slav proto-homeland) corresponded very well to the three basic groups discovered by Ukrainian archaeologists in the ancient artifacts of Scythian times. Archaeological finds explain the mistake made by Greek merchants who extended the general name of Scythians to the Slav Scoloti: there are many Scythian traits in the material culture of the Slav land-tillers ("Scythian ploughers"). The fact that this part of the Slavs were neighbours of the Scythian-Sarmatian Iranian world for a long time also influenced the language: there are many words of Scythian origin in the East Slavonic languages—*topor* (axe) instead of the Slavic *sekira, sobaka* (dog) instead of the Slav *pyos*—and so on.

The social system of the Slavs living in the middle reaches of the Dnepr was on the threshold of statehood one and a half thousand years before Kievan Rus. The fact is attested to not only by the reference in Herodotus to Scoloti kingdoms and kings but also by the knightly features of buried warriors, the enormous tsar burial mounds in the Kiev area, and the imported luxury of the Slav tribal chiefs.

Most probably the Slavs in the middle reaches of the Dnepr were on friendly terms with the tsar Scythians in the Black Sea area, which enabled them to trade with the seaside towns and borrow some of the mores from the nomad Scythians.

The Slavs can take pride in the fact that a corner of the Slav world in the middle reaches of the Dnepr was described by the Father of History, Herodotus, and apparently described on the basis of first-hand knowledge: he not only had seen the Slav Borysthenes in Olviopol but knew exactly the length of their lands (eleven days in a boat along the Dnepr), was familiar with the taste of the water in the upper reaches of streams, was acquainted with the fauna of the partly wooded steppe and wrote down the tales of three brothers and three kingdoms which have come down to our day in the *bogatyr* fairy-tales. He even wrote down the names of the mythical founding heroes who were also retained in East Slav folklore.

The Slavs of Scythian times were not uniform. While the forest and steppe Slav tribes of Dnepr Scoloti acquired many features of Scythian culture, next to them, in the forest zone on the northern outskirts of the Slav proto-homeland, adjacent to the

Balts (Lettish-Lithuanian tribes) there lived Herodotus's Nevrs (Milograd archaeological culture) lagging behind their southern neighbours the "Scythian ploughers" in many respects. The contrast between the way of life of the "well-ordered Polyanians" and their forest neighbours "living like beasts", noticed by Nestor, had emerged in Scythian times.

In the 3rd century B. C. the Scythian state in the steppe fell under the onslaught of the more primitive, also Iranian tribes of Sarmatians. The Scythians were divided in half by the new stream of nomads: some of them retreated south into the Crimea while others moved northwards into the partly wooded steppe where they were assimilated by the Slavs (perhaps this was the time when Scythian words appeared in the Slavonic language?).

The new masters of the steppe — the Sarmatians — behaved quite differently from the Scythians: whereas the Slavs lived with Scythian neighbours more or less peacefully for five hundred years and we have no evidence of serious hostile actions, the Sarmatians behaved aggressively. They intercepted trade routes, plundered Greek towns, attacked the Slavs and pushed the zone of crop-growing settlements northwards. Archaeologically the Slavs of Sarmatian times were characterised by what is known as the Zarubintsy culture of the 3rd century B. C., a quite primitive culture. Geographically it included not only the middle reaches of the Dnepr but also more northern areas of the forest zone colonised by the Slavs.

At the turn of the Christian era the Sarmatians spread terror throughout the thousand-kilometre Black Sea steppe. It is possible that the Sarmatian raids during which the land-tilling population was driven into captivity, were instigated by the Roman Empire which, in its very extensive conquests (from Scotland to Mesopotamia), needed large numbers of slaves for the most varied purposes — from ploughmen to rowers in the fleet.

The "wife-ruled" Sarmatians so called because of strong survivals of matriarchy among the Sarmatian nobility also left their trace in the Slav folklore as had the Cimmerians: the fairy-tales have preserved narrations about the Serpent Woman, about the Serpent's wives and sisters, and about the Baba Yaga (witch) that lived not in a forest hut on chicken legs but in an underground house near the sea, in the tropical sea land of the hostile "Maidens' Kingdom" where "Russian heads are displayed on poles".

The Sarmatian onslaught continuing for several centuries resulted in a decline of the Slav lands and the population moving northward from the partly wooded steppe to the forest zone. It was at this time that patronymic names of tribes such as Radimichians or Vyatichians appeared in the newly settled areas.

It was here, in the dense forests defended from invasion by impenetrable swampland, that new Slav tribal centres began to form. They left cemeteries with hundreds of tombs where bodies were buried according to the ritual of burning described in detail by Nestor.

We see newly built forts, such as Goroshkov on the Dnepr between the mouth of the Sozh and the Berezina, which might have been the tribal centres of the Dregovichians—the swampmen (*drygva* means swamp). The forts were situated directly after the wide strip of Pripet and Lower Desna marshes, north of them, totally inaccessible from the Sarmatian south in the land of the ancient Nevres.

The earliest references by ancient authors to the Slavs-Venedae date back to the first centuries A. D. Unfortunately, they provide very little information about the East Slavs blocked from view by the Sarmatians who had already reached the middle reaches of the Danube, and the forests in which the Slavs had hidden resettling outside their ancient proto-homeland.

A new and brilliant period in the history of the Slavs was linked both to the gradual overcoming of the results of Sarmatian raids and new events of European history in the first centuries A. D. A great deal in the history of the Old World was related at the time to the growing might of the Roman Empire. Rome exerted a strong influence on the Germanic tribes and part of the West Slav tribes along the Rhine, Elbe and Oder. The Roman legions seized Greek towns on the northern

Earthenware of the Chernyakhovo culture made on the potter's wheel. Middle reaches of the Dnepr, 2nd-4th centuries A. D.

shore of the Black Sea and used them as a market to buy local grain and fish.

Rome's relations with the peoples of Eastern Europe grew considerably in the reign of Emperor Marcus Ulpius Trajanus (98-117 A. D.) when the Romans conquered all of Dacia and forced its population to speak Latin. The Empire became the immediate neighbour of the Slav lands where, due to this proximity, export agriculture was revived again, this time on a large scale.

The scope of Slav export in the 2nd-4th centuries A. D. may be judged above all by the enormous number of finds of Roman coins in the land-cultivating Slav partly wooded steppe. The influx of Roman silver increased abruptly under Trajan, and the high level was sustained for several centuries. No wonder the author of *The Lay of Igor's Host* recalled Trajan's age when speaking of the bygone times of prosperity. The monetary wealth of the Slav nobility in the 2nd-4th centuries was obtained from the Romans in exchange for an equivalent amount of local grain which is proved by the Slavs' adoption of the Roman unit for measuring capacity: the Roman quadrantal under the name of *chetvert* used in measuring grain survived in Russia to 1924.

In Trajan's age the Slavs of the middle reaches of the Dnepr (the northern partly wooded steppe area of what is known as the Chernyakhovo archaeological culture) were experiencing a very marked upsurge. The crafts were developing, the potter's wheel appeared as well as furnaces for reducing iron ore and revolving millstones. The Slav nobility made wide use of imported luxury items: varnished earthenware, decorations, and various household goods. A situation was re-emerging similar to the one existing before the Sarmatian invasion in the epoch of the flourishing of the neighbouring Scythian state.

One of the trade centres on the Dnepr was the future site of the city of Kiev.

The routes to the south, to the Black Sea, were revived in connection with export agriculture. Roman road maps mentioned the Venedae in the lower reaches of the Danube, and in the mid-3rd century Roman sources frequently referred to naval expeditions in which "Scythians" took part on a par with the Goths (southern coastal part of the Chernyakhovo culture). The former were apparently the southeastern part of the Slavs.

In the social respect the Dnepr Slav tribes once again reached the pre-state level at which they were in Scythian times. The possibility is not to be excluded that in the 2nd-4th centuries, before the invasion by the Huns (about 375), a state system had emerged in the southern part of the territory of Eastern Slavs who occupied the same fertile partly wooded steppe areas where the "kingdoms" of the Scoloti land-tillers had been situated. This assumption is supported by such factors as the wealth of the Slav nobility based on export agriculture, the appearance of *ognishcha*, large houses for bondservants, unfortified villages possibly in view of the state-wide defence line, and the beginning of expeditions by fighting men far beyond the borders of their own lands.

In this part of the Slav world, which was closest to the centres of world culture the level of social development twice reached the line between primitive and class society long before Kievan Rus, and perhaps even passed that line. Further development was interrupted the first time by the Sarmatian invasion in the 3rd century B. C., the second by the invasion of the Turkic speaking Huns at the end of the 4th century A. D.

The Origins of Rus

The end of the 5th century and the first half of the 6th century A. D. saw three interrelated events which bore directly on Kievan Rus and which answer the questions Nestor put down in the title of *The Tale of Bygone Years:*

> From whence comes the Russian land,
> Who was the first prince to rule Kiev
> And how was the Russian state formed?

The most important event of the late 5th and mid-6th centuries was the beginning of the great migration of the Slavs to the south, beyond the Danube, to the Balkan Peninsula, when the Slav warriors conquered and settled in nearly half of the Byzantine Empire. The flow of colonists came from both the western half of the Slavs (Slovenians) and the eastern one (Antians). The tremendous large-scale movement of the Slavs towards and beyond the Danube changed the entire ethnic and political map of early medieval Europe and, in addition, considerably altered the historical process on the main Slav territory (the proto-homeland and the zone of early northern colonisation).

The second event, which was in line with the first, was the founding of Kiev on the Dnepr. The chronicle conveys the ancient legend about three brothers—Kii, Shchek and Khoriv—who built the town on the Dnepr in the land of the Polyanians in the name of the eldest brother Kii. That legend, dating back to times immemorial already in Nestor's lifetime (early 12th century), gave rise to doubt among the chroniclers of Novgorod, the town that rivalled Kiev in the 11th and 12th centuries, and they inserted the legend about Kii into the chronicle under the year 854. Such a late date is totally out of line with reality, because modern scholars have at their disposal irrefutable proof of a much earlier origin of Kiev built in the land of the Polyanians. The proof comes from the Armenian 8th-century history by Zenob Glak in which the author included a legend having nothing to do with the history of the Armenian people: three brothers—Kuar, Meltei and Khorevan — built a town in some country called Paluni. The Armenian description coincides with the one in the chronicle both in substance and in detail (hunting grounds, a town on a hill, and a pagan shrine). The question arises: how did the Slav legend find its way onto the pages of an Armenian chronicle in the 8th century? The answer is quite simple: in that same century (in 737) the Arab military leader Mervan waged war against the Khazars and managed to reach the Slav river (the Don) where he captured 20,000 Slav families. The prisoners were driven away to Transcaucasia and settled not far from Armenia. All this means that the legend about the founding of Kiev by Kii and his brothers in the land of the Polyanians arose in the Slav land of the Polyanians itself some time before 737.

The chronicler Nestor who put down the question "who was the first prince to rule Kiev" in the title of his work did not know the Armenian manuscript which included the ancient Slav legend and could not refer to it in his argument with the people of Novgorod who deliberately sought to understate Kiev's age. There even appeared an idea, quite insulting to the Kievans, that Kii was not a prince but simply some man who ferried people across the river. An educated and versatile historian well read in Greek historical literature and familiar with local Slav tales dating back to the 5th and 6th centuries A. D., Nestor did some special research and found that Kii was indeed a prince; he proceeded from the fact that Kii met the Emperor of Byzantium.

> Were Kii a common ferryman, how could he have travelled to Tsargrad?*
>
> No, Kii was a prince in his tribe and when he went to the Emperor of Byzantium he was received with great honour.
>
> On his way home he built a small fort on the bank of the Danube which the Danubians still call Kievets.
>
> Kii returned to his Kiev and died there; his brothers Shchek and Khoriv and sister Lybed

---

* The Russian name for Constantinople.— *Ed.*

Silver figurines (6th century) from the Martynov treasure on the Ros River

also died in Kiev. After them, their descendants were the princes of the Polyanians.

The conscientious historian unfortunately did not know the name of the emperor but refused to invent it. A situation when the emperor of the largest world power invited a Slav prince and showered him with the greatest honours, was possible not earlier than the end of the 5th century when the Slavs began to assault the Danubian frontier of Byzantium in the reign of Emperor Anastasius (491-518). The situation would be quite suitable for the age of Justinian (527-565), but Russian scholars knew that emperor very well and could hardly call him an unknown emperor. Perhaps it was Emperor Anastasius.

Let us turn to authentic archaeological data of the time. It was at this time, at the turn of the 6th century, that an important event occurred in the life of the inhabitants of the hills along the Dnepr. The earliest fortified site here was the so-called Zamkovaya (Castle) Hill which dominated the Podol; it was situated on the Kiyanka stream. As we remember, the chronicle says that at first, before the town was built, Kii lived on a hill. Archaeologically Kii's Hill is determined as Zamkovaya Hill which has an ancient cultural layer dated by the coins of Emperor Anastasius.

The building of a small fort on the high Starokievskaya Hill where Rastrelli's St Andrew's Cathedral stands today became an important event. That high hill which dominates the entire valley of the Dnepr and offers an excellent view of Vyshgorod at the mouth of the Desna River, became the historical centre of Kiev. It was here that the prince's palaces stood under

Vladimir I, this was the site of the Cathedral of All Russia—the "Tithe" Assumption Church of 996, and it was here that the statues captured and brought out of Khersones were displayed after the victory over Byzantium.

The reasons for the transfer of Kii's residence at the turn of the 6th century from the flat hill near the Dnepr quays to the high impregnable hill and for the development of a new small fort into the capital of an enormous state lie in the great migration of the Slavs in the 5th-7th centuries about which the chronicler wrote:

> After a long time had lapsed the Slavs settled on the Danube where the Hungarian land now is...

Taking part in the settlement of the Balkan Peninsula were not only the tribes of the southern fringe of the Slav world but also the more distant, inland tribes such as the Serbs (who had lived near present-day Berlin) or the Dregovichians who had lived north of the Pripet marshes next to the Lithuanians.

If we take a look at the map of Eastern Europe, we immediately realise the important strategic role played by Kiev in the age of the mass-scale, many-thousand-strong movement by the Slavs southwards to the rich Byzantine cities and the fertile cultivated lands. All the largest rivers of the Dnepr basin converged on Kiev; the Berezina, the Sozh, the enormous Pripet, the Desna and the Teterev flow into the Dnepr above Kiev. The basin of these rivers included the lands of the Drevlyanians, Dregovichians, Krivichians, Radimichians and Severyanians with a total area of about a quarter of a million square kilometres! And all these boundless expanses, all the routes from them southwards to the Black Sea were blocked by the fortress on the Kiev Hill.

The boats, dug-outs and rafts of the Slavs sailing in the 5th and 6th centuries to the borders of Byzantium from half of the East Slav lands could not avoid passing the Kiev heights. Prince Kii had acted with acumen in locating the new fort on a hill lower than the mouth of the full-flowing Desna; he was now the master of the Dnepr, without his consent the Slav warriors could not make their way south, and most likely paid him a tribute to be allowed to pass, and if they returned from a distant expedition, shared their spoils with him. Prince Kii could head these expeditions to the south, gathering together the boats of the northern tribes at the Dnepr quays, and then, having mustered sufficient forces, move down the Dnepr where it was necessary to overcome the dangerous nomad cordons of the Avars and Turks-Bulgars.

One chronicle has a supplement to Nestor's story about Kii: the Prince of the Polyanians had to wage war against the Turks-Bulgars, and during one expedition Kii led his forces up to the Danube and allegedly even reached Constantinople (Nikon chronicle).

The builder of the fort on the Dnepr became a leader of the general Slav movement to the Balkans. No wonder the unknown emperor attempted to appease the powerful Slav prince. The time of Byzantine expeditions was a time when Slav tribal alliances emerged and developed. Some of them, such as the Duleb alliance, fell under the onslaught of the Avar hordes in the 6th century; other Slav tribal alliances survived and grew stronger in the fight against the steppe peoples. Among these strengthened unions, as we see it, was the alliance of Middle Dnepr tribes resulting from the merging of two groups of Slav tribes—Rus (the basin of the Ros) and the Polyanians (Kiev and Chernigov). The merger was reflected in the chronicle's sentence: "Polyanians, now called Rus".

The name Rus or Ros appeared in the sources for the first time in the mid-6th century, at the height of the Slav settlement. One author, Jordanes, recalls the Rosomons who struggled against the prince of the Goths Hermanarich in the 370s. Another distant author writing in Syria listed the steppe nomads along the Black Sea and mentioned the people ROS who lived northwest of the Amazons, i. e. in the middle reaches of the Dnepr (the legendary Amazons were supposed to be on the Maeotis, the Sea of Azov).

The two variants of the name (ROS and RUS) have existed since ancient times: the Byzantines used the name ROS, and Arabic-Persian authors of the 9th-11th centuries the name RUS. Russian medieval written sources had both forms: *Russkaya* land and *Rosskaya Pravda*. Both forms have come down to our day: in Russian the country is called *Rossiya* but its inhabitant is a *Russky*.

It is interesting to define the original geographical meaning of the notion Russian land, because it is quite clear that the broader meaning denoting all Eastern Slav tribes from the Baltic to the Black Sea could have appeared only when that area had been embraced by some degree of unity.

Carefully considering the geographical terminology of the chronicles of the 11th-13th centuries we find a curious ambiguity: the expression Russian land is used, alternately, to denote all Kievan Rus and the whole ancient Russian people on an equally broad scale, or to refer to a much smaller area in the partly wooded steppe which was never a political entity in the 10th-12th centuries. Thus, for example, it is frequently written that someone went from Novgorod or Vladimir to Rus, i. e. Kiev; that Galich troops fought against the "Russians", i. e. the Kiev warriors, that Smolensk towns were not Russian while Chernigov towns were, and so on.

If we were to mark all the references to Russian and non-Russian areas on the map, we would see that the words Russian land were also used in a more narrow sense: Kiev, Chernigov, the Ros River and its banks, Pereyaslavl Russky, the land of the Severyanians and Kursk. Since this forest area did not coincide with any of the principalities of the 11th-13th centuries (it was the site of the Kiev, Pereyaslavl, Chernigov and Severyanian principalities), we must regard these persistent ideas of 12th-century chroniclers from different towns as a reflection of an earlier tradition still firmly existing in the 12th century.

A search for the time when the name Russian land in the narrow sense could reflect some really existing unity led us to only one possible historical period, the 6th and the 7th centuries when a definite archaeological culture spread within these bounds; characteristic of that culture were fibulas resembling a palm with outspread fingers, spiral temporal rings, certain details

Slav decorations (8th century). Middle reaches of the Dnepr

of female headdresses and the existence of imported Byzantine objects.

This was the culture of the Russian-Polyanian-Severyanian alliance of Slav tribes inhabiting the forest and partly wooded steppe. It emerged in the age of the Byzantine expeditions and the building of Kiev. It is not surprising that the ROS people were heard of in 6th-century Syria, that the prince of that powerful tribal alliance received gifts from the Byzantine Emperor, and that it was from this time that the Kiev annalist of the Monomakh epoch dated the history of Kievan Rus.

In subsequent times the names Rus, the Rus and the Ros referred to the Slavs inhabiting these lands and the foreigners who were in Kiev or served the Kiev prince. Appearing three hundred years after the first mention of the Ros people, the Varangians also began to be called Rus, because they were in Kiev.

The richest and most interesting finds of the artifacts of the Rus of the 6th and 7th A. D. centuries were made in the basin of the Ros and Rossava rivers. It is quite probable that the original tribe of the Ros-Rus was situated along the Ros River, and the name of that river is associated with the name of the tribe dating back, according to Jordanes, to at least the 4th century A. D.

The original land of the ROS people was situated, first of all, on the territory of the Slav proto-homeland,

and second, at the site of one of the most important "kingdoms" of the Scoloti in the 6th-5th centuries B. C. Third, it was a centre of the Chernyakhovo culture of Trajan times. In the 6th century A. D. the alliance of the inhabitants of the Ros and the Polyanian Kiev and Severyanian Sejm River became the nucleus of the emerging state of Rus with its centre in Kiev. Apparently, the argument concerning the place where the Russian state arose, in the Novgorod north or the Kiev south, is definitely and quite objectively decided in favour of the south which had taken its historical road and started to communicate with the areas of world civilisation earlier than any other area.

The Rise of the State of Rus

Extensive material from varied sources convinces us that the Eastern Slav state developed in the south, in the rich and fertile partly wooded steppe zone along the middle reaches of the Dnepr River. Land cultivation was known here a thousand years before Kievan Rus. The rate of historical development here, in the south, was much higher than in the distant forests and swamps with poor sandy soils. The "kingdoms" of the Borysphenite land-tillers who should be regarded as the proto-Slavs arose in the south, at the site of the future nucleus of Kievan Rus, a thousand years before the founding of Kiev; export land cultivation reappeared here in the Trajanus times (2nd-4th centuries A. D.) resulting in a very high level of social development.

The areas to the north of Smolensk, Polotsk, Novgorod and Rostov had no such rich legacy and developed incomparably slower. Even in the 12th century, when south and north had levelled out to a large degree, the southerners still ironically referred to their forest neighbours as living like beasts.

In analysing the obscure and frequently contradictory historical sources the historian must take into account the axiom of uneven historical development which, in our case, stands out in particularly bold relief. We must be highly suspicious of the sources which refer to the north as the place where the Russian state arose, and it is up to us to find the reasons for such obvious bias.

The second comment to be made before considering the early state of Rus concerns not geography but chronology. Medieval annalists impermissibly compressed the process of the rise of the state reducing it to one or two decades, attempting to fit the thousand years during which the preconditions about which they had no idea were created into the lifespan of one hero, the founder of the state. This involved an ancient method of mythological thinking, a medieval habit to replace the whole by its part, its symbol: in pictures a town was replaced by a depiction of a tower and a whole army by one horseman. The state was replaced by one prince.

The compression of historical time was reflected in the fact that certain annalists attributed the founding of Kiev, which we have now established as dating back to the late 5th or first half of the 6th century, to the year 854, making Kii a contemporary of Rurik and reducing to naught a timespan of 300 to 350 years. Such a mistake is tantamount to making Mayakovsky* a contemporary of Ivan the Terrible.

Among the Russian historians of the 11th and 12th centuries Nestor was the closest to the historical truth in describing the early phases in the life of the state of Rus but his work reached us in a form strongly distorted by his contemporaries precisely in the introductory part.

On the basis of surviving fragments of Nestor's *Tale of Bygone Years* supported, as we saw, by numerous materials of the 5th-7th centuries and retrospectively by 12th-century sources, the first stage in the rise of Kievan Rus is portrayed as the forming of a powerful alliance of Slav tribes in the middle reaches of the Dnepr River in the 6th century A. D., an alliance which assumed the name of one of the tribes, the ROS or RUS people, known in the 6th century beyond the Slavic world as consisting of strongmen.

---

* Vladimir Mayakovsky (1893-1930), famous Russian Soviet poet.— *Ed.*

As a sort of epigraph to the first stage in the history of the Russian state the Kiev annalist included two sharply contrasting stories about two tribal alliances, two different fates. The Dulebs were attacked in the 6th-7th centuries by the Avars. The latter "conquered the Dulebs, a Slav tribe, and treated the Duleb women very badly: if they needed to go somewhere, they harnessed not horses or oxen but several Duleb women to their carts." The Dulebs fled to the Western Slavs, and splinters of their alliance were introduced into the Czech and Polish tribes.

The tragic image of Slav women pulling a cart with Avar nobles was opposed by the glorious picture of the Polyanian prince welcomed with honour in the palace of the Byzantine Emperor in Constantinople.

The founding of Kiev in the land of the Polyanians-Rus was compared by another annalist to the founding of Rome, Antioch and Alexandria, and the head of the Russian-Polyanian alliance of tribes, the Grand Prince of Kiev, to Romulus and Alexander the Great.

The historical road of the further development of the Slav tribes in Eastern Europe was traced and predetermined by the situation of the 6th-7th centuries when the Russian alliance of tribes withstood the onslaught of the war-like nomad peoples and took advantage of its favourable position on the Dnepr which served as a route to the south for several dozen northern tribes in the Dnepr basin. Holding the key to the Dnepr itinerary and protected from steppe raids by the entire breadth of the partly wooded steppe zone ("there was a forest around the town and a big pine forest") Kiev became the natural centre in the process of the integration of Eastern Slav tribal alliances and the emergence of socio-political entities going beyond the most developed primitive society.

The second stage in the historical life of Kievan Rus was the transformation of the Dnepr alliance of forest and steppe Slav tribes into a super-alliance including within its bounds several dozen separate lesser Slav tribes unknown to us, united into four larger alliances. On the example of the Vyatichians we can see what an alliance of tribes was like in the 9th century: relations of domination and subordination emerged here independently, from within, hierarchies of power were formed, such a form of levying tribute as *polyudye* linked to foreign trade was established, and wealth was accumulated. The other alliances of Slav tribes ruled by princes were approximately the same.

The process of class-formation occurring in each tribal alliance was preceded by a process of further integration when one prince ruled not a principality uniting about a dozen primary tribes but several such alliances-principalities. The emerging new enormous union was in a direct, mathematical sense an order higher than each individual alliance of tribes such as the Vyatichians.

It was approximately in the 8th-early 9th centuries that the second stage in the development of Kievan Rus set in marked by the subordination of a number of tribal alliances to the power of Rus, the Kiev prince's rule. Rus did not include all the alliances of Eastern Slav tribes; there were also the independent southern Ulichians and Tivertsians, the Croats in the Carpathian area, the Vyatichians, the Radimichians and the mighty Krivichians.

> The [state of] Rus included only these Slav alliances of tribes: Polyanians, Drevlyanians, Novgorodians (introduced later, such a tribe did not exist), Polochanians, Dregovichians, Severyanians, Buzhanians later called Volynians (i. e. not after the Bug River but the town of Volyn).
>
> *The Tale of Bygone Years*

Although the chronicler defined this stage as a period of incomplete uniting of the Eastern Slav tribes, if we look at a map of Eastern Europe we see a large territory extending to the entire historically significant partly wooded steppe and a broad zone of woodland stretching from Kiev northwards to the Western Dvina and Ilmen. In area (but not population of course) Rus at the time was equal to the whole Byzantine Empire of 814 or the Carolingian Empire of the same time.

If there existed within the individual alliances of tribes both a hierarchy of the prince's power (princes of the *volost*-tribes and the prince of princes) and *polyudye* which, as we will see below, was an extremely complex and bulky state undertaking, then the rise of the alliance of alliances raised all these elements to a higher level. Oriental travellers who saw Rus in the first half of the 9th century with their own eyes describe it as an enormous state the eastern borders of which reached the Don River while the northern borders were believed to be at the edge of the "uninhabited desert of the North."

Indicative of the international position of Rus in the first half of the 9th century was, first of all, the fact that the head of the entire complex of Slav tribal alliances standing above the princes of the princes possessed a title equal to that of emperor—he was called Kagan, like the kings of Khazaria or the head of the Avar Kaganate (839). Second, the scope of the foreign trade carried on by Rus (the sale of *polyudye*) was vividly described by Oriental geographer Ibn Khurdadhbih who wrote *The Book of Roads and States*:

> As to the Russian merchants, and they are a sort of Slavs, they take beaverskins and the pelts of Polar foxes and swords from the most distant parts of the Slav country to the Rumnian Sea (Black Sea, also called the Russian Sea at the time), and the tithe is levied on them by the King of Byzantium, and if they wish they go along the Tanais(?), the river of the Slavs, and go through the straits of the capital of the Khazars, and their ruler levies the tithe.

The capital of Khazaria could be reached by merchants from certain tribal alliances favourably situated along the routes leading to the Lower Volga River. The Slavs (Vyatichians and others) were full-fledged contractors for the Khazars in their capital. As to the Rus, subjects of the Kievan state, it is said that they went south, far beyond the bounds of Khazaria, crossing the Caspian Sea 500 farsangs long:

> Then they set out for the Jurjan Sea and land on any shore... (and sell everything they bring along, and it all goes to Rey. Sometimes they bring their products on camels from Jurjan

Oriental artifacts found on the territory of Ancient Russia

      to Baghdad where Slav slaves serve as interpreters for them. And they claim to be Christians...
      (Ibn-al-Faqih's text is in parenthesis).
At first glance it may seem incredible that the Russian merchants travelled from the most distant parts of Slavonia to the very heart of the Moslem world, Baghdad. But the distant lands of the Polochanians already belonged to Rus; this was confirmed, as we saw, by the list of tribal alliances. The route along the sea and the long expedition from the southern shores of the Caspian

47

to Baghdad were documented by an eyewitness account: Ibn Khurdadhbih did not write on the basis of hearsay—he was chief of the post in Rey, a major trading town, and the Jebel area through which the Rey-Baghdad road went was within his jurisdiction. The author must have seen with his own eyes the ruins of the ancient zikkurat in the outskirts of Baghdad and knew the exact measurements of the ruins—"Its ruins are between Assyria and Babylonia. The height and breadth of the pyramid equal 5,433 cubit."

In the languages of European peoples (including the descendents of the Varangians, the Swedes) the word meaning camel is derived from the Greek ($\chi\alpha\mu\varepsilon\gamma o\varsigma$) or the Latin *camelus*. The Iranian peoples had the form *ushtra*. The Slavs called this tough animal with their own Slav word, *velblud*, easily etymologized: it was formed by the merging of two roots meaning much (vel) and wandering (blud). In order to give the camel a name reflecting its endurance and ability to cover large distances, it was not sufficient to see the humpbacked beasts somewhere at the bazaars: their abilities had to be tested on the road. Apparently it was along the caravan route from Rey to Baghdad (about 700 kilometres) that the new word appeared among the Slav merchants. It is not to be excluded, however, that the Slav *velblud* was an interpretation of the Arab word for camel, *ibilun*. If this proved to be so, it would be further proof of the familiarity of the Rus with the caravan routes of the Orient.

The Russian nobility sold *polyudye* not only to the countries of the Middle East but also to the Byzantine possessions along the Black Sea, a fact referred to in passing by Ibn Khurdadhbih when he speaks of the tithe the Rus pay to the emperor. It is possible that Byzantium's blocking of the mouth of the Dnepr and the part of the Black Sea coast which the Rus needed for coastal sailing to the Kerch Strait or Constantinople was the reason for the Russian expedition against Byzantine possessions in the Crimea described in *The Life of Stephan of Surozh*.

Scholars believe that the expedition of "Novgorod Prince" Bravlin had taken place at the end of the 8th century or the first thirty years of the 9th century. The Rus captured Surozh (modern Sudak), and their prince was baptized; perhaps it is the adoption of Christianity by some part of the Rus that explains Ibn Khurdadhbih's words about the Rus claiming to be Christians and paying tribute like Christians in the countries of the Caliphate.

The armed fleets of the Rus appearing on the Black Sea did not confine themselves to the southeastern shore of the Crimea lying on their usual way to Khazaria and the Caspian Sea. They also undertook sea expeditions to the southern Anatolian coast of the Black Sea in the first half of the 9th century as described in the *Life of St George of Amastris*.

The Black Sea, the Rumnian Sea—the Sea of Byzantium—was becoming the Russian Sea as our chronicler called it. He called the Caspian Sea Khvaliskoye, i. e. Khorezm Sea, referring to the link with Khorezm lying beyond the Caspian from which it was possible to travel to the Arab lands of the Caliphate. Linked directly with Kiev the Black Sea is described by the chronicler in the following terms:

> The Dnepr flows into the Pontus (Black Sea) in three arms. The sea is called Russian.

Despite their fragmentary nature reports about Russian fleets on the Black Sea in the 8th and early 9th centuries point to the intense activities of the Rus state along its southern trade routes. The famous expedition of the Rus against Constantinople in 860 was not the first time that the Greeks encountered the Russians, as the Constantinople Patriarch Photius exclaimed rhetorically, but the first landing by Rus forces at the walls of the Second Rome. The aim of the Russian squadron's expedition to the Bosphorus was to conclude a peace treaty with the Emperor.

The second stage in the historical existence of Kievan Rus (8th-mid-9th century) was marked not only by enormous territorial expansion from the uninhabited deserts of the North, from the remotest parts of the Slav world to the boundary with the steppe, but also by unprecedented activity in the area from the Russian Sea and the Slav river to Byzantium, Anatolia, the Transcaspian and Baghdad. The state of Rus had already risen to a much higher level than that of contemporary separate alliances of tribes ruled by princes.

The domestic life of Kievan Rus at that time can be traced, due to the absence of contemporary sources, only by studying the subsequent period and considering in retrospect the phenomena which arose at the second stage and were documented only for the subsequent period.

The third stage in Kievan Rus' development was not associated with any new quality. What had arisen at the second stage continued and developed: the number of Eastern Slav tribal alliances included in Rus increased, Rus' international trade relations were slightly expanded, and the confrontation with the steppe nomads went on.

During the third stage in the life of Kievan Rus the rumours about its established regular links with the countries of the Orient became known to the Slavs' northern neighbours of whose existence Oriental geographers of the 9th century knew absolutely nothing. Reports about these travels in some form reached the remotest parts of the Slav world, where tribute was collected among the Polochanians or the Slovenians by warriors who had just returned from thousand-*verst* expeditions to the southern overseas lands. After all, the anonymous Persian author of *Parts of the World** believed that the warm Gulfstream washed the lands of the Slavs and not the Scandinavians and Lapps.

From the "uninhabited desert of the North" the Varangians began to appear in the southeast Baltic area, attracted by rumours that, somewhere beyond the forests, there existed Rus which undertook annual trade expeditions to Byzantium and to the countries of the Khvalyn Sea from where the stream of Oriental silver coins went northwards.

Concerning the lively relations of Rus with the Orient reflected in numerous numismatic finds prominent Soviet historian V. L. Yanin writes: "The pattern of the movement of Eastern coins through the territory of Eastern Europe seems to be as follows. European-Arab

---

* *Parts of the World*, a geographical work of the first half of the 9th century.— *Ed.*

trade arose at the end of the 8th century as Eastern European trade (i. e. involving Rus, the Slavs and Volga Bulgaria—*B. R.*) with countries of the Caliphate... The myth about the initial organising role of the Scandinavians in European-Arab trade is not substantiated in the sources." All this also holds for the second stage.

The seafaring Normans sailed around Europe, ravaging the coasts of France, England, Spain and Sicily and reaching Constantinople; the peoples of the West had a special prayer: God save us from the Normans! Accustomed to travelling by sea the Scandinavians had no difficulty in organising fleets of hundreds of ships which terrorised the population of the rich seaside towns taking them by surprise. The Normans did not venture to go deep inland.

All the Eastern Slav lands were situated far from the sea, and it would have involved tremendous difficulties for the Baltic seafarers to reach Smolensk or Kiev: they had to sail up rivers and the fleets could be attacked from both banks. The greatest difficulties had to do with the watersheds where the boats had to be dragged over dry land. It made the Norman armada even more vulnerable: there was no question of suddenness.

It was sufficient for the Kievan prince to set up an outpost at the portages and forks in the routes (for example, on the sites of Novgorod, Rusa or Smolensk) to block the way for the seafarers travelling over dry land. Therein lay the major difference between Eastern and Western Europe. The Varangians began to penetrate the Eastern Slav lands much later than the coasts of the European seas. Searching for ways leading to the East the Normans rarely made use of the route "from the Varangians to the Greeks", but, bypassing Rus' distant possessions from the northeast, reached the Volga and went down the Volga to the Caspian.

As to the route "from the Varangians to the Greeks" allegedly leading from the Baltic to Lake Ladoga, and from Lake Ladoga to Lake Ilmen and further along the Dnepr to the Black Sea, it was an invention of the Normanists who convinced all the learned people of the 19th and 20th centuries to such an extent that the description has become canonical. Let us turn to the only source where the expression is used, *The Tale of Bygone Years*. It opens with a general title which indicates that the author intends to describe the roundabout way through Rus and round the European continent. He begins the actual description with the route from "the Greeks" northwards up the Dnepr:

> There is a route from the land of the Varangians (Sweden) to Byzantium and from Byzantium along the Dnepr and in the upper reaches of the Dnepr a portage to the Lovat River and along the Lovat to the large Lake Ilmen from which the Volkhov River flows falling into the large Lake Ladoga, and from that lake a wide channel (the Neva River) leads to the Varangian (Baltic) Sea.

This is a detailed and competent description of the way from Byzantium, through all of Rus to the north, to the Swedes. It is the route "from the Greeks to the Varangians". It is shown by the annalist in only one direction — from south to north. This does not mean that the itinerary was not passed by anyone in the opposite direction: up the Neva, up the Volkhov, up the Lovat and then along the Dnepr, but the Russian scholar traced the itinerary of ties between the southern lands and the Scandinavian North, and not the route of the Varangians.

The route "from the Varangians to the Greeks" is also indicated by the annalist later, and it is of great interest to us:

> It is possible to sail to Rome on the same Varangian Sea (the sequence of seas washing Western Europe), and from Rome along the same sea to go to Constantinople (contemporary Istambul), and from Constantinople to the Pontus Sea into which the Dnepr River flows.

The real route "from the Varangians to the Greeks" turns out to have nothing to do with Rus and the Slav lands. It reflected the real itineraries of the Normans from the Baltic and the North Sea (both could be united under the name of Varangian Sea), round Europe into the Mediterranean, to Rome and the Norman possessions in Sicily and Naples, further east "along the same sea", to Constantinople and then the Black Sea. We have come full circle.

The Russian annalist knew the geography and history of the Normans much better than the later Normanists.

The first indication of contacts between the Normans and the Slavs is dated 859 in the chronicle (the date is tentative).

> The Varangians (Normans) coming from overseas (the Baltic) imposed tribute on the tribes of Chud, Slovenians, Merya, Ves and Krivichians.

The list of areas attacked by the Varangians refers, first of all, to tribes living on the seacoast (Chud — Estonians) or near the sea, along large rivers, and, second, to the roundabout way bypassing Rus from the northeast mentioned above (Ves and Merya).

The Slavic and Finnish tribes resisted the Varangians:

> In 862 they drove the Varangians beyond the sea and stopped paying tribute. The Slavs became independent.

Subsequently in *The Tale of Bygone Years* and other ancient chronicles there is a confusion of fragments with different trends. Some fragments were taken from the Novgorod chronicle, others from the Kiev chronicle (strongly diluted when it was edited), still others were added in place of those which were edited out. The desires and bias of various annalists were not only different but often directly opposite.

It was from this confusion that the founders of the Normanist theory snatched individual phrases without any critical approach; these were arrogant 18th-century Germans who had come to "wild" Russia to introduce European culture into it. S. Bayer, G. Miller and A. Schlözer snatched from the chronicle the phrase about the animal-like way of life of the ancient Slavs, attributing it to the contemporaries of the annalist, although in actual fact the contrasting description of the "intelligent and wise" Polyanians and their forest neighbours should be attributed to the first centuries A. D. The scholars were overjoyed to find the legend about the inviting of the Varangians by the northern tribes which enabled them to maintain that the Normans-Varangians brought the wild Slavs elements of statehood. During its entire subsequent two-hundred-years history Normanism was increasingly turning into a frankly anti-Russian and later anti-Soviet political doctrine which its advocates carefully guarded from any contact with real scholarship and critical analysis.

Anti-Normanism was founded by Mikhail Lomonosov*; his followers destroyed, step by step, the conglomeration of arguments which the Normanists resorted to in order to retain and strengthen their positions. Numerous facts, particularly archaeological data, appeared showing the secondary part played by the Varangians in the rise of the Rus state.

Let us return to the sources from which the Normanists derived their initial assumptions. In order to do this we must first consider the historical situation in which the annalistic concepts of Russian history were created, i. e., when the introductory chapters to the chronicles were written in the times of Yaroslav the Wise and Vladimir Monomakh. For the Russian people of the time the meaning of the legend about the inviting of the Varangians lay not in the Varangians but rather in the political rivalry between ancient Kiev and the new town of Novgorod which was catching up with Kiev in its development.

Thanks to its favourable geographical position Novgorod very quickly came close to being the second town of Rus after Kiev. But its political position was not adequate. In primitive olden times the town did not have its prince; the town and its excessively growing region were regarded in the 11th century as the domain of the Kiev prince where he usually appointed his eldest son as ruler. Novgorod was a sort of collective castle for the numerous northern *boyars* for whom distant Kiev was only a collector of tribute and obstacle on the way to Byzantium.

The Novgorod people agreed in 1015 to help their prince Yaroslav in his expedition against Kiev and took advantage of the occasion to obtain deeds protecting

---

* M. V. Lomonosov (1711-1765), great Russian scholar, naturalist, enlightener and poet.— *Ed.*

Novgorod from the outrages perpetrated by the Varangians the prince had hired. Kiev was conquered by Yaroslav and his Novgorod-Varangian force: "there were a thousand Varangians and 3,000 Novgoroders".

That victory, first of all, laid the foundations for the separatist seekings of the Novgorod *boyars* and, secondly, put Novgorod in the eyes of its people ahead of conquered Kiev. From here it was only one step for the Novgorod people to assume in their historical outlook that Novgorod had the priority in state development. A. A. Shakhmatov singled out the Novgorod collected chronicle of 1050 which, judging by several features, should be regarded as the chronicle of the Novgorod town elder Ostromir.

The author of the Ostromir chronicle begins Russian history with the building of Kiev and from the start places this event, of importance for the whole of Russia, chronologically on the same footing as his own northern history, saying that the Slovenians, Krivichians and other tribes paid tribute "in those same times". Telling about expelling beyond the seas the Varangians who perpetrated violence the author further describes wars between tribes.

> The Slovenians formed their own region (built a town, called it Novgorod and appointed Gostomysl the elder). The Krivichians had their own region, the Merya their own, the Chud theirs. But wars and quarrels began, town fought against town and there was no order.
>
> Then it was decided to seek a prince who would rule us and administer justice fairly. They set out overseas to the Varangians and said: "Our land is great and rich, but there is no order in it. Come to us as prince and rule over us!"

Further on, the chronicle describes how Rurik, Sinaus and Truvor came to the above-mentioned northern tribes: Rurik was prince of the Slovenians, Truvor the Krivichians (at Pskov in Izborsk) and Sinaus the Ves at the Beloozero; the legend leaves the Merya without a prince.

Historians have long ago pointed to the anecdotal nature of Rurik's "brothers". While Rurik himself was a historical personality, the "brothers" proved to be Russian transliterations of Swedish words. It was said about Rurik that he came with his relatives (sine use, Sinaus) and loyal fighting men (tru war, Truvor).

Sinaus—sine hus—his clan.

Truvor—thru waring—loyal fighting men.

In other words, the chronicle includes the rendering of some Scandinavian tale about Rurik's activities (the author of the chronicle, a man of Novgorod who did not know Swedish well, mistook the traditional entourage of the konung mentioned in an oral saga for the names of his brothers. The authenticity of the legend as a whole and, in particular, of its geographical part, is not very great as we can see. There were no mythical princes in Izborsk, a small town near Pskov, and in distant Beloozero, there were merely collectors of tribute.

Legends about three brothers invited to rule in a foreign land were widespread in North Europe in the Middle Ages. We know legends about the voluntary inviting of the Normans to Ireland and England. Three brothers arrived in Ireland with peaceful aims under the pretext of trade (like Oleg in Kiev). The Irish council decided to have them stay.

Widukind of Corvey in his *Res gestae Saxonicae* (967) tells about an embassy of the Britons to the Saxons who said that they offered them to rule their large and great country abounding in all kinds of goods (recall the chronicle: "our land is large and abundant"). The Saxons sent three ships with three princes. In all instances the foreigners arrived with their relatives (sinaus) and loyal fighting men (truvor).

The similarity between the legend in the chronicle about the inviting of the Varangians and the North European court folklore is not to be doubted. And the court of Prince Mstislav, as will be seen below, was similar to the one about which Widukind wrote.

Were the princes, or to be more precise, Prince Rurik invited? The answers may only be tentative. It is indisputable that the Normans raided the northern lands at the end of the 9th and in the 10th century. A proud patriot of Novgorod could have depicted the real raids of the surprise attackers as voluntary invitation of the Varangians by the northern inhabitants in order to maintain order. Such an interpretation of the Varangian expeditions for tribute was not as shameful to the proud Novgorod people as acknowledgement of their helplessness. The invited prince would have to administer justice fairly, i. e. it was thought, in the spirit of the 1015 events, that like Yaroslav the Wise, he would grant his subjects a deed.

It may have been otherwise: seeking to defend themselves from the unregulated extortions of the Varangians, the inhabitants of the northern lands could have invited one of the konungs to rule as prince so he would protect them from the other Varangian parties. Rurik, whom some scholars believe to be Rurik of Jutland, would be an appropriate figure for the purpose, because he came from the most distant part of the Western Baltic and was a stranger for the Varangians from Southern Sweden situated closer to the Chud and East Slavs.

Historical sciences have insufficiently studied the question of the relationship between the Varangians of the chronicles and the Western Baltic Slavs. The archaeological links of the Baltic Slavs with Novgorod are traced to the 11th century. Written sources of the 11th century refer to trade between Western Baltic and Novgorod. It may be supposed that if the invitation of a foreign prince really took place as an episode of the anti-Varangian struggle that prince could be Rurik of Jutland whose initial principality was located in proximity to the Baltic Slavs. Yet the above considerations are insufficiently substantiated to build a hypothesis on their basis.

Let us now continue our review of the 1050 chronicle which introduced the legend about the inviting of the Varangians for the first time in Russian written sources:

> And it was from the Varangians, newcomers, that the name was derived. Even now there are descendents of the Varangians among the Novgorod people.

This ordinary sentence explaining the presence of Swedes among the townsfolk of Novgorod (confirmed by different versions of the Russkaya Pravda) underwent changes in the works of other chroniclers, as we will see below, and the Normanists have taken advantage of the fact.

Further the 1050 chronicle says:

> And they (the Varangians) had a prince named Oleg, a wise and brave man... [there follows a description of the pillaging of the capital of Rus Kiev by Oleg]. He had fighting men from among the Varangians and the Slovenians. Since then they have been called Rus.

It is quite clear from the sentence that Oleg's force consisting, as was the case later with Yaroslav the Wise, of Varangians and Slovenians, came to be called Rus after the capture of Kiev. From the time that Oleg became the provisional prince of Rus his warriors began to be called Rus, Russians.

Of exceptional interest in determining the relationship of the Varangians to the North Russian political system is the report about the tribute paid to the Varangians:

> From Novgorod came tribute 300 grivnas so the Varangians would not attack; it is still paid now.

The tribute was paid to avoid raids and not as a duty by subjects. A similar tribute was later paid by Kievan princes to the Polovtsi to prevent sudden raids. In the 10th century Byzantium paid such tribute to the Rus. Novgorod's tribute to the Varangians was paid up to the death of Yaroslav the Wise in 1054 (the chronicler writing circa 1050 said that it was still being paid).

The paying of this tribute can hardly be interpreted as political domination of Novgorod by the Varangians. On the contrary, it presupposes the existence of local power in the town capable of collecting a large sum of money (in the prices of the 11th century the sum sufficient to buy 500 boats) and paying it to an outer force for the sake of peace. Those who receive tribute (in this case the Varangians) always appear to be more primitive than those who pay it to secure themselves from raids.

Following the victorious outcome of the expedition against Constantinople (911) Oleg returned not to Kiev but to Novgorod and "therefrom to Ladoga. There is his tomb in Ladoga". As already mentioned above other chronicles describe his burial place otherwise: "he went overseas and a snake bit him in the leg and he died".

There are different accounts of the place where the founder of the Russian state (as Oleg is referred to by the Normanists) died: in the mid-11th century Russian people did not know where he had died—in Ladoga or in his own country overseas. Seventy years later another unexpected version appeared: Oleg's tomb turned out to be in the outskirts of Kiev.

All the data in the Novgorod Ostromir chronicle are such that they do not allow us to conclude that the Varangians played the organising role in Kievan Rus, which had formed a long time before, or even in the federation of northern tribes which had suffered most from the Varangians' raids. Even the legend about the inviting of Prince Rurik here seems to display the wisdom of the Novgorod people in matters of state.

Let us consider the historical situation of another age when Nestor's detailed and monumental work was twice revised, first with the participation of Father-Superior Sylvester Vydubitsky and then by a writer whose name is unknown and who was an agent of Mstislav (son of Vladimir Monomakh). That writer, in the first person, described his visit to Ladoga in 1114 (there he showed an archaeological interest for ancient beads washed out of the soil). Let us call him tentatively Ladozhanin (man of Ladoga). In the opinion of A. A. Shakhmatov he revised Nestor's annals in 1118; this is now known as the third edition of *The Tale of Bygone Years*.

A talented statesman and military leader Vladimir Monomakh ascended to the Kiev throne of Grand Prince not by right of dynastic seniority—he was the son of the youngest of Yaroslav's sons, Vsevolod, and descendants of the older branches were still alive. The relationship between Monomakh and the powerful Kievan *boyars* was a complex one. In the last years of the life of Vsevolod Yaroslavich, Vladimir was with his ill father and in effect ruled the state. After Vsevolod's death in 1093 the *boyars*, dissatisfied with Vladimir, gave the Kievan throne to the inept Svyatopolk (according to seniority), and Monomakh attempted to win the throne for twenty years without success. It was only in 1113 (after Svyatopolk's death), at the height of the popular uprising, that the *boyars* sent an invitation to Vladimir who was the prince in Pereyaslavl Russky (now Pereyaslav-Khmelnitsky) to come to the Kievan throne. Monomakh agreed, arrived in Kiev, and immediately added special *Rules* to the Russkaya Pravda which eased the position of the common townsfolk.

As a true statesman acting among rival princes, Monomakh was always concerned with affirming his rights and describing his deeds in a proper manner. Without excessive modesty he personally wrote the famous *Sermon* which is, in part, a memoir (where, as in any memoir, the author is concerned with showing his activities in a favourable light) and, in part, a summary for an annalist describing Vladimir's 83 expeditions to different ends of Europe.

Monomakh's concern about the chronicle, about how his doings, laws and expeditions would be presented to contemporaries and posterity, led him to read Nestor's chronicle (written under his predecessor) and he transferred the manuscript from the Pechersky Monastery to the Vydubitsky Cloister founded by his father. The Father-Superior of that monastery Sylvester altered certain things in the manuscript (in 1116), but this, apparently, failed to satisfy the high client. The new revision was ordered to be done by Ladozhanin.

Monomakh was attracted to three ideas in the Novgorod Ostromir chronicle: first, a prince invited from another place (as he had been himself) has lawful authority; second, the prince comes to put down unrest resembling the 1113 situation in Kiev ("big war and quarrels; one town fights another", 1050 chronicle); third, the invited prince eliminates lawlessness ("and they had no order") and must "rule according to law". By this time Monomakh had already issued his new *Rules*.

There was a rather close consonance between the 1050 Chronicle and the situation in Monomakh's time. There is nothing about the Varangians as such here;

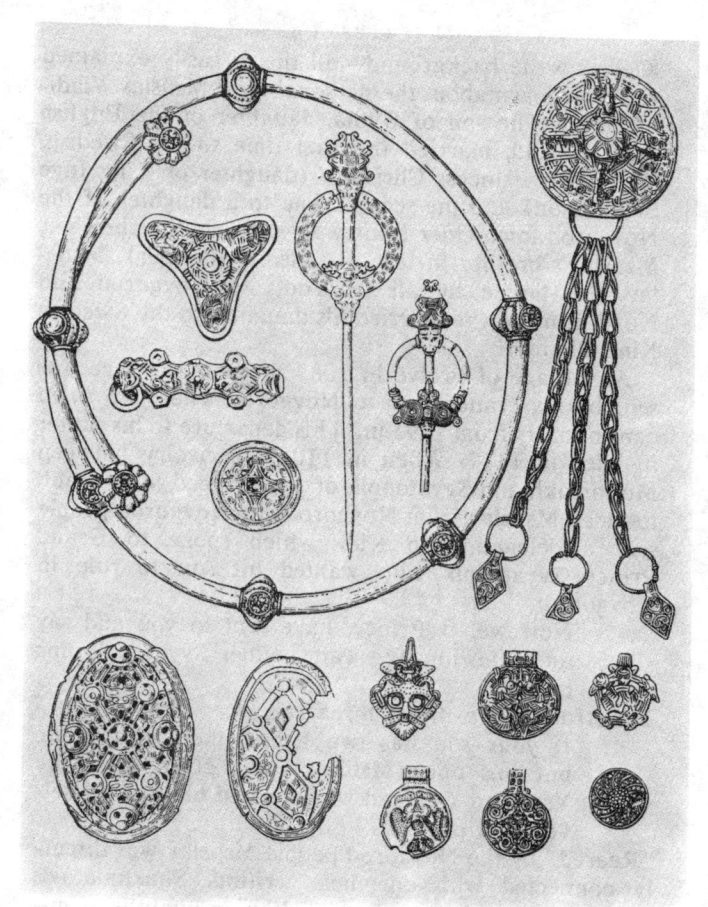

Scandinavian silver and bronze decorations (10th and 11th centuries) found in East Europe

as we can see, the significance of the analogy lies elsewhere. However, the revisions in Nestor's manuscript (1113) made by Ladozhanin were clearly pro-Varangian. At this point we must mention Monomakh's son Mstislav with whom A. A. Shakhmatov associated the 1118 text produced under Mstislav's supervision.

The northern bias of the insertions into *The Tale of Bygone Years*, all the pro-Varangian elements in them and the efforts to put Novgorod in first place and push

Kiev into the background—all this is easily explained when we learn about the personality of Mstislav Vladimirovich. The son of Gytha, daughter of the English King Harold, married the first time to the Swedish, Varangian Princess Christina (daughter of King Inge Stenkilsson) and the second time to a daughter of the Novgorod town elder Dmitry Zavidovich (her brother, Mstislav's brother-in-law, was also town elder), Mstislav was linked by all his roots to Novgorod and North Europe (he married his daughter to the Swedish King Sigurd).

At the age of twelve in 1088 the young prince was sent by his grandfather to Novgorod where he ruled continuously from 1095 until his departure to his father in Kiev in 1117. When in 1102 the rivalry between Monomakh and Svyatopolk of Kiev forced Monomakh to recall Mstislav from Novgorod, the Novgorod people sent a delegation to Kiev which spoke to Grand Prince Svyatopolk who wanted his son to rule in Novgorod:

> Now we, O Prince, have sent to you and say the following: We want neither Svyatopolk nor his son.

Then followed a direct threat:

> If your son has two heads, then send him... but this one (Mstislav) was given to us by Vsevolod (...) and we educated him for ourselves as a prince.

"Reared" by the Novgorod people Mstislav was directly connected with chronicle writing. Shakhmatov's arguments may be supplemented by an analysis of miniatures from the Radziwill Copy of the chronicle. It paid extensive attention to Mstislav's affairs since his arrival in Kiev in 1117; the illustrator devotes miniatures to events in his life and a new architectural style appears in the pictures which continues until Mstislav's death in 1132. During this period the artist uses symbolic figures of animals (Polovtsi—a snake; arguments and quarrels—dogs; victory over a neighbour—a cat and a mouse, and so on).

Apparently in the times of Mstislav a special illustrated chronicle of Mstislav Vladimirovich was kept in Kiev. Let us now see how all this affected the account of the episodes of early Russian history in *The Tale of Bygone Years*.

There is no doubt that the circle of people involved in revising Nestor's chronicle in a spirit desired by Monomakh knew the 1050 Novgorod chronicle quite well (the latter was continued to 1079). The Novgorod chronicle was used chiefly because it contained the legend, unknown to the Kiev people, about the voluntary invitation of princes similar to the invitation of Monomakh to Kiev in 1113 and election of Mstislav by the Novgorod people in 1102. The grudge Monomakh held against the Kiev *boyars* who, for two decades, would not let him ascend "the golden paternal throne" resulted in another trend of the 1118 edition — to relegate Kiev to second place in the initial phase of the Russian state's history replacing it with Novgorod and exaggerating the role played by the Varangians invited from overseas. It was important for the editor to disavow the Kiev Russian tradition.

In his version Ladozhanin identified Varangians with Rus, and presented it as the chronicle's original feature. The author of the 1050 chronicle wrote quite clearly that the newcomers from the North, Oleg's Varangian and Slovenian forces, began to be called Rus only after they had asserted themselves within Rus in Kiev which they conquered. Yet Ladozhanin claimed that there was a Varangian people called Rus such as the Norwegians, the English or the Gotlanders. Actually there was no such people in the north of Europe, and all searches made by scholars failed to yield results. The only possibility was that the author had mistaken the Frisians living west of Jutland for the Varangians.

Nestor pointed out the closeness of the Old Slavonic written language and the Russian language. Ladozhanin introduced his own conjecture that the name Rus was derived from the Varangians, a conjecture which resulted from an incorrect interpretation of one point in Sylvester's partly revised manuscript.

The only possible explanation for the fact that Rus was identified with Varangians was that the editor had in his hands the treaty between Rus and Byzantium of 911 extracted from the prince's archives which opened with the words: "We of Russian kin." Then comes a list of names of the delegation members authorised to conclude the treaty. There were purely Varangian names among them: Ingeld, Farlof, Ruald and others. The first phrase of the treaty, however, meant not the ethnic origin of the diplomats but the legal aspect, the power on behalf of which the treaty was concluded with another power: "We of Russian kin (people)... are sent to you, Leo, Alexander and Constantine, from the Russian Grand Prince Oleg and all the grand princes and *boyars* he rules..."

The legally binding phrase "We of Russian kin" is also present in the 944 treaty as there were many Slavs not related to the Varangians among the ambassadors: Uleb, Prasten, Voist, Sinko Borich and others. If Ladozhanin knew Varangian names, he could conclude that Russian kin was Varangian kin. But the point is that throughout the text of the treaty the word Russian means a Russian person generally, Russian princes, Russian towns, citizens of the Rus state, and the word *rod* (kin) meant people in the broad sense of the word. The text of the treaty is an excellent illustration to the story that, having come to Kiev, the Varangians began to be called Rus as subjects of the Rus state. Three decades had lapsed since the appearance of the Varangians in Kiev to the time the treaty with emperors Leo and Alexander was concluded.

One important reservation must be made—nowhere does Ladozhanin say that the Varangians ruled the Slavs; he only claims that the Slavs received their name from the Varangians-Rus he had invented. This was not an historical concept, rather these were ethnonymic comments made in passing which were not unusual in the 12th century, in a situation when the Varangians-Swedes were trade neighbours and part of the prince's courtiers (the court of Princess Christina) and a certain part of the townsfolk.

To assert, on the basis of only one phrase, which, however, is repeated like a leitmotif: "the Russian land received its name from the Varangians", that the Normans were the founders of Kievan Rus was possible only when history had not become a science yet and was at the level of alchemistry.

The appearance of the Normans at the edge of the "uninhabited deserts of the North" was reflected in yet another Russian source which came to the attention of historians rather late. These were the entries in the Nikon 16th-century chronicle about the years 867-875 absent in the other chronicles known to us, including *The Tale of Bygone Years* (in the 1116 and 1118 versions which have come down to us). These entries were mixed with excerpts from Russian and Byzantine sources, somewhat revised in terms of language but still retaining the old orthography differing from that of the 16th-century historians who had compiled the Nikon chronicle.

The additional data for 867-875 could have been regarded as an invention of 16th-century Moscow historians, but the fragmentary nature of the entries, the presence of minor insignificant details (for example, the death of Prince Askold's son) and the complete absence of any idea which could, from the viewpoint of the compilers, lend meaning to these entries prevent us from doing so. Moreover, the entries about Rurik contradict, by their anti-Varangian tone, both the nearest articles taken from *The Tale of Bygone Years* (1118) and the overall dynastic tendency of the 16th century which regarded Rurik as the direct ancestor of the Moscow Tsar. As to the assumption that these entries were invented, we can say that they differ sharply from the style of the age of Ivan the Terrible. In the 16th century a great deal was invented, but it was in the form of whole compositions ornamented by "the intertwining of words". From the viewpoint of 16th-century authors, individual isolated factological references were of no value.

The chronology of these additional entries is very complex and confused, and it differs from that of *The Tale of Bygone Years*. It can be deciphered only after an analysis of the Byzantine system of chronology of the 9th and 10th centuries and reference to facts we have precise knowledge about.

It is rather interesting that the entries of the Nikon chronicle make up for gaps in *The Tale of Bygone Years* where considerable intervals exist between the events of the first recorded years.

Let us consider all the first-dated (tentative dates) events in Russian history in both groups.

The Tale of Bygone Years (1118)

859
> The Varangians levied tribute on the Chud, Slovenians, Merya, Ves and Krivichians.
> The northern tribes expelled the Varangians. Quarrels. Inviting of the Varangians. Rurik settled in Ladoga (1118 edition) and two years later in Novgorod.
> Rurik distributed towns among his men: Polotsk, Rostov, Beloozero. Two of Rurik's *boyars*—Askold* and Dir—set out for Kiev and began to rule there.

866 Askold and Dir launched an expedition against Constantinople.

Nikon chronicle

867 (tentatively)
> The beginning of the annual entry is quite similar to the text of *The Tale of Bygone Years*. There is a difference in the description of the search for a prince:
> "Let us seek and choose a prince from among our people (Russians) or among the Khazars or among the Polyanians or among the Danubians or among the Varangians. And, after deliberation, sent to the Varangians."

870
> Rurik's arrival in Novgorod.

872
> "Oskold's son was killed by Bulgars (Black Bulgars, in the lower course of the Dnepr)."
> "In the same year the Novgorod people were angry and said: 'It seems we must be Rurik's slaves, experience much and suffer from him and his kin'." "In the same year Rurik killed Vadim the Brave and executed many Novgorod people his supporters."

---

* In Nikon's chronicle the name is spelled as Oskold.— *Ed.*

873

> Rurik distributed towns: Polotsk, Rostov, Beloozero. "In the same year Oskold and Dir fought against the Polochanians and did much evil."

874

> "Expedition of Oskold and Dir against the Greeks..."

875

> "Oskold and Dir returned from Constantinople with the survivors of their force and there was a great lament in Kiev." "In the same year Oskold and Dir defeated numerous Pechenegs." "In the same year many Novgorod *boyars* fled from Rurik, from Novgorod to Kiev."

The above fragmentary entries which do not constitute a compact whole in the Nikon chronicle but are diluted by excerpts from the 1512 Chronology and other sources are of undoubtable interest in their entirety. The events artificially grouped in *The Tale of Bygone Years* under the year 862 are here attributed to different years filling the gap that exists in *The Tale* from 866 to 879.

The precise dates of comparable events in these two sources do not coincide (and generally cannot be regarded as final) but relative dates are observed. Thus, in *The Tale* Rurik arrived first not in Novgorod but in Ladoga; this was written by Ladozhanin who visited Ladoga four years before the editing of the chronicle and, apparently, drew on certain local legends. In actual fact Rurik came to Novgorod two years later which was reflected in the notes of the Nikon chronicle.

The chief difference between *The Tale of Bygone Years* (second and third editions) and the Nikon notes lies in various views of the events. Sylvester and Ladozhanin both describe affairs from the standpoint of the Varangians: the Varangians levied tribute, they were expelled; quarrels began—they were called, the Varangians settled in Russian towns and then conquered Kiev.

The author of the notes included in the Nikon chronicle regards events from the viewpoint of Kiev and Kievan Rus as an existing state. The Varangians appeared somewhere in the far Slavic-Finnish north. By joint force the northern tribes made the Normans return overseas to their country, and then, after a period of internecine strife, began to ponder over their new state order intending to appoint one prince to head the newly formed alliance of tribes. Several possibilities were discussed: the prince could be chosen from among the united tribes but therein, apparently, lay the reason for the conflict, because the anti-Varangian alliance consisted of different tribes speaking various languages.

Possibilities of inviting a prince from other places were also pointed out; the first place went to the Khazar Kaganate, a powerful nomad state in the Caspian steppe. The Polyanians, i. e. Kievan Rus, were in the second place. Third place was taken by "Danubians", a mysterious but very interesting notion linked geographically to the lower course and delta arms of the Danube regarded as Russians (in historical references) up to the end of the 14th century. And the last place was occupied by the Varangians to whom the delegation was sent. The invitation of a Swedish konung could be explained by the fact that the Varangians appeared in these northern parts without invitation but with arms. The invitation of a Varangian (the reference is to one prince) was, apparently, due to the principle of paying tribute to secure peace.

We do not know what reality was like, but the tendency here differs sharply from that described by the annalists of Monomakh who considered the Varangians the sole claimants upon the title of prince in the alliance of northern tribes. This tendency may be defined as pro-Kievan, since the first country to which it was intended to send for a prince was the Kievan principality of the Polyanians. The subsequent text confirms it, because all the additional notes are devoted to the activity of the Kiev princes Askold and Dir.

In *The Tale of Bygone Years* Askold and Dir are introduced to the reader as Varangians, Rurik's *boyars* who obtained his permission to undertake an expedition against Constantinople and allegedly conquering the Polyanian land and Kiev along the way. A. A. Shakhmatov showed a long time ago that the version of the Varangian origin of Askold and Dir was incorrect and that these 9th-century Kievan princes should be regarded as the descendants of Kii and the last members of the local Kievan dynasty.

The Polish historian Jan Dlugosz (died in 1480) who knew the Russian chronicles quite well wrote about Askold and Dir:

> After the death of Kii, Shchek and Khoriv, their sons and nephews ruled for many years among the Russians until the throne passed to two brothers Askold and Dir.

Shakhmatov's scholarly analysis of chronicles distorted by editing without reference to Dlugosz's text, and the notes made by the Sandomir historian from a Russian chronicle unknown to us, both reflect the same annalistic tradition to regard these princes killed by Varangians as the last link in the dynastic line descending from Kii. The Byzantine Emperor Basil I (867-886) called Askold the vainglorious Kagan of the northern Scythians. The name of the Kagan (a title equal to that of emperor) is written by Ladozhanin as Askold and in the Nikon chronicle (in its unique entries) as Oskold.

Although this cannot be proved it may be supposed that the name of this aboriginal prince who ruled along the Middle Dnepr might have retained the ancient proto-Slav form going back to Herodotus' Scoloti, "called after their king". In toponymy the name Scoloti has come down to our day in the names of two outlying rivers: Oskol at the edge of the proto-Slav land, and Vorskla, a proto-Slav river separating the Slavs from the nomads. In the 12th century the name of the river was written as Vorskol, the etymology of which is easily defined as (*vor*, fence) Fence of the Scoloti. It would be interesting indeed if subsequent analysis were to confirm the connection of the name Oskold to the archaic Scoloti.

The personality of Prince Dir is not clear. It seems that his name was artificially added to Oskold, because in describing their allegedly joint actions the singular instead of the plural grammatical form is used.

The Kievan Rus of Prince Oskold (the 870s) is

depicted as a state with complex foreign policy tasks.

Kievan Rus organises expeditions against Byzantium. These are well known both from Russian and Byzantine sources (860-1043).

An important task of Kievan Rus was to defend the thousand-kilometre-wide steppe frontier from various warlike peoples: the Turks-Bulgars, Magyars, and Pechenegs. And the Nikon records tell about Kiev's wars against these nomads. From Russian chronicles we know nothing about the war against the Bulgars whom we should regard as the Black Bulgars of Russian chronicles called the Inland Bulgars by Oriental authors. These Turko-Bulgar nomads occupied an enormous area all along the Rus' southern frontier. According to the Persian anonymous author, they were "a brave, warlike people instilling terror... they owned sheep, arms and implements of war".

The first reference in the Nikon notes to Oskold is connected with that warlike people: "Oskold's son was killed by Bulgars". The war against the Bulgars about which Russian sources are silent could be questioned, but it is confirmed by the same Persian anonymous author: "Inland Bulgaria is in a state of war with all of Rus."

The Nikon 872 entry has been confirmed: 16th-century historians offer information which became known to science only at the very end of the 19th century.

In 875 Prince Oskold defeated numerous Pechenegs. At the time the Pechenegs had already started to drift from the Azov Sea area westwards following in the footsteps of the Magyars who had gone to the Carpathians. Wars waged by the Dnepr Slavs against the nomads (in this case against the Bulgars and the Pechenegs) were an old and important function both of the Russian alliance of tribes in the 6th and the 7th centuries and of the state of Rus in the 9th century.

In the last twenty five years of the 9th century the Kievan state was beset by another problem: Varangian newcomers from overseas appeared in the extreme north of the Slav world. Despite their brevity the Nikon notes describe three groups of interesting events: first, the Novgorod people headed by Vadim the Brave waged an active struggle against Rurik in their town refusing to be his slaves. The name Vadim gives rise to some doubt, but the fact of anti-Varangian actions may well be believed, because it had a precedent—the expelling of the Varangians beyond the seas.

The second group of events is the flight of the Novgorod men to Kiev from Rurik. Kiev granted asylum to the refugees.

The third group of events is the most interesting. Kievan Rus organised resistance to the Varangians in the northern outskirts of its possessions. Recorded in one year we have: Rurik sends his *voivoda** to Polotsk, and Kiev responds—Askold fought against the Polochanians and did much evil. This is also probably connected with Kiev's war against the Krivichians mentioned by V. N. Tatishchev under the year 875. ("Oskold went on an expedition against the Krivichians and also defeated them.")

The Polochanians had already been a part of Rus, and the war against them after they had accepted Rurik's envoy was explained by Kiev's desire to return its possessions on the Western Dvina. The war against the Krivichian alliance was also prompted by the strategic importance of Smolensk, where the portage began from the Dnepr to the Lovat. It was a war for the Dnepr, so that the route from the Greeks to the Varangians would not turn into the route from the Varangians to the Greeks.

The strategic purpose of the Kiev princes was to prevent, to the best of their ability, the newcomers from overseas from advancing southwards or at least, to put their movement under the control of Kiev which had long been the master of the Dnepr. It was possible to prevent the invasion of Varangian forces only by setting up military strongholds along the principal routes. The first such stronghold of Rus before Rurik's arrival was Polotsk which blocked the Dvina; Smolensk could be the second, closing the very beginning of the Dnepr route. The Gnezdovo archaeological site with an enormous burial ground dating back to the 9th century was probably such a stronghold. The third stronghold

---

* Military commander.— *Ed.*

securing the approaches to Smolensk and the Dnepr in the north could be Russa (Staraya Russa) on the southern bank of Lake Ilmen (near the mouth of the Lovat which flowed from the Smolensk lands). The very name of the town, Russa, could have something to do with the original Rus. Russa's ties with the Kievan Prince and his personal domain can be traced very well in later treaties between princes of Novgorod and Kiev. The fourth, most important stronghold was undoubtedly Novgorod, built either by the Slovenians themselves during the war against the Varangians or by the Kiev prince as a small fort which prevented the Varangians from reaching Lake Ilmen, i. e. both trans-European routes—along the Volga to the Caliphate and down the Dnepr to Byzantium. In its subsequent history Novgorod was regarded by Kiev for quite a long time as a lesser town, the prince's domain, ruled by the elder sons of the Kiev princes.

It is probable that the supplement to the list of Slav peoples included in the state of Rus (there was only the Slovenian language in Rus) made not according to the name of the tribal alliance (Polyanians, Dregovichians and others) but according to the name of the town—Novgorodians—appeared in the original text after the building of the town which became the centre of a federation of different tribes. The remark preserved in Sylvester's variant should also be attributed to this group of events: "Since the time of those Varangians Novgorod began to be called the Russian land", i. e. was included in Rus, about which an additional note was made in the list of alliances of tribes constituting Rus.

The building of Novgorod by the Varangians (1118 edition) was excluded because the Scandinavians had a different name for that town completely unknown in Rus. Only Ladoga was a stronghold of the Normans; it was where Oleg returned after the successful expedition.

The Nikon notes' special value lies in the fact that, as distinct from *The Tale of Bygone Years* distorted by the Normanists' of the early 12th century, they depict Rus (in accordance with the surviving fragments of Nestor's text) as a large state which has existed for a long time and led an active foreign policy both in respect to the steppe, to rich Byzantium, and to the distant northern newcomers who were forced to bypass the possessions of Rus along the Volga route. In the intermediary points between Lake Ladoga and Kiev there were such strongholds as Novgorod, Russa and Gnezdovo-Smolensk; only individual trade missions or Varangian groups specially hired to serve Kiev could pass through them.

Archaeologists have found Varangian burial sites in Smolensk and on the Upper Volga, but these trading Varangians had nothing to do with the building of the Russian state which had already existed and established routes leading deep into Asia. It may be assumed that it was these routes which had attracted the Normans to the expanses of Eastern Europe.

The Varangians also appeared in Kiev but almost always as a hired army, rowdy, scandalous, and terribly cruel with the vanquished. We know this from the oldest Russkaya Pravda. The overland portages and strongholds reliably protected Kiev from unexpected incursions by large masses of Varangians as it was with their fleets on the West European coasts. Only Konung Oleg managed to outwit the townsfolk disguising his force as a trade caravan, and he seized power in Kiev and annihilated the Kii dynasty. Due to the fact that he led the enormous combined force of nearly all the Slav tribes (most of them had long formed part of Rus) Oleg succeeded in undertaking successful expeditions against Constantinople documented by the treaties of 907 and 911.

However, in the Russian chronicle Oleg features not so much as an historical figure but rather as a literary hero whose image is patched together out of recollections and Varangian sagas. The Varangian saga makes itself felt in the story about the successful deception of the Kievans and in the description of the situation, unusual for the seafaring Varangians, when the ships are put on logs and dragged overland and even sails raised when the wind was right. The story about Oleg's predetermined death was also borrowed from a saga — "you shall die from your horse".

The abundance of epic tales about the leader of the

successful joint expedition was explained by contemporaries as follows:

> And Oleg returned to Kiev, bringing gold and silk and fruit and wine and all sorts of ornaments. And Oleg was called the Oracle (enjoying the support of the supreme forces), because people were still ignorant pagans then.

The Novgorod chronicle contains a direct reference to the epic story of the successful Varangian:

> Oleg went to Novgorod and thence to Ladoga. Others say in tales that he went overseas and there a snake bit him and he died. There is a burial mound of his in Ladoga.

However, while there are so many epic tales on the subject, it is amazing that Russian people knew very little about Oleg's actual fate. Immediately after the expedition which made him rich and during which the joint force of Slav tribes and Varangians imposed a contribution on the Greeks, the Russian Grand Prince, as the 911 treaty read, disappeared not only from the capital of Rus but also from the Russian scene altogether. And he died in an unknown place: either in Ladoga, according to the Novgorod people, or in Kiev.

The epic of Oleg the Oracle was carefully pieced together by the editor of *The Tale of Bygone Years* in order to present the prince not only as a newcomer and usurper but also as a wise ruler freeing the Slav tribes from payment of tribute to the Khazar Kaganate. The annalist Ladozhanin juggled with the facts, knowing the version about Oleg's grave in Ladoga (having visited Ladoga in 1114 and discussed historical matters with the town elder Pavel, he could not have been ignorant of it), he nevertheless says nothing about Ladoga or Sweden because this would not have fitted the image of the founder of the Russian state and builder of Russian towns. The editor introduces a whole legend into the chronicle ending with the mourning of the Kievans and Oleg's ceremonial burial in Kiev's Shchekovitsa. In Kiev, however, another grave of some Oleg was known, in quite a different place. Besides, Ladozhanin inserted into the chronicle the authentic text of the treaty with the Greeks (911) taken from the prince's archives.

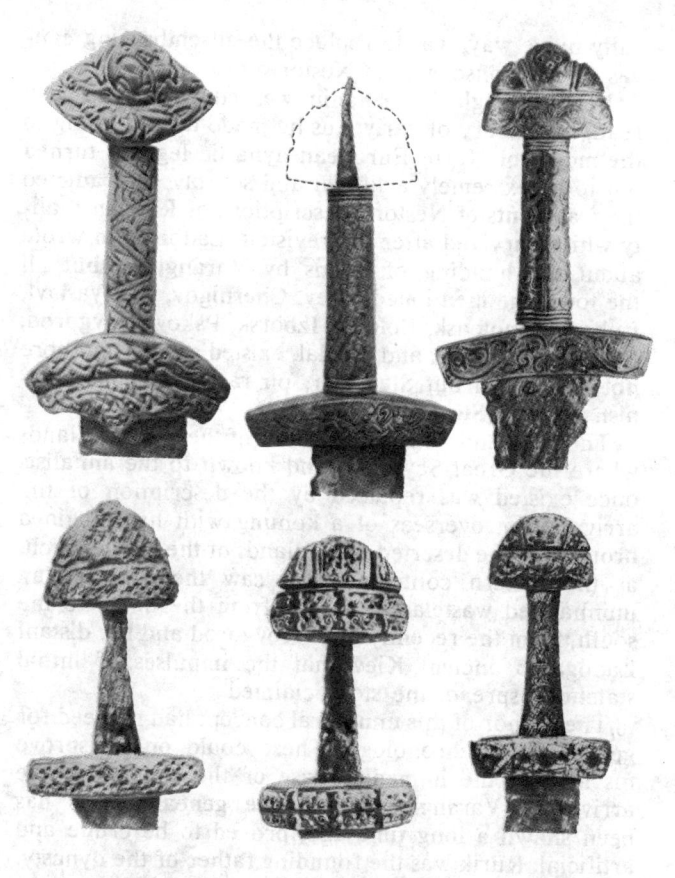

Swords (10th century and first half of the 11th century)

As a result of the editorial and literary efforts of Ladozhanin a new special concept of an early history was created; it was based on two heroes, two Varangians, Rurik and Oleg. The former headed a number of northern Slav-Finnish tribes (on their request) and established law and order for them, while the latter conquered southern Rus, did away with Khazarian tribute and headed the successful expedition of 907 or 911 against the Greeks which enriched all the participants.

This simple concept, presenting history in a medie-

75

vally naive way, was to replace the all-embracing canvas of the conscientious Nestor.

Yet, although Ladozhanin was educated and well read, the history of early Rus he made up according to the model of North European dynastic legends turned out to be extremely artificial and sharply contradicted the fragments of Nestor's descriptions of Russian reality which survived after the revision. Ladozhanin wrote about the building of towns by Varangians, but all the towns he mentioned, Kiev, Chernigov, Pereyaslavl, Lubech, Smolensk, Polotsk, Izborsk, Pskov, Novgorod, Rostov, Beloozero, and Suzdal, existed earlier and bore not Varangian but Slavic or, on rare occasions, Finnish names (Suzdal).

The thousand-year-long history of the southern lands where the Great Scythian land known to the annalists once existed was replaced by the description of the arrival from overseas of a konung with his imagined brothers to the deserted swamplands of the north which, as the eastern contemporaries saw them, were "an uninhabited wasteland". It was from the north to the south, from the recently built Novgorod and the distant Ladoga to ancient Kiev that the impulses of initial statehood spread, the story claimed.

The author of this unnatural concept had no need for genealogy or chronology. These could only disprove his idea of the immediate rise of the state after the arrival of Varangian ships. The genealogy, as has been shown a long time ago, proved to be crude and artificial: Rurik was the founding father of the dynasty, Igor was his son, Oleg a relative, alhough the writer closest in time to these figures (Iakov Mnikh who glorified Yaroslav the Wise) started the new dynasty of Kiev princes (after the Kii dynasty) from Igor the Old (died in 945) ignoring the short rule of usurper Oleg and not considering it necessary to mention Rurik who never reached Kiev.

The 1118 editor made Igor Rurik's son. The chronology of events and of the princes' reigns in the 9th and early 10th centuries is extremely vague and contradictory. Fortunately for science, the editing of the chronicle was done unceremoniously yet not consistently enough: too much of Nestor's detailed and interesting text had survived for the reader to regard Ladozhanin's concept as the only possible version.

Considering from this vantage point the fragmentary notes of the Nikon chronicle we discover in them the antithesis of the pro-Varangian theory. The author of the original notes was undoubtedly a Kievan, as was Nestor. He knows what was happening in the south—the struggle against the Pechenegs and the Turks-Bulgars; he knows everything happening in Kiev, and most importantly, he views the appearance of the newcomers on the Western Dvina River and Lake Ilmen through the eyes of a Kievan: the Kiev prince sends troops against the Polochanians and the Krivichians in whose lands the Varangians appeared, the Kiev prince receives the Novgorod refugees fleeing from the violence perpetrated by Rurik. This is quite a different view of the early years of the Russian state's contacts with Varangians!

The question naturally arises, could these Nikon notes be an indirect rendering of surviving fragments of Nestor's text removed by one of the editors of 1116-1118?

The thought is prompted not so much by the Kievan viewpoint of the author of the fragments (not every Kievan is Nestor) but rather by the presence in both the fragments and Nestor's genuine text of such a rare geographical notion as Danubians in reference to the population of the Lower Danube. Nestor writes that the Danubians "to this day" indicate the Kievets site as the place where Kii stayed. In the Nikon records the word appears during the discussion of the question where to search for a prince—among the Khazars, the Polyanians or the Danubians. In this context the Danubians appear to be some sort of state union equal in importance to Rus (which had not yet included the Slovenians) or the Khazar Kaganate, but undoubtedly distinct from Bulgaria and the Bulgars about whom Nestor had written at great length under their own name. The mystery of the Danubians will be solved later when we study the route of the Rus to Byzantium and the crossing near the mouth of the Danube.

Having acknowledged the concept of the editors of *The Tale of Bygone Years* to be artificial and trivial we must seek an answer to the question, what was the real role played by the Varangians in early Russian history?

1. Varangians were attracted to the almost untractable Russian lands by reports about Rus' lively trade with the countries of the Orient; the fact of the trade is proved by numismatic finds. In the second half of the 9th century the Varangians began their raids against the northern Slav and Finnish tribes and levied tribute on them.

2. The Kiev princes of the 870s undertook a number of serious measures to resist the Varangians (expeditions against the Krivichians and Polochanians). It was probably then that such strongholds as Russa and Novgorod were built in the north.

3. Oleg (Swede? Norwegian?) was based in Ladoga but gained possession of the Kiev throne for a short time. His victorious expedition against Byzantium was carried out as a joint venture by many tribes; following the expedition, testified to by the text of the 911 treaty, Oleg disappeared from the Russian scene and died in an unknown place. Legends indicate his graves in the most different places. The Varangians had nothing to do with the building of Russian towns.

4. For a long time Novgorod paid the Varangians tribute to avoid new raids. Byzantium paid a similar tribute to the Russians "to secure peace".

5. The existence of overland portages between the river routes in Eastern Europe prevented the Varangians from taking advantage of their being a seafaring people (as they did in Western Europe). The Kiev princes' countermeasures contributed to the turning of the principal Varangian routes towards the Volga River instead of the Dnepr. The road from the Varangians to the Greeks was the way around the European continent. The route from Kiev to Novgorod and the Baltic was called the road from the Greeks to the Varangians.

6. Kiev princes, as well as the Byzantine emperors widely used Varangian hired detachments, specially sending for them to the North Baltic area, overseas. Even Oskold had sent for Varangians, if we are to believe *The Tale of Bygone Years*. Planning another expedition against Byzantium in 941, Igor "sent men to hire Varangians overseas inviting them to fight

against Byzantium". Pechenegs were hired simultaneously with the Varangians. Varangian warriors carried out diplomatic missions for Kiev princes and took part in concluding treaties. Varangians were hired for wars and to commit political murders: hired Varangians knifed Prince Yaropolk in 980, and Varangians also killed Prince Gleb in 1015.

7. Part of the Varangian nobility was included among the Russian *boyars*. Some Varangians such as Sveneld gained high positions but were very cruel to the Slav population. Cruelty, often senseless, was frequently displayed by the Varangian forces fighting under the Russian flag. For that reason they were identified with the Rus, i. e., with the population of the state they served.

Thus the Rus' trade with the countries of the Caspian coast for a long time was peaceful, and local authors described how the Rus came out on any coast and traded there or travelled on camels to Baghdad. But at the very beginning of the 10th century (Oleg's time) when it may be assumed that the number of Varangians in the Kievan forces grew indefinitely the sources report terrible atrocities perpetrated by the Rus on the same coast of the Caspian Sea. The real Rus-Slavs in the expeditions of that decade (903-913) turned out to be strongly diluted by undisciplined groups of Varangians who were taken by the local population for the Rus.

The cruelty of the Varangians is described by the French annalist from Normandy Dudon of St Quentin:

> Carrying out their banishments and expulsions, they (the Normans) first made sacrifices in honour of their god Thor. The sacrifice is not cattle or some animal, not the gifts of Father Bacchus or Ceres but human blood... That is why the priest appoints people for the sacrifice from a lot. The people to be sacrificed are clubbed over the head with a bull's yoke. Each person whose lot it is to be sacrificed has his brains blown out of his head in a special way, laid out on the ground, and then turned over to find the vein leading to the heart. Having squeezed out all the blood they, according to

> custom, smear their heads with the blood and quickly unfurl the sails on their boats...

The warriors of Oleg the Oracle displayed equal cruelty in the expedition against the Greeks:

> Many of the Greeks were killed... And among those who were taken captive, some were hacked to death, others tortured ... and a lot of evil was done.

8. At the end of the 10th and beginning of the 11th centuries a foremost task of the Russian state was to resist the rowdy gangs of mercenaries. They were quartered not in the towns, but outside the town walls (for example, in Shestovitsy at Chernigov). In 980 when Prince Vladimir went overseas to hire Varangians and captured Kiev from his brother with their help, the Varangians demanded a very high price for their services. Vladimir banished the Varangians to Byzantium and asked the emperor not to return them: "And do not let one come here (to Kiev)!"

Acute conflicts arose in Novgorod in 1015 when Yaroslav hired many Varangians intending to launch a war against his father. The Novgorod folk defended their wives' and daughters' honour with arms.

9. The second stage in the development of Kievan Rus, marked by the appearance of the Varangians, did not introduce any significant changes into the course of the Russian historical process. Rus expanded by including the northern tribes' territories as a result of these tribes' consolidation in the course of the struggle against the newcomers and Kiev's joining in that struggle.

The two early stages in the development of Kievan Rus of which the first is described by the chronicle only in a fragmentary manner and the second is distorted, should not be sharply separated from each other. During the entire 9th and first half of the 10th centuries there was a single process of the rise and strengthening of the state element in Rus. Neither raids by the Magyars or the inland Bulgars, nor visits by Varangians, nor attacks by the Pechenegs could stop the process or considerably change it. It is necessary to take a better look at what was occurring in the Slav lands generally and in the Rus super-alliance in particular.

Early Rus (9th to mid-10th centuries)

Polyudye

Polyudye is the key notion to the understanding of the early Russian state structure. It is highly important for us to establish the existence of *polyudye* at the level of one tribal alliance, i. e. at a lower level than the alliance of alliances, Rus. Concerning the tribal alliance of the Vyatichians it is known that there was a full circle of *polyudye*—the prince's annual rounds of the entire ruled territory, the collection of "apparel" (probably furs) and the sale of the collected wealth by floating it down the Don to the Itil River in exchange for which the Vyatichian nobility obtained large amounts of Oriental silver coins, and the Oriental decorations which influenced local tribal crafts.

On a par with the tribal alliance of Vyatichians (Slavs) there existed the super-alliance of Rus uniting five or six tribal alliances similar to the Vyatichian alliance. *Polyudye* was also widely practiced here (the Rus carried their furs "from the most distant parts of the Slav world") but it differed significantly from the Vyatichian alliance in the size of the ruled territory, and therefore the collecting of tribute had more developed organisational forms.

The Rus, just as the Vyatichians, had a second major task, that of selling the results of *polyudye*. The 9th-century Oriental author described the enormous scope of Rus trade expeditions, much larger than what we could expect with the Vyatichians. The Rus sold their goods to Byzantium and to the lands of the Caliphate reaching Rey, Baghdad and Balkh (!).

The phenomena occurring in each of the independent tribal alliances and in the super-alliance of Rus which existed simultaneously, were similar in many respects, but differed in scope, i. e., what occurred in the alliance of alliances was of an order higher than what occurred within the individual alliances which had not yet reached the highest degree of integration.

Perhaps, here lies the starting point of new social

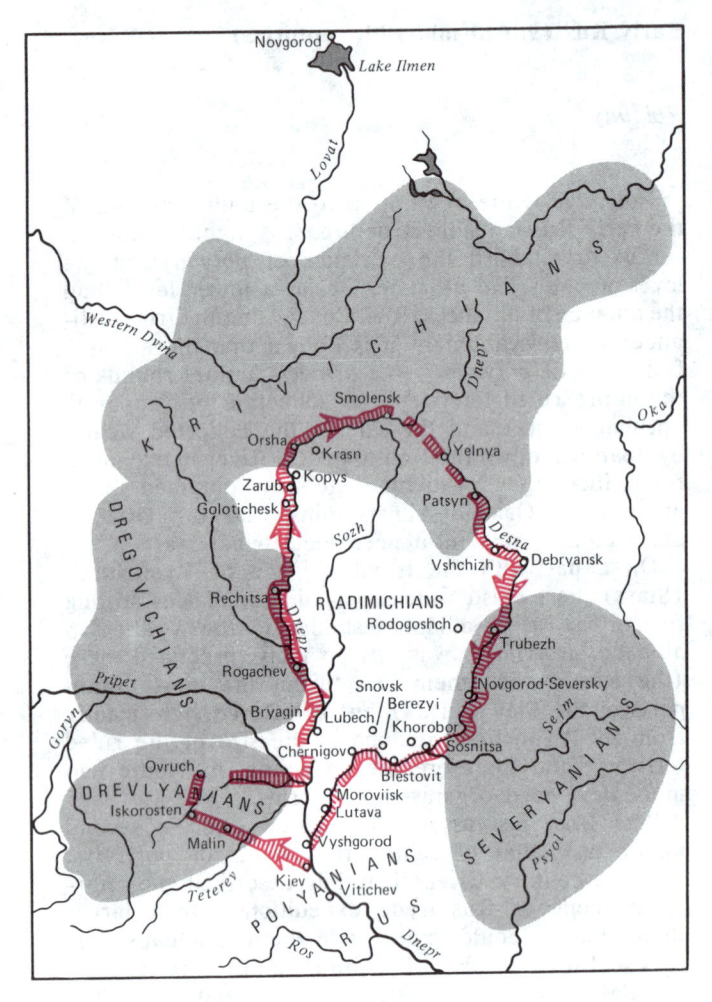

Polyudye Levied by the Kiev Princes in the First Half of the 10th Century According to Emperor Constantine Porphyrogenitus

and economic relations, the new formation. The alliance of tribes was the highest stage in the development of the primitive communal system which prepared certain tribes for the forthcoming historical stage of living in large communities where ancient patriarchal forms of relations inevitably and rapidly disappeared giving way to new, broader ones. The formation of an alliance of tribes had paved the way to statehood. The "head of heads" leading a dozen tribes and called the "high sovereign", translated as "king" by foreigners, was not just the ruler of primitive tribes but rather the head of the rising state. When society rises one step higher and creates a new association out of the tribal alliances, new both in terms of quantity and quality, i. e., the alliance of tribal alliances, the question of statehood can be settled only in one way: the state is considered to exist where integration of tribes has reached such a high level.

When the annalist described in detail which of the Eastern Slav tribal alliances were included in Rus, he described the state of Rus at one of its development stages (the first half of the 9th century) when Rus extended to only a half of the tribal alliances. *Polyudye* is the first, most clearly revealed form of domination and subordination, of implementation of the right to the land, and establishment of the notion of citizenship. If in the tribal alliance *polyudye* could to some extent be founded on the former tribal relations, in the super-alliance it was completely abstracted and separated from any patriarchal memories.

In view of the falsifications the Normanists perpetrate in respect to Russian history it should be noted that in the sources *polyudye* is presented as a purely Slav institution with Slav terminology. *Polyudye* is known, for example, in Poland where it was called *stan* (bivouac) and the tribute levied *goshchenye*.

The Russian word *polyudye* is found both in chronicles and in deeds. *Polyudye* has nothing to do with the Varangians; on the contrary, the Russian, Slavic word was used in Scandinavian lands to denote this phenomenon. In the Scandinavian saga about Harald such rounds are denoted by the borrowed Slav word *poluta (polutasvarf)*. The Emperor Constantine Porphyrogenitus denotes the prince's rounds by the same Slav word.

Polyudye was known to Oriental authors as the visiting of the remotest Slav lands long before the Normans appeared in Rus. It may be regarded as typical of the entire 9th century, perhaps even the late 8th century, and of the first half of the 10th century, although it is known even in the 12th century as a local survival. A detailed description of *polyudye* in the mid-10th century has been left by Emperor Constantine, and a tragic event—a prince's murder during the collection of *polyudye*—was described at great length in the chronicle under the year 945.

Analysing *polyudye* of the 940s we should extend the idea of it to an earlier time, to the turn of the 9th century; the difference in the size of lands ruled by Rus did exist but it did not make any qualitative differences. The super-alliance of the early 9th century consisting of five or six tribal alliances and the super-alliance of the mid-10th century consisting of eight to ten alliances did not differ fundamentally.

Let us begin an account of *polyudye* with Emperor Constantine's description (circa 948), rearranging some of the parts topically.

Constantine Porphyrogenitus

"About the Rus, Who Come to Constantinople from Russia in "One-tree' Ships *(Monoxyla)*."

The severe manner of life of these (same) Rus in winter time is as follows. When the month of November begins, their chiefs together with all the Rus at once leave Kiev and go off on the *polyudye* which means rounds, that is, to the Slav regions of the Drevlyanians and Dregovichians and Krivichians and Severyanians and the rest of the Slavs who are tributaries of the Rus. There they are maintained throughout the winter, but then once more, starting from the month of April, when the ice of the Dnepr River melts, they come back to Kiev. Then they take their ships, equip them, and set for Byzantium.

The monoxyla which come down from

outer Rus to Constantinople are from Novgorod, where Svyatoslav, son of Igor, prince of Rus, had his seat, and others from the fortress of Smolensk and from Lubech and Chernigov and from Vyshgorod. All these come down the river Dnepr, and meet at the town of Kiev, also called Samvatas(?). Their Slav tributaries, called Krivichians and the Lenzanenes (Polochanians) and the rest of the Slavs, cut the monoxyla on their mountains in time of winter, and when they have prepared them, as spring approaches, and the ice melts, they bring them on to the neighbouring lakes.

And since these lakes debouch into the river Dnepr, they enter thence on to the same river, and come down to Kiev, and draw the ships ashore to be finished and sell them to the Rus. The Rus buy the frames only, furnishing them with oars and rowlocks and other tackle from their old monoxyla which they dismantle; and so they fit them out.

Emperor Constantine's highly interesting account of *polyudye*—the Emperor saw the Russian one-tree boats with his own eyes every year—has long been known to historians, but there has not been a single attempt to recreate mid-10th century *polyudye* in its full scope as a Russia-wide annual phenomenon. Yet it is impossible to understand the crux of the Rus state in the 8th-10th centuries without *polyudye*.

Let us begin with the one-tree vessels which were frequently regarded as small Slav dugouts hollowed out of one tree thus explaining their Greek name *monoxyla*. The small dugouts intended for only three people did exist at the time as we know from *The Notes of a Greek Toparch*, Constantine's younger contemporary. But here we have something quite different: from the above text it is clear that the vessels were furnished with rowlocks and oars while the dugouts had only a paddle and never had rowlocks and oars: the dugout was too narrow for them.

It becomes clear what the one-tree ships were like when the source describes how they pass the Dnepr rapids: the people get out of the vessels where the load is left and push them through the rapids; some push the bow, others the middle and still others the stern with long poles. In each case we have the plural: one boat is pushed by a crowd of people; the boat contains not only the load but also chained slaves. It is obvious that these are not dugouts, but ships carrying 20 to 40 people, as we know from other sources.

The large size of the Russian boats is also attested to by Constantine's words that having covered the most difficult part of the route, dragging their ships through the rapids, the Rus "furnish their one-tree ships with the missing gear again: sails, masts and yards which they bring along". The masts and the yards are final proof that these are not dugouts but rather large ships. They are called one-tree ships because the keel of the ship was made out of one tree, 10-15 metres long. A ship built in that way was capable not only of sailing of rivers but also suited for long sea trips.

The annual process of making several hundred ships points as it is to a state approach to this important matter. The ships were built throughout the Dnepr basin and even in the basin of the Ilmen. The source mentions large areas of the Krivichians and the Polochanians where the ship-builders worked all winter.

We are already quite familiar with this enormous area of the Dnepr basin all the rivers of which come together at Kiev; that town became the master of navigation on the Dnepr back in the 5th-6th centuries when the spontaneous movement of the northern Slav tribes southwards began. Now the "tributaries" of the Rus were hewing one-tree ships in "their hills" throughout the region. Constantine, however, writes that the tributary Slavs sold their newly-made ships in Kiev. But it is not accidental that the emperor linked ship-building to being subjects of Rus; apparently this was a duty of the tributary Slavs who were paid something for their work.

In creating the merchant fleet the state principle was also displayed in the fact that Constantine lists local sites where ships were assembled in an area 900 kilometres long: Novgorod (the basin of the Ilmen, Desna and Sejm), Smolensk (the basin of the Upper Dnepr),

Chernigov (the basin of the Desna and the Sejm), Lubech (the basin of the Berezina, part of the Dnepr and the Sozh), and Vyshgorod (the basin of the Pripet and the Teterev). A special site was set aside in Kiev (apparently Pochaina?) where all the ships delivered from these rivers were finally furnished. The name of the fortress Samvatas, still remains undeciphered by scholars.

Thus, the building of the fleet occupied wintertime and part of spring (floating it downriver and equipping it) and demanded the efforts of many thousands of Slav carpenters and shipbuilders. The process was under the control of five regional heads one of whom was the son of the Grand Prince, and it was completed in the capital itself. In addition to the work of the men who made the wooden hull of the ships there was the toil of the Slav women who wove the sails.

The number of vessels in the merchant fleet is unknown to us; the military fleets numbered up to 2,000 ships. The annual trade expeditions that carried the results of *polyudye* were, obviously, smaller in size, but could not be too small because they had to make their way through the lands of the Pechenegs who pillaged the Russian caravans at the Rapids.

Let us tentatively set the number of one-tree ships at 400-500. One sail required about 16 square metres of *tolstina* (a rough but strong canvas) or about 150 cubits of cloth. This was a job for two weavers during the entire winter. Taking into account the fact that below the Rapids additional sails were unfurled we obtain the following estimate: the work of 2,000 looms all winter was necessary to make all the sails, i. e. the work of the women of 80 to 100 villages of the time. Add to this the growing and spinning of the flax and hemp and the making of about 2,000 metres of *uzhishcha*, a rope for the ships.

All these calculations, yielding very approximate results of course, show, however, that behind the terse lines of the source we should see phenomena in their full and real scope. And it turns out that only one part of the social complex called *polyudye* for short constituted quite a considerable duty. The making of the looms, carrying of the tribute to Kiev, making of the ships and sails for them—all this was an early form of corvée the full burden of which fell upon both the prince's servants and the communal peasants.

Let us consider, from the same positions, *polyudye* itself as an annual state undertaking and reveal, as far as possible, its practical organisational importance. Emperor Constantine's treatise contains sufficient material.

First of all, we know the lands of the tribes, or tribal alliances, to be more precise, through which *polyudye* passed. These belonged to the Drevlyanians (between the Dnepr, the Goryn and the upper reaches of the Southern Bug), the Dregovichians (from the Pripet in the north to the watershed with the basins of the Neman and the Dvina, in the east up to the Dnepr inclusive), the large area of the Krivichians in the upper courses of the Dnepr, the Dvina and the Volga, and finally, the Severyanians extending to the Middle Desna, the banks of the Sejm and the basin of the Upper Psyol and Vorskla.

If we were to draw the four areas on the map we would see that they involved a region of 700 by 1,000 kilometres and were almost adjacent to each other leaving a "blank spot" about 300 kilometres in diametre. That spot falls on the lands of the Radimichians. The latter were not included by Constantine Porphyrogenitus among the tribes paying tribute to Kiev. The Emperor was absolutely accurate: the Radimichians were subjugated by *Voivoda* Vladimir the Wolf's Tail only in 984 after the battle on the Peschana River 36 years after the writing of the treatise.

Second, we know that *polyudye* lasted for six months (from November through April), or about 180 days.

Third, we can supplement Constantine's report with the speed at which *polyudye* travelled, keeping in mind that it is highly tentative, equal to approximately 7-8 kilometres a day.

Fourth, we know that it formed a circuit, and if we follow the order in which the tribes are listed, went by the sun.

Multiplying the number of days by the average daily speed (7-8 kilometres) we obtain the approximate length of the entire course of *polyudye*—1,200 to 1,500 kilometres. What could have been its actual itinerary? The route along the perimeter of the four tribal alliances should be rejected outright, because half of it passed through the trackless forest and swampland fringes and the length would be about 3,000 kilometres.

The account of Olga's reforms in the chronicle has two groups of precise geographical identifications: near Novgorod in the north—the Msta and the Luga, and near Kiev in the south—the Dnepr and the Desna. Setting out from Kiev in autumn and returning in the spring the prince might have taken advantage of these same Kievan rivers which form an almost continuous ring: at first the route goes up the Dnepr to Smolensk and then down the Desna to Olga's town Vyshgorod standing at the mouth of the Desna.

Let us check these calculations: the route from Kiev to Smolensk along the bank of the Dnepr, or over the ice, makes up about 600 kilometres. The turn to the Drevlyanians, to Iskorosten, where Igor collected tribute, increases the distance by another 200-250 kilometres. The way from Smolensk to Kiev along the Desna to Yelnya (the town is mentioned in the 12th century), Bryansk and Chernigov constituted about 700-750 kilometres. The total distance (1,500-1,600) could be travelled from November to April.

The route also satisfies us in respect to all four tribal alliances Constantine mentions. The Vervianians (Drevlyanians) stand first in his list; it is most likely that *polyudye* began with the land closest to Kiev, that of the Drevlyanians, a day's travel from Kiev to the west. On the way from Kiev to the capital of the Drevlyanian land, Iskorosten, lay the town of Malin not mentioned in the chronicle but quite probably the residence of the Drevlyanian prince Mal who sought Olga in marriage. In addition to Iskorosten *polyudye* could visit Vruchy (Ovruch) lying 50 kilometres north of Iskorosten.

Collected in November when the rivers had not frozen over yet the Drevlyanian tribute could well be floated down the Uzha into the Dnepr to Chernobyl and from there to Kiev so as not to be an additional burden during the circular journey.

From the Drevlyanian Iskorosten (and Ovruch) *polyudye* must have moved in a northeastern direction to Lubech which served as the northern gates of Constantine Porphyrogenitus' "Inner Rus". Advancing north up the Dnepr *polyudye* entered the lands of the Druguvitians (Dregovichians) living along both banks of the river, and further westwards. On the eastern bank of the Dnepr the Dregovichians neighboured the Radimichians.

In the upper reaches of the Dnepr the prince's expedition entered the extensive lands of the Krivichians; it passed along their southern fringe and reached the Krivichian capital of Smolensk. Further the route could turn to the ancient Yelnya, to the Desna, and enter the northwestern edge of the Severyanian land (Novgorod-Seversky and Sevsk) somewhere near Bryansk. Then it went along the Desna to Kiev through Chernigov which lay outside the Severyanian lands.

This circuit did not cross the central part of the lands belonging to the tribes listed, but went along the inner edge of the possessions of each of the four tribes bypassing all along the blank spot of the Radimichians not mentioned by Emperor Constantine among the subjects of Rus. It does not seem possible to shift the supposed route to any side, because in that case one of the tribes inevitably drops out or the speed changes greatly as compared with 1190 when, as has been established, the *polyudye* expedition moved with an average speed of 7-8 kilometres a day.

The average speed of the *polyudye* expedition does not mean, of course, that the riders and carts travelled only 7-8 kilometres a day. In such wooded parts usually a day of travel equals 30 kilometres. In that case the entire circuit may be divided into 50 daily laps: the day on the road and resting at night. It is probable that places where the night was spent were called *stanovishches* in the 10th century. Another 130 days remain for longer stops.

Thus we should regard *polyudye* as a movement

with a usual speed of horse travel and average stops of 2-3 days in places where the expedition spent the night. The stops could be longer in larger towns while the expedition could stay for a shorter time in lesser *stanovishches*. The slow advance made it possible to undertake incursions away from the principal route; therefore, the itinerary of *polyudye* is not a line but a 20- to 30-kilometre-wide strip crisscrossed by the tribute collectors.

The strip within which the larger *polyudye* described by Constantine Porphyrogenitus moved included a number of towns and settlements known from 10th-12th century sources (according to archaeological data frequently dating back to the 10th century) which could have been *stanovishches* for *polyudye*:

The route from Kiev	*The route from Smolensk*
Iskorosten	Dorogobuzh (?) Luchin (?)
Vruchy	Yelnya
Chernobyl	Rognedino
Bryagin	Patsyn
Lubech	Zarub
Strezhev	Vshchizh
Rogachev	Debryansk
Kopys	Trubezh
Odrsk	Novgorod-Seversky
Kasplya	Radogoshch
Krasny	Khorobor
Smolensk	Sosnitsa
	Blestovit
	Snovsk
	Chernigov
	Moraviisk
	Vyshgorod
	Kiev

Five towns (Kiev, Vyshgorod, Lubech, Smolensk and Chernigov) in this list were mentioned by Constantine, the rest were pointed out on various occasions and at different times by the annalists and in the deed of Rostislav of Smolensk.

Polyudye was remembered as late as the 12th century in one of the towns, Kopys. Among the large number of places mentioned in Rostislav's deed (1136) tribute called *polyudye* was collected only in two. "At Kopys *polyudye* is four grivnas..." Kopys is situated on the Dnepr, along the route of our *polyudye*.

Smolensk was the furthest place and turning point, half of the prince's circuit. Somewhere near Smolensk the *polyudye* expedition had to pass into the Desna River system. A visit to Dorogobuzh was possible, but the Desna route most probably began in Yelnya. Smolensk is indicated by Constantine as one of the major centres from which the monoxyla ships set out for Kiev in spring, after the rivers had been cleared of ice. It is quite possible that the tribute collected during the first half of *polyudye* was not taken along but remained in *stanovishches* until spring when it could easily be taken down the Dnepr. Smolensk, the town which Constantine called a fortress, could have been the main storage place for the tribute.

Polyudye undoubtedly involved many people. Constantine writes that the princes set out in November "with all the Rus". Igor left for the Drevlyanian land with all his men and, having collected the tribute, sent most of the men with the tribute to Kiev and stayed in the hostile land with "a lesser troop". The assumption is that the smaller force seemed sufficient to the prince to maintain the authority of the Grand Prince and provide for his security.

Grooms, cart drivers, various servants, cooks, craftsmen who mended the saddles and harness and so on had to accompany the warriors on the *polyudye* expeditions. Some idea of the numbers involved may be provided by the words of Ibn Fadlan (922) concerning the Kievan prince: "Together with him (the king of the Rus) there are 400 men in his castle from among the warriors, his companions and the loyal people with him..." Even if we take account of the fact that the prince had to leave some of his warriors in Kiev to defend the capital from the Pechenegs, *polyudye* should have consisted of several hundred warriors and "loyal people". All of them had to be accommodated at the *stanovishche*.

In wintertime the *stanovishche* had to have *izbas*, warm houses for the people, stables, storehouses to keep and sort out the tribute, storage facilities for the grain and fodder. The *stanovishche* had to be equipped with stoves to bake bread, millstones, a forge for the weaponry.

Many of the things necessary at the *stanovishche* had to be prepared beforehand, while the *polyudye* had not arrived yet. There must have been people doing various jobs to prepare the *stanovishche*, to service it during the *polyudye* and to guard the *stanovishche* (perhaps with the tribute left there until spring) until the time when the prince and his warriors arrived again.

The fact that *polyudye* did not travel deep into the tribal areas but only went along the edge of the territory of each tribal alliance makes us ponder over the way in which the tribute was collected. Most probably, the mechanics of collecting tribute directly from the peasant population were sufficiently well regulated by the local princes and a certain amount of tribute from the remote areas was taken beforehand to the places through which the *polyudye* of the Kiev prince passed.

We should not imagine *polyudye* as a frenzied indiscriminate raid by the prince's warriors of the towns and villages. The amount of tribute was strictly fixed, as we know from the events of 945, and it is most likely that annual *polyudye* visited the same *stanovishches* from year to year, and the local princes delivered the required tribute there beforehand.

The *polyudye* route went 200 to 250 kilometres from the outer boundaries of the tribal alliances of the Drevlyanians, Dregovichians, Krivichians and Severyanians. It is difficult to imagine such a large and bulky mechanism as *polyudye* without the preliminary delivery of tribute organised by the local tribal chieftains. If the voracious and greedy mass of Kiev warriors were to regularly devastate the same areas along the Dnepr and the Desna, the population of these parts would simply disperse, going deep into tribal territory, far away from the dangerous circular itinerary. Since this did not occur, it means that the local princes, safeguarding their position in the tribe and seeking to distribute the Kiev tribute evenly, guaranteed the delivery of a definite amount of tribute to the *stanovishches*.

Violation of the agreement with Kiev concerning *polyudye* could turn *polyudye* into an expedition against some tribal alliance. Therefore *polyudye* should be regarded not as a primary form of collecting tribute but as the final phase of the process also involving local tribal armed force.

The largest tribal alliance were the Krivichians. The tribute they owed was to be brought to Smolensk, their capital. That town stood at the crossroads between Novgorod and Kiev and, as we already know, the turning point of the larger *polyudye*. Therefore we should not be surprised by the existence of an enormous camp and town of Gnezdovo in the 9th and 10th centuries near Smolensk. The burial mound cemetery of the 9th-11th centuries contains about 5,000 graves, being the largest in Europe. A. N. Nasonov[*] had every reason to say: "Undoubtedly a powerful feudal nobility arose in old Smolensk of the 9th-11th centuries; its wealth is revealed by the contents of the Gnezdovo burial mounds. The nobility grew from the local root: the Gnezdovo mounds belonged predominantly to the Krivichians as all the archaeologists acknowledge. It may well be that the wealth and power of local nobility was founded on the exploitation of the dependent and semi-dependent population." It was that locally rooted nobility which could have been the intermediary between the Krivichian countryside and the *polyudye* of the Kiev prince which could not be extended to the whole enormous territory of the Krivichians.

Quite an interesting and vivid account of *polyudye* is contained in the Russian chronicle under year 945. Prince Igor the Old had just completed two

---

[*] A. N. Nasonov (1898-1965), Soviet historian, expert on Russian chronicles.— *Ed.*

expeditions against Byzantium. During the first sea expedition of 941 Igor led a fleet of 10,000 ships. The figure may be exaggerated, but the Russian squadron then conquered the entire southwestern coast of the Black Sea: Wiphinia, Paphlagonia, Pontian Heraclia and Nikomydia. Even Bosphorus suffered. Only the famous Greek fire-throwers which shot like lightning drove the Russians away from Constantinople.

Immediately after the defeat Igor began preparations for a new expedition. The Kiev Prince hired overseas Varangians and steppe Pechenegs (even taking hostages from among them); he invited the distant northern forces of the Slovenians and the Krivichians and the southern forces of the Dnestr Tivercians. The army advanced in 943 both by land and by sea. The Khersonian Greeks reported to Emperor Román: "The Russian ships are coming: they cover the whole sea."

When Igor had reached the Danube the emperor sent him ambassadors to sue for peace. Igor sought the advice of his men who were glad to obtain tribute from the empire without battle. "Who knows who will win, we or they (the Greeks)? Who has heard the advice of the sea? We do not tread the earth but the depths of the sea and death stalks us at every step." Having received a ransom from the Greeks Igor returned to Kiev, and the next year signed a treaty with Román and Constantine Porphyrogenitus which allowed Rus to send to Constantinople for trade "any amount of ships ... so long as they come with peaceful aims". The treaty was approved in Kiev in the St Ilya Cathedral on the Podol and on the hill at the idol of Perun.

The double onslaught against Byzantium in 941 and 943 was possibly provoked by obstacles the Greeks set up against Russian trade despite the 911 Treaty signed with the father of Román and Constantine. Some restrictions were still preserved in the 941 treaty, but the way to the trade centre of the world, Constantinople, was open for Russian ships. Having spent so much on the furnishing of two such enormous fleets, one of which suffered great losses, and on paying mercenary forces, the Kiev government had to replenish its resources generally, and its export in particular.

The appearance in Kiev of Varangian forces hired by Igor should be attributed to the late 930s when the Varangian leader Sveneld is mentioned. In order to pay the mercenaries Igor assigned them the tribute from the Drevlyanians and the Ulichians provoking a war between these tribal alliances against Kiev. The Ulichian town of Peresechen (at the Dnepr) resisted Igor for three years, but Igor finally "overcame the Ulichians, imposed tribute on them and passed the tribute to Sveneld".

The above-said is sometimes interpreted as the passing of the right to collect tribute, but its grammatical form allows us to understand it only in one way: tribute obtained by Igor was passed to Sveneld in 940. Participation of Varangian warriors in the collection of Drevlyanian or Ulichian tribute is not to be excluded, but here it is a legal question. When five years later Igor set out to collect Drevlyanian tribute himself, the annalist makes not a hint at the fact that he was infringing upon Sveneld's right. The Varangian simply did not have that right: he had received pay and not become a beneficiary.

In 942, following the defeat of the Russian army by the Greeks, and perhaps as compensation for the Varangians who had taken part in the ill-fated expedition, the Varangian leader received the Drevlyanian tribute provoking the discontent of the Kiev warriors: "He has given much to one *boyar*." The Kievans envied the Varangians: "Sveneld's warriors received arms and apparel, while we are naked. Let us, Prince, go together to collect tribute, both you and we will get it."

After the treaty of 944 was concluded, which strengthened the positions of Rus, the need for the Varangian mercenary force was greatly reduced (Igor ruled "being in peaceful relations with all countries"), and in autumn 945 the Kievan prince returned the land of the Drevlyanians to the former system of his Kiev *polyudye* when the prince began his rounds right from the Drevlyanians.

> 945. Autumn came and Igor planned an expedition against the Drevlyanians, hoping to get much tribute...
>
> Arriving in the Drevlyanian land Igor and his men forcibly increased the former tribute and collected more.
>
> Having collected the tribute Igor set out for his town and on the way back, on second thoughts, told his men: "Go home with the tribute and I shall return and travel some more", and with a small group he turned back to obtain more wealth.

The tribute had obviously always been fixed, because Igor increased it by inventing new taxes. When Igor appeared again "to obtain more wealth", all sections of the Drevlyanian community demonstrated a striking consolidation in opposing the Kiev prince together with their local princes headed by the prince of princes Mal.

> Having learned that Igor was returning the Drevlyanians sought council with their prince Mal: "If a wolf falls into the habit of stealing sheep, he will carry away the whole flock if he is not killed. So is it now, if we do not kill Igor, he will destroy us all!"
>
> And they sent messengers to Igor: "Why do you come again?
>
> You have collected all the tribute already." Igor did not heed them. Then the Drevlyanians came out of their town Iskorosten and killed Igor and his men, because they were few. They buried Igor. His mound is near Iskorosten even to this day.

The Byzantine author Leo the Deacon reports one particularity about Igor's death: "...having marched against the Germans (?) he was captured by them, tied to trees and torn into two."

The Drevlyanians who executed Igor according to the sentence passed by the *veche* regarded themselves as being in their right. The envoys who arrived in Kiev to propose the Drevlyanian prince as husband for Igor's widow Olga told her:

> "Your husband was like a wolf: took away and

plundered, but our princes are kind; they rule the Drevlyanian land very well."

Once again, as in the case with the Vyatichians, we have an alliance of tribes with a hierarchy of local princes. There are many princes; in the conflict with Kiev they are somewhat idealised and described as kind pastors. The alliance is headed by Prince Mal of the same rank as the head of heads among the Vyatichians. Mal regards himself as equal to the Kiev prince and boldly seeks his widow's hand in marriage. Archaeologists know his domain town in the Drevlyanian land which still bears his name, Malin.

It is notable that at the beginning of Igor's *polyudye* none of these princes protested against the collecting of tribute, and they did not resist Igor. Everything apparently was in the order of things. The "kind" princes killed Igor only when he began to violate the existing order and exceeded the fixed rent. This shows us once again that *polyudye* was not a disorderly jaunt but a well-arranged important state undertaking in the course of which the feudal class was consolidated and a multiple feudal hierarchy was simultaneously established.

The local princes of various ranks (themselves living at the expense of the tribes they supervised) helped in the collecting of *polyudye* by their suzerain, the Grand Prince of Kiev, and the latter, in turn, did not forget his vassals in diplomatic representations to the emperors of Byzantium. A year before his death Igor sent an embassy to Constantinople on his behalf as "the Grand Prince of Russia and on behalf of the princes he ruled over and all the people of the Russian land". The treaty of 944 provides for the lawlessness of vassals and arrière-vassals usual for a society with a feudal hierarchy: "If someone among the Russian princes or the Russian people violates this deed (treaty), what is written on this parchment, then he will die of his own arms and will be damned by God and by Perun."

Polyudye existed in each tribal alliance; it marked a departure from patriarchal tribal relations and traditions when each member of the tribe knew his tribal prince personally. Within the framework of the tribal alliance *polyudye*, probably appearing simultaneously with the alliance itself, was a transitional form on the way to class society, to statehood. The power of the prince of princes was torn away from ancient local traditions and relations of kin and became multitiered (prince of princes, prince of a tribe, chief of a clan).

When several tribal alliances were included, voluntarily or not, in Rus, the supreme power completely broke away from the direct producers. State power became completely abstract, and the right to the land, always associated in the land-tiller's mind with labour and inheritance law in his microscopic world, was now related to the right of supreme (alienated) power, to the right of military force.

As a system, the feudal hierarchy to some extent cemented the new society, forming a chain of links: the highest links (the high princes) were connected, on the one hand, with the Grand Prince and, on the other, with the princes of individual tribes. The tribal princes were connected with the *boyars*. A vassalage growing out of the microstructure of primitive society was the natural form for the feudal state.

The sum total of sources dating back to the early 9th century enables us to make a general review of the social and political stratification of Rus:

1. The Grand Russian Prince. Khakan Rus (a title equal to that of emperor).
2. The heads of heads, the high princes (princes of tribal alliances).
3. Any princes, princes of individual tribes.
4. Grand *boyars*.
5. *Boyars*, men, knights.
6. Merchants.
7. People. *Smerds*.
8. Servants. Slaves.

The bulky and complex mechanism of *polyudye* was able to function provided all its parts were smoothly running and coordinated. Any disruptions led to wars. The chronicle repeatedly describes how some tribal alliance rebelled and waged a war against the Kiev prince. Statehood in Rus as a whole was established in the course of a difficult struggle between various forces.

Constantine Porphyrogenitus described the Rus

state at a time when *polyudye* as a primary form of obtaining rent was passing through its last years. But the beginning of the *polyudye* system should be sought in the transition from separate tribal alliance to super-alliances-states, i. e. the turn of the 9th century. It was quite natural that this was also the time of the emergence of extensive trade relations between Rus and the Orient and Byzantium: *polyudye* was not only a way for the prince and his men to secure their livelihood but also a method of obtaining the values which the rising Russian crafts were still unable to produce.

Polyudye sustained the Kiev warriors and their servants for half a year; most likely *polyudye* secured the food supplies for the second, summer part of the year, when the most valuable part of the tribute was sold in the shape of marten, beaver, silver fox and squirrel pelts. *Polyudye* is referred to in a passage an incorrect understanding of which had led some scholars to conclude that the Rus did not know land cultivation:

> The Rus have no ploughed land, but eat what it brought from the land of the Slavs (Ibn Ruste).
>
> Always 100 to 200 of them (Rus) go to the Slavs and forcibly take from them what they need while they are there (Gardizi).

All this is easily explained by *polyudye*. The part of *polyudye* which was exported consisted of fur, wax and honey; the products of hunting and apiculture were supplemented by servants and slaves eagerly bought at international markets both in the Moslem Caliphate and in the Christian Byzantium. The system of the sale of *polyudye* provides particularly convincing evidence of the state nature of Kievan Rus' actions in the 9th-10th centuries.

The Sale of Polyudye

Kiev was, undoubtedly, the centre of international trade relations in Eastern Europe. Kiev and Russian merchants, the *rusari*, were well known in Central and Northern Europe and were granted important benefits, because, by force of arms, they made their way through the nomad barriers of the Khazars, Magyars, Pechenegs and Inland Bulgars and supplied the Europeans with the luxuries of Oriental bazaars. Kiev did not lose its importance as a major trade centre of Europe up to the Crusades.

A well-trodden route led from Kiev westwards to Cracow and further to Regensburg on the Danube. It was through Kiev (and thanks to it) that the route went "from the Greeks to the Varangians" linking Byzantium with Scandinavia. The route from Kiev to the Bulgars on the Volga was important and well organised. It was divided into 20 stations situated about 70 kilometres from each other. It took messengers riding without any load one day to travel from station to station, and for merchants with heavy loads it was two days' travel and one day of rest at the station.

The route through Russian lands went through the following station towns: Kiev—town site on the Supoya—Priluk—Romen—Vyr(?)—Lipitsk town site — Gochevo and several anonymous town sites towards the Don River. In two cases contemporary villages have retained the names of ancient road stations of the 9th-11th centuries: Istobnoye (from *istba*, warm place); they are precisely 70 kilometres from each other.

The tenth station located halfway from Bulgar to Kiev was somewhere on the Don River south of Voronezh. According to Oriental sources (Jeihani, Idrisi) this was where the eastern border of Rus was. Moving from Bulgar to the west, Oriental travellers first crossed the deserted Mordovian forests and meadows and then came to the Don where this overland route intersected the Don River route from the Vyatichians to the Volga and Itil. It was along this road that they observed the life and habits of the Slavs.

Reaching the western end of their 1,400-kilometre itinerary two months later the Bulgarian or other Oriental merchants came to Kiev on the banks of the Dnepr which they called either Duna or Russa. It is here, in the Middle Dnepr area near Kiev, that Oriental authors point out three Russian towns that have become the apple of discord for several dozen con-

temporary scholars. One of the most reliable sources, Hudud al-'Alam, reports:
> There is also the river Russa (Duna) flowing from the depths of the land of the Slavs and eastwards to the border of the Rus. Then it goes through the places Artab, Salab and Kuyab (Kiev) which are Rus towns...

Possessing an enormous library of Oriental geographical literature of the 9th-11th centuries Idrisi is the only author to indicate the distance between these three towns situated along one river: it is four days' travel from the town of Artan to Kiev; and it is also four days to the town of Slavia.

Ignoring the above precise directions researchers have regarded the alleged "three centres of ancient Rus" as certain political entities each extending to a large area. Kiev (Kuyab, Kuaifa and others) did not give rise to any doubts and was usually identified with the historical Kiev, the centre of South Rus.

As a rule Slavia was identified with the Novgorod Slovenians and Novgorod, although not a single Russian, Scandinavian or Greek source calls Novgorod Slavia. This idea was due to the influence of Normanism which sought to artificially create a state centre in the north. These broad interpretations were also facilitated by the fact that the concept of town was frequently confused with that of country.

Identification of the third town whose name was given in about a score of transcriptions proved to be particularly varied. Equally varied was the search for Artania or Arsania (both names are highly tentative) on the geographical map of the 9th-10th centuries. Artania was identified with Mordva-Erzya, Tmutarakan, Ryazan and Rostov.

Leaving aside the extensive literature devoted to the "three centres" let us indicate lines along which they should be sought according to the above directions.

1. All three towns are on the same river as Kiev, i. e. on the Dnepr.

2. All of them are located not far from Kiev, at a distance ranging from 140 to 280 kilometres.

Such a galaxy of Russian towns along the Middle

Dnepr is well known to us from 10th-century documents, they are the towns mentioned in the treaties with the Greeks: Kiev, Pereyaslavl and Chernigov. The distance from Kiev to Chernigov is 140 kilometres; to Pereyaslavl about 100 kilometres; from Pereyaslavl to Chernigov—170 kilometres. This triad is continually mentioned as the chief towns of the Russian land in the narrow sense. The town of Slavia should not be looked for in the north about which the Oriental geographers had no idea. Slavia is Pereyaslavl (or Pereslav), the ancient town standing near the Dnepr and the closest one to the Inland Bulgars. There is only one thing that does not conform to the source in the case of Chernigov: it is situated not on the Dnepr but on the Desna River. After studying the description of all three towns one might offer another possibility of Artania's identification.

Hudud al-'Alam describes the three towns of Rus thus:

> 1. Kuyaba is the Rus town closest to the countries of Islam, a pleasant place and the residence of the king. Various furs and valuable swords are brought from it.
> 2. Slava is a pleasant town and in peacetime merchants travel from it to the Bulgarian area.
> 3. Artab is a town where foreigners are killed when they reach it. Here, valuable blades for swords are made which can be bent in two and if one let it go the blade returns to its original state.

Other authors offer additional information. Ibn Haukal compares Kiev with Bulgar indicating that Kiev is larger than Bulgar.

It is always very important for us to find out the viewpoint of the informant. One of the earliest authors Ibn Haukal writes: "People reach Kuyaba and its area with the aim of trade." That is why Kiev was regarded as the closest to the countries of Islam; that is why it is compared with Bulgar—this was done by merchants travelling along the 20-station road beginning in Bulgar and ending in Kiev.

The merchants went to Kiev through the town of Romen (modern Romny, called Armen by Idrisi) which was indeed on this highway. Idrisi describes the town of Slavia as the most important one. Perhaps this was due to the name of the town Preslav meaning Very Glorious or an analogy with the Bulgarian capital Preslav.

The more difficult case is the third town tentatively called Artania or, as the anonymous Persian author names it, Urtab. In addition to the above, having told about the killing of foreigners Idrisi goes on to say that "no one is allowed to enter the town with the aim of trade ... merchants from Kuyaba take fur and lead from the town." Ibn Haukal also writes that the inhabitans of Arsa do not let foreigners come to the town, but "go down the river for trade and say nothing about their affairs and their goods and do not allow anyone to follow them and enter their country".

On the Dnepr, 120 kilometres away from Kiev (three and a half days of travel along a straight line), at the mouth of the Ros River, there was a town by the name of Roden only the site of which remains today on a high hill, Knyazhya Gora. The town was abandoned when Christianity was adopted and is never mentioned in the chronicles throughout the 11th-13th centuries, although many events took place in its vicinity. Judging by its location in the centre of the ancient area of the Rus in the 6th-7th centuries, Roden could have been the tribal centre of the Rus and named after the most important god of the ancient Slavs, Rod. The latter was compared to Osiris, Bahad-Gad and the Biblical Sabaoth. Rod was a more important god than Perun who was a god of princes and their men and who had replaced Rod.

This assumption could well explain the place in the chronicle (possibly taken from Greek sources of the 9th century) "the Rodi called Rus". The naming of a tribal alliance according to a common god can also be seen in the name of the Krivichians called after the ancient local (Lithuanian) god Krive—Kriveite. The Rus on the Ros River might have received their name from the god Rod who was worshipped in Roden on the Ros.

In Svyatoslav's time this was, apparently, the prince's domain because it was the site of his courtyard. During the struggle for the Kievan throne in 980 Prince Yaropolk hid here (perhaps, he hoped that this sacred place would be respected), but after a long siege was killed by hired Varangians. The town was probably well known in Rus, because after the difficult siege a proverb appeared which existed more than a century: "there is a saying to this day: the troubles of Roden," wrote a contemporary of Monomakh.

The god Rod was the supreme deity of the heavens and the universe. Bloody sacrifices were offered to him. A particular holiday falling on July 20 (the day of the thunder god) is documented for the Slavs of the Roden area by a 4th-century calendar, and in 983 a young Varangian living in Kiev was sacrificed. Offering foreigners, prisoners, conquered enemies to their gods as a sacrifice was usual in ancient times among many peoples and was specially called xenochthonia (Greek). Obviously it was this annual offering of sacrifice that caused some foreign authors to write chapters providing an exaggerated account of the killing of foreigners in general.

The ban on entering the Urtab area with the aim of trade is easily explained if we identify Urtab (Artania) with Roden. It was here, near Vitichev (a town mentioned by Constantine in connection with *polyudye*), that the voyagers on one-tree ships gathered before setting out for Byzantium. It was here, in the last stretch of the Dnepr protected by wooded islands, that the final equipping of the fleet took place and the goods were sorted out for sale on distant international markets. Merchants and idle observers were not needed here. Urtab-Roden was not excluded from trade, but the local trade was conducted by Kiev, the people from "Kuyaba"; no wonder Prince Svyatoslav's courtyard was situated in this town, almost on the very border of Rus.

It seems that the following identification of the three towns of Rus would be most logical:

Kuyaba—Kiev

Slava—Pereyaslavl

Arta—Roden at the mouth of the Ros River.
All three towns are on one river, the Dnepr.

Kuyaba, the closest town to the countries of Islam,

is described in this way because the informants reached it along the highway from Bulgar to Kiev. The two other towns were situated to the side of this highway: Artania was four days' travel away (downriver) from Kiev, while Slavia was four days from Artania sailing up the Dnepr from the mouth of the Ros to Pereyaslavl.

The account of the export of the flexible steel swords from Kiev and Urtab which passed from one historical work to the next is confirmed by the legend about the attempt by Khazars to impose tribute on the Polyanians. Responding to the demand to pay tribute,

> having discussed the question at the *veche* the Polyanians decided to give a sword from each household. And the Khazar elders told the Kagan: "Such tribute is a bad sign (double-edged swords); they, the Polyanians, will later collect tribute from us and other countries. And so it was.

The legend could be known in the Khazarian East.

Slavia trades with the Bulgars. Pereyaslavl is located closer than the other towns to the Inland Bulgars on the left bank of the Dnepr who are constantly fighting against the Rus; that is why the source say that trade is carried on in peacetime.

Urtab-Roden, the place where the fleet with *polyudye* is concentrated and which was controlled by the Grand Prince of Kiev (still called Knyazhya Gora, Prince's Hill, today), did not permit foreigners to enter. It was here, in the sanctuary of Rod (after whom the town was named), that aliens were offered as sacrifice. All this taken together gave birth to various legends concerning the Knyazhya Gora area which Kiev could deliberately support. The name of this town varies so much in Arabic writing, such different towns are proposed in deciphering it that, perhaps, identification of Urtab with Roden is the most successful version.

Kuyaba, Slavia and Urtab are not three states, not the three centres of Rus, but simply Kiev and two neighbouring towns which played an important part in the life of Kievan Rus and interested the Oriental

The walls of Constantinople

merchants who arrived in Kiev from Bulgar. They considered the prince's vicegerents (or their sons) to be kings and repeated the legends of the most distant town of Roden where they were not allowed to go. In the early 10th century the place of Roden was taken by Chernigov which was included in the triad of the most important Russian towns.

Every year, in springtime, Kievan Rus fulfilled its second major state function: to export the enormous amount of goods collected during the half-year-long *polyudye* circuit. The collectors of tribute turned into seafarers, caravan-bashaws, warriors making their way through the nomad cordons and merchants selling their wares and buying everything that the rich Orient produced, and that dazzled the Europeans of that time with its luxury.

The ships filled with barrels of wax and honey, beaver and fox skins and other products were prepared to set sail for the distant seas in Kiev itself and in neighbouring towns on the Dnepr—Vyshgorod, Vitichev which had a signal tower to warn of the approaching Pechenegs by means of a bonfire, Russian Pereyaslavl and Roden. The southernest fortress port on the border river, the Sula, ten kilometres from the Dnepr, was the town of Zhelni (the town site Voin), a peculiar stronghold in which the ships coming from Rus could take shelter in case of bad news entering the area of coastal fortifications directly from the river.

> In the month of June, setting out along the Dnepr River, they (the Rus one-tree ships) go down to Vitichev, a fortress belonging to Rus. Waiting two or three days there until all the one-tree ships arrive, they set out and go down the above-mentioned Dnepr River (Constantine Porphyrogenitus).

Further Constantine describes at length (apparently proceeding from what he was told by a Varangian in Russian service) the difficult and dangerous passing of the fleet through the Dnepr rapids. He refers both to the Slav and the Russian names of the rapids, mistaking the post of Sveneld's contemporary who served Rus for his ethnic identity.

The "Russian" names of the rapids (indeed Scandinavian in a number of cases) overjoyed the Normanists, but actually prove nothing more than the fact that Varangians were in the service of the Kiev Prince, something already known both from the treaty between Rus and Constantine and from the chronicle which reports that Igor at the time hired Varangians to fight in the war against the Greeks.

> The first rapids were called Essupi which means 'Don't sleep!' in Russian and in Slavonic. These rapids are so narrow that they are no wider than a hippodrome. In the middle of it tall and steep rocks stand out like islands. Rushing towards them and upwards, and falling down from them, the water makes a loud noise and provokes fear.

Dragging their ships through rapids with difficulty the Rus even sometimes unloaded them and portaged the ships along the bank. In this way they reached the

Krarian crossing (Kichkas) used by Khersones merchants going to Rus. This entire route went through an area constantly attacked by the Pechenegs.

Having passed the rapids, on Khortitsa Island (near the modern Zaporozhye),

> the Rus offer their sacrifice, because an enormous oak grows there. They bring live cocks, drive arrows into the ground all around it, and some put bits of bread and meat...

From Khortitsa Island the Rus sail to Berezani Island by the mouth of the Dnepr and additionally furnish their ships before going out to sea. Further on their route lies to the mouth of the Dnestr and from there to the Selina, arm of the Danube.

> Until they pass the Selina River the Pechenegs chase them along the bank. And if the sea throws the one-tree ships on the coast, they pull their ships out on land to fight against the Pechenegs all together.

The sailing along the western shore of the Black Sea (to which we will yet refer) ends in Constantinople where the Russian "guests" spent the whole summer returning to Rus only for the next *polyudye*.

From the mouth of the Dnepr or Berezani Island the sea route of the Rus split up into two: one went to Constantinople while the other was a complicated route to Khazaria and on to the distant countries of the Caliphate about which we already know from the account by Ibn Khurdadhbih of the mid-9th century.

> The Rus merchants are a part of the Slavs. They bring the furs of squirrels, foxes and swords from the outskirts of the Slav world to the Black (Roman) Sea and the Byzantine ruler levies a tithe on them. Or they set out along the Don River (Tanais), a Slav river, reach Hamlijas (the Khazarian capital), and then its ruler levies a tithe on them.

Ibn Fakih's account is an interesting version:

> Byzantium's ruler levies a tithe on them. Then they go by sea to Samkish-Jewry after which they turn to Slavonia. Then they take the road from the Slav Sea (Azov) until they reach the Khazarian channel where the Khazarian ruler

> levies a tithe on them. Then they go to the Khazarian Sea along the river called the Slav River...

It is important to note here that, first, the Russian fleet passed through the Kerch Strait which belonged to the Khazars who had adopted Judaism (Samkish-Jewry) and, second, there are very many Slav qualifications: the Sea of Azov is called Slavic; the lower reaches of the Tanais-Don is the Slavic River, the North Azov Sea area—Slavonia (?) and even the Lower Volga in its undoubtedly Khazarian course is referred to as the River of the Slavs. Without attempting to specify these definitions, let us indicate only that, apparently, the Azov Sea area and the Lower Dnepr were indeed overflowing with Slavs at that time.

Annual expeditions by the Rus through the Kerch Strait past Kerch and Tmutarakan led to the appearance of new geographical names connected with Rus, if not among the local inhabitants then in the works of foreign geographers:

Kerch—Rusia Town.

Kerch Strait—Rusia River.

The part of the Black Sea near Tmutarakan (five days' sailing from Trebizond), the Russian Sea.

It is not surprising that scholars frequently linked another mystery of Oriental geographical works with this area, the Island of the Rus believed to be Tmutarakan. Undoubtedly in view of a considerable scope of its trade operations in the south Kievan Rus needed some strongholds on the Black Sea, but Tmutarakan which was ruled by the Khazars until the 960s could hardly be defined as the Island of the Rus (although it was called an island).

Having travelled the difficult (and expensive in terms of duties) way to Khazaria (300 kilometres on the Sea of Azov, 400 kilometres up the Don River and by the portage, and 400 kilometres down the Volga), the Russian fleet came out on the Caspian Sea called either Khazarian or Khorezmian (Khvalisskoye in the chronicle) or Jurjan or Khorasan.

Continuing his narration concerning the Rus Ibn Khurdadhbih reports interesting data about the distant sea and land routes of the Russian merchants:

From Khazaria "they go to the Jurjan Sea and land on any shore. And the diameter of that sea is 500 farsangs. (Ibn Fakih has retained another particularity of this text: ' ...and they sell everything they have with them; and it all reaches Rey'.) And sometimes they bring their goods on camels from Jurjan to Baghdad where Slav slaves serve as interpreters for them. And they claim to be Christians and pay a poll tax." Another variant: "they go to the Jurjan Sea, then to Balkh and Maverannahr, then to the nomad area of the Toguz-Guz, then to China."

There is reason to believe Ibn Khurdadhbih's account, because he himself was in Rey and the route of the Russian merchants from Rey to Baghdad (about 700 kilometres) passed through the Jebel area which Ibn Khurdadhbih had charge over as the director of posts. The Russian caravans passed before his very eyes every year. The author of *The Book of Ways and States* knew what he was writing about.

In addition to these far routes involving sea trips, there was another overland trans-European itinerary one of the important links of which was Kiev. The itinerary started on the eastern fringe of Europe, on the Volga River, in the capital of Volga Bulgaria, the town of Bulgar. The caravan routes led from Maverannahr and Khorasan through the gates of the Guz northwards to Bulgar. The Volga River way brought the northern merchants here. The Volga flowed from Bulgar to the Itil and further to the Caspian.

The informants of Oriental geographers frequently took Bulgar as their point of departure. Numismatists believe that Bulgar was one of the most important points where Oriental coins circulated in the 9th and 10th centuries.

We have already seen what an important highway was the well-trodden, carefully measured road from Bulgar to Kiev furnished with *mansils* (messenger stations), according to Jeihani. But that route did not end in Kiev; Kiev was merely the limit of the Oriental geographers' knowledge in the 10th century. Most probably, it was here, in the capital of Rus, that the active role passed to the Russian merchants who were known as the Rusari in Western Europe.

The road from Kiev to the west was evidently more than just the way along which the tribute collected in the Russian lands was exported; it is likely that the Russian furs exported to the west were supplemented by some share of Oriental goods brought by Moslem merchants from Bulgar to Kiev or bought by the Rus during their overseas travels.

A French poet of the time, singing praises to a beautiful damsel, said that she wore apparel from Russian silk. Of course, actually, the silk was only brought through Russia from Byzantium or Khorasan (where the silk, in turn, came from China), but it is important that the last suppliers were the Rusari, otherwise the silk would not be called Russian.

The road from Kiev to the west went through Drogichin on the Western Bug, where numerous commercial seals have been found, and into Poland of somewhat more to the south towards Crakow which was a major political and trade centre at that time. Then the Kievan Rusari headed for the Middle Danube, to a major economic centre of Europe, Regensburg.

Kiev was linked to Northern Europe by the route described by annalist Sylvester as the way from the Greeks to the Varangians, but historians have turned it upside-down and called the way from the Varangians to the Greeks, although the annalist clearly indicated that the latter referred to the trip round Europe by sea in which the seafarers first came to Rome and only then "to the Greeks".

Sylvester described the route having to do with Kiev in the following terms:

> There is a way... along the Dnepr to its upper reaches, and then a portage to the Lovat River, and along the Lovat it is possible to reach the big Lake Ilmen from which the Volkhov River flows into the great Lake Ladoga (Nevo), and an arm of that lake (the present Neva River) falls into the Varangian (Baltic) Sea.

Among the five trade highways leading from Kiev to Constantinople, to the Caspian and Baghdad, to Bulgaria, to Regensburg and Novgorod and Scandinavia,

Mould for making imitations of Oriental dirhams

the most important, of state significance, were the first two. We have already considered in detail one of these most important routes of Kievan Rus foreign trade taking Russian caravans on camels to Baghdad and Balkh. The Russian warrior merchants here were the distant predecessors of Afanasy Nikitin*, because they almost reached the very gates of India which were 10-days' travel away from Balkh and intersected the future itinerary of the Tver merchant in Rey. Now let us consider another important route of trade and military expeditions—the southwestern, "to the Greeks".

That route was known to the Slavs at the dawn of their historical life: Tacitus writes about the expeditions of the Venedians to the mouth of the Danube to the Pevkins: the sea expeditions of the mid-3rd century

---

* Afanasy Nikitin, Russian traveller and merchant. Went to Persia and India in 1471-1474.— *Ed.*

went to the western coast of the Black Sea. The colonisation of the Balkans by the Slavs also occurred along the same routes.

For Rus which had just emerged as a state, trade with Byzantium was a highly important section of state activities. Beginning with 860, military expeditions were undertaken not in order to conquer Byzantine land but to secure a free route, which was then closed by the Greeks at the mouth of the Dnepr and the ports of the Black Sea. The expeditions were also due to the desire to obtain contributions in gold and brocade as if to compensate for the obstacles in trade.

As we see from Constantine's description, the entire route from the Russian border at the Sula where the fortress and port of Voin was located and to the Danube, was a defensive military expedition intended to resist the hordes of forty Pecheneg tribes which owned the whole steppe within a distance of "thirty days' riding". Only the ramified delta of the Danube held back the steppe nomads. The Selina River, at the present time the middle, and in ancient times the first arm of the Danube from the north, was the nearest to the steppe which explains the defensive frontier role of that river.

Also of interest is the subsequent route along the Bulgarian coast indicated by Constantine. That annual coastwise navigation remained in the memory of Russian people for a long time, and in a list of "Russian towns near and far" a scholar of the late 14th century, completely unexpectedly for the situation of the 1390s, included sea harbours of the ancient Bulgarian coast as if he were supplementing and correcting Constantine's work which he had never known.

The enumeration of Russian coastal towns goes up almost to the same place as Constantine's—the Dichina, which should be regarded not as the town on the Danube but as the river between Varna and Mesembria, as Constantine rightfully says, where Khan Omurtag built a palace in 821. As a result we have an extremely interesting historical list of Black Sea piers visited regularly by the Russian merchant, and, perhaps, military fleet:

In the mouth of the Danube (on the southern bank of the ancient Selina), it is Kilia, on the Black Sea—

Constantsa (ancient Tomy), Cape Kaliakra (Akolyakra), Kavarna, Karna, Varna, Dichina, and Mesembria.

When this list of piers is transposed on a map, their uneven distribution becomes obvious: such harbours as Kilia, Constantsa, Varna, and Mesembria are located at large distances from each other. This reflects the nature of Russian coastwise sailing. But on the section between Cape Kaliakra and Dichina there are five piers on sixty kilometres of coastline. It is almost certain that this is due to Russo-Bulgarian trade, because the above coastal towns were located closer to the vital centres of the first Bulgarian kingdom—Pliska, Preslav and Shumen, where there was some sort of "Russian office". It is only about three days' riding from Varna to Preslav and only two days to Pliska.

The large number of piers near Varna continually used by Russian trade expeditions indicates that even before it reached Byzantium, Russian *polyudye* was partly sold in Bulgaria. The Russian trade bases in Bulgarian harbours were apparently so well developed by the fleet of the Kiev princes that the Russian author of the 14th century included them in the general list of Russian towns.

The "difficult and long-suffering" route of the Russian merchants was marked by several sites of heathen sacrifice. Constantine mentioned one of them (on Khortitsa Island). There is a village Volos (Vlas) at the end of the Bulgarian part of the sea route between Dichina and Mesembria whose name is associated with the Slav god of wealth, Volos. Whether these were the local Slavs or foreign Slav seafarers that founded the shrine of that god, the members of the sea expeditions described by Constantine, who indicated that the frightening and difficult sailing trip ended at Mesembria, could have offered sacrifice in gratitude to their "cattle god", by whose name they swore in concluding the treaty with the same Constantine.

Having left the Bulgarian harbours, part of the Russian merchant fleet set out for Constantinople, the capital of the Byzantine Empire. The Emperor did not describe the life of the Rus in the second Rome, but here we are assisted by the Russian annalist who included in the chronicle the invaluable text of the treaties between the two states—Rus and Byzantium.

Rus had a vested interest in regular peaceful trade with Byzantium which, however, sought to play an active part in its foreign trade and not allow foreigners into the country and to its markets. The Greeks had many means at their disposal to prevent Russians from entering the Empire: the outpost at the mouth of the Dnepr controlled from Khersones (modern Sevastopol), the closure of Black Sea harbours the Russians needed for coastwise navigation, urging the Pechenegs to attack the Russians, and finally, the closure of the entrance into the Bosphorus. Kievan Rus overcame all these obstacles by force of arms as was recorded in diplomatic documents. The siege of Constantinople by the Russian forces in 860 reflected the confrontation between the two mighty adversaries which left a deep mark upon the memory of European peoples. The annalist began his chronicle of the historical life of Rus with that unprecedented event.

The treaties between Rus and the Empire (907, 911 and 944 were to formalise the success of Russian arms (or the success of their threat) and secure the possibility of peaceful trade, the chief aim of the Russians, since Rus made no territorial claims after the victory.

In concluding the treaties the executors of the Kiev prince's orders, as seen above, were both the Varangians and the Slavs, but the treaty itself was drawn up in two copies and in two state languages — Greek and Slavonic (Russian). The treaties were concluded by Byzantium in the name of the Emperor and on the Russian side on behalf of the Grand Kiev Prince and his vassals, various high princes heading the tribal alliances, and "all kinds of princes" — numerous tribal princes. The treaties frequently refer to the Russian Law, the text of which has not come down to us, but was apparently well known to the Greeks (even the fines were fixed in Greek money), otherwise there would be no sense in referring to it.

The 907 Treaty introduces us to the daily life of the Russian "guests" in Constantinople in the political situation when Kievan Rus imposed its terms on Byzantium, while the latter protected its rights as best it could. The Russians received ambassadorial pay from the Greeks.

The merchant-guests were paid every month for half a year. This was the summer half of the year when the Russian visitors sold everything that had been collected in the winter half, in the course of *polyudye*. It follows from the above that the sale of *polyudye* was not a wholesale operation but was carried out without hurry, in the course of six months, while visitors from Kiev, Chernigov, Pereyaslavl, Polotsk, Rostov and Lubech lived in the suburbs of Constantinople and received from the Greek government "bread and wine and meat and fish and fruit". There was even a clause stipulating that they could visit the city thermae.

The Byzantinians who feared armed Rus inserted only one restriction into the treaty concerning the capital's security. The emperor's official drew up a list of Russian visitors in order to distribute the allowance, and accompanied them into the city. The Russians were to enter the city only through one of the gates in groups of no more than 50 persons and without arms, but they were allowed to conclude trade deals without any tax.

When the Russian visitors prepared to leave for home at the end of the summer, the Emperor was obliged to provide them with food, anchors, rope and sails if they were needed. Such a highly advantageous situation was, of course, due to a certain balance of power in favour of Kievan Rus and was maintained by the threat of war.

Under the year 907 the chronicle presents the part of the agreement between Rus and Byzantium concerning the normal life of the Russian warrior merchants in the Empire's capital during the six summer months. The 944 Treaty concluded after the threat of a new expedition against Byzantium (Igor only reached the Danube in 943) also contained these everyday regulations with minor changes. When the Russians entered the Constantinople fortress a Greek "policeman", a state official, was to guard them and to observe the lawful behaviour of both Russians and Greeks.

The purchase of silk fabric (the silk monopoly belonged to the emperor's workshops) was limited to 50 units; each purchase was sealed by the official.

In addition to regulations concerning the usual life of the Russians in Constantinople, the treaties of 911 and 944 provide for a large number of special legal clauses having to do with property and criminal law. The actions of the sides are specified in case of merchant shipwrecks; many clauses are devoted to imprisoned slaves (ransom, return of fugitives, cost and so on); the existence of rich and poor persons is provided for on the Russian side, the possibility of eluding creditors is considered, a rich Russian can draw up a written will. Possible cases of theft, fights and murders are not forgotten. In certain cases there are references to the Russian Code and Law and whoever the criminal may be, "let him submit to the Russian and the Greek law".

As we see, Rus' foreign trade, a direct continuation of the collecting of the prince's *polyudye* in all the lands ruled by Kiev (both Slav and non-Slav), in the 9th and mid-10th centuries reflected the presence of a strong state element in Kievan Rus, because of its scope, organisational complexity and inevitable support lent to it by the military force of the young state.

The State Grows Stronger

The first one and a half centuries in the historical life of Kievan Rus are known to us from scanty references in the sources which require close attention and cautious treatment. The sum total of references and deductions again reveal the same process of the rise of body politic and the state itself.

The state system, class relations and the development of lands into principalities had already started at the level of tribal alliances, i. e. approximately in fifteen separate centres. An example is provided by the tribal alliance of the Vyatichians on the Oka River where, according to Oriental geographers, there were princes (tribal chiefs) and the supreme prince of the alliance (chief of chiefs) corresponding to the "high prince" of the 911 Treaty. The annual rounds of the dependent tribes and collection of tribute ("offerings") constitute established legal relations of domination and subordination, a display of the real power of the "high prince" supported by mounted warriors in "excellent chain mail". It is assumed that the information about what was taking place within the "Vantit country" was obtained from an anonymous treatise of the mid-9th century.

It is possible to extend what we know about the distant (and not the most advanced) alliance of Vyatichian tribes to all the other known alliances of Slav, Lithuanian-Lettish and Finnish tribes in Eastern Europe taking account of certain local differences concerning the rates and chronology of the general process of primary feudalisation.

Simultaneously with this universal process of tribal alliances, this highest form of primitive society, turning into primary feudal bodies, there was a process of alliance integration which had dramatically stepped up historical development. The forming of tribal alliances could be voluntary in some places, as, for example, in the zone of nomad raids, but occasionally could be implemented by direct force. Quite naturally the centre of integration was the Russian alliance of tribes which united Rus proper, the Polyanians and the Severyanians as early as the 6th century A. D. That alliance had extended its power by the 9th century to the Drevlyanian, Dregovichian, Volynyanian (?), and Polochanian alliances.

The political frontiers of Kievan Rus, the alliance of tribal alliances, changed quite often, however; first one, then another alliance rebelled and insisted on its sovereignty. For a whole century Kiev had to wage repeated wars to put down Drevlyanians, Ulichians, Tivercians, Radimichians, Vyatichians, and Volynyanians. The local tribal nobility undergoing the process of feudalisation resisted the Kiev warriors

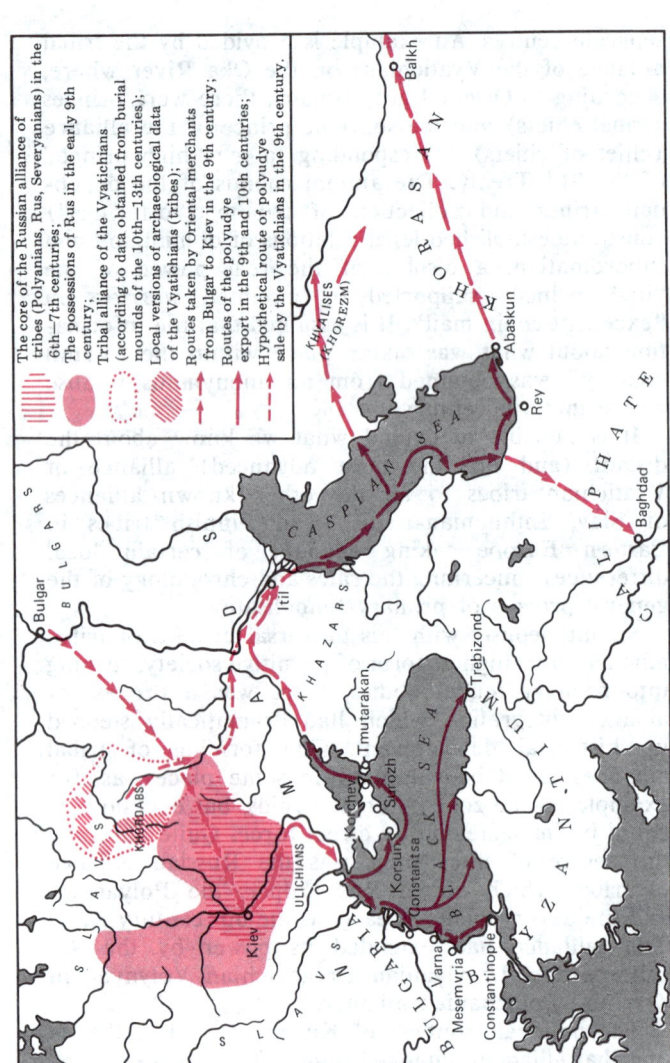

Russia in the Early 9th Century and Its External Links

and, as we saw from the example of the Drevlyanian princes, could rally the popular masses against the Kiev forces (945). The feudal hierarchy of minor princes was formed not by means of grants but rather by involving the local tribal nobility in the general process.

The first state-wide undertaking exceeding in scope all the tribal affairs of the local princes was *polyudye*. No wonder the Russian word passed into the language of the Greek Emperor and the Scandinavian sagas. The Kiev prince and his warriors devoted half a year to travelling about 1,500 kilometres through the enormous territory of a number of tribal alliances, and the other, summer half of the year organised large-scale military and trade expeditions which carried the results of *polyudye* along the Russian Sea either to Bulgaria and Byzantium in one direction or to the Caspian in another. In the latter case Russian land caravans reached Baghdad and even Balkh on the way to India.

Systematic annual expeditions to Byzantium and the Caliphate through the steppes occupied by the war-like Khazars, Magyars and Pechenegs required a complex and bulky system to implement them. Powerful Russian strongholds had been set up in the Black Sea on the "island of the Rus" in Dobruja, and in the channels of the Danube (the "Danubians" in Russian chronicles).

It is possible that hired groups of Varangians took part in some expeditions, but this led to inner quarrels, for instance between Igor's warriors and Sveneld's Varangians, and serious troubles in foreign relations. For dozens of years the Russians landed on any shore of the Khorezm (Khvalyn, or Caspian) Sea and carried on peaceful trade, and at the very beginning of the 10th century when Kiev was ruled by Oleg, the Rus (in this case, obviously, Varangians in Russian service) made a number of cruel and senseless attacks against the inhabitants of the Caspian coast.

Kiev's military strength and the resulting foreign political power reflected in treaties with the Empire impressed the minor princes of distant tribes who, under Kiev's patronage, gained access to world trade and partly weakened the separatism of the local nobility. Such was the situation in the mid-10th century when the Kiev Prince Igor attempted to extort tribute over and above the fixed amount, was taken prisoner by the Drevlyanians and executed. Igor's widow Olga, herself from Pskov, became head of state as regent over the young Svyatoslav.

The chronicle completed at the end of the 10th century contains many tales written in an epic form about the three generations of Kiev princes: Igor and his wife Olga, their son Svyatoslav and grandson Vladimir whom the clergy proclaimed a saint and the people sung praise to as the defender of Rus.

The first action Princess Olga undertook was to seek revenge against the Drevlyanians for killing her husband. The revenge assumed the form of a state ritual. This part of the chronicle, however, is to such an extent filled with the spirit of epic tales that it, perhaps, reflects a desirable form of didactic story rather than historical reality. As the story goes, the Drevlyanians sent an embassy on ships (along the Teterev and the Dnepr) to Kiev which made an unexpected proposal for the young widow to become the wife of the Drevlyanian Prince Mal. "The Drevlyanian land has sent us to tell you: your husband was killed because he was like a wolf purloining and plundering, while our princes are good, because they rule the Drevlyanian land very well. Marry our Prince Mal!"

The author based the story on contrasts: first the Drevlyanians kill the head of state, then seek the widow in marriage. Further on the play on contrasts continues. Olga perfidiously advises the ambassadors to demand to be taken to her palace in a boat. The credulous Drevlyanians dressed up and, seated in the boat, allowed themselves to be carried to Olga's stone tower-chambers. A pit had been dug in the courtyard, and the ambassadors were thrown into it and buried alive.

Olga sent messengers to the Drevlyanian land to tell the Drevlyanians (who knew nothing about the killing of the first embassy) that the princess gave her consent for marriage and asked an honourable embassy consisting of noble *boyars* to be sent for her, because otherwise the Kievans would not permit her to leave Kiev. The Drevlyanians "chose the best *boyars* who ruled the Drevlyanian land". Olga, according to Russian custom, offered them to visit the bathhouse. Russian stories say: "Take the guest to the bathhouse, give him to eat and drink, and only then speak with him." Then the ambassadors were locked in, the bathhouse set afire and "they were burned to ashes".

Both forms of vengeance recreate the ritual burials of the time: travellers who died along the way were buried in boats; a customary form of funeral was to burn the body in a small house. The next act of the ritual was to make an enormous mound over the boat or the burned house, and it was completed with the funeral feast.

The tale of the vengeance of Igor's widow was written as an antithesis to the unheard-of fact of the murder of the Grand Prince during *polyudye*. The author, first, pointed out that there was a departure from the usual fixed amount of tribute, and second, indicated the reason for the departure, mainly the exceptional luxury of the Varangian mercenaries and the envy of the Russian warriors.

In the third, most important part of the tale the author resorts to heathen burial symbols in order to intimidate the rebellious Drevlyanians: the ambassadors were buried in a boat before the very eyes of Olga who mocked them. The second embassy consisting of noblemen was burned.

For the concluding part of the burial ritual, the putting up of the mound, Princess Olga goes to the Drevlyanian land herself. Here as well, the author remains true to himself in his love for contrasts: when the princess' desire is proclaimed, the listeners accept everything at face value, as the Drevlyanians were intended to, without suspecting the perfidy and cruelty of her real designs which are revealed at the end of each episode.

The princess travels to the Drevlyanians "to weep over his (Igor's) coffin". Upon arrival Olga ordered "a large mound to be made and when it was done bid a funeral feast to be held". The funeral feast consisted of warrior games and contests in honour of the diceased military chieftain. Then the feast proper began in the course of which the Drevlyanians got drunk and the Kievan men attacked and hacked 5,000 of them to death.

It is difficult to vouch for the truth of all the particularities mentioned in the chronicle, but it is quite clear that the Drevlyanians could not have been ignorant of what had happened in Kiev. The Drevlyanian land came very close to Kiev from the west (one or two days of travel), and the public burning of the embassy in the centre of the capital could not have remained secret.

The Drevlyanians remaining in the dark was a literary device intended to link the different parts of the invented story together. It is probable that the death of the Grand Prince during *polyudye* was avenged in some way by the Kievans, but the *Tale of Olga's Vengeance*, as we can call it, did not reflect real events, but was an intimidating epic produced in the interests of the Kievan rulers. The heathen Kievan author could not say: "He who takes up the sword shall perish by the sword," and he drew a terrible picture of vengeance resorting to heathen symbols of the funeral fire and feast.

The final part of the tale is connected with the real siege of the Drevlyanian town Iskorosten (modern Korosten) by Olga's forces. For a whole year the Kievan troops besieged the town near which Igor had been killed, but the inhabitants refused to surrender fearing vengeance. Here again, Olga acted wisely as the medieval poet saw it. She told the townsfolk: "I no longer seek vengeance but want to collect a small tribute and, having made up with you, will return home." The idea of a small tribute again demonstrates the perfidy of the Kievan Princess which the author regards as wisdom: "I do not want a heavy tribute as my husband, but ask only for small tribute... give me three doves and three sparrows from each household."

The inhabitants of Iskorosten were overjoyed at the truly unprecedentedly easy tribute. Having received the birds Olga ordered bits of sulphur to be fastened to each of them, and in the evening, at dusk, the sulphur was set aflame and the doves and sparrows were set free to return to their nests in the dovecotes and under the roofs.

The town burst into flames. The sheds, towers and sleeping chambers were consumed by fire, and "there was no household that did not burn". The people fled from the town and were either massacred or turned into slaves. Two embassies of Drevlyanian nobility murdered, 5,000 Drevlyanians killed at Igor's mound, and an insurgent town burned to the ground — such was the outcome of the Drevlyanians' rebellion against Kiev.

The author of the *Tale of Vengeance* resorted to primitive artistic means to influence the semi-primitive consciousness of his contemporaries, and to the swords of the Kievan warriors he added ideological weapons, forcing his readers to believe in the wisdom and invincibility of the Kiev princely dynasty. Deception, perfidy and unprecedented cruelty of the tale's main heroine apparently did not go beyond the moral restrictions of the time. Her actions are not condemned but, on the contrary, praised as reflecting the properties of the supreme intelligent being.

In this respect the *Tale of Vengeance* is an exceptionally interesting literary and political work, the first deliberate, and probably, originally oral account of the strength of Kiev. The fact that under Olga's grandson Vladimir the story was included in the chronicle indicates its value for official state chronicle-writing.

One and a half centuries later the chronicler of the late 11th century turned to the age of Princess Olga and her son Svyatoslav as to a certain political ideal. He was dissatisfied with the contemporary situation (the time of Vsevolod Yaroslavich), when the princes' officials "robbed and sold people". The chronicler (the Father-Superior of the Kiev-Pechersky Monastery?) recalled the heroic olden times when "the princes did not hoard large wealth, did not use invented, false fines, but if the fine was fair, gave the money to the men for weapons".

In his introduction to this historical work the author addresses the readers: "Turn the ears of your reason to the times when former princes and their *boyars* defended the Russian land and conquered other lands." If in the military respect the ideal of the chronicler was Svyatoslav, then in respect to domestic government it was obviously Olga, because immediately after the *Tale of Vengeance* the chronicle includes innovations introduced by the princess. Vengeance was fine but the state needed order and regulation of duties which would make the annual collection of tribute lawful.

> Olga and her son and their warriors passed through the Drevlyanian land establishing the size of duties and corvée. Her *stans* (camp sites) and hunting grounds are known. In 947 Olga set out for Novgorod and established the taxes and corvée on the rivers Msta and Luga and built *pogosts*, warehouses for storing the tribute. Olga's *pogosts* and hunting grounds are known throughout the land. Her sled is preserved in Pskov to this day. Her *perevesy* (places for catching birds with nets) have been preserved along the Dnepr and Desna. A village called Olzhichy exists to this day.

The chronicle contains the most valuable information on the prince's domain in the mid-10th century. It stresses the possessive nature of Olga's establishments, "her *stanovishches*", "her hunting grounds", "her town Vyshgorod", "her own village". What the chronicle reports here does not contradict the large *polyudye* of the Kiev princes mentioned above. That *polyudye* probably went in a large circle down the Dnepr to Smolensk and further on down the Desna; it is not even mentioned here. The Dnepr and the Desna are mentioned only in connection with the *perevesishches*, i. e. enormous nets for catching birds for the prince's feasts, which most probably, extended geographically to the virgin parts between the Desna and the Dnepr in the upper point of which stood the prince's Vyshgorod.

Order was established in the conquered Drevlyanian land, duties were imposed, two thirds for Kiev and one third for Vyshgorod. The duties, "rules" and "lessons" (i. e. court duties and penalties) — were determined. Olga set up her *stanovishches* — the strongholds of *polyudye* — in the interests of security during the collection of tribute. In addition, the limits of the prince's hunting grounds were strictly defined; thirty years later Olga's grandson killed the Varangian Lut Sveneldich for having violated them. As we see here, the outlines of the domain which will be fully established by the Russkaya Pravda a century later have already appeared at that point.

Extensive prince's possessions were indicated in the north (outside the large *polyudye*), in the Novgorod land. Olga introduced duties and corvée to the west, of Novgorod along the Luga, and to the east along the Msta. Olga set up *pogosts* on the Msta, an important trade artery linking the Baltic basin with the Caspian basin, and lakes Ilmen and the Volkhov with the Upper Volga. Msta was singled out specially, apparently due to its exclusive position, but the chronicler adds that *pogosts* were set up throughout the land (meaning the Novgorod land). Besides, the principal grounds providing "honey, wax and fur", hunting grounds and "places" which probably mean fishing sites, have been enumerated. To implement all of Olga's innovations and reforms it was necessary to divide the grounds, guard the borders of the preserves and assign servants to make regular use of them.

In the list of the princess' innovations the most interesting is the mentioning of the organisation of *stanovishches* and *pogosts*. *Stanovishches* are indicated in connection with the Drevlyanian land where *polyudye* was held earlier as well. It is possible that under Igor the Kiev warriors stopped in the towns and settlements of the Drevlyanian princes, such as Ovruch, Malin and Iskorosten, and did not build their own strongholds in the Drevlyanian land. The conflict with the local nobility and the Drevlyanian uprising made it necessary to establish new relations. Now new *stanovishches* had to be built for the security of the future *polyudye* expeditions, and Olga built them.

In the north, beyond the limits of the large *polyudye*, beyond the Krivichian land, in the Novgorod land, the Kievan Olga not only chose the grounds for herself, but also set up a network of *pogost*-strongholds to make her northern domains a thousand kilometres away from Kiev more secure.

The difference between a *stanovishche* and a *pogost* must not have been great. *Stanovishches* accommodated the prince and a large crowd of his warriors, servants, riders, messengers numbering probably many hundred people and horses once a year. Since *polyudye* was carried out in wintertime, the *stanovishche* must have had stores of fodder and food supplies, and warm premises. The fortifications of the *stanovishche* did not have to be very strong because the *polyudye* expedition itself constituted a formidable military force. Defensive walls were necessary only in case part of the *polyudye* were stored inside.

A *pogost* two months away from Kiev was a feudal body in miniature introduced by the prince's power into the thick of peasant communities and villages. It must have had all the facilities required in the *stanovishche*, but we must take it into account that the *pogost* was farther from the prince's centre and more independent than the *stanovishches* along the *polyudye* itinerary.

Polyudye intimidated the local peasant population; annual visits by the whole of prince's court was a guarantee of safety which did not exist in the *pogosts*. Riders, tribute collectors, *virniki* visiting the *pogost* were also armed but they were not as numerous as the *polyudye* expeditions. Therefore the *pogost* must have been a small fort with its garrison.

The people living in the *pogost* must have been not only servants but also warriors. The fact that they were far from the domains made it necessary for them to engage in agriculture, hunting, fishing and animal husbandry. As to the cattle and horses there must have been the prince's horses to transport the tribute and cattle to feed the tribute collectors. It is to be supposed that the *pogost* had more premises for storage than the *stanovishche*; it was necessary to store tribute (wax, honey and fur), food supplies for the garrison and tribute collectors (meat, fish, grain and so on), and fodder (oats and hay).

The system of the *pogost* can hardly be imagined without some sort of fortifications. The very idea of founding *pogost* in the midst of the lands conquered by the prince required defence works, "the town", "the lesser town". Therefore, we find it possible to identify certain town sites of the 9th-11th centuries in Slavic and neighbouring lands as *pogost*.

The only instance when a *pogost* mentioned in a deed of 1137 was excavated by archaeologists was that of Vekshenga, at the confluence of the Vekshenga River with the Sukhona, 89 kilometres to the east of Vologda. "Vekshenga gave 80 pelts to St Sophia." A. V. Nikitin explored the place near the village which is still called *pogost*. It is a usual cape-like town site of triangular shape two sides of which are bordered by ravines and the third one, joining the plateau, by a moat. It is a town site of small size, probably fortified by a stockade. There is almost no cultural layer on the town site itself. The people probably lived at the site of the modern village of Vekshenga.

The number of *stanovishches* and *pogosts* of the 9th-11th centuries cannot be determined precisely. There must have been at least fifty *stanovishches* for the large *polyudye*. Each *stanovishche* must have had several dozen people to serve it. This list should be supplemented by the villages situated around the stronghold (either the *stanovishche* or the *pogost*) in which the people servicing it lived and ploughed the land.

The number of *pogosts* was probably much larger than the number of former *stanovishches*, but it is not possible to determine it. It would seem that the density of *pogosts* in the northern part of the Russian lands could be very great, but their overall number for the Pskov, Novgorod, Vladimir-Suzdal, Ryazan, and Murom lands may be estimated, on the basis of the deed of 1137, at 500 to 2,000.

In the sociological sense the *pogost* originally constituted a cell of the prince's domain transferred to undeveloped remote lands. The *pogost* was at the same time an element of the feudal state structure since both types, the domain and the state, were closely interrelated in practice and in the legal consciousness of the medieval people.

Pogosts were the knots of an enormous net thrown by the princes of the 10th-11th centuries over the Slav and Finno-Ugric lands of the North; the meshes of this net could embrace *boyar*'s domains and communal ploughed lands, and the *pogosts* were the basic knots which held together the net and enabled it to retain these lands in submission.

Each *pogost* with its houses and stockade and adjacent villages and ploughed lands where the people maintaining order in the *pogost* carried on their economic activities constituted a miniature semi-independent state standing over the peasant *mirs-vervs* (communes) of the aboriginal population. Its strength lay not in the people who lived in the *pogost* and the surrounding settlements but in its links with Kiev, and later with the local new capital, and with the *state* in the widest sense of the word.

It is to be assumed that each mesh in the net, i. e. each *pogost* was linked to the next *pogost*, and all the *pogosts* together constituted the primary form of the vital links of the capital with the remote outskirts: messengers from Kiev could have received fresh horses at each *pogost* to reach the next *pogost* faster; other news might be transmitted by the local people who knew the nearest paths and swamps better.

In our medieval sources the concept of *pogost* is a part of a set: *pogost, selo, smerds*. The latter refers not to the entire peasant population who were called *lyudi* (people), but to a certain layer related to the prince's domain and directly subjected to the prince ("*smerds* shall not be punished without the prince's word") and obliged to fulfill certain duties in favour of the prince. The *smerds* paid tribute. The most honourary duty of the *smerds* was military service in the prince's cavalry which placed the *smerds* one level higher than the usual communal peasants.

Smerds ploughed the land, lived in villages and were assigned to *pogosts*:

> He who is considered a *smerd* is assigned to his *pogost* (deed of 1270).

Our contemporary word *selo* has a wider meaning of a rural settlement in general and is close to "village". In ancient Rus the usual village was called by the ancient Indo-European word *ves* and the word *selo* meant a domainal village of a prince or a *boyar*. *Smerds* lived in *selos* and not in *veses*.

> I said about the *smerds* who lived in the *selos* (Kirik's Lament, 12th century).

The data in the chronicle concerning the reforms of Princess Olga in 947 are valuable in that they provide us with the starting point in the historical life of such a set as *pogost-selo-smerds*.

The system of exploiting peasants consisted of the tribute collected during *polyudye* and a number of duties in the form of corvée, such as transporting goods, making ships and sails, and building *stanovishches*. Tribute was levied, most likely, by the local princes who were forced to share it with the Kievan prince.

Besides, from the mid-10th century, we learn about the structure of the prince's domain. Beyond the large *polyudye*, in the north of Rus, the prince's power was introduced in the form of a network of *pogosts* surrounded by *selos* populated by *smerds* paying tribute to the prince.

The time of Princess Olga was, indeed, a time when feudal relations grew more complex and a number of memorable reforms had been introduced, strengthening and legally sustaining the extensive prince's domain stretching with intervals from the outskirts of Kiev to the Luga River which flowed into the Baltic Sea, and the Msta which linked the Baltic with the Volga River.

The crucial nature of the age of Igor and Olga, the mid-10th century, can also be felt in the attitude to Christianity; the official adoption of Christianity as a state religion took place later, in 988. The first contact with Christianity and the individual baptising of some Rus people began in the 860s, but in the mid-10th century we already witness the introduction of Christianity into the state system. Let us compare two treaties with the Greeks: in concluding the 911 Treaty the Russian envoys swore only by the name of the heathen Perun (the Varangian envoys also used the name of this god who was foreign to them). Yet in the 944 Treaty the oath was made both to the heathen Perun and the Christian god.

> We, those that are Christians, vowed in the St Ilya Church, to the just cross that was there.

The Church of St Ilya, the saint likened to the Perun God of Thunder, was in the commercial part of Kiev on the Podol, "over the stream". It is important to note that the church is called a cathedral, which implies the existence of other Christian churches. In addition to baptised Russians, baptised Khazars and Varangians are mentioned.

Christianity represented a considerable political and cultural force in Europe and in the Middle East. Being Christian made it easier to trade with Byzantium; Christianity introduced the country to writing and an extensive literature. A number of Slavic countries had already adopted Christianity by that time.

Of greatest importance for our lands was the Christianisation of Bulgaria (864?) and invention of the Slavonic alphabet by Cyril and Methodius in the mid-9th century. Bulgaria had produced an extensive religious literature by the mid-10th century making it easier for Christianity to penetrate into Rus. It is quite possible that a link between Bulgaria and Kievan Rus was "the island of the Rus", the land of the "Danubians" which was often politically dependent on the Bulgarian kingdom. It was here that the most ancient Russian Cyrillic inscription of 943 has been discovered. The second point of contact between the Rus and Bulgarian cultural centres was the concentration of Russian harbours on the Bulgarian coast between Constantsa and Varna.

Prince Igor was a heathen: he swore not in the St Ilya Church but "on the hill where Perun stood and put his arms, shields and gold"; and he was buried by Olga according to the heathen ritual, under an enormous mound. But there were some Christians among his *boyars* and envoys to the emperors of Byzantium.

Igor's widow Olga, regent of the young Svyatoslav, subsequently adopted Christianity and, perhaps, intended to make it the state religion, but at this point a sharp contradiction came to the fore because of the Byzantine clerical-political concept according to which the Emperor was God's vicegerent and head of both the state and the Church.

A conclusion very advantageous for Byzantium was drawn from this assumption: any people adopting Christianity from the hands of the Greeks became the vassals of the Greek Emperor, a politically dependent people or state.

Kievan Rus which regarded Christian beliefs calmly, preferred equal relations with Byzantium, which should have been determined by mutual profit and balance of power, and would place no additional obligations on Rus associated with the divine origin of the Emperor, rather doubtful for the Russians.

The intention to adopt Christianity proclaimed by Olga in 955 should be regarded not as an episode of her personal life but as a political step in the duel between monarchs standing at the head of the two largest powers of the time; in this each side sought to clarify its positions in the forthcoming situation. We do not know the subject of the argument, and we do not know what each side wanted, because the negotiations were secret and only hints and references have come down to us in the sources. Yet we must say that the author of one of the sources was a direct participant in these talks, Constantine Porphyrogenitus, the same emperor who left us a detailed description of Russian *polyudye*. Apparently the Emperor knew how to keep secrets.

The Russian chronicle includes a special account of the Russian regent princess' trip to Constantinople:

> in 955 Olga went to Byzantium and arrived in Constantinople. Then ruled Constantine, Leo's son, and Olga came to the Emperor. Having seen her, beautiful in appearance and sharp-witted, the Emperor was amazed and said to her: it befits you to rule with us in this city.

The account was written down not immediately after the events; in some manuscripts the Emperor was called Tzimisces (969-976), but the latter began to rule only after Olga's death; in the above passage we have another hitch: the Emperor sought the Russian princess in marriage while his wife was alive and spoke with Olga.

Olga answered that she was a heathen and wanted the Emperor himself to baptise her.

"I am a heathen. And if you want to baptise

me, then you must do it yourself. If someone else does it, I will refuse!" And the Emperor with the Patriarch baptised her. Her Christian name was Helen after the mother of Constantine the Great."

The choice of Christian name was highly symbolic: Olga was given the name of Empress Helen who took part in introducing Christianity as the state religion of the Empire in the 4th century A. D. For that deed Emperor Constantine the Great and his mother Helen were acknowledged by the Greek Church to be Apostles. Giving the name to Olga, Byzantine rulers obviously hinted at the fact that they would like, with her help, to introduce Christianity in Rus as an official religion, thus placing the young but powerful Rus state in vassal bondage to Byzantium. Further on the account develops the author's favourite theme, highly improbable but romantic: Constantine Porphyrogenitus officially proposed to Olga: "I want to take you as my wife".

Misled by V. N. Tatishchev who thought that Olga was of quite an advanced age when she arrived in Constantinople, some 68 years old, historians believed that this was the main reason why she could not have been sought in marriage.

Let us calculate approximately Olga's age proceeding from reliable data and what we know about the customs in ancient Rus. Svyatoslav was Olga's only child. In 946 he symbolically began the battle against the Drevlyanians by throwing his lance, but it fell right next to his horse, for he was very small. Svyatoslav was born in 942 and was only four years old at the time when that war started.

Women married in ancient Rus usually at the age of 16-18. Olga, therefore, was born in 923-927. At the time of her conversation with the Emperor she must have been 28-32. She was a young widow rather that an aging princess.

Olga answered the Emperor who sought her in marriage: "How could you take me as your wife if you yourself baptised me and called me your daughter!?" According to church rules a godfather could not marry his goddaughter. According to the author

Olga had thought of the baptism beforehand to avoid the undesirable marriage with the Emperor. Having heard this clever answer the Emperor is said to have exclaimed: "O Olga, you have outwitted me!' And generously bestowed gold, silver, silk and various precious vessels on her. Then he let her leave having called her his daughter."

Constantine described his meeting with Olga in his book *On Ceremonies* under 957. Here he mentions gifts to the Russian embassy, a golden plate on which 500 miliarensis were brought. That plate was also mentioned by Russian merchant Dobrynya Yadreikovich who visited Constantinople in 1212. He wrote that in the St Sophia he saw a "large golden plate for church services presented to the Russian princess when she took tribute in Constantinople".

The Emperor describes the ceremonies of Olga's reception in the palace mentioning two visits: on September 9 and October 18. Olga arrived with her priest Grigory. The Emperor says nothing about the baptising of the princess. If Olga were really baptised in Constantinople by the Emperor and the patriarch it would be difficult to believe that Constantine, who had listed the members of the embassy, the size of tribute, the receptions and conversations and feasts would not have hinted in his text at that important event.

It is most probable that Olga arrived in Byzantium already a Christian (this must be the reason why she was accompanied by a priest), and the colourful account of the baptism of the Russian princess by the Emperor was also a fantasy of the author as was the proposal made to Olga by the married Emperor. Something quite different that had nothing to do with marriage or baptism was the subject of the long negotiations which apparently satisfied neither of the sides. It follows from the words of Dobrynya Yadreikovich that Olga took tribute from the Greeks, but most probably, these were merely rich gifts.

The chronicle reveals more:

> As we said Olga arrived in Kiev and the Emperor sent her a message: "I bestowed generous gifts on you and you promised to send

me, when you return to Rus, slaves, wax, fur, and also auxiliary forces." Answering the envoys Olga said: "If you were to stay in the Kiev harbour at the Pochaina as long as I did in Constantinople in the straits, I would give you what I promised."

Two important details become clear: first, the Russian embassy was kept for too long in the Constantinople harbour; second, Olga promised to present many gifts for something. In the end Olga received some sort of tribute; she refused to send gifts and warriors from Kiev and spitefully promised Constantine that if he were to come to Kiev he would be kept in the Kievan harbour.

Obviously the main point on the agenda was Russian military assistance to Byzantium. Many historians believed that the reason for tensions during the negotiations was the issue of the independence of the newly established Russian church.

Two years later, in 959, judging from West European sources, Olga sent ambassadors to the German Emperor Otto I allegedly with the request to send a bishop with priests, a request that turned out to be false subsequently.

However, the monk Adalbert, already named the bishop of Rus, set out for Russia. In 962 Adalbert, unable to fulfill any of the missions he had been sent for and seeing that his labours were in vain, returned to his country. On the way back from Kiev some of his companions were killed; he himself escaped death only by a miracle.

It is possible that Olga really intended to organise a church in Rus and hesitated between the two centres of Christianity, Constantinople and Rome. An envoy from the Roman curia was banished from Rus and just managed to survive. No envoy was sent from the Constantinople patriarchy. This could have been a result of the Byzantine concept of clerical-political vassalage.

The Russian chronicler naively rejoiced at the fact that the Patriarch and the Emperor called Olga daughter. It was not an indication of the prestige of a ruler, but rather it meant a certain distance between father and son or daughter. When some 12th-century Russian prince requested the Grand Prince to accept him as a vassal, he asked for the right to be called his son and to ride next to his stirrup as for a great favour.

Constantine's instructions to Olga at the conclusion of all the negotiations ("called her his daughter") could hardly be viewed as the words of a Godfather to his aging granddaughter. It was the definition of the situation by the head of the Empire and the church: the Russian princess was considered by him not as an equal sister but merely as a subordinate daughter. It was probably this conclusion of negotiations that provoked Olga's refusal to send Russian goods and the Russian auxiliary corps to Byzantium, and the flirtation with the Roman church. This also explains the princess' unpleasant recollections of the talks and the long time she had to spend not in the palace but on a ship in the Bosphorus.

Olga's rule was apparently marked by a number of innovations: in addition to the former *polyudye* carried out by the prince together with his warriors and the local princes, the prince's domain proper was organised. Far in the north, in the Novgorod land, along lively international routes, on the Msta, the Kievans set up *pogosts*, a new form of involving the lands outside the *polyudye* zone in the sphere of prince's influence.

Two measures were applied to consolidate the prince's power over the lands proclaimed to belong to the Kievan Prince: first, more definite duties and their size were established ("rules", "lessons", corvées and tribute) and, second, epic works were written praising the Grand Princess and her foreign policy (for instance, the historically inaccurate account of baptism in Constantinople), and the intimidating *Tale of Vengeance*, the first monarchic work in Rus intended to cast fear on the popular masses and local nobility by showing the tragic doom of any attempt to resist Kiev. Olga's attempt to introduce Christianity should apparently be viewed as yet another state protective measure.

The Kievan Rus state appears to be well established and, under the existing historical circumstances, properly organised. The time of Olga concluded a large, 150-year-long lap in Russian history from the Kaganate of the Rus in the early 9th century to the Kievan Rus of the mid-10th century described by authors in different countries.

The Russian chronicler describes the short rule of Svyatoslav Igorevich (964-972) in the most laudatory colours of a court panegyric. The pages devoted to this prince are not the chronicle of events but rather a praise to the valour, wit and knighthood of the young prince, "praise and glory to him", where admiration prevails over truthful description of the facts. The author is very careless in dates and is not concerned with the location of the theatre of military operations. He lets out such famous towns as Philippopol, Preslav the Great, and Arcadiopol. Even the Emperor of Byzantium remains unnamed, just as in the account used by Nestor to obtain information about Prince Kii's trip to Constantinople "to an emperor whose name was not retained". The name of Emperor John Tzimisces is only mentioned in the review of the 971 Treaty by another person.

The account of Svyatoslav in the chronicle has retained the style of the epic warrior poem similar but not identical to the *bylinas*; as was already mentioned, Svyatoslav's name is absent from popular epic works.

The author of the warrior tale shows his hero to listeners (and later readers) as a small child. But the 3 to 5-year-old boy is described as a real military leader—he opens the battle against the Drevlyanians by throwing his lance, and the military chiefs say: "The prince has started the battle, let us follow the prince!"

On the subsequent pages of the chronicle the voice of the clerical chronicler praising Olga for adopting Christianity mixes with the voice of a warrior singing the glory of the military leader for being faithful to his heathen men. In answer to his mother urging him to follow her example the 15-year-old prince replied: "How can I decide to accept the new faith alone? The warriors would laugh at me."

Christianity was rejected by Svyatoslav and his *boyars* because they knew very well that Christianity would entail vassal dependence on Byzantium, and the next Emperor would gladly call him "son" in the feudal sense.

Under 964 the chronicle gives an epic description of the beginning of Svyatoslav's independent rule, possibly retaining the original rhythm of the oral narration:

> When Prince Svyatoslav reached adulthood and came to man's estate, he began to muster a large force of brave *bogatyrs*; he was a very brave man himself. In many wars he moved swiftly like a cheetah and took along no wagons and heavy cauldrons for boiling meat. They cooked any kind of meat—horse-flesh, beef and the flesh of wild animals—cutting thin pieces and roasting them on coals.
>
> Neither did he carry tents but slept on his felt *shabrack* with his saddle under his head. All his warriors lived likewise on the march.
>
> Setting out on an expedition Svyatoslav warned his adversary: "I march against you!"

Before going into battle Svyatoslav inspired his warriors with speeches which later became classical examples of this genre. Greek authors, contemporaries of the events, also indicate these speeches addressed to all the warriors.

Byzantine chronicler of the 10th century Leo the Deacon quotes one speech:

> Let us be inspired by the valour bestowed on us by our ancestors, let us remember that the strength of the Ross has been invincible so far, and let us fight bravely for our lives! It does not befit us to return home fleeing to save ourselves. We must either win and remain alive or die with glory performing feats worthy of valorous knights!

The chronicler's rendering of Svyatoslav's speeches circa 969 is close to the following account by a participant in the emperor's expeditions:

> We have no other way—whether we want to or not we must engage in battle. Let us not dis-

> grace the Russian land and lay down our lives here; the dead cannot be ashamed! But if we flee, then we will deserve shame.
>
> No, we shall not flee but will stand firm! I shall ride ahead of you and if I die, take care of yourselves.
>
> And his warriors said: "Where you die, there shall we also die."

Svyatoslav fought in the Volga Bulgaria, in Khazaria on the Caspian, in the Pecheneg steppe, on the territory of Bulgaria and Byzantium.

According to the most modest estimate Svyatoslav marched 8,000-8,500 kilometres in a few years. Sometimes historians accuse Svyatoslav of being too war-like and senselessly quarrelsome, calling him an adventurist and the leader of a nomad force. Usually they refer to the events of 968 when in his absence, the Pechenegs besieged Kiev and Olga and her grandchildren proved to be in danger.

> The Kievans sent messengers to Svyatoslav to say, "You, O Prince, seek foreign lands and take care of them but have neglected your own land. We here in Kiev were nearly captured by the Pechenegs".

Sleek as a cheetah the prince was on the Danube at the time.

> He and his warriors rapidly saddled their horses, and arriving in Kiev he kissed his mother and children being sorry that the Pechenegs had attacked. Mustering all his troops Svyatoslav drove the Pechenegs away into the steppe. And there was peace.

Despite the happy outcome of the episode with the siege of Kiev, the accusation of adventurism and lack of state wisdom stuck to Svyatoslav. We should consider the activities of Svyatoslav in greater detail and against a broader historical background.

To begin with, we must say that Svyatoslav's military activity, although unprecedented in scope, was subordinated to two directions—Volga-Caspian (Khazar), and Constantinople. Both were, as we repeatedly saw, the basic directions of trade expeditions organised by Kievan Rus as a state. State export as a form of selling primary feudal rent and securing its safety was a most important task of the young state.

Rus' trade with the Orient acquired a transitory nature by the 10th century. Many states in Northern Europe and France which did not have direct access to Oriental goods had a vested interest in obtaining silk, spices, arms, decorations, race horses and a lot more: Byzantium regulated and centralised its export too strictly. The straight overland road to the Anatolian Eastern lands was blocked by a powerful semicircle of nomad tribes of Magyars, Turks-Bulgars, Pechenegs, Khazars, Kipchaks and Guzes inhabiting the areas from the Middle Danube to the Lower Volga.

In the course of the crusades in the 11th-13th centuries West European knights blazed a trail to the Orient, but before the Crusades only Kievan Rus was capable of carrying the heavy loads through the nomad cordons to Baghdad, Constantinople, Reffelschtetten and Regensburg on the Danube.

The struggle for the security of trade routes from Rus to the Orient was becoming a common task for all Europeans.

The parasitical state of Khazars living from customs duties held all the routes from Eastern Europe to the Orient, to the land of the Guzes, Khorezm and the other possessions of the Caliphate. The Kagan of Khazaria levied enormous duties on the merchants going eastwards and back, and when the balance of force was favourable, it simply robbed the returning Russian caravans as it happened in 913.

Byzantium initiated systematic aggressive actions against Bulgaria (the first Bulgarian Kingdom) establishing its influence from time to time in those places on the Balkan Peninsula past which went Rus' old trade route to Constantinople.

Both directions of Russian overseas expeditions still required military support.

The chronology of Svyatoslav's expeditions is not very precise in the sources, but it is possible to single out two consecutive groups:

first, the expedition against the Vyatichians, on the Volga, and against Khazaria (according to the chronicle in 964-966, according to Ibn Haukal in 968-969);

second, the expedition against Danubian Bulgaria and the war against Byzantium jointly with the Bulgarians (967-971).

The description of the Khazarian expedition of Svyatoslav in the chronicle is preceded and followed by references to the Vyatichians who previously had paid tribute (customs duties?) to the Khazars. To some extent, this determined the route of the expedition during which Russians fought in the Volga Bulgaria, in the land of the Burtas and in Khazaria where Itil and the ancient capital of the Kaganate, Semender on the Caspian, were taken. Then the peoples of the North Caucasus were conquered: the Yassy (Ossetians) and the Kasogi (Adyge tribes). The expedition ended on the Taman Peninsula which since then became Russian Tmutarakan. On the way back the Rus captured Sarkel on the Don and from there Svyatoslav went not directly to Kiev but along the roundabout Vyatichian way to the north, so as to avoid the Dnepr nomad Pechenegs; that is why the Vyatichian land is mentioned twice, under the year 964 and 966.

The length of the expedition was about 6,000 kilometres. It is to be assumed that it took about three years with winters spent somewhere on the Volga and in the North Caucasus. It is difficult to say precisely which years they were. Combining the data from the chronicles and from Ibn Haukal, it is possible to assume that this grand-scale expedition took place in the lap between 965 and 968. Ibn Haukal already knew that following the victory over the Khazars the Rus set out for "Rum" (Byzantium), and to Andalus (Anatolia, the southern shore of the Black Sea).

The results of the expedition were exceptional: the huge Khazarian Empire was destroyed and disappeared from the political map of Europe for good. The way to the Orient was cleared. The Volga Bulgaria ceased being a hostile barrier, and besides, Sarkel and Tmutarakan, two major towns in the southeast, became Russian centres.

The balance of power in the half-Byzantine and half-Khazarian Crimea also changed, and Kerch (Korchev) also became a Russian town. A hundred years later, Prince Gleb, the great grandson of Svyatoslav measured the frozen Kerch Strait and left the famous chronicle about how he measured the sea over the ice from Tmutarakan to Kerch, as if marking the hundredth anniversary of the Russian victory along this most important route.

The growing power of Kievan Rus following these victories, the appearance of the Russians in the Crimea and the selling of *polyudye*, accumulated during the years of the expedition, in Byzantium and its possessions in Asia Minor might have given rise to a confrontation unknown to us, merging very vaguely in 967-968. In 969 it assumed the shape of a major war of Rus and Bulgaria against the Byzantine Empire. Opinions concerning that war are also contradictory due to the incomplete Russian chronicles and extreme bias of the Greek sources which sought to depict the Rus as adversaries of Bulgaria and Byzantines as its friends and liberators. But precisely these events caused the Russian chronicler to write his famous dictum about the untruthful Greeks so frequently referred to by historians: "The Greeks are deceitful to our day".

Everything began with that part of the Black Sea area where the Island of the Rus was supposed to exist formed by the bend and the delta of the Danube, the sea and the enormous Trajan wall and moat.

In 943, when Igor of Kiev received tribute from Byzantium here on the Danube, this area belonged to Bulgaria. The 943 inscription mentions Zhupan Dimitry. But due to its colonisation by the Ulichian Rus it could be claimed by Kievan Rus which possessed several harbours here. However, the ethnic closeness of the island's inhabitants to Kievan Rus did not determine their political sympathies, since the Ulichians had resettled on the Danube as a result of a three-year war with Kiev.

The existence of a Greek population in the Black Sea towns and the abundance of Roman-Byzantine forts gave ground for the Greek Empire to claim this strategically important area.

The 100,000-strong Russian population of the "island", like the Don Cossacks later, could seek independence, but due to various external events, it inevitably had to vacillate between two related countries, Kievan

Rus and Bulgaria. It was least of all interested in being subordinated to Byzantium, because this, first, imposed on them many obligations connected with guarding the Danubian frontier and second, deprived the local ports of the advantages of Russo-Byzantine trade.

The situation was further aggravated by the existence within Bulgaria, among the nobility, of adversaries and allies of Byzantium. It is quite possible that the reasoning went along the following lines: the further from the empire some area was situated the less was the immediate danger coming from the empire, and the less dangerous it was to appeal for its patronage. In any case the rulers of the Pereyaslavets on the Danube, the capital of the island of the Rus, on several occasions revealed their hostility to Svyatoslav during his war against Byzantium.

The Russian chronicle describes the beginning of Svyatoslav's expeditions in the following terms:

> 967. Svyatoslav marched to the Danube to fight the Bulgarians; Svyatoslav triumphed and captured 80 towns on the Danube. He stayed here ruling in Pereyaslavets and exacting tribute from Byzantium.

This short account is rather contradictory. It would seem an exaggeration to refer to so many Danubian towns; partly it can be explained by the fact that in his time Emperor Justinian built many towns on the Danube some of which were subsequently abandoned.

It would seem strange that having defeated the Bulgarians Svyatoslav exacted tribute from Byzantium. This is probably explained by the abrupt turn in Byzantine-Bulgarian relations at the end of the reign of Nicephorus II Phocas (963-969). Byzantium became aware of its strength and abolished the 927 treaty with Bulgaria which was disadvantageous for it, in 966. Nicephorus began to address the Bulgarian king Peter as his vassal. It was also in June 966 that the emperor, in the words of the chronicle of John Scylitzes, "set out to inspect the towns located in Thracia and arrived at the Large Moat. He wrote to the Arkhont of Bulgaria Peter for the latter to prevent the Turks (Magyars) from crossing the Ister and devastating the lands of the Romeis".

Subsequent events are described as follows by the Greek author: King Peter refused to carry out Nicephorus' orders. Byzantium and Bulgaria became enemies.

At that time Svyatoslav twice appears with the Rus on the Lower Danube and, allegedly on a request by Nicephorus, occupies Bulgarian lands after which he breaks the treaty concluded with Nicephorus and answers the emperor with words full of barbaric bragging.

Another Greek author, Leo the Deacon, reports a different version: the emperor's ambassador Patrici Kalokir began to act in his own interests in negotiations with Svyatoslav, and persuaded Svyatoslav to take his forces into Bulgaria to subsequently launch a war against Byzantium to help him, Kalokir, to depose Nicephorus and seize the throne.

Greek sources abound in incongruities and hints and are reluctant to acknowledge the Russo-Bulgarian alliance which, judging by the number of Bulgarian towns passing to Svyatoslav (80), had emerged already during the first appearance of the Russians on the Danube. The Greek authors wrote at the time when Byzantium, having driven Svyatoslav from the Balkans, completely conquered the Bulgarians, and in their numerous diatribes against the Russians they merely proceeded from political instructions. This should be taken into account in analysing the sources.

Judging from the way Emperor Nicephorus, who allegedly invited Svyatoslav in order to bring the Bulgarians to submission, received the news that the Rus had appeared at the delta of the Danube it becomes clear that there was no invitation or friendly treaty aimed against the Bulgarians between Kievan Rus and Byzantium.

Having learned of the appearance of the Rus, Emperor Nicephorus began to hastily prepare to defend his capital: "furnished cavalry with armour, made catapults and deployed them on the towers of the city wall"; the Bosphorus was spanned by an enormous iron chain. It is hardly the way to welcome allies allegedly loyal to the emperor.

It follows from the words of Leo the Deacon that Svyatoslav's appearance on the Danube was regarded by the Emperor himself as "the beginning of war against both peoples", i. e. against the Rus and the Bulgars. "It seemed to him that it would be useful to attract one of these peoples to his side." The cunning Byzantines decided to obtain hostages from Bulgarian nobility, and under the pretext of inviting brides for Emperor Roman's sons lured Bulgarian girls of noble birth to Constantinople. As a result a certain part of Bulgarian feudallords were in Nicephorus' hands. This explains a great deal in the events of the late 960s.

Apparently the references in the chronicles to Svyatoslav's battles against the Bulgars in 967 refer not to Peter's kingdom or Bulgaria in general but to individual feudal rulers whose daughters became the Emperor's hostages. Among them we should certainly include the rulers of Pereyaslavets on the Danube who were hostile to Svyatoslav. Here, on the site of the former Khan Omortag's palace (mid-9th century), there might still have remained contingents of the Turcs-Bulgarian horsemen who lived somewhat apart from the rest of the population.

In view of the information concerning Byzantium's supporters among the Bulgarian nobility, we must take a guarded attitude to the deliberate statements of Greek chroniclers about the war of the Rus against the Bulgarians. If Svyatoslav's lower Danube operations resulted in tribute imposed on Byzantium, according to the chronicle, it becomes clear who his real enemy was.

In 969 the Bulgarian king Peter died and Emperor Nicephorus was killed by his cousin John (Ioann) Tzimisces who fatally wounded him with a sword on December 10, 969. John became the emperor.

The situation in 970 was as follows: the Bulgarian king Boris, son of Peter, lived in the capital of Bulgaria, the Great Preslava, in the royal palace, possessing all the treasures. The Varangian in Russian service Sveneld was his military commander.

Svyatoslav ruled in Pereyaslavets, on the Danube, in the middle of the Island of the Rus. He left his elder son Yaropolk in Kiev, and appointed another son, Oleg, to rule in the rebellious land of the Drevlyanians; he sent the third son, Vladimir, to Novgorod. Svyatoslav himself was quite satisfied with the new land

Sacred horn from the Black Tomb
Below: the upper part of the horn

where he had gone in 967-969. This was a transfer not of the capital but of the residence, and consolidation of a new very advantageous position at the crossroads of important routes.

> I don't like living in Kiev: I want to live in Pereyaslavets on the Danube because it is the very heart of my land, all sorts of goods come here—silk, gold, wine and different fruit from Byzantium, silver and horses from Hungary and Bohemia, and fur, wax, honey and slaves from Rus.

The Russian and Bulgarian forces not only dominated Bulgaria but also assumed a large-scale offensive along the entire northern border of the Byzantine Empire. They turned up in places where Emperor Nicephorus only recently carried out his inspections. Svyatoslav's forces marched over the Balkans, crossed the Byzantine border and found themselves in the "valley of roses", in the basin of the Maritsa River. It was here that they captured Philippopol (modern Plovdiv), and the allies reached Arcadiopol. "Svyatoslav failed to reach Constantinople only by a small margin." It was only four days of travel along the plains to Constantinople.

In the main battle at Arcadiopol the Pechenegs and the Hungarians who were part of the Russo-Bulgarian army faltered and the battle was lost. John Tzimisces launched a tremendous offensive in 971 after recalling the Asian forces from Syria and training them all winter. The Greeks managed to repulse the onslaught, capture Great Preslav where they took King Boris prisoner, take Pliska and move northwards to the Danube.

Having captured Bulgarian towns the Greeks plundered them without mercy. Thus, when Preslav was taken the "Romeis rushed into the town all at once, dispersed among the narrow streets, killed the townsfolk and plundered their possessions." (Leo the Deacon).

Svyatoslav made Dorostol (Silistria) his stronghold on the Danube where the concluding phase of the war against Byzantium took place. A number of major battles occurred here after which the Slavs lit burial bonfires to their dead warriors. This was the theme of a famous picture by Semiradsky. It was here that Tzimisces besieged Dorostol for more than two months waiting in vain for it to surrender, it was here that the Emperor personally met the famous Kiev prince described by Leo the Deacon.

The Russians began their last decisive battle on the Day of Perun, July 20, 971, but neither side could claim victory. Peace talks began: the emperor sought to impress the Slav military leader by the splendour of the imperial regalia, but was himself struck by the simple attire of the Grand Prince:

> Emperor John Tzimisces in gilded armour rode to the bank of the Istra leading a large group of armed horsemen in dazzling golden attire (the "immortals"). Svyatoslav also appeared crossing the river in a Scythian boat. He was seated rowing just like the rest of his men.
>
> This is what he looked like: of average stature, not too tall but not too short, with thick eyebrows and light blue eyes, snubnosed, beardless with thick and very long hair over his upper lip (a moustache). His head was completely bare, but a strand of hair hung from one side, a sign of nobility.
>
> The back of his head was strong, his chest wide, and all the other parts of the body were well proportioned. He appeared to be grim and wild. A golden earring was in one ear; it was decorated by a carbuncle and two mother-of-pearl.
>
> His attire was white but differed from the others' clothes only by its cleanliness. Seated in the boat on the place of a rower he spoke with the emperor for a while about the peace terms and then departed.

Tzimisces, as the same author writes, accepted the terms of the Rus eagerly. The peace terms were set down in the treaty included in the chronicle: Svyatoslav promised no longer to wage wars against Byzantium. The prince departed "having taken much property from the Greeks and innumerable prisoners". It was an honourable peace.

However, the Byzantines took measures: they informed the Pechenegs about Svyatoslav's movements and the latter attacked him at the Dnepr Rapids in the spring of 972. From his skull the Pecheneg khan "made a cup, lining it with gold, and the khan drank from that cup".

With Svyatoslav's departure from Bulgaria, the independent Eastern Bulgarian Kingdom was conquered and occupied by Byzantium. When Tzimisces took prisoner the lawful king of Bulgaria Boris, Svyatoslav's ally, he hypocritically honoured him, calling him the ruler of the Bulgars. But as soon as Svyatoslav and his force which had defended the Bulgars left the banks of the Danube, Tzimisces showed his true face.

> He (John Tzimisces) walked into the Great Cathedral of the Lord's Wisdom (St Sophia in Constantinople) and, having delivered prayers of thanks, devoted to God the first part of the booty, the splendid Bulgarian crown. Then he went to the Emperor's palace and led the King of the Bulgars Boris into it and ordered him to remove his royal regalia. Then he bestowed the rank of master upon Boris.

Bulgaria's capital was renamed Ioannopol in honour of the emperor, ancient Dorostol was renamed Pheodoropol and the whole of Danubian Bulgaria was turned into the Byzantine province Paristrion.

Summing up the short but brilliant reign of Svyatoslav we see that he was not "a thoughtless adventurist" roaming the steppe. His Volga-Khazar expedition was of vital importance for the young state of Rus and his operations on the Danube and beyond the Balkans were a manifestation of friendship and solidarity with the Bulgarian people whom he assisted in defending their capital, their king and political independence against the encroachments of the Byzantines.

Svyatoslav's defeat was the end of independent Bulgaria which was revived only two centuries later.

In respect to Rus, all of Svyatoslav's dynamic activities proceeded not from lack of attention for his country and its interests, but were aimed at resolving important state problems that required quite an effort to be made. The most important mission, to secure Rus against the Khazar Kaganate, was fulfilled quite successfully. The second mission, to set up a peaceful trade stronghold on the western coast of the Rus Sea, in collaboration with Bulgaria, was not implemented, because Rus was opposed by two strong forces here: Byzantium and the Pechenegs, whose territory spread out through the steppe for a month of travel on horseback.

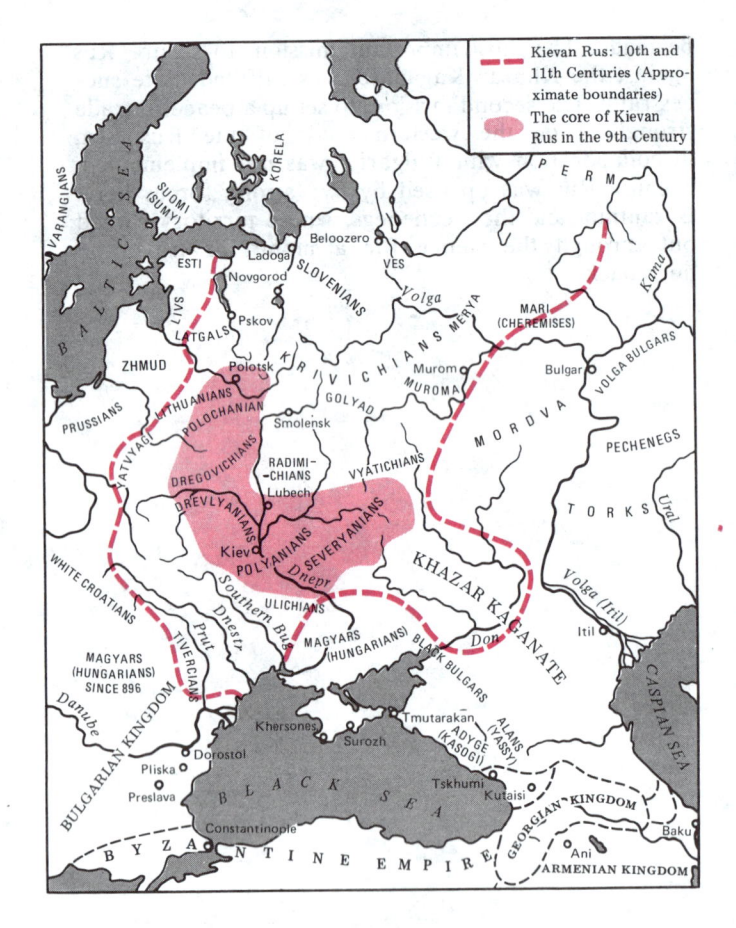

Kievan Rus

THE GOLDEN AGE OF KIEVAN RUS

Vladimir the Red Sun

In the 10th century it became urgently necessary for Rus to wage a struggle against the Pechenegs. The whole of the partly wooded fertile steppe area densely covered with Russian settlements and towns was opened towards the steppe and suffered from sudden raids by the nomads who were spread across the Russian Plain "for a month of travel on horseback" from the Danube to the Zhiguli.

As a result of the raids villages were burned, fields destroyed and the population driven away into slavery. That was why defence against the Pechenegs was not only a state matter but also a popular cause easily understood and supported by all sections of the population. And it was only natural that a prince who succeeded in heading that defence would become a popular hero whose actions were praised in popular epic tales, the *bylinas*.

Svyatoslav's illegitimate son Vladimir became that prince.

In the mid-10th century a certain Malko the Lubechanin lived in the picturesque town of Lubech which served to defend the Kievan land from the north. His daughter Malusha was Princess Olga's house-keeper, and his son Dobrynya was apparently in the service of the prince. In *bylinas* it is indicated that Dobrynya was a "groom and guard" but subsequently became a courtier — "he served food and drinks at the court for nine years".

Malusha the Lubechanka became one of Svyatoslav's concubines and gave birth to a son named Vladimir who was mocked for his origin continuously and

153

called a "slave" or "bondsman". Were it not for a stroke of good fortune, the housekeeper's son might have been lost in the crowd of youngsters and servants at the prince's court. But on one occasion his uncle Dobrynya took advantage of the fact that the prince's legitimate sons Yaropolk and Oleg refused to go to a remote northern factory belonging to Rus, Novgorod, and suggested that his nephew be sent there instead. Thus, the son of a common woman Vladimir became the vicegerent prince in the small town on Lake Ilmen.

After Svyatoslav's tragic death, quarrels flared up between his legitimate sons fanned by the Varangian Sveneld, and the Drevlyanian Oleg was killed. Then Dobrynya and Vladimir marched from Novgorod against Kiev capturing Polotsk, a major trade centre on the Western Dvina, along the way. In this town Vladimir forced the daughter of the Polotsk Prince Rogneda to marry him. Russian *bylinas* reflect the struggle between Oleg and Sveneld and Vladimir's marriage with Dobrynya as the intermediary.

Yaropolk was murdered in the palace by two Varangians from Vladimir's troops, and the son of a slave woman became the Grand Prince of Kiev, and Dobrynya the military leader of Rus.

The first state undertaking of Vladimir was to drive the Varangians out of Kiev. Then he established a heathen cult of six gods headed by the god of thunder and war Perun.

A number of successful expeditions against Poland, the Vyatichians, Lithuania, the Radimichians, the Bulgarians and the Croatians in Transcarpathia considerably strengthened and extended Rus as a state of all the Eastern Slavs.

Vladimir's government sought to involve the rather amorphous early feudal state of Kievan Rus in a new administrative system built, however, on the typical for the time merging of the state element with the personal: instead of the former "high princes" heading the tribal alliances Vladimir appointed his sons:
Novgorod—Yaroslav;
Polotsk—Izyaslav;
Turov—Svyatopolk;
Rostov—Boris;

Silver coin of Prince Vladimir with the inscription "Vladimir on the Throne"

Murom — Gleb;
The Drevlyanian land — Svyatoslav;
Volyn — Vsevolod;
Tmutarakan — Mstislav.

Highways were laid from Kiev to these distant towns described in the *bylinas* and linked to the name of Ilya of Murom.

The main problem of Rus foreign policy, however, remained unsolved: the defence against the Pecheneg tribes advancing along the entire forest-steppe frontier had not been organised. The chronicle ascribes the following words to Vladimir:

> It is very bad that there are few forts around Kiev. And they began to build forts along the Desna and the Oster Rivers and along the Trubezh and along the Sula and the Stugna. And they chose the best warriors from among the Slovenians (Novgorod land), the Krivichians (Smolensk land), the Chud (Estonia) and the Vyatichians (lands along the Oka River).
>
> The warriors from these lands made up the garrisons of the newly built towns. The war against the Pechenegs was being waged at the time and they were defeated.

These words from the chronicle contain exceptionally interesting information about the organisation of state-wide defence. Vladimir managed to involve all of Rus, almost all the peoples constituting it, in the struggle against the Pechenegs. The garrisons for the southern forts were recruited in distant Novgorod, in Estonia (Chud), Smolensk, and in the basin of the Moskva River, in lands where not a single Pecheneg ever reached. It was Vladimir's achievement that he managed to make the whole forest north defend the southern frontier which ran along the lands of the Polyanians, Ulichians and Severyanians.

Of the five rivers on which the forts were being built, four flowed into the Dnepr from the left. The reason why forts were needed on the left bank was that there were less natural obstacles here and the steppe almost reached Chernigov.

Now, when the defensive lines were built, the Pechenegs were forced to overcome four obstacles. The first was the line on the Sula which served as the border between Rus and the nomads for 200 years. In the *Lay of Igor's Host* the Sula is praised as flowing in silver streams while the Polovtsi land was depicted as being "across the Sula River".

Archaeologists have excavated a fort-and-harbour at the mouth of the Sula River where Dnepr ships could seek refuge in case of danger: the fortified harbour had the characteristic name of Voin (Warrior). Further up the Sula the forts stood at a distance of 15-20 kilometres from each other.

If the Pechenegs overcame this line, they encountered a new barrier on the Trubezh where one of the largest towns in Kievan Rus, Pereyaslavl, was located. If the Pechenegs managed to capture or bypass this line as well, the road was open to Chernigov and Kiev. But in front of Chernigov were the defensive lines along the Oster and the Desna, obstructing the enemy's approach to that ancient and rich town.

In order to pass from the left bank of the Dnepr to Kiev the Pechenegs had to ford the river near Vitichev and then cross the valley of the Stugna. But it was along the banks of the Stugna that Vladimir set up his forts.

Archaeological excavations in Vitichev revealed a powerful fortress of the late 10th century with oak stockade and signal tower on the top of a hill over a ford on the river. A huge bonfire was lighted on the tower at the first sign of danger, and since Kiev was visible with the naked eye from that tower, the appearance of the Pechenegs on the Vitichev ford was immediately known in the capital.

The Stugna line went along a "great forest" which surrounded Kiev from the south. This was the last defensive line consisting of the towns Trepol, Tumash, Vassilyev and the ramparts linking these towns. In 991 Vladimir built an enormous bivouac town deep inside that line, between the Stugna and Kiev, which became a reserve of all Kievan forces. This was Belgorod.

The building of several defensive lines according to a specially devised system of forts, ramparts and signal towers made it impossible for the Pechenegs to make sudden attacks, and helped Rus assume the offensive. Thousands of Russian towns and settlements were rid of the horror of Pecheneg raids.

The Russian chronicler, a contemporary of Vladimir, wrote about this frontier line, as well as the western Bishop Bruno travelling from Kiev to Pechenegia, and these "border fortresses, strongholds" were also the subject of folk songs.

Prince Vladimir had an acute need for large military forces and gladly accepted common folk who had displayed their valour in action. He even invited the *izgois*, people who had to leave their native communes and were unable to set up their own households; thereby the prince contributed to the further deterioration of tribal relations in the countryside. The position of an *izgoi* ceased to be a terrible punishment: the *izgoi* could find himself a place among the prince's warriors.

Victories over the Pechenegs were celebrated in public with great pomp. The prince and the *boyars* and warriors feasted on the high gallery of the palace and tables were laid for common people in the courtyard. The elders from all the towns and innumerable other folk arrived for the celebrations.

Vladimir's famous feasts which were a specific way of recruiting men for the *druzhina* were described in the *bylinas* in full accordance with the chronicle.

The common folk created a whole cycle of *bylinas* about Prince Vladimir the Red Sun, about Dobrynya,

Fortress wall of Belgorod. Late 10th century. Reconstruction

about Ilya of Murom and about the struggle against the Whistling Robber who symbolised the tribal princes, about expeditions to distant lands, about the struggle against cruel heathen customs and about the strongholds of the *bogatyrs* defending Kievan Rus from the pagan force.

People have preserved the solemn and majestic songs of the *bylinas*, this oral textbook of Russian history, in the course of a thousand long-suffering years, supplementing them with new heroes, new events, and turning to them in grim years of trials.

The heroic age of Vladimir (980-1015) was praised both by the feudal chronicler and the common folk because in its principal events the feudal element merged with the popular, and the Prince's policy objectively coincided with the popular interests.

A certain Russian scholar of the 12th century travelling aboard a ship sailing through the blue waves of the Aegean Sea decided to write a treatise about Slav paganism, *The Story of How the Pagan Peoples Worshipped Idols and Offered Sacrifice*. Our traveller was acquainted with the ancient Egyptian cult of Osiris, Mohammed's teachings in the Moslem lands, the customs of the Seljuk Turks, and the crusaders' music of the organ in Catholic churches, unfamiliar to the Russian ear.

His ship sailed from the south to the north, through the Aphon and Constantinople, and at the beginning of the journey which may have started in Palestine or even in Egypt, the scholar must have seen the island of Crete known in ancient times by its worship of Zeus-Dios, and the ancient palaces of Aphrodite, Artemis, Athena and the site of the famous Delphian tripod which served for the Oracles to make predictions.

It is possible that the abundance of ancient ruins of pagan shrines encountered during the journey inspired the scholar to compare the Slav, pagan faith with the other ancient beliefs.

The periodisation of Slav beliefs proposed by this highly educated and intelligent author is of exceptional interest to us.

1. Initially the Slavs offered sacrifice to the *upirs* and guardian spirits.

2. Then they began to offer sacrifice to Rod and to the mother figure.

3. Subsequently, the Slavs began to worship mostly Perun, while retaining their faith in other gods.

The *upirs* were vampires, fantastic creatures, werewolves symbolising evil. There were also "beregynis", who were kind and helped people. The attribution of a living soul to all natural elements, and their division into good and evil ones were very ancient ideas which emerged among the hunters of the Stone Age. Various enchantments were used and charms worn against the *upirs*. Folk art has retained numerous symbols of the good and fertility; they were depicted on clothes, dishes and in the living quarters. Ancient people thought they would drive away the spirits of evil. Such symbols include the sun, fire, water, plants and flowers.

The worship of Rod and the mother figure, the gods of fertility, was undoubtedly linked to land cultivation and reflected a later stage in mankind's development—Neolith, Eneolith and the subsequent epochs.

Later, after the Christianisation of Rus, the mother figure was identified with Our Lady.

Rod was the supreme god of the heavens and the earth commanding all the vitally necessary elements—the sun, rain, thunder, and water. The belief in one supreme divinity provided the basis for the later Christian monotheism.

The cult of Perun, the god of thunder, war and weapons, appeared relatively late, and was associated with the development of the warrior, military caste in society.

As we can see, the stages in the development of primitive religion were indicated by the seafaring author quite correctly and accurately. He also depicted the last stage correctly as one of dual faith — the Slavs adopted Christianity "but even today those living in the outskirts worship the accursed god Perun and other pagan gods".

Worship of their gods by the pagan Slavs was rigorously scheduled according to the seasons of the year and agricultural periods. The year was determined by the phases of the sun, because the sun played a tremendous part in the beliefs and world outlook of the ancient land-tillers.

The year began, as it does today, on January 1. New Year celebrations lasted for 12 days including the end of the old year and the beginning of the new. At first all the fires in the hearths were extinguished, then the "living" fire was obtained through friction, special bread was baked, and people engaged in fortune-telling; from various signs they tried to guess what the coming year would be like.

In addition the pagans always actively tried to influence their gods by means of prayers, requests and sacrifice. Feasts were held in honour of the gods at which bulls, goats and sheep were slaughtered, the whole tribe engaged in making beer and baking cakes. It was as if the gods were invited to these feasts to share the food with the people. Special shrines existed for such ritual feasts.

The church combined the pagan celebrations with

Christian holidays of Christmas and Epiphany or Twelfth Day (December 25 and January 6).

The next holiday was *maslenitsa* (Shrovetide), a boisterous and orgiastic celebration of spring solstice, welcome of the sun and exhortation of Nature on the eve of spring ploughing. The church opposed this holiday but was unable to overcome it and only managed to have it put off till before the Lent.

In the time of ploughing, sowing of summer crops and the germination of grain in the ground the thoughts of the ancient Slav were turned to his grandparents also lying in the ground. People visited the cemeteries on those days bringing their grandparents boiled sweetened wheat, eggs and honey believing that the ancestors would help the wheat grow. In ancient times the cemeteries resembled settlements of the dead. A wooden structure was set up over the ashes of the dead, food was brought in spring and autumn to these miniature houses. Later mounds were built over the graves. The custom of offerings on parental days was retained until the 19th century.

In the course of spring and summer the ancient land-tiller's concern for the harvest increased: rain was needed on time as well as the sun. The first spring holiday was on May 1 and 2 when the first sprouts of the summer crops appeared.

The second holiday that subsequently merged with the Trinity was the day of the god Yarilo, the god of the vital forces of Nature; on that day, June 4, a young birch was decorated with ribbons and houses with branches.

The third holiday marked the summer solstice, June 24, the day of Ivan Kupala.

An insistent request for rain is felt in all these holidays. Dances by young girls, rituals and songs in sacred groves, offerings of sacrifice to rivers and springs — all this was aimed at obtaining the gift of the heavens, rain. The Kupala Day was preceded by a week of mermaids, the nymphs of the water and the fields on whom, as the Slavs saw it, depended the watering of the ground by rain.

It is well known to Slav ethnographers that on the days of such mermaid celebrations the most beautiful girls were chosen, decorated with green twigs and water poured over them imitating rain which the Slavs sought to provoke by these actions.

The Kupala holiday was the most solemn in the spring-summer cycle. Water was worshipped, the girls threw wreaths into the water, and fire was worshipped—enormous bonfires were lighted on the hills, and young boys and girls jumped over the fire in pairs. These celebrations were retained for a very long time turning from a ritual into joyful youthful games.

Ethnographers of the early 19th century described the splendid panorama of Kupala bonfires in the Western Ukraine, Poland and Slovakia when from the high peaks of the Tatras and the Carpathians hundreds of bonfires could be seen.

The culmination of the Slav agricultural year were the hot July days with their usual thunderstorms just before the harvesting time.

Powerless in the face of the elements, the land-tiller watched the heavens in fear: the harvest grown by his hands thanks to the prayers to the gods, as he thought, was nearly ready but the grim and capricious sky could destroy the harvest. A drought could make the ears too dry, pouring rain would shake loose the ripe grain, lightning might burn the dry field, and hail destroy the harvest completely.

The god governing the heavens, thunder and clouds was particularly frightening on these days; his displeasure could doom whole tribes to hunger. The day of Rod-Perun (St Ilya Day on July 20) was the most grim and tragic in the whole annual cycle of Slavic worship. Cheerful dances and songs were not performed on that day, but bloody sacrifice was offered to the overbearing god, the immediate precursor of the Christian God. The pagan priests and witch-doctors who first appeared back in the primitive age were the greatest experts in all the rituals and the calendar of worship.

Along with heathen prayers requesting a good harvest, which constituted the annual cycle of holidays, Slav paganism included primitive animism, belief in woodgoblins, spirits of water swamps, and forest, and worship of ancestors and house-spirits.

Marriages and funerals involved complicated rituals. Wedding ceremonies abounded in magical acts aimed at safeguarding the bride who passed from the protection of her family to another clan and at securing the wellbeing of the family and the fertility of the couple.

The funeral rituals of the Slavs grew very complicated at the end of the pagan period in connection with the development of the warrior caste. Arms, armour and horses were burned together with noble Rus. According to Arabic travellers who witnessed Rus funerals, there existed a ritual of killing a rich Rus' wife at his grave. All these accounts were fully confirmed by excavations of mounds.

As an example we can refer to an enormous mound, the Black Barrow in Chernigov where many different 10th-century objects were found in the course of excavations: golden Byzantine coins, weapons, female decorations and an aurochs' horn bound in silver with chased designs depicting *bylina* themes, the death of the fabulous monster, Koshchei the Deathless, in the Chernigov forests.

The Black Barrow where, according to legend, the Chernigov Prince was buried, was located on a high bank of the Desna and the enormous funeral bonfire must have been seen for dozens of kilometres.

Having ascended to the Kievan throne Vladimir carried through a kind of pagan reform. Seeking to raise the former popular beliefs to the level of state religion Vladimir ordered the wooden statues of six gods to be set up on a hill next to his chambers: Perun with a silver head and golden moustache, Khors, Dazhdbog, the god of rain, Stribog, the wind god, Semargl and Mokosh.

It was alleged that Vladimir even introduced human sacrifice to these gods which made the rituals tragic but highly solemn. "And the Rus land was desecrated by blood," the chronicle says.

The cult of Perun was also introduced by Dobrynya in the northern fringe of Rus, in Novgorod. Eight bonfires burned constantly around the idol of Perun and the memory of that eternal fire was retained by the local inhabitants until the 17th century.

Stribog, the wind god, was most likely the god of the

heavens, Dazhdbog the deity of light, fertility and warmth like the ancient Apollo; Khors, the god of the Sun as the source of light. Semargl was a god close to the mermaids who secured water for the fields; it was the god of the soil and roots of plants, one more god of fertility.

Mokosh was the only goddess and apparently symbolised the female element in nature and women's household chores (shearing of sheep and weaving).

An attempt to turn paganism with its cult of Perun into a state religion apparently failed to satisfy Vladimir although Kievans eagerly supported even the most extreme forms of the bloody worship of the war-like god.

Christianity and its main dogmas had been well known in Kiev for a long time already, and suited quite well to the needs of the feudal state. The first references to Christianity among the Rus go back to the 860Б-70s. In the 10th century there was already a church in Kiev of the Christian Saint, the St Ilya Cathedral (St Ilya was the Christian counterpart of Perun). In the times of Svyatoslav and Vladimir an extensive clerical literature existed in neighbouring Bulgaria written in old Slavonic, which could be easily understood by all Russians.

The Kiev princes, however, delayed the adoption of Christianity, because, according to the theological-legal views of the Byzantines, adoption of Christianity entailed the vassal dependence of a newly converted on the Empire.

Vladimir I invaded the Byzantine possessions in the Crimea, occupied Khersones, and from there he dictated his terms to the Emperor. He sought to marry a daughter of the Byzantine Emperor and adopt Christianity. Under the circumstances there could be no question of becoming vassals of the Empire.

Circa 988 Vladimir was baptised himself and baptised his *boyars* and forced all the Kievans and all Russians in general to be christened. In Novgorod the same Dobrynya who had introduced the cult of Perun now baptised the Novgorod folk.

Officially, Rus became a Christian country. The ritual bonfires on which the killed slave women were burned were put out, the bonfires of Perun who required human sacrifice like the ancient Minotaur were extinguished, but for a long time to come pagan mounds were built in country settlements, and Perun and the god of fire were worshipped, and the boisterous celebrations of olden days held in the villages.

Paganism merged with Christianity.

The church in Rus was organised in the following manner: it was headed by the Kievan metropolitan appointed by Constantinople or by the Kiev prince himself with subsequent election by the council of bishops. The large towns had bishops who supervised all the church affairs on a large area, an eparchy. When the independent principalities began to emerge each prince wanted his capital to have its own bishop.

The metropolitan and bishops owned lands, villages and towns: they had their own servants, slaves and *izgois* and even their own troops. Princes paid a tithe, i. e., the tenth part of all their duties and corvée to the church. The church had its own courts and special law by means of which it interfered in the family and personal affairs, into the thoughts and behaviour of people.

There were many stone and wooden churches in the towns of the 11th and 12th centuries in which priests and their assistants deacons served. The service was held daily, three times a day, matins, liturgy, and vespers. The clergymen sought to regulate life and continuously influence their flock. Particularly solemn services preceded by nocturnal prayers were held on holidays: the pomp of the service was intended to impress the common folk.

However, for a long time to come the clergy complained that their churches remained empty: "If a dancer or musician or comedian calls the people to pagan assemblies everyone goes there and spends whole days in revelry. If we are called to church we yawn, scratch and stretch ourselves sleepily and say it is rainy or cold, or find some other excuse. There are neither roofs nor protection from the elements at the games, but we are happy and enjoy the spectacles that are destructive to our souls.

"There is a roof and pleasant air in the church but people refuse to go there."

All the means of the arts were used by the church to assert its views on life and the social structure.

Orators persuaded listeners that rulers were of divine origin and that a person had to gain eternal bliss after death by submission.

Artists depicted the Last Judgement when, according to the prophets, all who had died over several thousand years would rise from the graves. And God would start the Last Judgement sending the righteous to paradise and dooming the sinners to hell and eternal suffering. The artist showed sinners being thrown into ovens by ugly devils who were tearing their bodies with their claws.

The harmonious singing and solemnity of the service were intended to show Christianity as a different, righteous road. Architects sought to raise the churches above the huts and palaces so that the churches would shape the architectural ensemble of towns.

In its art the church continuously condemned secular amusements and interests: "Woe to those who look forward to the night with its tambourines, flutes and psaltery, to those who pretend not to know the harm caused by the psaltery, dancing and singing."

The church prophet censures the prominent townsfolk who are outwardly decent but enjoy the performances by the street musicians, singing and dancing, and even take children to the feasts: "But ask these shameless old men how the prophets and apostles lived. And how many apostles and prophets there were? They do not know and will not answer. But if we talk about horses or birds or something else, here they are philosophers and knowledgeable."

The monasteries were among the most important organisations playing an important part in the history of medieval states.

The monastery was intended as a voluntary brotherhood of people rejecting family and ordinary life and completely dedicated to serving God. In actual life, the monasteries were major landowning feudal lords and owned villages, carried on wholesale trade, lent money for interest and were in the thick of life, taking a direct part in secular affairs and major political events.

The Fathers-Superior of monasteries, on a par with bishops, played the part of diplomats and intermediaries.

There was acute inequality in the convents between the poor and those who came from the *boyar* or merchant milieu.

The highest church authorities—bishops and metropolitans—could be appointed only from among the monks who, as opposed to the ordinary priests, were called the black clergy.

Some central convents such as the Kiev-Pechersky Monastery founded in the mid-11th century became religious academies, and the sons of courtiers who sought to make a career eagerly entered them. There were excellent libraries in such convents, chronicles were written and sermons composed, the inner life of the convents was recorded, and hermit monks were praised.

The rich economic life of the monasteries and the existence of an aristocratic stratum which did not have to do dirty work compelled the administration to create a screen which would obscure the class nature of the convent and distract the attention of the townsfolk and peasants. Such a screen was provided by the simple, invalids, i. e. mentally deranged God's fools whose defects were demonstrated shamelessly to the monastery's visitors.

The story of one such simlpe man, Isaac, who lived in the 1060s and 1070s in the Kiev-Pechersky Monastery, has come down to us. He was weak in mind and body, suffered from hallucinations, and was wearing rough goatskins; the convent cooks mocked him and made him catch crows. Isaac would gather children and dress them in monk's apparel, or stood on a burning oven with his bare feet, or walked among the people behaving like a fool. The story of this wretch was introduced into the chronicle and the monk who wrote it deliberately presented him as God's chosen man.

At the beginning of the 13th century we see manifestations of anti-church and anti-monk views. The Smolensk priest Avraam known for his education and eloquence addressed his sermons to a wide circle of townsfolk among whom were craftsmen, the poor and slaves. His teaching was similar to that of the West European Waldenses who opposed the clergy. Bishops and Fathers-Superior brought Avraam to trial.

The Russian church played a complicated and many-sided role in the history of the 11th-13th centuries. The church was undoubtedly useful as an organisation promoting the consolidation of the young state in the age of the rapid advance of feudalism. Its part in developing Russian culture, introducing Rus to Byzantine culture, spreading education and creating major literary and artistic values is really great.

Yaroslav the Wise and His Sons

The state of Kievan Rus had existed for two hundred years by the beginning of the 11th century. It had developed from an alliance of Slav tribes to a major feudal power with a population consisting of different tribes. It was dominated by Eastern Slav tribes all of which were included in that state, but also included Lettish-Lithuanian Baltic and Finno-Ugric tribes.

In his famous introduction to the history of Rus Nestor listed all the Slav tribal alliances constituting Rus and then added the peoples speaking other tongues. Each entry in the list apparently refers to a stable alliance of several tribes.

Here is a list of other, non-Slav, peoples paying tribute to the Rus state:

        Chud (Esti and Komi-Zyryanians)
        Merya (Finno-Ugric tribes along the Klyazma and the Volga rivers)
        Ves (Veps)
        Muroma (Finno-Ugric tribes on the Lower Oka River)
        Cheremises (Mari)
        Mordva
        Perm (Komi-Permyakians)
        Pechera (Ugric tribes of the north Urals)
        Yam (part of the Finns-Suomi)

Litova
Zimegola (part of the Lettish tribes)
Kors
Noroma
Liv

The area of the state was enormous. Its perimeter was about 7,000 kilometres. It stretched from the Vistula in the west to the Kama and the Pechora in the east; from the Black Sea (the mouth of the Dnepr) to the White Sea and the Arctic Ocean. Half of these boundless expanses consisted of sparsely populated forests of the North with hunting grounds, but the cultivated part settled by land-tillers was sufficiently large and it was extremely difficult to rule the whole state. For example, if some event happened at Beloozero, and the Kiev prince had to send his men there, they would have arrived at their destination some three or four months after the event. Roads of brushwood, bridges and established fords were only being introduced. It was regarded as a deed of valour to travel from Kiev to the land of the Vyatichians by the "highway".

The state element could be asserted only provided there was the support of the local tribal nobility which was slowly being transformed from the "highwaymen" into the Grand Prince's administration without losing the prerogatives in respect to fellow tribesmen which dated back to primitive times.

The greatness of the territory gave rise to a number of factors influencing historical development: first of all, there existed considerable reserves for expanding land cultivation for quite a while; second, there were opportunities for extensive spontaneous colonisation outside the feudal zone. Third, large distances made it easier for the local authorities to pursue independent policies and remain free of central control.

As we have already seen Prince Vladimir's government did a great deal to implement the state element: laid out roads, fought robbers and settled the "best men" in the strategically dangerous border zone. One of the measures asserting the state element, in the form typical of the Middle Ages when the state element frequently merged with the personal one, was appointment of the Grand Prince's sons to rule the large towns along the fringes which had formerly been tribal centres. However, that measure did not help destroy local separatism. Nearly the entire 11th century was a time of acute conflict, fraternicidal quarrels made worse by foreign invasions and tense social relations. Immediately after the death of Vladimir Svyatoslavich a ten-year-long internecine war began between his sons, the principal character of which was Yaroslav, the eldest son of the Grand Prince.

Yaroslav was born approximately in 978 or somewhat later. The proud Polotsk princess Rogneda was his mother; as the chronicler wrote she had refused Vladimir but had been taken captive when Polotsk was seized. In childhood Yaroslav became lame and because of it was often the object of ridicule.

The story of Yaroslav described in the chronicle which was generally hostile to him begins with 1014, the last year of the rule of Vladimir.

Yaroslav lived in Novgorod and collected a tribute of 3,000 grivnas every year; he left 1,000 grivnas to pay his men and sent two thirds to the capital of Rus. Such was the *urok*, the annual norm, but having lived for many years in the large distant town linked by active commercial ties with overseas countries Yaroslav decided to cease paying the *urok*. This act provoked the anger of his father who vigilantly tried to preserve the unity of Rus, and, in his time, had forced the Novgorod people to build forts for defence against the Pechenegs far in the south. Vladimir ordered bridges to be made and forest roads cleared, preparing to march on Novgorod, but fell ill.

Yaroslav, as it turned out, intended to wage a real war against his own father and hired large Varangian forces. Married to the daughter of King Olaf he was directly linked to the Varangians. The Scandinavian sagas telling about konung Jarisleif (Yaroslav) mention the names of the Varangian leaders Ejmund and Ragnar invited by him to Novgorod and report interesting details concerning the terms of the contract and the greed and perfidy of the Varangians.

The mercenaries behaved rowdily and wildly in the Russian town: "And the Varangians began to perpetrate

Prince Yaroslav the Wise. Reconstruction by M. M. Gerasimov on the basis of Yaroslav's skull

violence against married women." One August night of 1015 the Novgorod townsfolk gathered and killed the Varangian offenders in Paramon's courtyard. Prince Yaroslav was angered by the townsfolk but did not show it immediately. He lured a thousand of the best warriors, possibly the *boyars* and *voivodas* of the Novgorod Thousand, and massacred them to avenge the Varangians. Part of the townsfolk fled. A messenger arrived in Novgorod from Yaroslav's sister Predslava at the end of the tragic night with the news that the old prince had died on July 15 and a bloody struggle for the throne had flared up between the brothers.

Morning began with reconciliation between Yaroslav and the Novgorodians. He gathered the surviving townsfolk on a field, opened a *veche* and delivered an unusual speech: "O my beloved and honest warriors

171

whom I killed yesterday in madness! Their deaths cannot be atoned for with any gold. Brothers! My father Vladimir has died. Svyatopolk rules Kiev. I want to march against him, support me!" Novgorodians produced 3,000 warriors and moved against Kiev headed by Yaroslav. The Novgorod prince remained for three months at Lubech on the Dnepr where Svyatopolk met him, and only in late autumn Yaroslav resolved to attack his brother. The battle of Lubech was won by the Novgorod people. Svyatopolk fled to the Pechenegs and Yaroslav entered Kiev with great ceremony.

Yaroslav's warriors were awarded: *smerds* one grivna, the elders ten grivnas and all the Novgorodians ten silver grivnas.

> And he let them all go home and gave them Pravda, the law and Rules saying: "Live according to this law as I wrote it."

There follows the text of the Russkaya Pravda of the 11th century, the first articles of which were, most probably, indeed linked to Yaroslav's obligations to the Novgorod people. The impact of the events in Novgorod in July-August 1015 described above is obvious in all the articles of the first part of the Russkaya Pravda. The legal document laying down fines for various crimes against individuals portrays the town filled with mercenaries provoking rows in the streets and houses as colourfully as the chronicle.

The town is inhabited by knights and *kholops*; the knights are on horseback and armed with lances, swords and shields; the *kholops* and servants often take part in fights helping their masters and beating free men with sticks and when they are beaten themselves they seek refuge in their masters' palaces. Sometimes a servant flees from his master and hides in a foreigner's house.

The knights for whose sake the law was written to protect them include Russians arriving from the Kiev land and the prince's warriors who received 1,000 grivna of Novgorod tribute, and the merchants who, as the custom of the time had it, wore swords, and high prince's officials—the *yabedniki* and swordsmen who supervised collection of taxes and were the judges of the prince's court of justice.

The law also protected broader circles of the Novgorod population: it mentions the *izgois* who came from the communes and had broken with the past but not found a place in the new life yet, and the common Slovenians, inhabitants of the immense Novgorod land. The latter sections of common folk remind us of Yaroslav's words of repentance at the *veche* when his appeal to Novgorod brothers, and apparently relevant promises, resulted in the mustering of a large force for the time, 3,000 men, including even common *smerds* (perhaps the Slovenians of the Russkaya Pravda).

The most ancient Russkaya Pravda as well as the chronicle for 1015-1016 portrays Novgorod split into two parts, two camps: one includes Novgorod's population from *boyar* to *izgoi* and the other the foreign Varangians and Kolbyaks (inhabitants of the Baltic area). Fights occur in the town, people threaten each other with swords, steal horses and ride them in the town, take other men's weapons, hide servants belonging to others, pull out whiskers and beards, slash arms and legs and murder people. Even at feasts people fight with goblets and auroch's horns.

All this supports the annalist's account about Varangian violence in the town.

Yaroslav's law relegated Varangians and Kolbyaks to an unequal status. Thus, if the offender was a Novgorod person, the offended person was to present two witnesses, but if the rowdy who pushed a Novgorod man turned out to be a Varangian or Kolbyak, it was sufficient for the Novgorod man to give his word of honour.

These restrictions are particularly obvious in comparing the Short Pravda of the 11th century with the Long Pravda of the 12th century where the Varangians were granted equal status with other people. The law provided for a fine in case of the harbouring of another man's servant only for the Varangians and the Kolbyaks. It is particularly important to point out that the detailed list of persons whose lives were protected by the ancient custom of blood feud or the high fine of 40 grivnas included all sections of the townsfolk, even visiting Kievans, but did not mention the Varangians or the Kolbyaks although these foreigners owned houses in Novgorod.

The very beginning of Yaroslav's Pravda seems to return us to that unfortunate night when the indignant townsfolk sought revenge against the Varangians. The Russkaya Pravda legalised the blood feud:

> If a warrior kills a warrior, he shall be avenged by his brother, or a son shall avenge his father, or a father his son. Nephews, sons of brothers or sisters may also seek revenge. If there are no such avengers (i. e. close relatives), then it is 40 grivnas for a head. If the killed person is a Rus (Kievan?) or from the prince's guard or a merchant or a prince's tribute collector or a swordsman (an executor of the prince's will armed with a sword) and even if he is an *izgoi* (one who has left his estate) or an inhabitant of the Novgorod land—in all cases the person guilty of murder shall pay 40 grivnas.

Expecting that he would have to defend Novgorod from his father's troops, Yaroslav played up to the hired Varangians and not only did not restrain them but also cruelly punished Novgorod people who took justice into their own hands. Princess Predslava's letter changed all that: Yaroslav could now intervene in the emerging internecine strife, the Varangians' role and Yaroslav's attitude to them changed. Now the mercenaries would seek to march against Kiev themselves because of the rich booty that they hoped for in that town. But Yaroslav would not dare fight against the half-Byzantine Svyatopolk with only a thousand warriors, particularly mercenaries who might sell their services to another prince for a higher price at the decisive moment or, having looted enough, go home overseas.

Under the circumstances Yaroslav needed a more reliable force. The only possibility was an alliance with Novgorod, with its *boyars* and even common folk, and this required guarantees and a law to protect all Novgorod people from the atrocities of the Varangian warriors of Ejmund or any other konung whom fate might bring to Novgorod. Thus appeared Yaroslav's Oldest Russkaya Pravda eighteen articles of which protected the lives, honour and property of the Novgorod men and common Slovenians from the impudent encroachments of the Varangians hired to take part in the internal struggle.

The specific instructions on fights and conflicts in Novgorod did not, of course, seek to encompass all aspects in the social life of the town and the whole Russian land. It concerned a very limited range of phenomena, and did not deal (and was not intended to deal) with the relationship between master and *kholops*, master and peasants, etc. It was by pure chance, in connection with street fights, the main subject of the instructions, that the document mentions a *kholop* hiding in the chambers of his master after a brawl.

That is why historians are seriously mistaken when they regard this most ancient Russkaya Pravda of 1015 as the first code of law allegedly reflecting life in its fullness at the time. From the fact that this legal document had nothing to say about agriculture, forms of peasant feudal dependence, *smerds* and *zakups* it was concluded simply and illogically, that these phenomena did not exist in real life.

Yaroslav's Rules were not the first legislative act. The treaties of 911 and 914 with Byzantium referred to the Russian Law, and it is quite possible that the articles of the Russkaya Pravda about the servant go back to that ancient law that has not come down to us but used the same terminology. A great deal in the Russkaya Pravda relied on common unwritten law. Created in the specific historical context of 1015 Yaroslav's Rules proved to be applicable in general to all cases of street fights so common in medieval towns and existed for several centuries being included in codes of the prince's laws in the 11th-12th centuries.

The Russkaya Pravda is a most valuable source for studying the history of feudal relations in Kievan Rus. It refers to a whole set of legal documents of the 11th-12th centuries reflecting the complexity of Russian social life and its evolution. The Russkaya Pravda was the object of the closest scrutiny by historians beginning with V. N. Tatishchev (in the 1730s).

The complicated set of laws brought together under the name Russkaya Pravda has been classified thanks to the efforts of scholars in the following way:

1. The Oldest Pravda or Yaroslav's Pravda of 1015-1016.
2. Supplements to Yaroslav's Pravda: Rules for Bridgebuilders (Pay), Tax Custom (Status on Collectors of Court Penalties).
3. Pravda of Yaroslav's Sons (Pravda of the Russian Land). Introduced by the sons of Yaroslav the Wise: Izyaslav, Svyatoslav and Vsevolod in about 1072.
4. Vladimir Monomakh's Rules, 1113.
5. The Long Russkaya Pravda. Approximately 1120-1130. Sometimes it is dated the beginning of the 13th century.

Certain parts of these main legal documents could have appeared in connection with one or another social conflict and been included in existing texts. The Russkaya Pravda is not a comprehensive or immutable code of laws but a whole series of legal regulations of different times gradually extending to a growing range of questions. The principal trend in that evolution was that originating from the law of the prince's domain, the Pravda gradually developed into a collection of norms of feudal law in general, a law which protected not only the prince's possessions but also those of any "master".

In addition to secular law ancient Rus had an independent church legislation which was binding first, for the people of the church (the clergy, monks, the the crippled, beggars and physicians) and second, the entire population in cases of crimes and controversies of a non-feudal nature: abduction of brides, divorce, family quarrels, witchcraft, pagan worship, heresy and so on. This legislation of the 11th-13th centuries brought together under the name of Rules was ascribed to Vladimir I and Yaroslav the Wise. Rules provide a wealth of material on Russian family law.

The appearance of the Oldest Pravda as the first chapter of the future code is explained not by the fact that fights between knights were the most important thing in the life of the state but by the fact that Prince Yaroslav had to provide the Novgorod people with guarantees of safety at that historical moment, at the height of the dramatic events of 1015-1016.

Yaroslav's capture of Kiev did not bring peace. Svyatopolk was linked to the Pechenegs and the Polish King Boleslav; and he took advantage of these two forces to regain the Kievan throne.

In 1017 Kiev was attacked by a large Pecheneg force. Ejmund's saga describes how the townsfolk prepared for the siege, dug a moat round the town and filled it with water and put logs over it; many green branches were fastened to the fortress wall so the Pecheneg arrows would not fly into the town. Two gates of Kiev were left open and forces stationed in them to sally forth. The Pecheneg assault was repulsed.

Soon, however, Boleslav the Brave moved from the west, and Yaroslav, defeated on the border in a battle on the Bug River, fled on horseback to Novgorod from where he attempted to flee to Sweden. At this point the Novgorod people acted resolutely once again; headed by the town elder Konstantin Dobrynich they hacked to pieces the boats prepared for the flight. The Novgorod folk collected money to hire a new Varangian force levying tribute on the free population: 4 kuns from a man, 10 grivnas from elders and 18 grivnas from *boyars*.

Meanwhile Svyatopolk drove Boleslav the Brave from Kiev. The Poles who had seen the capital of Rus left an interesting description of Kiev preserved by the medieval historian Thietmar: "The large town that was the capital of that state (*Kiev*—B. R.) had more than 400 churches, 8 marketplaces and an unusual multitude of people consisting, as in the entire area, of fugitive slaves coming here from everywhere and very agile Dans. It (Kiev) continuously resisted the Pechenegs who inflicted much damage and conquered others."

In this description fugitive slaves are obviously the *izgois* who came to the towns from all parts of Rus and became either warriors or palace servants of the feudal lords. The agile Dans are to be regarded as different Varangians serving one or another prince. This description is important for us because it refers to the town's enormous size.

As soon as Svyatopolk was left without Polish support, he was unable to retain Kiev in his hands. Yaroslav captured the town again, but in 1019 Svyatopolk made his last attempt to seize the throne of Grand Prince with an enormous Pecheneg force. Yaroslav defeated Svyatopolk in the battle on the Alta River.

The internecine strife did not abate however. In 1021 Vladimir's grandson Bryachislav captured Novgorod, and in 1024, when Yaroslav was suppressing an uprising in the Suzdal land, Mstislav Vladimirovich moved from Tmutarakan to Rus at the head of a Russo-Caucasian force. The Battle of Listven (near Chernigov) ended in victory for Mstislav: Yaroslav and his Varangians fled.

Mstislav, however, did not claim Kiev. He proposed to his brother to divide the ancient Russian land as follows: "You be the prince in your Kiev ... while I shall possess this (left) bank of the Dnepr." In 1026, having come together to make peace, the brothers "divided the Russian land along the Dnepr: Yaroslav took the right (western) bank and Mstislav the left (eastern)". Mstislav gained the entire left bank of the Dnepr with Chernigov and Pereyaslavl, while Yaroslav retained Kiev and the right bank. The ten-year-long internal war was abated.

Of Vladimir I's 12 sons many met a tragic end: Prince Gleb of Murom was killed on a ship near Smolensk. He was slaughtered by his own cook bribed by Svyatopolk who had just become the prince in Kiev and sought to get rid of his rival brothers.

Prince Boris, the favourite of his father's elder *druzhina* and for that reason the most dangerous rival for the other brothers was killed when he was returning from an expedition against the Pechenegs. According to the chronicle the murder was carried out by two Varangians sent by Svyatopolk, but according to the Scandinavian sagas he was killed by Yaroslav's allies already known to us, the Varangians Ejmund and Ragnar. Ejmund rushed into Boris' (Borislef) tent and killed the prince at night. He brought Yaroslav the young prince's head.

Svyatoslav of the Drevlyanian land fled from Kievan Rus to Bohemia, to his mother's native parts, but the murderers hired by Svyatopolk caught up with him in the Carpathians and killed him.

Vsevolod of the Volynian land did not die in internecine strife but also met a tragic end. According to the saga he proposed to the widow of the Swedish King Erik—Sigrid the Murderess—and was burned by her together with all the other suitors during a feast. This episode of the saga resembles the story of Olga who burned the embassy of her suitor Mal of the Drevlyanian land.

Prince Svyatopolk nicknamed the Accursed who led the Poles and the Pechenegs upon the Russian land became deranged after losing his third decisive battle for Kiev. "When he rode away the devil attacked him and weakened his bones, he was unable to sit in the saddle and the men had to carry him." The murderer prince was beset by a mania of persecution and, having passed Brest, he rode all the way through Poland and died somewhere far from Rus in 1019.

Sudislav of Pskov, one of the most obscure princes, was put in a *porub** on a slanderous accusation by his brother Yaroslav. He was kept there for 24 years and only four years after Yaroslav's death he was let out by his nephews to be made a monk right away. He died in a convent in 1063 having outlived all his brothers. As we have seen most of Vladimir's sons fell victim to fraternicidal wars, conspiracies and secret murders.

Having fallen ill on a hunting expedition in the Chernigov forests, Prince Mstislav died in 1036; he was a powerful prince who had defeated the North Caucasian Prince Rededya in his time. Mstislav had no heirs and all the left-bank land were united under Kiev's rule again: "Yaroslav gained all of Mstislav's lands and became the autocrat of Rus."

The "autocrat" strengthened his power in Novgorod and Pskov, the northern foreposts of Rus, appointing his elder son prince of Novgorod, assigning a new bishop and arresting Sudislav in Pskov. Yaroslav managed to defeat the Pechenegs in the South and drive them away from the borders of Rus.

Having grown rich and strengthened his position on the throne Prince Yaroslav spent much money to

---

* *Porub* — a prison, a wooden tower without doors built around a prisoner.— *Ed.*

embellish his capital in the manner of Constantinople. The Golden Gates were built in Kiev and the enormous St Sophia with frescoes, mosaic and marble (1037). The Western chronicler Adam of Bremen who lived at the time called Kiev the jewel of the East and Constantinople's rival.

The court chronicler described flatteringly and at length Yaroslav's church buildings and his love for the priests and monks.

Many books were rewritten under Yaroslav, many manuscripts were translated from Greek into Russian. Among these translated works we find the Chronicle of Georgy Amartol. It is possible that schools to teach elementary reading and writing were organised at the time, and perhaps more serious studies were carried on to prepare persons to become priests.

Subsequently, Yaroslav was called the Wise. The autocrat of All Rus, the Kiev Prince whom the royal houses of France, Hungary and Norway sought to have as their relative, was not satisfied to be called the Grand Prince: his contemporaries used the Oriental title of Kagan and finally Yaroslav started to be called a Tsar as was the Emperor of Byzantium.

The rivalry with Byzantium was reflected not only in Kiev's architecture or in titles but also in the attitude to the church. In 1051 Yaroslav the Wise did something only the Byzantine Emperor had done until then. Without informing the Patriarch of Constantinople he appointed the intelligent Kievan author Illarion Metropolitan of Rus.

Being aware of the ideological strength of Christianity Yaroslav paid much attention to the organisation of the Russian church and the regular clergy. It was under Yaroslav that Antony of Lubech founded the subsequently famous Kiev-Pechersky Monastery.

Yaroslav died in 1054 at the age of 76. An inscription was made on the wall of St Sophia on the Assumption of Our Tsar.

The Queen of France Anna, daughter of Yaroslav the Wise. Sculpture

The Feudal Castle of the 11th-12th Centuries

The first fortified estates separated from the surrounding common houses and occasionally standing over them on a hill date back to the 8th-9th centuries. From the scanty traces of old life archaeologists manage to discover that the inhabitants of the estates led a somewhat different life from their fellow villagers. Weapons and silver ornaments are found more often on the estates.

The system of building was the chief difference: the estate-fortress was built on a hill surrounded at the foot by one or two hundred dugout huts scattered around. The castle was a small fort formed of several wooden houses adjoining each other in a continuous circle. The circular houses *(khoromy)* also served as a stockade surrounding the yard. About 20 to 30 persons could live here.

It is difficult to say whether it belonged to a tribal elder with his householders or a master with servants collecting *polyudye* from the surrounding villages. But it was in this form that the first feudal castles appeared and in this form that the first *boyars*, "the best men" of the Slav tribes were to emerge from among the land-tillers.

The castle was too small to take in all the inhabitants of the settlement at times of danger but quite sufficient to rule the settlement. All ancient Russian words referring to castles are quite suitable for these round forts: *khoromy, dvor, grad* (a stockaded, fortified place).

Thousands of these *khoromy* appeared all over Rus in the 8th-9th centuries marking the rise of feudal relations; it was a material expression of the advantages gained by the warrior estate. But it was only a few centuries later that we learned about them from legal documents—legal norms never come before reality but always appear as a result of life's demands.

Class contradictions came clearly to the fore by the early 11th century, and the princes sought to protect themselves not only by military force but also by written law. In the course of the 11th century the first version of Russian feudal law was compiled, the well-known Russkaya Pravda. It was written on the basis of old Slav customs which had existed for many centuries but it also included new legal norms arising from the new feudal relations. Relations between the feudal lords and the peasants and the relations between the warriors as well as the status of the prince in society were for a long time determined by oral, non-written law—customs supported by the real balance of power.

As far as we know this oral common law, written down by ethnographers in the 19th century, it was highly ramified and regulated all aspects in human relations from family affairs to border conflicts.

For quite a while there did not exist a need to write down these established customs or to register the payments annually made to the master within the small isolated *boyar* estate. Up to the 18th century most *boyar* estates lived according to their own unwritten laws.

The recording of legal norms was to begin either in a context of foreign relations where the Russian custom encountered the custom and law of other countries or in the prince's domain with its hunting grounds scattered about different lands and a ramified system of tribute and penalty collectors continuously visiting the dependent tribes and executing justice in the prince's name according to his law.

The first isolated notes of certain Russian legal norms arose on the basis of Yaroslav's Rules for Novgorod, in connection with individual cases, in instances of special need, and were not intended to reflect all aspects of Russian life. It must be noted once again how profoundly mistaken were the historians who compared parts of the Russkaya Pravda dating back from different times and mechanically drew the conclusions that if some phenomenon was not mentioned in the earliest sources, then it did not exist at all. This major logical mistake was based on the outdated idea that state and social life was shaped as a result of laws promulgated by the autocrat.

Actually social life develops according to its own inner laws and legal laws only reflect existing relations formalising the de facto domination of the class over another.

In the mid-11th century acute social contradictions emerged, particularly in the prince's entourage, which led to the appearance of the law of the prince's domains, what is known as the Pravda of Yaroslav's Sons (circa 1054-1072) dealing with the prince's castle and its economy. After the Kiev rebellion of 1113 Vladimir Monomakh (1113-1125) supplemented that code with a number of wider articles intended for the town middle sections, and at the end of his rule or the rule of his son Mstislav (1125-1132) an even broader code of feudal laws was compiled known as the Long

Russkaya Pravda reflecting not only the prince's but also the *boyars'* interests. The feudal castle and the feudal estate are given much emphasis in this code. Soviet historians S. V. Yushkov, M. N. Tikhomirov and particularly B. D. Grekov revealed the feudal essence of the Russkaya Pravda during its entire century-long development.

B. D. Grekov described the feudal castle and estate in the following terms in his fundamental work *Kievan Rus*:

"...the life of the prince's estate is outlined in its principal traits in the Pravda of Yaroslav's sons.

"The prince's court is the centre of that estate ... which includes, first of all, the *khoromy* where the prince lived at times, the houses of his high-ranking servants and premises for lower servants, various facilities—stables, cattle and poultry houses, hunting lodges and others...

"The prince's estate is headed by a *boyar-ognishchanin* whose duty it is to supervise the course of life at the estate and in particular to guard the prince's property. The collector of all sorts of tribute was probably under him. It is supposed that the *ognishchanin* commands the high-ranking prince's servants.

"The Pravda also mentions the Senior Groom who looks after the stables and prince's herds.

"All these persons are protected by a 80-grivna fine which points to their privileged status. This is the highest administration of the prince's estate. Then come the village and the military elders. Their lives are valued at 12 grivnas... Thus we can speak of the true agricultural physiognomy of the estate.

"These observations are supported by the details scattered through the Pravda of Yaroslav's Sons. They mention sheds and the range of draught, meat and dairy cattle usual for such estates. There are prince's and peasants' horses, bulls, cows, goats, sheep, hogs, chicken, doves, ducks, geese, swans, storks.

"The pastures on which the cattle and prince's and peasant horses graze are not mentioned but are obviously implied.

"On a par with the agricultural economy we see the bee-hives that are called the prince's.

"The Pravda lists the categories of direct producers serving the estate: *ryadoviches, smerds* and *kholops* whose lives are valued at five grivnas.

"It may be assumed that the prince visits his estate from time to time. This is indicated by the hunting dogs and hawks and falcons trained for hunting.

"The first impression from the Pravda of Yaroslav's Sons, as well as from the Long Pravda, is that the master of the estate with a multitude of servants of various ranks and positions, the owner of the land, the hunting grounds, the cattle and poultry and owner of his serfs concerned with the possibility of murder and robbery, seeks to find protection in the system of serious punishments provided for each encroachment against his rights. The impression is not misleading. Indeed, the Pravdas defend the master of the estate from attacks against his servants, land, bulls, slaves, peasants, ducks, chicken and dogs, hawks and falcons, and others."

Archaeological excavations of authentic feudal castles of the 11th century fully support this portrayal of the prince's estate.

An expedition headed by the author of this book excavated an 11th-century castle in Lubech in 1957-1960 probably built by Vladimir Monomakh at the time when he was the Prince of Chernigov (1078-1094) and when the Pravda of Yaroslav's Sons had only come into force.

The Slav settlement on the site of Lubech had existed already in the first centuries A. D. A small town with wooden stockade appeared here by the 9th century. It is probable that this town was taken by Oleg on the way to Kiev in 882. It was here that the estate of Malko the Lubechanin, Dobrynya's father and grandfather of Vladimir I must have been placed.

There was a pier at the end of Dnepr backwaters where the monoxylas mentioned by Constantine Porphyrogenitus were assembled and further on was a pine grove where these one-tree ships might have been built. Behind the hills was a mound indicated by legend as a pagan shrine.

All these ancient places are dominated by a tall hill bearing the name of Zamkovaya (Castle) Hill even today. Excavations showed that the castle's wooden stockade was built in the second half of the 11th century. The strong clay and oak wall encompassed the whole town and castle, but the castle also had its own cleverly devised defence system. It was like a kremlin.

Castle Hill is not very large, its upper part is only 35 by 100 metres and that is why all the structures on it were huddled close together. Exceptionally favourable archaeological conditions made it possible to trace the foundations of all the buildings and the number of storeys in each building determined, judging from the amount of soil filling the space between storeys which collapsed during the fire of 1147.

The castle was separated from the town by a dry moat over which a draw-bridge was lowered. Having passed the bridge and its tower a person found himself in a narrow passage between two walls. A road laid with logs led up to the Main Gates of the fortress and the adjacent walls.

The gates with two towers had a rather long tunnel with three more gateways which could block the way for the enemies. Having passed through the gates one found himself in a small courtyard where probably the guards were stationed; from here there was a passage onto the walls, rooms with small hearths on pediments for the guards to warm themselves and an underground room with a stone ceiling next to them.

To the left of the "hard-surface" road went a blank paling behind which were numerous warehouses for all sorts of food supplies: fish stocks, storerooms for honey and wine, with remains of amphoras, and storehouses without any trace of the food kept there.

The highest structure in the castle, the tower, rose in the rear of the guards' courtyard. Standing alone and not linked to the walls it served as the second gates and could also, in case of siege, be the defenders' last refuge, like the dungeons of Western Europe. There were pits for storing grain and water in the depths of the Lubech dungeon.

The tower-dungeon was the hub of all the routes inside the castle: it was the only way to get into warehouse area; the path to the prince's palace also went through

Lubech castle. Reconstruction by B. A. Rybakov

the dungeon. The person living in this massive four-storey tower saw everything that was happening in the castle and outside it; he controlled the movement of all people in the castle, and it was impossible to go into the prince's palace without his knowledge.

Judging from the splendid silver and gold ornaments hidden in the underground part of the dungeon the owner was a rich and noble *boyar*. The clauses of the Russkaya Pravda concerning the *ognishchanin* come to mind, which describe him as the ruler of prince's household whose life was protected by the enormous fine of 80 grivnas (4 kg of silver!). The central position of the tower in the prince's courtyard corresponded to the place of its owner in controlling the courtyard.

A small court of ceremonies opened up behind the tower and in front of the prince's palace. A tent stood in that courtyard, apparently for the guard of honour and there was a secret passage to the water here.

The palace was a three-storey building with three high chambers. The lower storey was divided into numerous small rooms; the ovens were there, the servants lived and stores were kept. The second storey was occupied by the prince's ceremonial apartments where there was a wide gallery, the site of summer feasts, and a large prince's chamber decorated with majolica and aurochs' and reindeer horns. If the Lubech council of princes of 1097 assembled in the castle, it must have taken place in this chamber which fitted tables for a hundred people.

There was a small church with a lead roof in the castle. The castle walls consisted of the inner row of living quarters and the higher outer row of stockades; the flat roofs of the houses served as the platforms for the warriors, flat wooden stairways led to the walls straight from the castle courtyard. There were large copper cauldrons dug in along the walls to pour boiling water on the enemies in case of an attack. In each inner section of the castle—in the palace, in the honey store and next to the church—there were deep underground passages leading in different directions from the castle. On the whole, according to estimates, 200-250 people could live here.

Many deep pits carefully dug in the clayey ground have been found in all the castle structures except the palace. We recall the Russkaya Pravda which punishes stealing grain from pits. Part of these pits could really serve for storing grain, but another part was intended for water, since no wells have been found on the territory of the castle. The total volume of the pits runs into hundreds of tons. The castle garrison could survive drawing on its stores for more than a year. Judging from the chronicle a siege was never continued for more than six weeks in the 11th and 12th centuries, therefore the Lubech castle of Monomakh was supplied with everything in plenty.

The Lubech castle was the residence of the Chernigov prince and was fully adapted for the life and service of the prince's family. The craftsmen lived outside the castle, both inside the walls of the town and outside it. The castle should not be considered separately from the town.

We also learn about such large prince's estates from the chronicles: in 1146 when a coalition of Chernigov and Kievan princes pursued the forces of the Seversky princes Igor and Svyatoslav (sons of Olga), Igor's village with the prince's castle near Novgorod-Seversky was plundered. "A fine castle was built there. Many different supplies were stored: honey and wine. There were so many heavy iron and copper objects that they could not even carry away all of them." The victors ordered everything to be loaded on carts for themselves and their warriors and then set the castle on fire.

Lubech fell victim to a very similar operation by the Smolensk prince in 1147. The castle was robbed, everything of value (except what was hidden) was carried away, and then it was burned down. Moscow was probably a similar feudal castle, and in the same 1147 Prince Yuri Dolgoruky invited his ally Svyatoslav, son of Olga, to the town.

In addition to large and rich prince's castles archaeologists have studied more modest *boyar* households situated not in the town but in the village. Often these fortified households included peasant huts and contained numerous agricultural implements — ploughs, sickles and so on. Such 12th-century households reflect the same trend of temporary enslavement of debtor peasants as the Long Pravda does when it refers to the *smerds* using their master's implements and being under the surveillance at their master's household from which they could leave only if they complained to the higher authorities against the *boyar*.

We must regard all of ancient Rus as a sum of several thousand feudal estates, large and small, belonging to princes, *boyars* and the church, and the junior warriors. All these estates were economically independent, each constituting a microscopic state hardly linked to any other and free of control from the prince. The *boyar*'s courtyard was the centre of such a small state with its economy, army, police and its unwritten laws.

In the 11th and 12th centuries, the prince's power could hardly unite these independent *boyar* worlds. It wedged its households and *pogosts* between them and appointed its elders in the towns, but nevertheless Rus was the *boyars*' element very weakly held together by the prince's rule; the prince continually confused notions of state with private-property feudal attitudes in relation to his ramified domain.

The princes' officials went riding through the land and were kept at the expense of the local population: they tried people, collected taxes for the prince, gained wealth for themselves, but hardly united the feudal castles or fulfilled any state-wide functions.

The structure of Russian society remained mostly "fine grain", it was dominated by the presence of these several thousand *boyar* estates with castles whose walls defended the masters not so much from foreign enemies as from their own peasants and *boyar* neighbours, and occasionally even from the prince's officials who carried out their function all too actively.

Judging from indirect sources the princes' and the *boyars*' estates were organised along different lines. The scattered possessions of the prince's domain were not always permanently attached to the prince—his departure for another throne in another town could entail changes in the prince's personal estate. That is why, if the princes frequently moved from one place to another, they regarded their estates as temporary possessions and tried to obtain as much as possible from the peasants and the *boyars*, which, in the final count, also meant the peasants, without being concerned about the reproduction of the unstable peasant economy, and in fact completely ruining it.

The executors of the prince's will cared even less about peasant economy. There were *podyezdniyes, ryadoviches, virniks* and *mechniks**—junior members of the prince's troop whose duty it was to collect the prince's revenues and wield part of the prince's own authority. Indifferent to the fate of the *smerds* and of the whole territory they visited, they were concerned with their own interests above all and, inventing false fines, enriched themselves at the expense of the peasants and partly the *boyars* for whom they were judges and administrators of the supreme power in the land.

The army of these prince's men grew rapidly and invaded the whole land, from Kiev to Beloozero, and their actions were not controlled by anyone. They had to bring the prince a fixed amount of quit-rent and tribute, but no one knew how much they took for themselves and how many villages they ruined or left to die of hunger.

If the princes plundered the peasants greedily and unreasonably by means of personal rounds *(polyudye)* and by sending their *virniks*, the *boyars* were more cau-

---

* These terms are not completely clear to us: *podyezdniyes* are probably messengers; *ryadoviches*, servants hired under contract for various needs; *virniks*, collectors of court fines; *mechniks*, armed servants of the highest rank.

tious. First of all, the *boyars* lacked the military force that would allow them to break the line between ordinary taxation and ruining the peasants. Second, it was not only dangerous but also unprofitable for them to ruin the economy of the estate which they intended to pass down to their children and grandchildren. That was why the *boyars* must have been more careful, restraining their greed and passing to economic coercion at the first opportunity, to the *kupa*, i e. a loan to the impoverished *smerd* which bound the peasant-*zakup* to the castle more strongly.

The prince's *tiuns* and *ryadoviches* were feared not only by the peasant members of the commune but also by the *boyars* whose estate consisted of the same peasant households. A scholar of the late 12th century advised *boyars* to stay away from prince's places:

> Do not build your castle close to a prince's, do not found a settlement near the prince's villages—his senior servants are like fire and the junior like sparks. If you save yourself from fire, you can't save yourself from the sparks!

Each feudal lord sought to secure the inviolability of his microscopic state and there gradually emerged the notion of feudal immunity, *zaboroni*, a legal contract between junior and senior feudal lords on non-interference of the senior in the affairs of the junior's estate. In respect to a later time, the 15th and 16th centuries, when the state was undergoing the process of centralisation, we regard feudal immunity as a conservative phenomenon contributing to the retention of feudal disunity, but for Kievan Rus the immunity of *boyar* estates was an indispensable condition for the normal development of the sound nucleus of feudal landowning—many thousands of *boyar* estates constituting the stable foundation of Russian feudal society.

Popular Masses. Smerd *and Craftsmen*

The people are the makers of history, by their persistent labour they create the values which enable society to advance. At moments of major upheavals, internal or external, it is the people who decide their own fate by straining their powers to the utmost. The rapid development of all Russian lands at the turn of the 11th century was due to the fact that the popular forces, to a greater extent than in other times, could take an active part in the building of the rising state and in the struggle against the Pechenegs.

Unfortunately, the feudal historians who saw their task in describing victorious battles and the life of the princes very rarely spoke of the people, the thousands of common working people who were the true founders of Kievan Rus and its highly developed culture.

Yet it is our good luck that the silence of the monk-chroniclers may be made up for by three kinds of materials. First, archaeological excavations have revealed numerous genuine monuments of popular life: settlements, homes, the economic system, utensils, clothes, customs and beliefs—all this has become accessible to Soviet historical science enabling it to write quite specifically about peasants and craftsmen. Russian bourgeois archaeology ignored the study of the modest remains of common life, being absorbed by the more effective excavations of the princes' burial mounds.

The second source of our knowledge of the people, of their thoughts and desires is their own folk art, folklore.

The majestic *bylinas* told the people of Kievan Rus about the recent heroic past, ancient written tales described the olden times before the state had appeared, fairy tales going back to distant primitive ages, riddles and sayings reflected folk wisdom and served to develop the mental facilities of the younger people. Folklore also retained a whole range of pagan ideas in its wedding songs and funeral laments, charms, and ritual round dances. Much of what was discovered by science in the 19th century dates back to the age of Kievan Rus and occasionally even to older times.

The third invaluable source is the language of the people; on the basis of its wealth ancient Russian literary written language was developed. The language shows the depths of the knowledge of nature, and gives an idea of the economic system, social relations, the complicated kinship system inherited from tribal times, cultural ties with neighbours, folk knowledge of mathematics and astronomy and a great deal more.

These three sources enable us to learn quite a lot about the popular masses of Kievan Rus.

Russian peasants of the 10th-12th centuries settled in small unfortified villages. The ancient name of a rural settlement was *ves*. The centre of several villages was called a *pogost*; it was a larger village where the collection of quit-rent was concentrated.

The peasant houses were small and heated by means of an open hearth warming the interior space with the smoke later going out through a small aperture. In the north, houses were made of logs and built straight on the ground; there was no wooden floor. In the south, taking advantage of the dry soil, a hut was cut into the ground, so that to enter it, one had to take two or three steps down as if it were a dugout. The stoves in the north were very large, known as Russian stoves, placed on a special frame of logs, while in the south a small adobe or stone stove was sufficient.

Sometimes there were household structures next to the home, small sheds for drying sheaves, deep covered pits for storing grain mentioned in the Russkaya Pravda.

Among household utensils mention should be made of hand-turned millstones in almost every house, wooden barrels, troughs, clay pots and larger vessels. The house was lighted up by a burning splinter or a lamp with an oiled wick.

Of interest among the archaeological finds are stone whorls for spindles made of pink slate in Volyn country, where there are large deposits of the stone; they were sold throughout Rus. Literate town ladies wrote their names on the whorls (perhaps not to mix them up when women got together to spin?), while illiterate peasant women made marks or drew pictures on them.

Fabric was made out of flax, wool and hemp. Complicated pattern weaving and embroidery were known. Women liked to wear decorations: silver or bronze temple rings suspended from the headdress, necklaces, bracelets made by local craftsmen from the neighbouring *pogost*. Beads made of overseas stones were probably purchased from wandering vendors who chanced to come to the village.

In order to reproduce the picture of life in the ancient Russian village on the basis of authentic but fragmentary archaeological data we must turn to the Russian serf village of the 18th and 19th centuries.

Despite the fact that seven centuries lapsed from the times of Monomakh to Radishchev's* lifetime, the Russian feudal village hardly changed at all. The centuries of progressive development of the feudal formation had an impact on the evolution of the city and the rise in the feudal culture, but the village remained nearly at the same level, being the embodiment of the routine Lenin wrote about. The peasants still tilled the land with the wooden or iron plough used in the times of Kievan Rus, sowed the same crops, bred the same animals, lived in the same smoke-filled homes lighted by a burning splinter, wore home-spun clothes decorated by women's skilful hands. Even grain was ground on hand millstones of the ancient type. Feudalism grew and developed at the expense of the serf peasants, giving almost nothing in return for a whole thousand years.

The feature of the village in the 11th-12th centuries distinguishing it from the later village was that the Christian church organisation had not penetrated it. The old pagan rites still prevailed in the village; high mounds were built over the dead, while in some places, such as the forest land of the Vyatichians, the ritual of burning dead bodies was still practiced. However, the church tithe and bishop's tax were probably paid by Christians and pagans alike.

The peasants of the age of Kievan Rus varied greatly in the degree of freedom or dependence. In remote places not frequented by *boyar* or prince *officials* there were completely free peasants who knew no form of subordination of individual peasant families. They had gained economic independence from the clan but had not grown strong enough yet and easily fell under the temporary or permanent authority of a larger, and therefore more stable and economically stronger landowner. With the emergence of these landed *boyars*

---

* A. N. Radishchev (1749-1802), Russian author, educator and public figure. The main work for which he is famous is *The Journey from St Petersburg to Moscow.— Ed.*

peasant freedom would have come to an end. No sources tell us about this in-depth process; it can only be guessed at.

Obrok or *povoz*, payment in kind of a part of the annual peasant income, was one of the relatively easy forms of peasant duties. The more difficult form was the corvée, unpaid labour on the lord's land instead of the peasant's own land or on the construction site of the lord's castle, town or chambers. At the time, the personal, feudal element was closely intertwined with state interests and there was no clear line between state taxes and feudal rent, and each feudal lord, the prince, the *boyar* and the Father-Superior of a convent fixed their own norm of exploitation.

Peasants were usually called *smerds*, although the term is not quite clear. Possibly it meant not the entire rural population but only those peasants who were dependent on the prince (and *boyar*?) The more vague term *lyudi* (people) was also used. The population divested of personal freedom and all personal rights was called *kholopy* and slaves. People temporarily deprived of freedom, the debtors who did not pay back their loans, were called *zakups*. Their position was incomparably worse than that of the *smerds*, because the *zakup* had to work in the lord's field, apparently supervised by an overseer, and live in the courtyard of the lord who had given him the loan. He was allowed to leave the courtyard only with the lord's permission on important errands — in search of money or to lodge a complaint.

The peasants were bound by collective responsibility: if, for example, a dead body was found near some village and the murderer was not known, the fine was distributed among all the members of the *verv*. Initially the *verv* was the tribal commune and subsequently the neighbourhood commune; it could include several villages. We do not know the precise meaning of the terms, but it may be assumed that the *pogost* was the centre of the *verv*.

The life of peasants in ancient Rus was difficult not only because the struggle with the natural elements was exhausting but also because the developing feudal relations fell on the peasantry with their full weight.

Decorations of Russian town ladies

Apart from the share of labour and product alienated from him which was spent on socially useful functions of the state such as the building of defensive lines and towns and laying of roads, much was spent on the prince's luxury and senseless internal quarrels.

The highhanded actions of the *princes'* and *boyars'* tax- and fine-collectors were appalling, their appetites boundless. Only the class struggle, armed action by the *smerds* could limit their encroachments. Judging by the severe clauses of the Russkaya Pravda *smerds* in the 11th century stubbornly fought for their rights and opposed the prince's administration with arms.

For a long time, historians interpreted the true purpose of the ancient Russian town in a variety of ways. Some regarded the town as a small administrative centre, others as a colourful marketplace, still others as a military fort. Soviet archaeologists have organised extensive excavations in such cities as Kiev, Chernigov, Pereyaslavl, Novgorod, Pskov, Smolensk, Moscow, Vladimir, Ryazan, Minsk and Polotsk.

As a result of many years of work the true image of the ancient Russian town was discovered. A combination of the following elements in the town should be regarded as typical: the fort, feudal owners' households, the craftsmen's section, trade, administration and churches. The craftsmen made up the largest group, of course; included among them were blacksmiths, potters, carpenters, builders, gold- and silversmiths, all in all, about a hundred of specialities could be found in large cities. Specialisation in the crafts conformed to a purely medieval principle — not according to the material but according to the finished product. Thus a craftsman making shields knew how to forge steel, make the wooden basis of the shield and furnish it with leather straps. A saddle-maker was skilled in tanning but also could forge stirrups and chase the saddle ornaments.

The craftsmen lived in groups by occupations. As a result streets and whole neighbourhoods in towns were called according to some trade.

Craftsmen's houses were somewhat larger than village huts, because frequently the workshop was combined with the home. Some town houses even had chimneys standing next to the stove and drawing most of the smoke out of the room. The household utensils were slightly more varied and rich in the towns as compared to those owned by *smerds*: the townsfolk had oil lamps, amphoras for wine, bronze crosses, intricate locks and keys, but craftsmen's wives also ground the grain on heavy millstones and spun yarn by means of spindles and whorls.

The craftsmen frequently inscribed their names on their articles and tools; that is why we know that they were literate and know the names of a number of first-rate craftsmen of the 11th-13th centuries.

Craftsmen mostly worked on order, but in the 12th century there are many signs pointing to the more progressive work for the market.

Differentiation in the crafts occurred at the time; the more well-off craftsmen emerged, perhaps owning a place at the market and selling their own goods, being simultaneously producers and traders.

A number of cheap common goods made in the towns went via wandering vendors to the village, to the remotest corners of the Russian land; among them were beads, glass bracelets, little crosses, whorls and so on.

The town craftsmen also experienced feudal oppression and frequently suffered acute need. There were cases when feudal lords owned craftsmen as *kholops*, or slaves, and in other instances imposed quit-rent on them.

The dependence on money-lenders was particularly hard. The interest paid on a loan sometimes exceeded half the original sum, and in cases when the townsman was unable to repay the debt he found himself in eternal bondage, being forced to pay interest to the money-lender permanently, although the sum he repaid could be much larger than the original loan. Only the uprising of 1113 forced the feudal lords to change the law in favour of those who needed loans.

The town craftsmen constituted a major social force. There is indirect evidence that they were united in corporations similar to the Western European guilds and that, of course, strengthened the positions of the common folk in the towns.

The craftsmen took an active part in the class struggle and urban anti-clerical movements of the 12th and 13th centuries. If the village was the basis for feudal routine, the town, the craftsmen above all—makers of tools of labour, weaponry, utensils and all sorts of ornaments—were the carriers of the winds of change; in the course of persistent struggle and uprisings they created the new elements which made the town the focal point of growth of the feudal social and economic formation.

The Uprising of 1068 in Kiev

Observing life from the windows of monastery cells or the prince's palace, chroniclers preferred not to include stories of mutinies on the pages of chronicles; they believed they should describe only battles and the valour of warriors. That is why we know very little about the class struggle in the age of early feudalism.

Even an approximate picture cannot be drawn from chance references in the chronicle. The story of the Drevlyanians' uprising in 945 against the prince who had violated the norm of tribute was retained by the chronicle because it ended in an unprecedented event, the killing of the prince. By pure chance, to explain the reason why Prince Yaroslav was absent from Kiev, the chronicler mentioned in passing the uprising of the poor in the Suzdal land in 1024 during a hunger.

The Russkaya Pravda offers a much fuller picture of social conflicts and the scope of the class struggle. Particularly significant are the instances in which severe laws and reticent chroniclers coincide: such were the 1060s and 1113. By the mid-11th century contradictions had grown acute chiefly in the upper part of feudal social hierarchy, in the system of the prince's domain; the Pravda of the Russian Land (the Pravda of Yaroslav's Sons) was drawn up specifically for the prince's domain by Yaroslav the Wise's three sons in the 1050s and the 1060s. Several *boyars* took part in compiling the code.

Without any introduction the code of the three princes opens with the articles protecting the lives of the prince's administrators and the inviolability of castle property.

"If an *ognishchanin* is killed..." is how the first three articles begin. The *ognishchanin*'s murder was punished either by the criminal's death (he is to be killed "like a cur") if he was murdered by a robber, or by an enormous fine of a quarter pood of silver in case if the *ognishchanin* had offended someone and was killed in revenge. If the *ognishchanin* was killed by robbers on the road, the same fine was imposed on the entire commune on whose territory the body was found. The fine for the murder of an *ognishchanin*, prince's messenger, *tiun* or stables *boyar* (80 grivnas) was equal to the annual tribute from a large district and, thus, doubled the tax burden for a whole area. The need for such resolute defence was due, apparently, to the fact that the desperate peasants were resorting to arms.

The transfer of princes from town to town which became more frequent in the second half of the 11th century inevitably aroused in them the desire to plunder the principality they were leaving without any concern for the future of the peasants. Internal strife and the struggle for the rich thrones ruined the people and increased the princes' expenditures and, therefore, aggravated relations between them and the peasantry.

Peasant economy was unstable in its very nature. Hail, draught or excess of rain were sufficient to leave thousands of people hungry for a whole year. The more the prince's *ryadoviches* and *ognishchanin* took from the *smerds* in such bad years, the greater was the danger for the village's last vital reserve, the grain left for sowing. If the exactions were so great that they threatened the seeds, the new agricultural year promised the *smerds* a hungry death regardless of the weather, and, realising this, the peasants were forced to resort to arms and wage an unequal struggle against the prince's messengers and servants and village elders which compelled Yaroslav's sons to issue a special law.

Crop failures aggravated all the contradictions in

the village, and forced the peasants to resist the tribute collectors or to turn in despair to the ancient gods and perform bloody rituals. There is a very interesting account by *boyar* Jan Vyshatich, probably an *ognishchanin* of one of Yaroslav's sons, who observed the consequences of a crop failure in the Rostov land; the account figures in the chronicle under 1071, but the events occurred at an earlier date, in the 1060s.

Once, during a hunger in Yaroslavl, two sorcerers appeared there saying that they could expose the women who were to blame for the hunger, and in a supernatural trance, pointed to wealthy peasant women saying: "That one hides grain, that one honey and that one fish, and that one furs." Allegedly they produced samples of these products from behind their backs—grain, fish, or a squirrel. The supposed witches were killed, and the sorcerers, together with about 300 people who had joined them, took their property.

Thus they reached Beloozero where they engaged Jan Vyshatich, but were defeated. The sorcerers were handed over to Jan, but they demanded that Prince Svyatoslav Yaroslavich himself decide their fate. After arguing with the sorcerers about the meaning of the pagan faith Jan gave them up to the relatives of those they had killed, and the relatives avenged themselves by having the sorcerers eaten by a bear.

The social implications of the events are clearly seen behind the grim romance of the rituals: in the time of hunger the poor *smerds* headed by the sorcerers resorted to witchcraft in order to confiscate the property of the richer part of the *pogost* population. This was not a movement against the feudal order in general, but only a struggle to redistribute vital supplies. The prince's envoy naturally took the side of the "better people". The attempt of the insurgents to kill Jan with a battle-axe could have resulted in the entire Beloozero district paying the heavy eighty-grivna penalty as provided for in the Russkaya Pravda for the murder of an *ognishchanin* by a gang of armed men.

During the 1060s the chronicler repeatedly mentions various ominous "signs". Pagan sorcerers predicting misfortune appeared in different places, in Beloozero, in Novgorod or in Kiev itself. Apparently there were crop failures not only in the Volga area, because the Kievan chronicler wrote a whole work on the importance of worshipping the Christian God and not a pagan one to secure good weather.

To crown it all, hordes of Polovtsi commanded by Khan Sharukan attacked Rus in 1068. Three of Yaroslav's sons, three authors of the Russkaya Pravda, Izyaslav, Svyatoslav and Vsevolod, fled from the Polovtsi after being defeated at the battle of the Alta River.

The Kievans taking part in the militia which was defeated by Sharukan realised the danger of a Polovtsi invasion of Rus and sought to continue the struggle, but they had neither weapons nor horses. A popular council, *veche*, convened in the marketplace on the Podol, far from the prince's fort, on September 15, 1068. The council decided to organise an expedition against the Polovtsi and sent envoys to the Grand Prince Izyaslav. The envoys told the prince: "The Polovtsi are doing what they like in our land... So, Prince, give us arms and mounts and we shall fight them again!"

The shortsighted prince rejected the proposal of the popular envoys which was so natural. It is difficult to say what were the causes for the refusal: either too many *smerds* from the vicinity sought refuge in Kiev and the prince was afraid that his supplies would fall into the hands of the peasants ruined by the war, or he did not want to open his arsenal for the Kievans who disapproved of the prince's policy of internal strife. Only a year before Sharukan's invasion Izyaslav and his brothers had cruelly murdered the Polotsk Prince Vseslav: "These brothers captured Minsk and cut down all the men and took away the women and children into slavery," writes the chronicler.

Prince Vseslav was defeated in battle, but then Yaroslav's sons decided to make up with him and swore on a cross that they would not do any harm to him. When Vseslav of Polotsk, relying on the words of honour of his kin, arrived in Izyaslav's camp near Orsha, he was perfidiously seized in the presence of the Grand Prince and together with his two sons taken to Kiev. In Kiev Vseslav was kept in a special log cell with only a tiny window for food; the prison was built somewhere not far from the prince's courtyard reminding Kievans for a whole year of the perfidy of their Prince Izyaslav.

The imprisoned Prince Vseslav enjoyed popular sympathy; he was famed for being a swift-acting and successful military leader, flying from one place to another as if by sorcery and displaying valour and wit, and taking first Novgorod in the north and then Tmutarakan in the south. Folk *bylinas* were devoted to Vseslav the Sorcerer, and he was mentioned with sympathy by the author of *The Lay of Igor's Host* who admired the prince's brave soul and regretted the misfortunes that fell to his lot. Vseslav is depicted as a grey wolf running from Kiev to the Black Sea in one night, a sorcerer hearing the Polotsk bells ringing in Kiev, or a lynx disappearing from a besieged fortress at night.

Prince the Sorcerer, capable of turning into animals, as he was depicted in the chronicles and songs, had a strong impact on the minds of 11th-century people. It is perhaps not accidental that chronicler Nikon, while telling about the Kievan uprising of 1068, opened it with a detailed introduction on the harm of paganism; it is possible that the Polotsk prince, engaged in strifes with Yaroslav's three sons, relied on popular discontent and supported folk pagan beliefs and rituals which then expressed class dissatisfaction, as we saw on the example of Yaroslav and Beloozero. If that is indeed the case, it is easier to understand the sympathy of the Kievans to the prince suffering in the log prison and the distrust for the common people by the Grand Prince Izyaslav. This also makes it clear why he refused to provide them with arms and horses.

Events of September 15 developed as follows: having learned of Izyaslav's refusal the council began to discuss the actions of military leader Kosnyachka (Constantine), one of the authors of the Pravda of Yaroslav's Sons. Apparently, the people decided to punish this courtier, and after the council they moved straight to the Kievan Hill, to the fortress. Now this was an uprising against the prince. The insurgents were unable to find Kosnyachka at his courtyard. Then the people split up into two groups—one went to free some warrior friends of theirs from prison, while the others crossed the bridge and went straight to the prince's courtyard.

The prison where the warriors were kept was situated near Bryachislav's palace (most likely he was Vseslav's father).

The story of the chronicler with all its reticence may be understood in approximately the following way: before the uprising on September 15, part of the Kievans or Polochanians who were close to the Kievans (from the entourage of the old Bryachislav or the young Vseslav) was arrested by Prince Izyaslav and locked up in a cellar near the Kievan quarters of the Polotsk princes. The insurgent people decided: "Let us go and free our friends from the cellar!" and the prison was opened.

At this point the courtyard in front of the Grand Prince's palace was already overflowing with people arguing with the Prince. Surrounded by *boyars* Izyaslav watched the crowd from a window at the gallery, and *boyar* Tuky, Chudin's brother, advised him to reinforce the guard at Vseslav's prison: "You see, Prince, the people have raised an uproar!" Obviously the court *boyars* knew about the Kievans' sympathy for Vseslav and advised the Prince to prevent the freeing of a dangerous prisoner. Just then, the group of Kievans who had been freeing their friends from the cellar appeared in the courtyard. The *boyars* told the Prince: "Things look bad. Send guards to Vseslav's prison, let him be called to the window by deceit and killed with a sword." The prince did not dare take the step, and the people rushed to Vseslav's prison with cries. Seeing this the Grand Prince and his brother Vsevolod fled from Kiev. Izyaslav went to Poland, and hired troops to reconquer the throne, using the gold and silver of the Grand Prince's treasury.

The insurgent people broke open the log walls and freed Prince Vseslav proclaiming him Grand Prince instead of Izyaslav.

The popular prince ruled in Kiev for seven months, but we know very little about his activities, because the chronicle of Prince Vseslav has come down to us in insignificant fragments.

The author of *The Lay of Igor's Host* says that having gained the Kievan throne, like the hero of a fairy story,

> *Vseslav the prince*
> *Judged his people,*
> *He assigned cities to princes,*
> *And himself would scour*
> *Through the night like a wolf:*
> *From Kiev speeding,*
> *Before cockcrow he reached*
> *Far Tmutarakan.*
> *Like a wolf,*
> *He would cross the path*
> *of Khors, the great god.*

The court singer of the 11th century Boyan had a negative attitude to the insurgent people's choice: "However skillful and lucky he may be, whatever success the fortune-teller predicted according to birds—he cannot escape God's judgement!"

The author of *The Lay of Igor's Host*, however, expressing popular views, defends Vseslav, praising him as an epic hero and even calling him a model to be emulated by contemporaries.

The Kievan chronicler hid the true nature of the events of 1068 from us. For example, he passed over in silence such an unprecedented episode as the murder of Novgorod bishop Stefan by his *kholops* which occurred in Kiev in the same 1068. The fact indirectly shows the scope of the popular movement at the time. The social element intertwined with the religious one once again—the Novgorod *kholops* who strangled the head of the Novgorod church were emulated: a wizard came out against Stefan's successor in Novgorod Bishop Fyodor in 1069-1070. "There was a great uproar in the town. And everyone believed the wizard and intended to beat Bishop Fyodor." Only the firm actions of Prince Gleb who hacked the wizard to death with an axe quelled the mutiny.

In 1071 a pagan oracle appeared in Kiev and predicted important changes in the life of Kievan Rus and Byzantium.

All this indicates a tense situation, ferment among the popular masses, in particular hatred for the feudal church and hopes for a true popular pagan religion. The people supported the wizards everywhere and believed them. As in Western Europe the class struggle in Rus often assumed religious forms.

Yet the class struggle was not aimed to return the old forms of the primitive system. The class struggle was not against feudalism as a formation but only against excessive tribute.

Izyaslav's immense wealth which struck the imagination of Europe's royal courts was apparently the result of unparalleled exploitation of the people. Crop failures and nomads' invasions ruined peasant economy completely and threatened to interrupt its normal reproduction. The return to paganism was an act of despair in the face of natural calamities, and the killing of *ognishchanins* and *ryadoviches* and driving away of one prince and his replacement by another were real actions in defence of popular rights, households and one's existence not as a *kholop* deprived of rights but as a direct producer owning a household or a workshop.

Popular uprisings provoked feudal opposition. Having returned to Kiev thanks to the support of Polish troops Izyaslav transferred the marketplace where the council of September 15, 1068, assembled, from the democratic Podol to the Hill in the immediate vicinity of the prince's and *boyars'* courts. Izyaslav's son, allegedly without his father's knowledge, dealt summarily with the Kievans: he executed 70 men who took part in freeing Vseslav and gouged out the eyes of others and "many innocent people suffered, because their guilt was not proved". The people continued to struggle: in the villages where Izyaslav quartered the Polish troops, the Poles were secretly murdered and eventually forced to leave Rus.

The Pravda of Yaroslav's Sons, rigorously defending the prince's domain, is frequently associated with the assembly of princes in Kiev in 1072 on the occasion of the transfer of the coffins of Boris and Gleb, victims of the conflict of 1015, to a new church in Vyshgorod.

Yet the Pravda of Yaroslav's Sons does not reflect in any way the unprecedented events such as the driving out of the prince and the pillaging of the prince's palace and prison as occurred in September 1068. There is not a word about the wizards frequently mentioned by the chronicle for 1065-1071 and nothing about the town. Obviously the Russkaya Pravda was compiled before these events, in response to the spontaneous and widespread actions by the people against the prince's administration with its "false fines".

In the uprising of 1068, in the centre of the capital of Rus the common people filling the courtyard in front of the palace and determined to defend their independence against the Polovtsi or the prince's tribute collectors were confronted by the feudal nobility headed by the prince who watched the insurgent people in fear.

The *boyars* and princes opposing the people on that day included several authors of the Russkaya Pravda: Prince Izyaslav and Vsevolod, *voivoda* Kosnyachko who barely managed to escape popular anger, and Chudin whose brother advised the prince to kill Vseslav treacherously.

The picture retained by the chronicler symbolically puts the authors of the rigorous feudal law against the common folk who had to submit to this law.

**Quarrels and Unity
(Late 11th and Early 12th Centuries)**

Princes "of Woe" and the Kievan Uprising of 1113

A brilliant poet and keen-sighted historian, the author of *The Lay of Igor's Host*, probed deep into the past and found material to be compared with his own times. One such view of the past was an excursus into the 11th century in which the poet singled out two contrasting figures—Vseslav Bryachislavich of Polotsk and Oleg Svyatoslavich of Chernigov. All his historical references to Kievan Rus were based on the juxtaposing of these two princes. The hero of the popular uprising of 1068 Vseslav is, as we have seen, described in an epic spirit of the folk *bylinas* about a young, brave and wise sorcerer prince. But Oleg, the founder of a whole dynasty of the greedy Olgovichi, a friend of the Polovtsi khans and fomentor of quarrels is described in grim tones in *The Lay*:

> *For he, that Oleg,*
> *Forged feuds with his sword,*
> *Sowed his arrows over the earth...*
> *Then, in the days of Oleg,*
> *The Son of Woe,*
> *Discord was sown and throve.*
> *Then perished the birthright*
> *Of the grandsons of Dazhbog...*
> *Then was the voice of the husbandman seldom heard*
> *Throughout the Russian land,*
> *But often, indeed,*
> *The ravens croaked*
> *Feasting on the dead...*

The courageous truthfulness of the poet and historian becomes particularly clear to us when we remember that these accusatory lines were written in the reign of Oleg's grandson Grand Prince Svyatoslav Vsevolodich. Motivated by true patriotic feelings, urging all Russian principalities to unite, the author of *The Lay* managed to rise above the feudal barriers and narrow dynastic interests, and take a broader view of the dark and bright aspects of the country's history.

Having been nicknamed Gorislavich (Famous for Bringing Woe) Oleg Svyatoslavich personified a large group of princes of the 11th and early 12th centuries who were concerned chiefly about their own enrichment, started wars to capture wealthy towns and ignored the interests of the people. Among them were also Grand Prince Vsevolod Yaroslavich and Svyatopolk Izyaslavich who replaced the latter and provoked the new Kievan uprising of 1113.

Let us consider more attentively the actions and designs of the prince whom the author of *The Lay of Igor's Host* chose 800 years ago to show to posterity as a negative hero. Oleg was the grandson of Yaroslav the Wise and son of Svyatoslav Yaroslavich. His father who owned the rich Chernigov land and collected tribute as far as Beloozero, possessed great treasures but kept them locked up and did not share them with his retinue. He pursued his aims shamelessly and, in the words of the chronicler, "started the deposing of brothers" from prince's thrones.

In his time Svyatoslav took part in the treacherous deceit of Vseslav of Polotsk, and in 1073 he attacked his own brother, the simple-minded Izyaslav. Only a year earlier in Vyshgorod all three of Yaroslav's sons peacefully feasted at one table celebrating the memory of their uncles, the saints Boris and Gleb canonised precisely in order to quell internal conflicts, and Svyatoslav soon conspired with Vsevolod, drove his elder brother Izyaslav from Kiev and took his place. Such was the father; we know little about the adolescent years of his sons, we don't even know when they were born and how they lived in their father's time. Not only the Chernigov chronicle of Svyatoslav has not reached us but even the chronicle of the three years (1073-1076), when he was the Grand Prince of Kiev, has not survived.

We first learn about Svyatoslav's whole family from the excellent encyclopedia known as *Svyatoslav's Izbornik* of 1073. The book had a page inserted with a miniature depicting the prince's whole family: Svyatoslav Yaroslavich in the prince's crown and brocade cape with a book in his hands stands in front, his wife with the little son Yaroslav is next to him, and behind them the four adult sons stand—Gleb, Oleg, David and Roman. The sons are already bearded; they were probably born in the lifetime of their grandfather, in the 1050s, and were taking an independent road at the time the *Izbornik* was compiled. The elder, Gleb, was already famous for having hacked a wizard to death with an axe in Novgorod.

Gleb Svyatoslavich was killed far away, in Zavolochye, beyond the Northern Dvina, probably while he was collecting tribute, as was his great-grandfather Igor. Roman, praised by Boyan, brought the Polovtsi to Rus and attempted to capture Voin, the frontier Russian port for Dnepr ships; he was killed by his treacherous allies, the Polovtsi, somewhere in the steppe.

How could the young prince Oleg have been brought up by his father in Chernigov or Kiev? Most probably, according to the old custom, he was put in the saddle at three, taught to read at seven and as a twelve-year-old boy taken on his first expedition by his father.

Oleg could have known about battles, conspiracies and betrayals of one's word of honour from the *bylinas* of his time and the Boyan's compositions. This famous 11th-century poet was Svyatoslav's court bard, he praised Oleg's brother, the handsome Roman Svyatoslavich, he offered his biased judgements concerning Oleg's contemporaries such as Vseslav who would, he predicted, succumb to the Last Judgement.

Oleg could read the Russian chronicle and Georgy Amartol's Byzantine chronicle translated into Russian by that time. One of the chief chroniclers of the time, Nikon, the founder of the cloister in Tmutarakan, was a close friend of Prince Svyatoslav. Oleg had at his disposal his father's library which included two encyclopedic *izborniks*: the already familiar *Izbornik* of 1073 and another one, compiled "from many books of the prince" in 1076.

The latter *Izbornik* reflected the spirit of social conflicts which dominated the Russian reality of the 1060s and 1070s. The *Izbornik's* sermons addressed in turn the wealthy and strong and the feeble. The poor and the weak are advised to be resigned and humble ("my yoke is my good fortune and my burden is light"), to remain "obedient unto death and toil unto death". The wealthy and noble are advised, first, to fear the prince ("be afraid of the prince with all your soul"), and second, not to irritate the poor excessively ("do not anger the man who is in poverty") and try as far as possible to abate social contrasts ("When in cold winter weather you sit in warm chambers and can easily remove your clothes, sigh and think of the poor who freeze huddling over a small fire and weeping from the acrid smoke.") All this had been prompted by the class battles of the 1060s. The editor of the *Izbornik* advises readers to hide their thoughts and guard their secrets reliably. In an age when some problems were solved by a blow of the knife wielded by a hired murderer the reader was warned: "Do not bring any person in your house—beware of the villain."

The *izborniks* were needed to supply a prince with proverbs on all and every occasion, so that, without leafing through many books, he could display his wit and knowledge, "pouring out his wisdom before the *boyars* like honey".

Reading such literature Oleg and his brothers learned to be hypocritical and outwardly cultivated, they wore a permanent mask of philanthropists allegedly concerned about the paupers and the feeble. Oleg's entire subsequent life showed that he did not intend to follow some of the advice. In the *Izbornik* of 1073 the editor, scribe Ioann, wrote: "Do not do unto others what you will not have done unto yourself." Oleg began his career by rejecting that noble principle.

Oleg is first mentioned in 1073 when he received the distant Rostov land to rule from his father. In 1076 together with Vladimir Monomakh, his cousin, Oleg was sent to Poland to fight against the Czech king Vratislav. The expedition lasted for four months. When the Poles made peace with the Czechs, Oleg and Vladimir decided that this was not in their interests and besieged Glogov taking a contribution of 1,000 grivnas in silver from the king.

To understand the unstable position of the Russian lands in that age let us take a look at the history of Chernigov, Kiev's neighbour: Vsevolod, the father of Monomakh, ruled the town in 1073-1076; Vladimir Monomakh ruled Chernigov from December 27, 1076, to May 4, 1077. He was driven out of the town by his cousin Boris Vyacheslavich who held out in Chernigov for only eight days. In July 1077 the town was ruled by Vsevolod again, and his nephew Oleg lived at court.

Oleg was an ambitious person, he could not remain in the position of a vassal for long, and he unexpectedly fled from Chernigov to Tmutarakan in 1078 where he was awaited by the unfortunate Boris Vyacheslavich and his brother Roman. Having concluded an alliance with the Polovtsi khans, "Oleg and Boris brought the pagans to the Russian land". With the assistance of the Polovtsi Oleg drove out his own uncle and became the prince of Chernigov for 39 days. But a new battle at Nezhatina Niva on October 3, 1078, during which both Boris and the Grand Prince Izyaslav who sided with Vsevolod were killed, forced Oleg to flee to Tmutarakan again.

This time he left his troops behind and did not entertain any hope for the future. The rich port proved to be an unreliable refuge: the Polovtsi killed Oleg's brother and the Khazars captured Oleg and took him to Constantinople. The prince in Chernigov was replaced again: Vladimir Vsevolodich had again ascended the throne.

Oleg spent four years in Byzantium. For two years he lived on a large and wealthy island of Rhodes near the coast of Asia Minor. While in exile, the young prince married the noble Greek lady Pheophania Muzalon and, apparently, ceased being a prisoner. In 1083 Oleg returned to Tmutarakan, dealt with the Khazars cruelly and drove out two minor princes who had seized the town at an earlier date; one of the latter, David Igorevich, became a pirate on the Black Sea and stole all the goods from merchants in the mouth of the Dnepr.

For ten years, Oleg ruled Tmutarakan, far from the main Russian lands. His name is not encountered during these years in the chronicles, but life could hardly have been quiet in the multinational coastal town. We know how frequently princes replaced one another here, and how devious were the Byzantine methods of eliminating rivals, as for instance, poisoning wine by a substance hidden under the nail of the person serving the goblet.

The social crisis in Rus was aggravated again at the time; the administration of the Grand Prince widely resorted to the right of trial and collection of taxes and was acquiring enormous wealth. The numerous army of junior warriors rode the width and breadth of the country also collecting fair and unfair fines, enriching themselves and ruining the people. Ignoring the advice of the "wise" noble *boyars* Grand Prince Vsevolod kept closer to the junior warriors who replenished his treasury: "They began to plunder and sell people."

The situation was made worse by the continual quarrels between the princes. Vsevolod's nephews demanded for themselves first one district and then another and took to arms on any pretext: either to fight in the open field or to drive a sabre stealthily into a dangerous rival as it happened with Yaropolk Izyaslavich killed by a hired assassin. The stronger princes acted impudently; peace with the Polovtsi enabled them to turn their strength against the common people. Weak princes engaged in continuous intrigues against each other, and their wars devastated Rus.

The inner contradictions were supplemented by objective factors: there was a terrible drought in 1092, "the land was scorched and many forests and swamps caught fire". Epidemics broke out first in the Polotsk land and then in the Kievan land where the number of the dead ran into thousands.

Aggravated by these outer circumstances the social crisis might have developed into an uprising not in 1113 but 20 years earlier were it not for one factor: a new dreadful invasion of Rus by the Polovtsi which was probably also linked to deteriorating living conditions in the steppe and an attempt by the Polovtsi khans to overcome their crisis at the expense of Rus. The Polovtsi assaulted the frontier line along the Sula and captured the Russian villages both on the left and on the right bank of the Dnepr River.

It was in this situation that the old and sick Prince Vsevolod, the last of Yaroslav's sons, died in 1093. Vast opportunities to fight for the Grand Prince's throne opened up: each of Yaroslav's grandsons considered himself a claimant to the Kievan throne. The closest to the Kievan throne was Vladimir Monomakh who came to the bedside of his ill father in Kiev, but he seemed to have voluntarily renounced his rights to the Grand Prince's throne to avoid internal strife and departed for his Chernigov. But apparently things were different, judging by the way they were subsequently depicted by Monomakh's court chronicler.

The *boyar* opposition was strong in Kiev; it was headed by the wealthy *boyar* Jan Vyshatich familiar to us from the uprising of 1071. The interests of this *boyar* group were reflected in the part of the chronicle where Vsevolod is accused of ignoring the advice of the noblemen. Dissatisfied with Vsevolod's policies the Kievan *boyars*, apparently, refused to put his son Vladimir Monomakh on the Kievan throne. They invited Svyatopolk, a minor prince from Turov, but he did not live up to the hopes pinned on him. A poor military leader, thoughtless politician, arrogant and greedy, suspicious and cruel, he set everyone against himself very soon, and his policies aggravated the crisis even further.

Vladimir had quarrelled and fought against the same Svyatopolk, his own cousin, from the very first days of the latter's rule, and the noblemen reprimanded both of them: "Wherefore do you two quarrel with each other? Yet the pagan Polovtsi lay waste to the Russian land."

In 1093 the Polovtsi dealt the Russian forces a crushing blow at Tripolye and reached the outskirts of Kiev; Svyatopolk fled from the battlefield with only two companions.

The Polovtsi were in command throughout Southern Rus, "burning villages and grain storages". A contemporary reports in horror: "All the towns and villages are empty. Let us go through the fields where herds of horses, sheep and oxen once grazed, and we shall see everything barren; fields are overgrown with weeds, and only wild animals live there." The Polovtsi force into slavery the population of towns and villages "and take many Christian folk to their yurtas where they live with their kin; the folk suffer sorely, they are tortured and numb from the cold, go hungry and thirsty, their faces swollen, bodies darkened, tongues sore, they walk through a foreign land without clothes, barefooted, bruising their feet against the thorns".

In the most difficult conditions the *boyars* sought to strengthen the Grand Prince's power, prevent new quarrels and provide resistance to an unprecedented Polovtsi onslaught which threatened all sections and classes in Rus from the poor *smerd* to the prince. The estates of many Kievan *boyars* were located in the black-earth and partly wooded steppe zone which was the scene of predatory raids by the Polovtsi, and this made the *boyars* particularly militant.

Their patriotism was not selfless, but viewed objectively, their position under the existing conditions was most in line with the interests of the people, because the Polovtsi raids involving the burning of villages, killing and driving away into slavery of the population were, undoubtedly, more fearful than the conflict between *smerd* and master.

Yet the princes "of woe" continued to settle their dynastic and personal accounts without regard for the interests of their native land and their people.

Currying favour with the powerful Polovtsi khan Tugortkan, the Grand Prince Svyatopolk married his daughter to him in 1095, but this did not save Kiev from the Polovtsi.

Edged away to the distant Tmutarakan under Vsevolod Oleg Svyatoslavich now decided to take advantage of a moment which was so difficult for Rus. Once again, as it had been sixteen years before, he marched against Rus at the head of the Polovtsi hordes. Having besieged Monomakh in Chernigov he burned all the surrounding settlements and cloisters, captured the town, and let the Polovtsi plunder the whole of Chernigov land. This was his repayment for the military assistance.

Contemporaries were appalled by Oleg's selfish actions: "It is the third time that he hounds the pagan Polovtsi onto the Russian land... Many Christians (Russians—*B. R.*) have been hacked to death, many driven away into slavery in distant lands."

In this period Oleg Svyatoslavich gave shelter to the Polovtsi khans in his principality, avoided taking part in Russian-wide expeditions against the Polovtsi and showed his obvious affinity for these enemies of Rus. Svyatopolk and Monomakh invited him to Kiev in order to consider problems of defence, but Oleg responded very haughtily, and it was understood in Kiev that the prince would not exchange his friendship with the khans for an alliance with the Russian princes.

A war began against Oleg. He fled from Chernigov to Starodub, and from there to Smolensk, and, driven out by the townsfolk, went further to Ryazan and Murom. While Monomakh himself repelled the attacks of Tugortkan and Bonyak in the south, his sons fiercely fought Oleg who had started to ravage the Northeast of Rus.

The result of the three years of struggle was that Oleg appeared at the assembly of princes in Lubech in November 1097. The town of Lubech, from which Vladimir I traced his lineage, was, first of all, the family town of all Russian princes, and second, it already belonged to Oleg once and it was not shameful for him to come here for the prince's assembly.

The principle of the dynastic division of Rus between the various princely branches was proclaimed at the assembly on condition of observing unity in the face of a foreign threat: "From hence on let us unite as if we had one heart and defend the Russian land!" But this was all based not on the real interests of individual lands and not on the real balance of power. The princes divided it into pieces in accordance with the haphazard borders of the possessions of Yaroslav's sons. The princes' assemblies were not a way out of the crisis. The noble principles proclaimed in the picturesque Dnepr town were not guaranteed and were violated a few days after the solemn "kissing of the cross" in the wooden church of the Lubech castle.

We know all the details of the events which occurred in 1097-1098 following the Lubech assembly, because, fighting Svyatopolk, Monomakh was concerned with compiling a most detailed description of his rival's conspiracies, secret alliances and bloody deeds. The pirate prince David Igorevich persuaded the Grand Prince that allegedly Prince Vasilko of Terebovl had conspired with Monomakh against Svyatoslav. The latter's men seized Vasilko and gouged out his eyes. A long, dramatic struggle began. Making up with Oleg, Monomakh marched against Svyatopolk. Poland, Hungary and the Polovtsi land, and dozens of Russian princes and towns were involved in the struggle which ended in 1100 with the princes' assembly in Uvetichi (Vitichev) where Prince David was tried for "driving a knife" amongst the princes; Vladimir Monomakh, armed with the detailed chronicle, acted as the prosecutor.

Prince Oleg had become quieter by that time. He was the father of adult sons, the Olgovichi, who were notorious in the 12th century for being adventurists just like their father. His elder son Vsevolod, a drunkard and lecher, was known in his younger years for his raids against the peaceful population and was even included in the *bylinas* as an anti-hero (Churila). Svyatoslav, the youngest son, married to a Polovtsi woman, continued to bring Polovtsi troops to Rus as his father had done. The middle son Igor, lover of books and church singing, unsuccessfully continued his father's policy and was eventually killed by an enraged Kievan crowd; he was the epitome of the unfortunate age when "in princes' quarrels the human life was shortened".

Oleg Svyatoslavich died in 1115 in Chernigov. Three months before his death the restless prince began a new quarrel with Monomakh concerning the site of the sarcophagi of Boris and Gleb in the new Vyshgorod Church. After his death the family patronymic of his sons and grandsons Olgovichi became a symbol of unprecedented internal strife, bloody deeds and treachery for a long time to come.

We have traced, from beginning to end, the fate of a prince who laid waste to Rus. The nickname of Gorislavich proposed by the author of *The Lay of Igor's Host* was fully borne out by all of the doings of Oleg Svyatoslavich. He was not alone in this; he was typical of the age.

Another sad figure in Russian history of the turn of the 12th century was Grand Prince Svyatopolk Izyaslavich with whom we are already familiar. "This prince was tall, dry, with dark and straight hair, long beard and keen sight. He was a reader of books and had an acute memory... He was not fond of war and although he angered easily he would soon forget. At the same time he was very fond of silver and miserly" (V. N. Tatishchev).

The latter words are confirmed by many sources. Prince Svyatopolk invented all sorts of ways to enrich the treasury. His son tortured monks to force them to show the place where treasures were buried. Despite the hopes of the Kievan *boyars* Svyatopolk failed to defend Rus from the Polovtsi and only ruined it by additional wars.

Immediately after prince Svyatopolk's death a popular uprising flared up in Kiev.

On April 17, 1113, Kiev was divided into two camps. The Kievan nobility assembled in the St Sophia Cathedral to decide the question of a new prince. There was a wide choice, many princes laid claim to the title, but the *boyars* gave preference to the Pereyaslavl Prince Vladimir Monomakh.

At the time when the *boyars* in the cathedral were electing a Grand Prince, the popular uprising was raging outside the walls of the cathedral. Exhausted by Svyatopolk's financial policy the people stormed the palace of the prominent Kievan *boyar*, commander of the Thousand Putyata Vyshatich (Jan's brother), and ravaged the houses of Jewish money-lenders.

At the peak of the uprising the *boyars* sent a second messenger to Monomakh asking him to arrive in Kiev as soon as possible. "Prince! Come to Kiev! If you do not come, great misfortunes will occur: then not only the household of Putyata and those of the Hundred commanders and money-lenders will be despoiled by the common folk but they will also attack the widow of the late prince, your sister-in-law, and all the *boyars* and the cloisters. You, O Prince, will be to blame if the common folk pillage the cloisters!"

The uprising raged for four days, until Monomakh arrived in Kiev. Soviet historians B. D. Grekov and M. N. Tikhomirov justly believe that the uprising was not restricted to the town but involved the villages of the Kievan land and the numerous *boyar* and princes' estates which formed a broad semicircle to the south of Kiev in the partly wooded steppe.

The uprising was undoubtedly successful, because Vladimir immediately issued a new code, The Rules of Monomakh, easing the position of the town lower strata indebted to the rich money-lenders and the peasant *zakups* in bondage to the *boyars*.

Vladimir Monomakh's Rules severely restricted the interest paid on loans. Let us explain this article by the following example. Say a peasant has loaned 6 grivnas of silver from a *boyar* in a bad year. Under the existing high interest rates (50 per cent) he had to pay the *boyar* 3 grivnas of interest every year (the cost of three oxen). And if the debtor was unable to repay the debt, in addition to the interest, he had to pay the lender interest for an endless number of years, falling into bondage.

Under the new Rules interest was paid only for three years—the debtor now paid 9 grivnas of interest which was one and a half times more than the original debt. Monomakh permitted the repayment to be ceased at that, because 9 grivnas included the debt and 3 grivnas of increment. The debt was annulled. In effect this reduced the annual interest to 17 per cent and saved the poor from the threat of long-term and eternal bondage. This represented a major victory by the insurgent people.

In the estate economy the new law defended certain human rights of the debtors *(zakups)*. The latter now had the right to leave the master's household if he set out in search of money or went to lodge a complaint to judges or the prince. The *zakup* was no longer held responsible for the master's property if it was stolen by others. The master had to pay a fine into the prince's treasury for "offending" or unjustly punishing the *zakup*. If the master sold the *zakup* as a *kholop* (slave) at his own will he was threatened by an even larger fine (12 grivnas). In this case the offended *zakup* was freed of his entire debt. The *zakup* peasant received the right to testify as witness in minor court cases. These were the gains of the insurgent people. The feudal lords were forced to make certain concessions improving the economic and legal position of the town craftsmen and the peasants.

Vladimir Monomakh, Prince of the Boyars (1053-1113-1125)

In appraising historical personalities it is more important for us to determine the objective significance of their activities: whether these activities went against the current or, on the contrary, contributed to the general progress, rather than analysing their subjective personal qualities which can be presented to us in a distorted way by biassed contemporaries.

Vladimir Monomakh is probably the only figure in Kievan Rus about whom so many vivid reminiscences had been written. He was remembered both in palaces and in peasant huts for many centuries to come. The people made up *bylinas* about him as the victor over the terrible Polovtsi Khan Tugortkan, and because he had the same name as Vladimir I these *bylinas* were included in the old cycle of Kievan epics about Vladimir I.

When the age of feudal splits and the Tatar-Mongolian invasion was replaced by the unexpectedly rapid rise of the Moscow centralised state, the Grand Prince Ivan III who liked to read the chronicles for political purposes turned to the majestic figure of Vladimir Monomakh who, just like Ivan himself, emerged at the turn of two epochs.

It is not surprising that at the end of the 15th century Moscow historians singled out the figure of Monomakh in Russian history, whose name was associated with the legend of the royal regalia allegedly received by Vladimir from the Emperor of Byzantium. The crown of Monomakh became the symbol of Russian autocracy, it was used to crown all the Russian tsars down to the Khodynka catastrophe* when the last tsar was crowned.

Under Vladimir Monomakh Rus defeated the Polovtsi many times, and for a while the latter ceased being a constant threat. The power of the Kievan prince extended to all the lands populated by the ancient Rus. Quarrels between minor princes were resolutely suppressed by the Grand Prince. Kiev was indeed the capital of an enormous state, the largest in Europe.

It is not surprising that in the grim years of internal strife Russian people sought consolation in their majestic past; their eyes turned to the age of Vladimir Monomakh. *The Lay of the Doom of the Russian*

---

* The catastrophe on Khodynka field in Moscow occurred on May 18, 1896, when the tsar's gifts were handed out on the occasion of the coronation of Nikolai II. Many people were killed in a crush.— *Ed.*

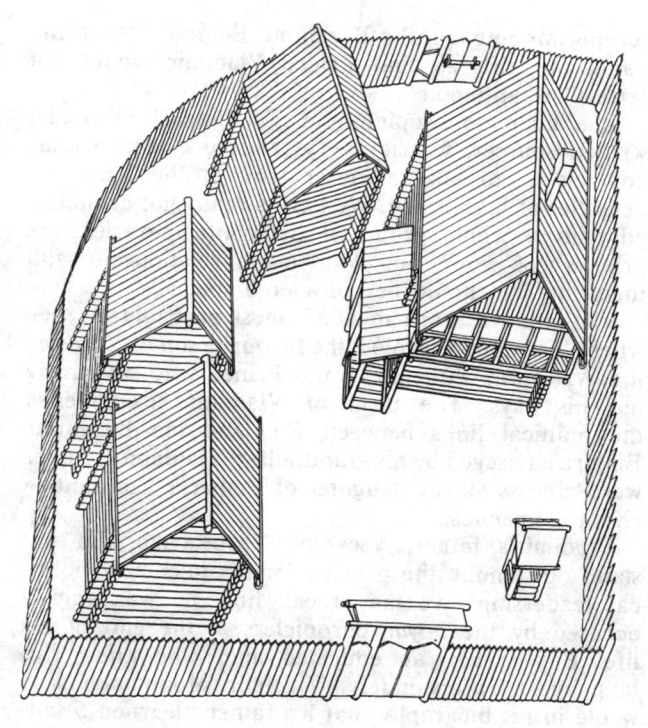

Reconstruction of 10th-century estate in Kiev (Podol)

Land written on the eve of the Tatar-Mongolian invasion idealises Kievan Rus and praises Vladimir Monomakh and his age. The poet outlines the borders of Rus in a gigantic semicircle: from Hungary to Poland, from Poland to Lithuania, further to the Baltic lands of the German Order, then on to Karelia and the Arctic Ocean, then to Volga Bulgaria, the Burtasi, Mordva and Udmurts.

All the lands inside these borders had long been obedient to Vladimir Monomakh "who was the bugbear the Polovtsi used to frighten their children in the cradle, while the Lithuanians did not come out of their swamps, and the Hungarians put iron gates into their stone fortresses so the Great Vladimir would be unable to enter them."

Mixing fact with fiction the poet even believed that,

fearing Monomakh, the Byzantine Emperor "sent him handsome gifts so that Prince Vladimir would not seize Constantinople".

The unanimous opinion of Vladimir II in feudal written sources, warrior verse and folk epic *bylinas* compels us to take a closer look at the long-time activities of that prince. We have already got acquainted with a whole group of his contemporaries, the princes "of woe", and Monomakh relationship with them, but he should be considered specially.

Vladimir was born in 1053, most probably in Kiev where his father Vsevolod, the favourite son of Yaroslav the Wise, was with the Grand Prince who was living out his days. The birth of Vladimir strengthened the political links between Rus and the Byzantine Empire envisaged by his grandfather: Vladimir's mother was Princess Maria, daughter of Emperor Constantine IX Monomachos.

Vladimir's father, Vsevolod Yaroslavich, did not stand out among the princes for his talents of political leadership—we may recall how he was angrily accused by the *boyar* chroniclers at the end of his life. But he was an educated man who knew five languages. Unfortunately, Vladimir Monomakh who wrote in his biography that his father "learned 5 languages sitting at home" did not mention which particular languages he knew. We may presume that the foreign languages he knew were Greek, Polovtsi, Latin and English.

Vladimir received an excellent education which enabled him to resort in his political struggle not only to the sword but also to the pen. He was well versed in the contemporary literature, possessed a good literary style and a vivid talent of a writer.

Vladimir spent his childhood years in the frontier town of Pereyaslavl, the starting point of the famous Snake Walls, ancient fortifications which for many centuries separated the country of the land-tillers from the "unknown country", the steppe stretching for many hundreds of kilometres.

At that time, changes were taking place in the steppe: the Pechenegs were pushed to the Danube, their place was temporarily taken by the Torks, while the innumerable tribes of the Kipchak-Polovtsi were already advancing from the east ready to sweep away everything in their way and lay waste to all of Rus.

Vladimir spent half his life, more than thirty years, in the frontier town of Pereyaslavl, and this inevitably affected his attitude to the disastrous Polovtsi invasions and the vital need for the unity of Russian forces.

Vladimir witnessed the wars against the Torks and the first Polovtsi raids ever since childhood. There was no other town in the entire Rus such as Pereyaslavl which was so frequently attacked by the steppe nomads. The most painful impression probably remained after the famous expedition by Khan Sharukan in 1068. The *bylinas* written about that invasion provide a very poetic description of herds of bay aurochs running through the steppe right from the very sea frightened by the hoofbeats of the Polovtsi force.

We do not know whether the fifteen-year-old Vladimir took part in the battle in which Sharukan defeated his father and uncles and whether he experienced the bitterness of flight, but in any case the rout which ended in an uprising in Kiev, the driving out of the Grand Prince and the death of the bishop must have left a deep imprint in his mind.

Vladimir went through a severe school; from his teens he had to help his father who was a minor prince for many years and a vassal of his brother. No wonder in his declining years Monomakh recalled his 83 major expeditions through Rus, the steppe and Europe. He made his first long journey as a thirteen-year-old boy travelling from Pereyaslavl to Rostov, through the wild Brynsk forests in which, according to the *bylinas*, the legendary Whistling Robber stalked travellers, where there was no straight road and the funeral ritual fires still burned, and pagans killed Kievan missionaries.

From the time of his first trip to his firm establishment in Chernigov at the age of twenty-five, Vladimir Monomakh changed at least five apanage towns, made 20 major journeys, fought in the most diverse places and, according to the most modest estimates, rode no less than 10,000 kilometres, not counting the rounds in the vicinity of towns which cannot be measured.

Already at an early age life showed him the negative sides of princes' quarrels, the vicissitudes of vassal service, and the terror of Polovtsi raids. Energetic, active, intelligent and cunning, he made good use of these lessons as subsequent events showed, because from his youth he knew life in Rus from Novgorod to the steppe and from Volyn to Rostov probably better than any of his contemporaries.

The Battle of Nezhatina Niva on October 3, 1078, abruptly changed the balance of forces in the enlarged family of princes. Vsevolod Yaroslavich became the Grand Prince asserting his power over the entire "Russian land" in the narrow sense: over Kiev which he ruled himself, over Chernigov where he sent his son Vladimir and over Pereyaslavl-Russky where the latter had ruled for several years before becoming the prince in Kiev in 1113.

Vladimir Monomakh ruled Chernigov for sixteen years, from 1078 to 1094. It was during his reign, most probably, that the stone chambers in the centre of the Chernigov Kremlin and the impregnable castle in Lubech on the Dnepr were built.

Vladimir was married to the English princess Gytha, daughter of King Harold who died in the battle of Hastings. The young couple arrived in Chernigov with a two-year-old first-born, Mstislav, subsequently a major figure in Rus.

In an autobiographical *Sermon* Vladimir often recalls this quite happy period in his life.

In his own words, the prince maintained very strict order and, not trusting his servants, checked everything himself:

> In war and in hunting I always did myself what my warrior could have done, giving myself no respite by night or by day, regardless of heat or cold. I did not rely on the town elders but looked after my household myself. I was concerned with the hunt, the horses, and even the hunting birds, the falcons and the hawks.

In the Lubech castle which we already mentioned all the parts of this enormous structure were well thought-out, every yard of space was rationally used, and all and every occasion of rough feudal life were provided for.

In medieval Rus, as in all countries at the time, hunt was the princes' favourite pastime and a fine school of courage. Occasionally the prince and his retinue, princesses and court ladies, went on boats to hunt the blue-grey ducks and white swans in the backwaters of the Dnepr or caught wild animals in nets beyond Vyshgorod, and the hunt could turn into a dangerous contest with a wild beast. Monomakh writes:

> When I lived in Chernigov I hobbled three dozen wild horses in the woods with my own hands, and when I had to ride through the steppe (the plain), I also caught them with my own hands. The aurochs twice lifted me and my horse on their horns. A reindeer hit me with its antlers, and elk stamped on me with its feet, and another attacked me with its antlers; a wild boar tore the sword off my side, a bear bit my knee, and a lynx pounced on my hip and threw me to the ground together with my horse.

A heavy golden snake-like amulet which had belonged to Vladimir was found in the woods near Chernigov in 1821. Apparently the prince had lost the expensive object during a struggle with a wild animal; perhaps an elk had stamped the prince's amulet into the ground.

In a letter to Monomakh Metropolitan Nikifor mentioned his habit of skiing.

Swift and resolute in his actions Vladimir Vsevolodich organised fast communications between Chernigov and Kiev: "and from Chernigov I rode hundreds of times to my father in Kiev in one day, arriving before vesper." Such a frenzied 140-kilometre ride could have been made only with a relay of horses along the way. As a study of the road from Chernigov to Lubech (60 kilometres) showed, the route ran through valleys and was divided into laps by special guard mounds where the horses could have been changed.

V. N. Tatishchev has the following description of the appearance of Monomakh, perhaps based on the notes made by contemporaries:

> He had a handsome face, big eyes, reddish and

curly hair, high forehead, wide beard, was not very tall but strong in body.

The sixteen years of life in Chernigov were not the years of quiet and isolation. Vladimir had to help his father many times in the struggle against internal and external enemies. Vsevolod's nephews fought for estates, demanded first one district then another. The cunning prince played a complicated chess game on the expanses of Rus: first he would withdraw Oleg Svyatoslavich from the game, then he would send away the elder of the nephews, Vladimir's dynastic rival, Prince Svyatopolk, to the distant Novgorod corner, or oust the outcasts, the sons of Rostislav, or the assassin would remove another rival, Yaropolk Izyaslavich.

All of this was done mostly by Vladimir Monomakh. It was Vladimir who drove away the sons of Rostislav, brought to Kiev his aunt, the widow of Izyaslav killed in a strife, and took the property of her son Yaropolk for himself.

It must be noted, however, that we learn about all these deeds from the chronicle of Nestor, the court annalist of Svyatopolk, Vladimir's rival. In order to correct this biassed chronicle, Vladimir began to keep notes for his own autobiographical chronicle. He put down many episodes of his struggle against the Polovtsi which had not entered the official chronicle. He described how he had taken the Polovtsi khans prisoner, recalled unexpected encounters with enormous Polovtsi forces in the steppe; wrote about successful pursuits, battles on Perepetovoye Polye, an enormous steppe clearing between the Ros and Stugna rivers. It becomes clear that the full weight of all military and police functions during Vsevolod's rule lay on the shoulders of his elder son, because in the last nine years of his life the Grand Prince no longer took part in expeditions.

Being in effect the ruler of the entire Russian land together with his father, Vladimir Monomakh could undoubtedly expect to become the Grand Prince by right of inheritance and ownership after his father's death. But when Vsevolod died in 1093 the Kievan throne was occupied not by Vladimir who was in Kiev at the time but Svyatopolk who was invited from Turov.

Possibly revised by Monomakh the chronicle explains the fact by his highly noble intentions; he was allegedly reluctant to start a new strife and respected the dynastic seniority of his cousin.

This was hardly the case: twenty years later Vladimir had no qualms about dynastic seniority, and as to the strife, we know that Vladimir and his brother Rostislav controlled the troops of the entire militant left bank, while Svyatopolk of Turov had only his eight hundred men.

The problem was quite different. As we will subsequently see, the chief force checking the princes' race from one town to another was the rich land-owning *boyars*. The choice of prince in the final count depended on "the best men" or the "sages".

Since the late 11th century the *boyars*' political role was growing steadily. More and more frequently it was the *boyars* who reviewed the motley crowd of princes, considered their doings and achievements, the wit and tractability of some prince, and invited a suitable candidate for the throne from another town, and occasionally even asserted their supremacy by signing a contract with the prince without which the latter was not regarded as fully authorised. The "sages" regarded themselves as the basis of the feudal army of Rus; they comprised the *boyar* duma, and it was up to them to decide whether to open the gates to a prince waiting by the walls of Kiev and lead him ceremoniously into the St Sophia Cathedral pledging allegiance to him ("You are our prince! Where we see your banner, there we are with you") or to tell the ruling prince firmly. "Prince, get thee gone, we do not need you!"

The policy of Prince Vsevolod for which Monomakh was also responsible provoked the acute displeasure of the "sages". The *boyars* were outraged by the arbitrary actions of the prince's judges and tax collectors who invented false fines and robbed the people. The *boyars*' concern for the common folk was, of course, a demagogic trick, but the fact that the trick was used shows that the actions of the prince's officials also infringed upon the interests of the *boyars*, apparently violating the immunity of their estates.

The difficult years of drought, epidemics and Polov-

Golden snake amulet of Vladimir Monomakh found on the Belous River where the prince frequently went hunting

tsi invasion which fell on the end of Vsevolod's rule should have aggravated social conflicts, and the Kievan *boyars* preferred to see on the throne of Grand Prince Svyatopolk Izyaslavich, the brother of Mstislav who in his time executed 70 participants in the 1068 uprising, blinding others and destroying the innocent.

When Svyatopolk ascended the throne Vladimir's hopes were dashed and he suffered many misfortunes: Svyatopolk's inexperience resulted in the Russian troops' terrible defeat by the Polovtsi at Tripolye. Monomakh recalled it as his only defeat in battle; his brother Rostislav drowned here, before his very eyes, in the waters of the Stugna. Forced to be content with

Chernigov instead of Kiev, Monomakh soon lost the former as well. Oleg Svyatoslavich and the Polovtsi drove him out of the town.

The forty-year-old prince with his wife and children, as we already know, had to leave Chernigov and go through the territory of the Polovtsi who were ready to rob the vanquished.

Vladimir found himself once again in the town of his childhood, where his father had started his life, where his younger brother ruled later, in Pereyaslavl, on the edge of the Polovtsi steppe.

The twenty-year Pereyaslavl period in the life of Vladimir Monomakh (1094-1113) was marked by two trends: first there was an active struggle waged against the Polovtsi advancing onto Rus through the Pereyaslavl principality, and second, Vladimir strove to draw to his side the Kievan *boyars* who to some extent held the key to the title of Grand Prince.

The struggle against the Polovtsi which Monomakh was forced to wage as the ruler of a frontier principality was always regarded by contemporaries as an all-Russian cause, the defence of Rus as a whole.

Monomakh was an advocate of decisive blows, expeditions deep into the steppe, and the final defeat of the steppe nomads.

The first victory was scored beyond the Sula River right after he had become prince in Pereyaslavl. Then, in 1095, Vladimir breached the short-lived peace with the Polovtsi, killed the Polovtsi envoy Itlar in Pereyaslavl and took part in a large expedition to the Polovtsi steppe where the Rus captured many prisoners, horses and camels. The next year Vladimir's troops defeated the Polovtsi at the Zarubintsy Ford on the Dnepr and killed Khan Tugortkan. The common folk made up *bylinas* in which it is easy to recognise Tugortkan as Tugarin Zmeevich (the Serpent) and Itlar as the Pagan Idol.

Three difficult years in Pereyaslavl proved to be the turning point in Russo-Polovtsi relations. Soon the struggle was transferred deep into the steppe, and the credit for this goes to Monomakh. The court chroniclers of Monomakh liked to repeat the story of how Vladimir persuaded Svyatopolk and his *boyars* to start the expedition in spring. The Kievan *boyars* refused to march against the Polovtsi under the pretext that it would distract *smerds* from ploughing the land. Monomakh delivered a speech: "It is strange, my friends, that you are concerned with the horses that are ploughing, but do not think that the *smerd* would begin to plough and the Polovtsi would come and kill the *smerd*, drive away his horse, and then take captive his wife and children in the village as well as all his property. How can you be concerned with the horses and not think about the *smerds*?"

These words, however, were dictated by clever calculation rather than real concern for the *boyars' smerds*. In any case, Monomakh managed to organise large, all-Rus expeditions in 1103, 1109, 1110, and 1111. Russian forces reached the Sea of Azov and reconquered the Polovtsi towns along the Seversky Donets inspiring such terror among the Polovtsi that they retreated beyond the Don and the Volga into the steppes of the Northern Caucasus and Southern Urals. Up to 20 Polovtsi khans were taken prisoner in some battles.

Occasionally expeditions against the Polovtsi assumed the form of a crusade—priests with crosses rode in front and sang hymns. Special tales were written about these crusades which said that "their fame would reach Bohemia, Poland, Hungary, Greece and even Rome".

The struggle against the Polovtsi was remembered for a long time and, a hundred years later, praising the great-great-grandson of Monomakh Prince Roman Mstislavich, the chronicler described how Vladimir drove Khan Otrok Sharukanovich beyond the Iron Gates at the Caucasus:

> Then Vladimir Monomakh drank the Don water with his golden helmet, took all their lands and drove out the pagan Agaryanians (Polovtsi — *B. R.*).

Regardless of Vladimir Monomakh's personal motives his victorious expeditions against the Polovtsi earned him widespread fame as a fine organiser and brilliant military leader.

Monomakh carried on his internal affairs with equal

vigour, although less successfully. He had to deal with such rivals as Svyatopolk of Kiev, on the one hand, and David and Oleg of Chernigov, on the other. Vladimir built the fortress Ostersky Gorodets between his rivals, on the road from Chernigov to Kiev he knew so well. He did it apparently to make communications between them more difficult. Monomakh's domain came to include Smolensk and Rostov where he often went after restoring order in the south. The Chernigov principality was surrounded almost on all sides by his possessions, and in 1096 Vladimir drove Oleg out of Chernigov and attempted to organise an assembly of princes which would condemn Oleg for having brought the pagans to the Russian land.

Vladimir managed to convene the assembly only at the end of 1097, and apparently the balance of forces was such that he was unable to dictate his terms: the assembly got together not in Kiev but at Oleg's estate, the ancient Lubech where it was probably not very pleasant for Monomakh to go. Most certainly, Vladimir Monomakh saw to it that special documents were written to win over to his side influential feudal circles: he himself wrote a letter to Oleg obviously intended for a wide range of people. Part of Monomakh's personal chronicle had been completed by the time, describing him as an untiring fighter against the Polovtsi and a person unjustly offended by Oleg. The chronicle of Ivan, the Father-Superior of the Kiev-Pechersky Monastery dates back to this time; it expressed *boyars'* negative attitude to Grand Prince Svyatopolk. Svyatopolk exiled Ivan to Turov, while Monomakh, seeking an alliance with the Kievan *boyars*, intervened on his behalf.

Monomakh prepared for the Lubech assembly not only as a military leader and strategist but also as a lawyer and polemical writer.

The Lubech assembly, however, did not bring Monomakh victory. The principle adopted there—let each one be the owner of his estate—left Kiev under the rule of Svyatopolk Izyaslavich, Chernigov under the sons of Svyatoslav, while the same frontier Pereyaslavl constantly ravaged by the pagans remained the only piece of Russian land belonging to Vladimir Vsevolodich. The campaign against Oleg was, in effect, lost, and Vladimir swiftly formed an alliance with the Polovtsi. The unexpected alliance was aimed against Svyatopolk, and Monomakh was the chief spring behind many events; apparently he was still harbouring the hope of becoming Grand Prince.

It is still possible to discern the real meaning of events occurring immediately after the assembly through the fanciful constructions of the biassed chroniclers whose writings were subsequently revised under Monomakh.

A rumour swept through court circles, probably not without reason, that Vladimir Monomakh had conspired with Vasilko Rostislavich of Terebovl against Svyatopolk. Although Vasilko's possessions were not large, his strategic designs were really grand: for example, as the chronicler writes, he intended to rally all the non-Polovtsi nomads (the Pechenegs, the Torks and the Berendei) and with them capture Poland in one year, then conquer the Bulgarian Kingdom beset by Byzantium, and transfer the Bulgars to his principality. Then he intended to make war against the entire Polovtsi land.

Vasilko was seized in Svyatopolk's palace when, travelling from Lubech to his land via Kiev, he reluctantly accepted the invitation of the Grand Prince to have breakfast with him.

As soon as it became known that Vasilko, in irons, had had his eyes gouged out and was taken under heavy guard to Vladimir Volynsky, Vladimir Monomakh, as if in justification of the rumours about his conspiracy with Vasilko, lead his troops against Svyatopolk. Vladimir and his new allies, Oleg and David Svyatoslavich, made camp outside Kiev.

Never had Vladimir been as close to the Kievan "golden throne" as on those November days of 1097. Svyatopolk was about to flee from the city. It seemed as if Vladimir's dreams were coming true. But this time, too, influential Kievan circles did not support Monomakh, did not open the Golden Gates for him, but persuaded Svyatopolk to stay in the city and sent a distinguished embassy to Vladimir and the sons of Svyatoslav. It consisted of the Metropolitan and Vladimir's stepmother the Grand Princess. The embassy proposed peace with great courtesy, and this meant dashed hopes again.

However, the cunning son of the Byzantine princess had already taken other measures which would provide him with evidence against Svyatopolk.

A certain Vassily, apparently one of Svyatopolk's courtiers who had taken the side of Monomakh was recording Svyatopolk's evil deeds. As a witness, he described the scene of Vasilko's arrest and put down the names of all those participating; he knew who had pressed a board against the prince, who guarded him and knew that it was Svyatopolk's servant who had blinded the prisoner. Subsequently, during the following two years (1097-1099) Vassily described at length the strife, laying stress on Svyatopolk's blunders.

Vladimir's old friends, chroniclers from the Pechersky Monastery, developed the theme of Svyatopolk's shortcomings. Around 1099 they wrote two stories about the stinginess and greed of Svyatopolk who enriched himself by means of a salt tax, and about the even greater greed of his son who tortured monks to learn where treasures had been hidden.

In 1099 Vladimir Monomakh wrote the principal part of his *Sermon* in which he, first, castigates the shortcomings Svyatopolk was accused of (lawlessness, inefficiency, breaking one's oath), and second, quite immodestly praises himself as if saying to the Kievan nobles: "here I am, the prince you need. I always fought the pagans. I did not give free rein to my junior warriors, did not allow them to do foul deeds, I am kind to merchants, I stand for just trial, I could calm the humiliated, I am true to my word, I manage my household well without relying on assistants, I seek the advice of my *boyars*, and I look after the church".

Vladimir seems to dissociate himself from all the evils his father had been accused of a few years before (and thereby he himself as co-ruler).

Vladimir's *Sermon* was addressed not to his own children. At the time they were giving their daughters in marriage and hardly needed their father's advice. It was intended for an extensive feudal audience.

Most probably, all the factual and literary materials were compiled for the next assembly of princes in 1100 in Uvetichi where Monomakh appeared as an accuser of David Igorevich and indirectly tried to destroy the reputation of his chief adversary, Grand Prince Svyatopolk.

The ambitious hopes did not come true this time either, but a great deal was achieved—a strong imprint was left on Kievan literature: contemporaries and posterity were to see Svyatopolk in a negative light, and Vladimir in a positive one.

Following the princes' assembly of 1100 which changed nothing in the fate of the elder princes, Vladimir Monomakh lost any desire to continue the literary struggle. He even abandoned his personal chronicle of travels making only seven entries in the subsequent 17 years: about new battles with the Polovtsi, about trips through the domain, about the death of his second wife, Yuri Dolgoruky's mother.

Among the events of these years mention should be made of the defeat of Bonyak and Sharukan the Old in 1107. Vladimir and Svyatopolk acted jointly in all these expeditions, but the initiative, apparently, belonged to Monomakh.

The Kievan uprising of 1113 frightened the feudal elité and forced them to turn to the only possible candidate, a popular prince known to all the people for his thirty-five-year-long struggle against the Polovtsi and famous in the *boyar* and clerical circles for his literary materials and speeches at assemblies of princes.

The sixty-year-old Vladimir Vsevolodich Monomakh became the Grand Prince. The new code of law, as we saw above, eased the position of debtors, in particular of *zakups*. But in addition, the Rules of Monomakh settled some questions of interest to merchants: the interests of foreign trade were provided for—privileges were granted to merchants who had lost their goods in a shipwreck, war or fire, and foreign merchants enjoyed preferential rights in liquidation of goods belonging to insolvent debtors.

Vladimir implemented the programme outlined already in the *Sermon*: "And honour the guest most of all from wherever he comes, whether he is a common man, a noble or an envoy; if you cannot honour him with gifts, then do so with food and drink: for all along the way they will extol the person as kind or reprehend him as evil."

Having become the Grand Prince and apparently enjoying the full support of the *boyars* Vladimir II held all of Rus firmly in his hands. The enormous military force mustered to fight the Polovtsi could now, after their retreat to the south, be used to retain Kiev's hold over Rus. As his namesake a century ago, Vladimir Monomakh ruled the country with the help of his sons, experienced princes.

The elder son Mstislav, "reared" by the Novgorodians, had long since ruled Novgorod. Having been called south by his father in 1117, he did not lose links with his town on Lake Ilmen. Mstislav took the men of Novgorod and Pskov to expeditions in the land of the Chud and together with them built mighty stone fortresses in Novgorod and Ladoga.

In the southern fringe, in Pereyaslavl, there was Yaropolk who marched from here to the Danube to retain the Danubian towns under Rus.

It was from Smolensk ruled by his son Vyacheslav that Monomakh marched against Vseslav's son Gleb (Vseslav of Polotsk had died in 1101).

In the east Yuri Dolgoruky who ruled the Rostov-Suzdal land waged a war against Volga Bulgaria.

Vladimir Volynsky was an important forepost in the west where Svyatopolk's son Yaroslav ruled at one time, but then Monomakh drove him out and put his son Andrei on the throne. Svyatopolk's son brought Poles, Czechs and Hungarians to Volyn but to no avail.

The princes of other branches were the true vassals of Vladimir II Monomakh: David of Chernigov and his nephew Vsevolod Olgovich obediently took part in expeditions under the leadership of the Grand Prince who retained the ability to lead troops to the age of 70.

Vasilko and Volodar Rostislavich, the heroes of the events of 1097, at one time served Kiev loyally, but sometimes took the side of Vladimir's enemies, taking advantage of the fact that their lands were far away from Kiev. But on the whole Kievan Rus at the time was a united state, and its frontiers outlined poetically in *The Lay of the Ruin* were not thought-up or exaggerated. Monomakh's son Mstislav (reigned 1125-1132) retained the unity for seven years after Vladimir's death; the state, however, fell apart immediately in 1132. That is why we should regard the rule of Mstislav Vladimirovich ("the Great", as the chronicle calls him) as a direct continuation of the rule of Monomakh, particularly since the son largely assisted his father in his lifetime.

It was during the rule of Mstislav that the Polotsk principality was incorporated into Kievan Rus in 1127; the principality had retained its independence up to that time.

Mstislav still managed to restrain the warring relatives, but with his death quarrels flared up again.

Further the chronicle describes how year after year certain princes and certain lands, one after the other, broke free of the authority of the Grand Prince. Kiev was losing its leading position; the age of feudal splits was beginning.

Being very particular about the literary recordings of his military and political successes and the shortcomings of his rivals, Vladimir Monomakh, upon becoming Grand Prince, could not avoid taking care of the state chronicle written under his predecessor Svyatopolk.

It was written by Nestor, a monk of the Kiev-Pechersky Monastery and a brilliant historian. His remarkable work *The Tale of Bygone Years*, embracing several centuries of Russian history, still remains our chief source in the study of Kievan Rus.

Of course, in describing the reign of Svyatopolk and his father Izyaslav, Nestor sought to smooth things over and present his whole branch of princes in the most favourable light. Vladimir Monomakh removed the chronicle from the rich and famous Pechersky Monastery and gave it to Sylvester, the Father-Superior of his court monastery. The latter revised some parts in 1116, but Monomakh was not satisfied with that and assigned his son Mstislav to supervise a new revision which was completed in 1118. The whole history of revisions and edition was ascertained in detail by Academician A. A. Shakhmatov.

As it was already pointed out above Mstislav fundamentally altered the introduction to Nestor's chronicle proceeding from the political situation in his day. He expunged from the old text much that had been written about the rise of the Rus state, as can be seen from surviving fragments, and instead inserted the biassed legend of the inviting of the Varangian princes to Novgorod.

The events of 1113 which ended in the inviting of a prince and additions made to the Russkaya Pravda were furnished with a distant chronological analogy which was intended to show that the Russian state was founded exactly in this way.

The literary inventions of Mstislav Vladimirovich have another aspect also explained by the urgent interests of Vladimir's rule. We remember how long, during two whole decades, Monomakh sought to win to his side powerful Kievan *boyars* who thought they could dispose of the Golden Throne of Grand Prince. Several times the Kievans dashed his hopes, leaving him to be a second-rate Pereyaslavl prince. The choosing of Monomakh could not eliminate all the collisions between the arrogant prince and the *boyars* who were used to wielding power. The arrival from Novgorod of Mstislav closely linked to the Novgorod *boyars* and merchants undoubtedly strengthened Vladimir's positions in Kiev.

In 1118 Vladimir and Mstislav jointly undertook an important step to consolidate relations between Novgorod and the Grand Prince—all the Novgorod *boyars* were summoned to the capital where they took the pledge of allegiance, and some, including *boyar* Stavr Gordyatich, a friend of Vladimir's younger years, were severely punished for selfwill, while others were left in Kiev. The alliance with the Novgorod *boyars*, subsequently strengthened by Mstislav's marriage to the daughter of a Novgorod *boyar*, was a countervailing force against the olygarchic tendency of the Kievan *boyars*.

Nestor's chronicle, quite justly assigning Kiev the leading part from the very beginning of Russian history and ascribing negative traits to the Varangians, a chronicle that relegated Novgorod to the extremely modest role of a minor northern trade factory, could not be to the liking of Mstislav who was related to all the Varangian royal houses and had lived in Novgorod for all of twenty years. Besides, in the 12th century Novgorod was no longer what it had been in the 9th century, now it was an enormous commercial city known throughout Europe. And the Varangians were no longer the robbers plundering North Russian, Estonian and Karelian lands, now they appeared in the role of merchants, and relations with them were peaceful, and, as we saw, Monomakh took care of foreign merchants both in word and in deed.

Supervising the revision of Nestor's chronicle Mstislav, perhaps, pushed Novgorod and the Varangians to the forefront at the beginning of the history of Rus to counter the haughty Kievan *boyars*. It was this trend that allowed the historians of later years to propose the Varangian, "Normanist" theory of the origin of the Russian state, and even link the very name Rus with the Varangians, regardless of the fact that the only reason for it was the gross and clumsy falsification of the Russian chronicle done under Monomakh with certain political aims.

The most complete code of feudal law, known as the Long Russkaya Pravda which embraced Yaroslav's deed to the Novgorod people of 1015, the Pravda of Yaroslav's Sons of the mid-11th century and the Rules of Vladimir Vsevolodich of 1113 was created on the eve of the final splitting up of Kievan Rus into separate independent principalities, i. e. in the reign of Monomakh or, more probably, Mstislav. This was not a simple compilation of variously dated documents. The editors revised them taking into account the demands of the 12th century.

In its final form the code's chronological accretions turned into thematical sections. The deed of 1015 was used to list punishments for crimes against the free men; the Pravda of Yaroslav's Sons provided material to defend the possessions and stewards of the prince. The Penalty Code determined the sustenance provided by the population for the prince's tax collectors all along their way; Vladimir's Rules, retaining its original name in this code, was concerned with foreign merchants, *zakups* and debtors. New articles developed the theme of protecting property, considered in detail issues of inheritance and the legal status of widows and daughters. The last section offers detailed legislation concerning *kholops* and fines for hiding other masters' *kholops*.

In the Long Pravda the articles which had put Varangians on an unequal footing were changed: this was quite in the spirit of Monomakh and particularly Mstislav.

The new code regulated the prince's share of fines more rigorously, so the collectors could not abuse their power. The attribute "princely" is mentioned here less frequently and *"boyar"* is occasionally added, but the rather indefinite word "master" is encountered dozens of times; it could refer equally to the prince and to any feudal lord.

The editors obviously sought to defend both the prince's domain and the *boyar's* estate. The legislation was acquiring a feudal-wide import, it defended the *boyars*, settled quarrels between *boyars* concerning fugitive *kholops*, protected the *boyars*' possessions from encroachments after the *boyar*'s death and to some extent restricted, or at least strictly fixed the prince's court incomes.

The late 11th and first thirty years of the 12th century was a time when the forces of all Rus were strained to the utmost due both to domestic troubles and foreign attacks and their rebuff. The united state could no longer exist in the form it had under Vladimir I or Yaroslav. It had to split into several independent principalities or be strengthened by some inner links; dynastic links destroyed the last semblance of unity. The split was rather untimely due to aggressive actions by Sharukan, Bonyak, Urusoba, Belduz, Tugortkan and many other Polovtsi khans. The latter, i. e. strengthening of inner bonds, required considerable effort and means, and was far from an easy task under the circumstances.

Vladimir Monomakh interests us precisely because

he used his indomitable energy, intelligence and undoubtable military talent to unite Rus which was falling apart and organise resistance against the Polovtsi. It is quite another matter that personally as the Pereyaslavl prince he had a vested interest in defending his possessions from Polovtsi raids, but objectively his policy of advancing into the steppe was important for all Rus. Uniting Pereyaslavl, Smolensk and Rostov in his hands and travelling almost every year 2,400 kilometres making rounds of his possessions he looked carefully after his tribute. Objectively this strengthened ties between several large areas of Rus and involved them in solving Russian-wide problems.

Vladimir is presented as a real living person. We know not only how he spent his day, how he arranged things in the palace, how he checked the guards, how he hunted and how he prayed or read the future in the Book of Psalms. We know that he was cruel at times—once together with the Polovtsi horde of the Chiteyeviches (just as Oleg) he captured Minsk, "laid waste to the town leaving neither slave nor beast in it". As we remember he could confiscate the personal property of a vanquished rival. Monomakh was undoubtedly ambitious and was completely unscrupulous in achieving supreme power. In addition, as we may judge from his literary works, he was hypocritical and knew how to present his actions demagogically in a favourable light to contemporaries and posterity.

The Chernigov period in the reign of Monomakh (1078-1094) saw him as an ordinary prince successfully ruling his land, taking part in quarrels and helping his powerful father, provoking the displeasure of the *boyars* as had Vsevolod himself.

The Pereyaslavl period (1094-1113) singled out Monomakh from among Russian princes as the organiser of active defence against the Polovtsi. At the time he sought to win over the Kievan *boyars*, posing as a more acceptable candidate to the post of Grand Prince than Svyatopolk Izyaslavich.

The epoch when Monomakh was Grand Prince (1113-1125) ends the tense 20-year-long struggle against the Polovtsi after which the existence of a united state temporarily lost its meaning and it continued to exist by inertia, because the head of the state had concentrated large military reserves in his hands and used them to maintain unity by force of arms. During the 20 years from the Kievan uprising of 1113 to Mstislav's death in 1132 the power of the Grand Prince was aimed at preventing quarrels and introducing order into the affairs of the feudal class as a whole by issuing a complete code of laws.

When Kievan Rus split into a score of independent principalities, all of them carried into the future the results of their united existence, embodied in *The Tale of Bygone Years*, the Long Russkaya Pravda, the Kievan cycle of *bylinas* where the image of Prince Vladimir combined both Vladimir I Svyatoslavich who saved Rus from the Pechenegs and Vladimir II Monomakh, a prince who ruled the whole of Rus and "wiped much sweat from his brow" for the Russian land in the successful struggle against the Polovtsi.

General Scheme of Russian Principalities in the 12th Century
(After I. A. Golubtsov)
Boundaries are approximate

THE RISE OF INDEPENDENT PRINCIPALITIES

Sovereign Feudal Lands

"And the entire Russian land fell apart," wrote an annalist in his chronicle under 1132 when, following the death of the Grand Prince of Kiev Mstislav, son of Monomakh, all the principalities broke free of Kiev and began to live independently. The princes of a score of sovereign states, equal and similar to West European kingdoms, set about "arranging their lands" which was reflected in the most interesting deeds-inventories of the 1130s laying down the duties of various towns and districts within the separate principalities. But to an even greater extent, the new age of feudal disunity was marked by lengthy and bloody quarrels between princes, wars to extend territorial possessions which a contemporary called "the ruin of the Russian land", because domestic wars were senseless from the viewpoint of the entire people and, in addition, weakened the defence of Rus in respect to foreign dangers (the Polovtsi, the Tatars and the German Crusaders).

The period of feudal splits lasted in Russia from the 12th to the end of the 15th century, but within that more than three-century lap there was a clear and grim watershed, the Tatar invasion (1237-1241), following which the natural course of Russian history was abruptly interrupted and sharply slowed down. The present book considers only the first phase frequently called as the pre-Mongolian period in the history of Rus.

The age of feudal disunity is filled with complicated and contradictory processes often leaving historians at a loss. The negative aspects of the age are particularly obvious: a clear weakening of the general military capacity facilitating foreign conquest, internecine wars and further splitting up of princes' possessions. In the mid-12th century there were 15 principalities, in the early 13th century, on the eve of Batu's invasion—about 50, and in the 14th century (when the process of feudal consolidation had already started), the number of major and minor principalities had reached about 250. The reason for such splitting was that princes divided their possessions between their sons; as a result the principalities grew smaller and weaker, which gave rise to ironic proverbs among contemporaries: "There's a prince in every single village in Rostov land" or "Seven princes have one warrior in Rostov land".

On the other hand, it is necessary to draw attention to the fact that the early phase in feudal disunity (before the invasion factor interfered in normal development) was marked not by a decline in culture as might have been expected, but on the contrary, an extensive growth of towns and a flourishing of Russian culture in all its manifestations in the 12th-early 13th centuries. It follows that the new political form, apparently, contributed (perhaps only initially) to progressive development.

Many things remain unclear in determining the causes of feudal disunity, and this also involves the issue of the time when it emerged.

Division of the principality among sons beginning with the testament of Yaroslav the Wise (1054) who assigned his sons to different Russian areas was regarded as one of the causes. But then we should begin with Vladimir I who distributed all his twelve sons throughout Rus as the Grand Prince's vicegerents. Quarrels between princes were considered to be another cause. But the internecine wars between princes-brothers also began in the time of Svyatoslav's sons: Yaropolk fought against Oleg, and the latter was killed; Vladimir fought against Yaropolk and hired Varangians to murder him. The second series of struggles lasting ten years (1015-1024) ended in the death of eight out of Vladimir's twelve sons.

Feuds between princes in Rus, as in European Middle Ages, accompanied (and to a considerable extent hindered) historical development, but did not fully determine one or another political form. The division of a prince's lands between the heirs which was felt beginning with the 13th century, deepened the split of principalities-states but was not a new phenomenon in the political life of Rus.

The subsistence economy is regarded as the economic basis of feudal division. This is correct as a statement of fact but cannot explain the causes of the transition from a united state to several independent principalities, because the subsistence economy prevailed both in primitive-tribal times, and when transitional forms (alliances of tribes) appeared, and on the enormous territory of Kievan Rus in the 9th-early 12th centuries. Moreover, it was precisely in the 12th century, simultaneously with the falling apart of Kievan Rus, that the original isolation of the economy was partly violated: town craftsmen increasingly began to work for the market, their products to a larger extent flowed to the village without, however, altering the economy's subsistence basis but creating fundamentally new contacts between town and the rising extensive village market.

The division of huge early feudal empires into a number of *de facto* (and occasionally *de jure*) sovereign principalities-kingdoms was an inevitable stage in the development of feudal society whether Kievan Rus in Eastern Europe or the Carolingian Empire in Central Europe (the latter was compared with Kievan Rus by Marx).

It is necessary to reject the interpretation of the age of feudal disunity as a time of regress, backward movement. Perhaps our usual academic terminology is not very appropriate: "Kievan Rus fell apart..." or "The powerful united state was split up into a number of principalities". The reader is immediately sorry that the wonderful state praised in the *bylinas* and the chronicles was "split up" or "fell apart": something whole ceased to exist and turned into splinters which, as the terminology implies, must be worse than the untouched whole.

If we take an attentive look at the meaning of the phenomena occurring in the 11th and 12th centuries, we would no doubt give preference to statements such as the following: "Kievan Rus was the kernel from which a spike of wheat with several new grains-principalities grew." Or "Kievan Rus was the mother who brought up many sons making up a new generation", and so on.

Paradoxical as it may seem at first glance, feudal disunity was not the result of differentiation but rather historical integration.

In dealing with feudal society built by the feudal class, we should be interested above all in the sum-total of feudalism's primary cells—landed estates, and their historical road. Unfortunately, they are insufficiently represented in the sources, but it is still possible to make some approximate estimates.

How many landed estates were there in Rus? There were 15 tribal alliances in the 9th and 10th centuries. An alliance was headed by the High Prince mentioned in the Treaty of 911, the tribal alliance (Vyatichians, Krivichians, Drevlyanians and others) corresponded in decimal terms to *tma*, i. e., 10,000. In later sources the same Russian word meant principality.

Each alliance consisted of approximately ten "thousands" headed by ordinary princes, the overall number of whom among the Eastern Slavs must have reached 150. Let us add 140 more tribal princes of the non-Slav peoples (by means of the same decimal estimate) who paid tribute to Rus. Thus we obtain more than two hundred minor princes in the 10th century. Each such prince may be regarded as a rising or existing feudal lord governing a certain district.

This does not end our estimates, however. Each "thousand" was divided into "hundreds", the latter being sets of several villages. The "hundred" was headed by the tribal elder or chief. This lower strata which ruled a village population of at least a hundred adult working men and warriors had every opportunity to become a feudal lord with an estate. So the number of landed estates of all ranks exceeded 3,000.

This should be supplemented by a certain number of seized land properties and benefices granted by the supreme prince and his warriors.

The *polyudye* we know so well had a considerable impact on this large number of potential and existing lords of estates. The formidable force of the Grand Prince's troops, making the rounds of the dependent tribes annually, intimidated everybody; they not only directly took away part of the harvest and products of hunting but also, since the Grand Prince himself was unable to reach the distant areas of all the tribes in the *polyudye* period, made the local nobility assist them. The princes ruling their lands as the pastor his flock had to organise the delivery of tribute by the tribal and "hundreds'" nobility to maintain peace.

The Kiev princes' *polyudye* stimulated intense alienation of the surplus product by the local nobility, and thereby stepped up the transition to feudal relations of domination and subordination in all the subdivisions of the decimal-tribal system. Back in the 9th and 10th centuries, when it was semi-feudal and semi-primitive, the local nobility faced the problem of organising mutual relations, relations with the supreme power and the peasant commune, the collective attack against which was stepped up by *polyudye*.

All this compelled the local *boyars* and minor princes to look for various measures to observe their own interests and fulfil Kiev's demands. It was here that they, in the language of the time, had "to take heed of the land order", i. e. their existence as a class. Vassal relations were established, and apparently there was a struggle everywhere for immunity, inheritance rights, etc.

The "turn" of princes in the second half of the 11th century, frequent change of princes in the capital towns which weakened the princes as a whole and ruined the local nobility must have heightened the concern of the landed *boyars* for their "land order". Local *boyars* needed consolidation to oppose the leap-frogging of the princes and their greed and, of course, the scale of all Kievan Rus did not conform to the possibilities of provincial feudal lords. The *boyars* of the 11th and 12th centuries could conceive of integration within a framework similar to the ancient tribal alliances, but not any larger.

The early feudal empire, a temporary political form

of the growth period, was particularly necessary to secure the initial feudalisation process in a setting of constant foreign dangers. Developed feudalism is marked by the need to arrange normal production along feudal lines in town and village. This did not require the enormous scale of Kievan Rus. The feudal economy was unable to unite effectively the enormous expanses of Kiev country, Polesye, Suzdal open land, Novgorod lake land, fertile Volyn area and Tmutarakan on the sea. The unity was insecure and partly due to external threat.

The time for a centralised state on this scale had not come yet; it occurred only on the threshold of capitalism, in the 18th century, when the scale of the European part of the Russian Empire approached that of Kievan Rus.

For young Russian feudalism of the 9th to 11th centuries, a united Kievan Rus was like a nursemaid who had brought up and safeguarded from misfortunes and calamities a whole family of Russian principalities. Within that state, the principalities had survived the two-century-long Pecheneg onslaught, invasions by Varangian forces, the prince's quarrels, and several wars with Polovtsi khans, and had grown to such an extent by the 12th century that they were able to begin an independent life.

The early feudal monarchy with the growing role played by the *boyars* led Russian lands onto the road of calm and normal development, overcoming both the swift Polovtsi and the no less swift princes seekers of fortune. The principal part of the ruling class—the many-thousand-strong landed (local) *boyars*—received in the last years of the existence of Kievan Rus the Long Russkaya Pravda, defining feudal rights. But the parchment kept in the archives of the Grand Prince did little to secure the *boyars*' rights in practice.

Even the power of the Grand Prince's tax collectors, swordsmen and warriors could not help the distant provincial *boyars* on the fringes of Kievan Rus.

The landed *boyars* of the 12th century needed their local power, capable of implementing the legal norms of Pravda and help the *boyar* in his conflict with the peasantry. A different scale of government, a different structure of the feudal body was required that would be better adapted to the needs of the basic class of feudal lords which was progressive for the time.

Such structure was offered by life itself; its scale and geographical limits were elaborated even prior to the rise of Kievan Rus. It was the tribal alliance, the principalities of the Krivichians, the Slovenians and Volynyanians listed by the chronicler and serving as geographical reference points for a long time to come.

Kievan Rus split into a score of independent principalities more or less coinciding with the score of ancient tribal alliances. The capitals of many of the largest principalities had in their time been centres of tribal alliances: Kiev was the centre of the Polyanians, Smolensk the Krivichians, Polotsk the Polochanians, Novgorod the Slovenians, Novgorod-Seversky the Severyanians. Tribal alliances were stable communities established over the centuries, and their geographical limits were set by natural landmarks.

During the early feudal empire feudal relations were established everywhere, the tribal nobility turned into *boyars*, towns developed and even began to rival Kiev. When the frequent, truly kaleidoscopic change of princes stopped, the local boyars could decide upon a certain prince asking him to stay and rule and not be tempted by the mirage of the Grand Prince's throne.

The princes settled down in the capital towns and founded their own local dynasties: the Olgovichi in Chernigov, the Izyaslavichi in Volyn, the Bryachislavichi in Polotsk, the Rostislavichi in Smolensk, the Yuryevichi in the Vladimir-Suzdal land and others. Each of the new principalities fully met the needs of the feudal lords—it was possible to ride from any 12th-century capital to the border of the principality in three days. Under the circumstances the sword of the ruler could quickly confirm the norms of the Russkaya Pravda.

Firmly settled down in some land, the prince had a different attitude to norms of exploitation and feudal duties, taking care, first, not to irritate the *boyars* who helped him become prince there, and second, to pass down his land to his children in good economic condition.

Each principality had its bishop, the princes issued their title deeds, a chronicle was written at the court of each prince, and various artistic and literary trends appeared in each capital town. This did not violate the unity of the ancient Rus, but enabled local creative energy to be realised. The crystallisation of independent principalities occurred against a background of rapid development of productive forces (mostly in the towns) and was largely due to that development. The growth of productive forces began long before the principalities were formed. The successes of the early feudal monarchy of Vladimir I enabled agriculture, the crafts, castle building, the towns and trade to develop particularly intensely.

However, in the second half of the 11th century, a time of instability and conflict, there occurred a break between the continuing development of the productive forces and the political form which temporarily slowed down the normal development of the feudal class. The revival of the feudal monarchy under Svyatopolk, Monomakh and Mstislav due to external causes, strengthened by the direct interference of the *boyars* somewhat improved the situation. However, despite the unquestionable personal talent of Vladimir Monomakh and his son, it turned out that the form of a single autocratic empire had already outlived itself, and for the superstructure to fully conform to the basis it was necessary to reduce the scale of the union, to bring state power closer to the feudal lords in localities, and to create several other centres on a par with Kiev.

Having selected the most suitable prince, the *boyars* of each principality had to be satisfied with their independence from Kiev and the share of participation in the governing of their land; they won this right by threatening their prince with broad opportunities that existed for a new choice—that is, that they could invite another prince to take his place from among his numerous relatives living in minor towns such as Klechsk, Vshchizh or Kursk.

As for the prince, he was satisfied because he was taking firm root; he knew that the *boyar* troops would support him (provided he suited the *boyars*); he realised that the *boyars* would oppose the tiresome and exhausting internecine struggles and would defend him (in their *boyar* interests) from rival princes; he also knew that under these favourable circumstances he would be able to pass his principality, landed estate and villages to his sons and the power of the prince in this land would remain in his family.

Feudal principalities of the 12th century were fully formed states. Their princes possessed all the rights of sovereign rulers; they "debated the land order and wars together with the *boyars*", i. e. ran domestic affairs and had the right to decide between war and peace, and to conclude any alliances, even with the Polovtsi. No one gave them those rights, the latter arose from life itself. Having become the first among equals, the Grand Prince of Kiev could not prevent Novgorod the Great from restricting (in effect, eliminating) the prince's power or to conclude a treaty with Riga, or Yuri Dolgoruky from conspiring with Vladimir of Galich against Kiev, or the Olgovichi in Chernigov from splitting their lands into landed estates or forming an alliance with the Polovtsi hordes.

The power of the Kiev prince had been left irrevocably in the past, as had a lot more in relations between princes. The former poorly observed dynastic seniority was replaced by new forms of vassal relations. Now a member of an elder branch frequently rode "by the stirrups" of the stronger prince who descended from a younger branch, and a brother called another brother "father", thus recognising him as his suzerain.

The restless tribe of princes was forced in the new circumstances to settle firmly on the land and occupy various rungs in the feudal ladder.

The highest rung was now taken not by the Kiev prince alone; in the 12th century the title of Grand Prince was applied to the Chernigov, the Vladimir and other princes. Their lands were not inferior to the West European kingdoms either in area or domestic structure. The process of their detachment from Kiev was completely in conformity with the general historical conditions.

The lands that were never threatened by the Polovtsi—Novgorod and Polotsk—separated sooner than the others. Each of these lands had its own trade route to Western Europe; this made them more independent, and in the 11th century they continually displayed separatist tendencies. In 1136 the townsfolk uprising ended in Novgorod turning into a feudal republic.

Following Novgorod and Polotsk, Galich, Volyn and Chernigov became independent. For Galich it was made easier by its location on the fringe, its remoteness from the main theatre of war against the Polovtsi and the proximity to Hungary and Poland from where it could expect support. Chernigov's separation was favoured by its links with the Southeast, Tmutarakan, and the Caucasus: when the Polovtsi appeared in the steppe, the Chernigov princes, more closely linked to the steppe world than the other, established friendly relations with the Polovtsi, intermingled with them and extensively took advantage of their support.

A new political map of Rus gradually came into being, with many centres. The Kievan land remained between the Dnepr and the Goryn, Polesye and the steppe.

Kiev itself was a major cultural centre in the 12th century, where new buildings were erected, literary works written, and the remarkable collection of articles of 1198 was compiled, which included a dozen chronicles of individual principalities. Kiev no longer ruled the Russian lands but retained the splendour of the "purple-mantled widow".

It was here, in Kiev, at the court of the "great and terrible" Svyatoslav that one of the best political poems of medieval Europe was written in 1185; this was *The Lay of Igor's Host*, presenting a popular programme of military alliance against the steppe nomads. The author angrily denounces princes' quarrels in past and present, and urges them to unite in an expedition to fight the Polovtsi.

Did the author of *The Lay* denounce the situation existing in his time—the existence of a dozen independent principalities on a par with Kiev? Was he attempting to revive the times of a united Kievan Rus about which he knew from the chronicles? Did he juxtapose his time to the past, condemning the new and idealising the old? There is nothing of the sort in *The Lay of Igor's Host*. The author was only concerned with the danger of scattered, separatist actions by the princes and pointed out the insistent need of uniting all the troops to set back a new Polovtsi attack in the 1170s and 1180s.

Without denouncing individual rulers but, on the contrary, showing full respect for their rights of grand princes, he praises the feudal lords, Russian "kings", turning first to the mighty Vsevolod Bolshoye Gnezdo (the Big Nest), then to the majestic Yaroslav Osmomysl of Galich, then to the descendents of the oracle Vseslav with the call to "stand fast for the Russian land".

After a short "honeymoon" of cohabitation between the boyars and the newly settled princes, a number of contradictions appeared already in the 1160s. On the whole, the *boyars* were inert and slow-moving, and mostly concerned with their own estates.

If the range of vision of the person under the tribal system was limited to a "microscopic world (commune) " within the boundaries of the tribal lands 10 to 15 kilometres from the settlement, the horizons of an ordinary *boyar* were extended to several such worlds, and no more. The landed estate was largely based on subsistence economy which could not contribute to a broader outlook. The chief tasks of the average feudal lord were, first, economic activities, i. e. alienation of part of the harvest in the few communes whose land the lord had proclaimed to be his own, and second, protection of the land of the estate from encroachments by equal but stronger feudal lords. The average feudal lord was an advocate of neither internecine struggles nor distant conquests. His cherished dream was to sit in his "family nest", in the landed estate that had belonged to his father and grandfather. If a prince called upon such *boyars*, their servants and *kholops* to set out for a war, the *boyars*, as the chronicler aptly put it, "going did not go", i. e. they pretended to be setting out but actually did not budge.

On the other pole of the feudal class there were the princes and the big land-owning nobility concentrated in the towns who generally got on well with the prince, but at times were displeased with his harsh temper. Those nobles frequently showed an interest in the affairs of neighbouring principalities, took part in quarrels, and undertook expeditions to foreign lands. Their outlook was broad, but their possibilities grew ever more limited.

The princes who founded new dynasties quickly took root in their principalities and sought to gain absolute power on the lands they had just obtained. However, only one generation of princes lived in friendship with the landed boyars who had invited them to rule. The sons of Yuri Dolgoruky, Izyaslav Mstislavich and Yaroslav Osmomysl fought for their lives against the *boyars* of their own land.

The princes needed a reliable support in that struggle, obedient forces ready to move anywhere at any time, "seeking glory for the prince and honour for themselves", i. e. regular troops living near the capital of the principality.

The degree to which feudal relations were developed was not the same as it had been under Vladimir I who supported enormous hosts of warriors: in the 12th century it was not necessary to keep all the reserves at court, the "warriors could be disbanded to live in the villages", i. e. provided with landed estates; this started the formation of the *dvoryane* or "boyar children" (as they were called in the 16th century) out of the prince's military servants. Many servants, the *ryadovichs* and *tiuns*, fulfilling economic, administrative and judicial functions in the principality, probably also received the prince's "benefices" and became tentative, temporary holders of the prince's land, and it is also possible that some of them received land in hereditary ownership for special services, thus entering the ranks of the *boyars*.

The lowest stratum of feudal lords—the *dvoryane* produced by the new conditions—was poor, economically unstable, greedy for land and peasants, but quite definite in their political sympathies and antipathies. From its very appearance the *dvoryane* were put in a position of rivalry in respect to the *boyars*, but as rivals they were much weaker, not sure of the future, and could fully provide for themselves only as long as they enjoyed the prince's favour; that was why in the eyes of the *dvoryane* of the 12th and 13th centuries, the prince was a clever helmsman, a reliable stronghold, a mighty oak standing firm in storms and winds, while the *boyars* were greedy and unscrupulous wrongdoers. "Better to live in bast-shoes at the prince's court than in morocco leather boots in the *boyar's* household," was how the situation was summed up by a prince's servant, Daniil the Exile.

In their quarrels with neighbouring states and everyday clashes with the *boyars* the princes could rely on "minors". At the end of the 11th century, Vsevolod Yaroslavich "favoured the junior warriors," and in the mid-12th century, a prince said directly that if the *boyars* disagreed with him, his *dvoryane* ("minors") would replace them and occupy theis position.

The largest reserve of mounted warriors similar in position to the *dvoryane* was at the disposal of the Kiev prince. On the enormous steppe expanses bordering on the forests of the Dnepr, Stugna and Ros, an area of 6,000 square kilometres, there lived nomad tribes of the Chernye Klobuki including the Torks, Berendei and Pechenegs, all settled there by the Kiev princes.

Thus the knightly 12th century pushed to the fore not only the *boyars* who were somewhat in the shade before, but also a variety of *dvoryane*, including palace servants, junior warriors and restless horsemen, the Torks and the Pechenegs.

The town was a particularly important element of medieval society, and it developed especially quickly at the time. The medieval town was a complex social body which cannot be described in terms of one trait.

The town was a fortress, a refuge for the *smerds* living in the vicinity in times of danger; it was a kind of collective castle belonging to the largest landowners in the area headed by the prince himself. A prominent place in the town was taken by the households of the *boyars* and princes.

In view of this, the town was a natural administrative centre of the area (or principality), the seat of the court and payments, the place where rulings were issued. It was the site of various crafts: the part of the

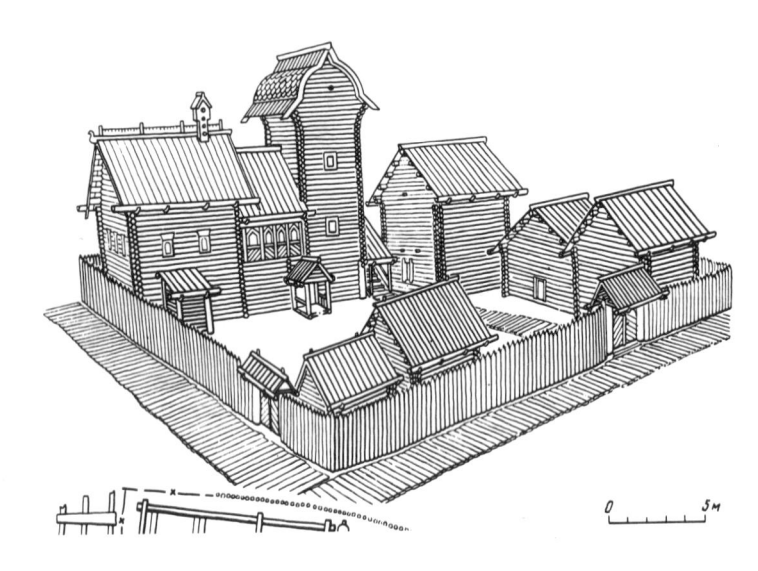

Novgorod homes. Workshop and chambers of Olisei Grechin, late 12th century

town where the craftsmen and merchants lived surrounded the aristocratic Kremlin in a wide ring. Everything needed for war and economic activities was produced in the town, as well as everything decorating the household or serving as a product for export. The town was also the most important (sometimes the only) place of trade in the area and a centre where supplies and wealth were accumulated; the town money-lenders spun their web in the poorest craftsmen's neighbourhoods lending their money at an exorbitantly high interest.

Another element of the feudal Middle Ages—the church—matured and developed in towns and in their immediate vicinity. In the 11th and 12th centuries the church not only became a means of ideological influence but also part of the ruling class. The church was headed by the Metropolitan appointed by the Grand Prince and approved by the council of bishops. The bishops ruled dioceses which coincided with the largest principalities in the 12th century and owned extensive landed estates, villages and towns.

If the Metropolitan partly corresponded to the Grand Prince (although he depended on the latter), and the bishop, to the prince of an individual land, the monasteries in the clerical sphere were somewhat like the *boyars*, becoming large landowners at the time. The land was not split up between heirs like the prince's and the *boyar*'s, and for that reason the former quickly grew rich. The bishops and the Fathers-Superior of big monasteries near towns were often rich and noble people closely related to court circles; they were given handsome gifts and were engaged in writing the prince's chronicle. The also carried on trade and money-lending operations.

All the links of the church organisation took an active part in political life, feudal strife and the class struggle. The Christian formula that slaves must submit to their masters was widely referred to in a context of acute social conflict.

All the listed parts of Russian feudal society were developing and constantly moving, forming various combinations of blocs and groups hostile to each other.

The princes created and supported the *dvoryane* to fight the *boyars*. The big *boyars* sought to restrict the prince's power by means of the *boyar duma* and simultaneously, with the same aim, applied pressure against the *dvoryane*, pushing them to the background. It is possible that the desire to create their own military strength and court servants compelled the *boyars* to revive the institution of *kholops* which is paid such extensive attention to in the Long Russkaya Pravda. As a result of the conflict between the *boyars* and the peasants falling into bondage the *zakups* were transferred to the fortified households of the feudal lords which follows from both the Russkaya Pravda and archaeological data concerning 12th-century households.

The towns were seething with revolt. The "black people" of the trade and craft strata suffered equally from the boyars and the merchants. The mighty princes became their unexpected allies ready to support any force that could be directed against the *boyars*. The craftsmen and the merchants formed "fraternities", "communities", and corporations

Prince's house (11th century). Chernigov. Reconstruction

similar to the craftsmen's and merchants' guilds in the West.

The class struggle flared up either in the form of direct uprisings or in the concealed form of anticlerical heresy.

In accordance with its specific historical development, each principality had its own balance of power, while its specific combination of the elements described above appeared on the surface. Thus the history of Vladimir-Suzdal Rus shows us the victory of the Grand Prince's authority over the landed aristocracy at the end of the 12th century.

At the beginning of the 13th century the irresistible process of feudal division of each principality became much more obvious, and smaller vassal principalities emerged.

The new Polovtsi onslaught of the 1170s and the 1180s only saw the beginning of this fatal process. The best people of Rus, such as the author of *The Lay of Igor's Host*, realised quite well that the threat from the steppes required complete unity of all forces, both within the separate lands and of large principalities between themselves.

Development of large economic regions, the overcoming of the isolation of the feudal subsistence economy, and the establishment of economic relations between town and village—all these progressive phenomena clearly apparent in Russian life even in the 12th and 13th centuries did not keep up with the catastrophic disintegration of the recently formed full-fledged and strong Russian principalities.

The Tatar-Mongol invasion of 1237-1241 found Rus as a flourishing, rich and civilised country which, however, was already afflicted by the decay of feudal disunity.

The heroic time of the joint struggle against the Pechenegs and the Polovtsi was in the past, there was no united military reserve, and Rus found itself in the same position as the other feudal states—the state of the Khorezm Shahs and the Georgian Kingdom—which were unable to put up resistance to the innumerable hordes of Genghis Khan and Batu.

The Tatar-Mongol invasion put an end to a major historical period in the life of the Russian people. That period was not forgotten, it was remembered as a time of prosperity, victories and brilliant international situation.

The Russian people derived confidence and faith in the future victory from the rich history of Kievan Rus and the Russian principalities of the 12th and 13th centuries.

Sources

Sources on the history of Russian feudal principalities of the 12th and 13th centuries are quite abundant and varied.

Of great interest are the 12th- and 13-century deeds that have come down to us, part of which reflect separate deals between feudal lords; some of them provide a broad picture of a whole principality such as the 1137 deed (rules) of Prince Svyatoslav Olgovich to the Novgorod bishopric which set the church's share in the prince's incomes and listed the villages and *pogosts* of the Novgorod land up to the Northern

Dvina and even to the Pinega and the upper reaches of the Vychegda.

Of even greater historical interest is the deed (rules) of Prince Rostislav Mstislavich to the Smolensk bishopric, providing a more detailed list of various feudal duties. This deed dates back to 1136 (previously it was incorrectly dated 1151).

A number of feudal affairs and relations was reflected in the birch-bark deeds of Novgorod the Great.

The birch-bark deeds proved to be an extremely important source when compared with chronicles, acts and the subsequent scribes' books.

Chronicles remain a most important historical source for the age of the existence in the 12th and 13th centuries of sovereign principalities which had separated from Kievan Rus. Both the general Russian chronicle and the chronicles of the individual principalities were studied from different angles in numerous works by Soviet historians and literary experts.

If the 10th century only left us the chronicle of Kiev, the 11th century, in which state chronicles continued to be written in Kiev, added the chronicle of Novgorod, frequently offering a different, local appraisal of events and personalities. The future *boyar* republic (beginning in 1136) obviously displayed an interest in the life of the town and took a negative view of some Kievan princes. It is possible that town elder Ostromir was the initiator of the first chronicle of Novgorod the Great.

In the 12th century, chronicle-writing ceased being a privilege of only these two cities and appeared in nearly every major feudal centre. The chronicles were continued in Kiev and Novgorod as well.

Literary works in various genres dating back to the 12th and early 13th centuries also serve as historical sources: special mention should be made of *The Lay of Igor's Host* and also two works (belonging to different authors) associated with the name of Daniil the Exile.

The Lay of Igor's Host was written in Kiev in 1185 by a person similar in his position in society, political views, dynastic sympathies and even language to Pyotr Borislavich, an annalist of the second half of the 12th century.

The author of *The Lay* was not only a poet but also a historian with a keen insight who looked back eight centuries from his time. This poem was imitated not only by contemporaries (the *Tale of the 1185 Expedition* in the chronicle) but also by authors of the early 13th century; it was quoted by the people of Pskov at the beginning of the 14th century; the poem about the victory over Mamai in the Kulikovo Battle was written in Moscow also in imitation of *The Lay*. Subsequently the manuscripts of *The Lay* existing in different parts of Rus were lost, and a collection including *The Lay of Igor's Host* was found in Yaroslavl only in 1792. The priceless manuscript was available for study during a mere two decades: in the Napoleonic fire of 1812 it perished in the flames in Moscow's Razgulyai. Fortunately, a copy had been made and, in addition, published in 1800.

Despite the fact that the original manuscript was studied by major scholars (Nikolai M. Karamzin, Czech scholar Josef Dobrovsky and many others), shortly after the manuscript was destroyed doubts arose as to the authenticity of *The Lay*. This poem displayed too high a level of culture. It was called a cluster of roses in a field of rye. But when the overall level of Russian culture of that period became better studied, *The Lay* proved to conform fully to that level. Doubts as to its authenticity were revived in the 20th century: during the German occupation of France, a book appeared whose author André Mazon attempted to prove that *The Lay* was an 18th-century forgery. But careful analysis of the poem's language and the Polovtsi words contained in it by experts of the Russian and Turkic languages showed that the Russian of *The Lay of Igor's Host* was the authentic language of the 12th century. As to the Polovtsi inclusions, that dead Turkic language became known to scholars (as a result of the discovery in Petrarch's library of a Latin-Polovtsi-Persian dictionary) in the middle of the 19th century after the original manuscript of *The Lay* had been destroyed.

The Lay of Igor's Host was written in connection

with the defeat of Seversky Prince Igor by the Polovtsi Khan Konchak in 1185 and Konchak's swift march against Kiev. There was discord among the princes who failed to support the Grand Prince of Kiev. The poem was directed against the princes' quarrels and disunity. Its author was an ardent patriot who was opposed not against the sovereign principalities existing at the time but against the confusion in the face of the common danger.

Two literary works are also very important for science: *A Word of Daniil the Exile* and *A Supplication of Daniil the Exile*, sometimes wrongly ascribed to one person.

Sources on the history of Russian principalities in the 12th and 13th centuries are numerous and varied. Their study and the obtaining of data from them on the economy, social structure, political order and social thinking are far from completed.

Unfortunately, this book could not include the history of all the score of Russian lands into which Kievan Rus fell apart in the 12th century. Only the most important principalities, which played a part in Russian-wide affairs are considered here (divided into two regions, the southern and most ancient part, and the northern part). The Pereyaslavl, Turov-Pinsk, Smolensk, and Ryazan principalities have remained outside this account.

South-Russian Principalities in the 12th and Early 13th Centuries

Kievan Principality

For the author of *The Lay of Igor's Host* the Kievan principality was the first among all Russian principalities. He views the contemporary world soberly, no longer regarding Kiev as the capital of Rus. The Grand Prince of Kiev does not order, but begs other princes to step into "the golden stirrup for the Russian land" and sometimes seems to ask, "Would you not fly here from afar to defend the paternal Golden Throne?" this is how he addressed Vsevolod the Big Nest.

The author of *The Lay* is highly respective of sovereign states, the princes of other lands, and does not propose to reshape the political map of Rus. In referring to unity, he has in mind something that was quite realistic at the time: a military alliance against the pagans, a single defence system and a common plan for a distant raid into the steppe. The author lays no claim to Kiev's hegemony, because a long time before, Kiev from the capital of Rus had turned into the capital of a principality and was on an equal footing with such towns as Galich, Chernigov, Vladimir-on-the-Klyazma, Novgorod and Smolensk. Kiev differed from these towns only in historic glory and the church centre of all Russian lands.

Before the mid-12th century the Kievan principality occupied a large area on the right bank of the Dnepr: almost the entire basin of the Pripyat and the basins of the Teterev, Irpen and Ros. It was only later that Pinsk and Turov separated from Kiev, and the lands to the west of the Goryn and Sluch passed to the Volyn land.

A specific feature of the Kievan principality was the large number of old *boyar* estates with fortified castles located in the old lands of the Polyanians south of Kiev. In order to defend these estates from the Polovtsi, large numbers of nomads expelled from the steppe by the Polovtsi—Torks, Pechenegs and Berendei united under the common name of Chernye Klobuki in the 12th century—had been settled along the Ros River in the 11th century. As if in anticipation of the future border *dvoryane* cavalry, they served on the border along the enormous steppe expanses between the Dnepr, the Stugna and the Ros. Towns arose along the Ros inhabited by the Chernye Klobuki nobility (Yuryev, Torchesk, Korsun, Dveren and others). Defending Rus against the Polovtsi, the Torks and the Berendei gradually adopted the Russian language, Russian culture and even the Russian epic *bylinas*.

First Kanev, then Torchesk, an enormous city with

two fortresses on the northern bank of the Ros, became the capital of the semi-autonomous Ros area.

The Chernye Klobuki played an important role in the political life of 12th-century Rus and frequently had a say in the choice of a prince. There were instances when the Chernye Klobuki proudly told a claimant to the Kievan throne: "O Prince, we have both good and evil for you," i. e. that his ascent to the Grand Prince's throne depended on them, border horsemen always ready to fight who lived two days away from the capital.

The Kievan principality had gone through a complicated period in the half-century separating *The Lay of Igor's Host* from the age of Monomakh.

In 1132, following the death of Mstislav the Great, principalities began to split away from Kiev one after another: first Yuri Dolgoruky came riding from Suzdal to seize the Pereyaslavl principality, then the neighbouring Chernigov Vsevolod Olgovich together with his friends the Polovtsi "went warring against villages and towns ... and hacked people with sabres; and they even reached Kiev...."

Novgorod freed itself completely from Kiev's authority. The Rostov-Suzdal land acted independently. Smolensk accepted princes of its own accord. Galich, Polotsk and Turov had their own princes. The range of vision of the Kievan chronicler was narrowed down to only Kiev-Chernigov conflicts in which, however, the Byzantine Prince, Hungarian troops, Berendei and Polovtsi took part.

Following the death of the unfortunate Yaropolk in 1139 the Kievan throne was ascended by the even more unlucky Vyacheslav who held out for only eight days—he was driven out by Vsevolod Olgovich, the son of Oleg.

The Kievan chronicle shows Vsevolod and his brothers as cunning, greedy and deceitful. The Grand Prince continuously engaged in intrigues, set his relatives at loggerheads, and granted remote lands to dangerous rivals to keep them further away from Kiev.

The attempt to return Novgorod failed, because the Novgorod people drove out Svyatoslav Olgovich "for his meanness" and "for his violence".

Igor and Svyatoslav, Vsevolod's brothers, were displeased with him, and all six years of his rule passed in a mutual struggle, oath-breaking, conspiracies and reconciliations. Major events included the stubborn struggle between Kiev and Galich in 1144-1146.

Vsevolod did not enjoy the sympathy of the Kievan *boyars*; this was reflected both in the chronicle and in the description V. N. Tatishchev derived from unknown sources: "This Grand Prince was a man of great stature and obesity, with little hair on his head, a wide beard, big eyes and a long nose. He was cunning in council and trial and could acquit or condemn anyone as he liked. He had many concubines and was better exercised in merriment than in quarrels. Through this the Kievans were heavily burdened by him. And when he died hardly anyone except loved wenches wept for him, but more rejoiced. But they feared even more troubles from Igor (his brother—*B. R.*) knowing his fierce and arrogant character."

The main hero of *The Lay of Igor's Host*, Svyatoslav of Kiev, was the son of this Vsevolod who died in 1146. Subsequent events clearly showed that the *boyars* were the chief force in the Kievan principality as well as in Novgorod and other lands at the time.

Vsevolod's successor, his brother Igor feared by the Kievans for his ferocity, was forced to pledge at the assembly that he would always heed their will. But the prince had hardly left the assembly to dine at home when the Kievans rushed to lay waste to the households of the officials and swordsmen they hated, which resembled the events of 1113.

The leaders of the Kievan *boyars*, head of the Thousand Uleb and Ivan Voitishich secretly sent envoys to Prince Izyaslav Mstislavich, grandson of Monomakh, in Pereyaslavl with an invitation to rule Kiev, and when Izyaslav appeared at the walls of the city, the *boyars* threw down their banner and surrendered to him as had been arranged. Igor was made a monk and sent to Pereyaslavl. A new phase in the struggle between the descendents of Monomakh and Oleg began.

The intelligent historian of the late 12th century Father-Superior Moses, who had at his disposal a whole library of chronicles from different principalities, compiled a description of these tempestuous years (1146-1154) consisting of excerpts from the personal chronicles of the warring princes. An interesting picture resulted: the same event was described from different viewpoints, one and the same deed was described by one chronicler as inspired by God and by another as the contrivances of the cunning devil.

The chronicler of Svyatoslav Olgovich carefully recorded all his master's economic affairs and after each victory of his enemies pedantically listed the number of steeds and mares driven away by the enemy, how many haystacks were burned, what utensils were taken from the church and how many jars of wine and honey were in the prince's cellar.

A particularly interesting man was the chronicler of Grand Prince Izyaslav Mstislavich (1146-1154). He knew military affairs very well, took part in expeditions and war councils and carried out diplomatic missions for his prince. Most probably he was the *boyar*, Pyotr Borislavich, head of the Kievan Thousand repeatedly mentioned in the chronicles. He seems to be writing the prince's political reports, trying to present the latter in the most favourable light, as a fine military leader, efficient ruler and caring suzerain. Praising his prince, he skilfully defames his enemies displaying outstanding literary talent.

In order to document his chronicles-reports intended, apparently, for influential prince and *boyar* circles, Pyotr Borislavich widely quoted from the real correspondence between his prince and other princes, the Kievans, the Hungarian King and the prince's vassals. He also drew on the minutes of princes' assemblies and diaries of expeditions. On only one occasion did he differ from his prince and began to denounce him—when Izyaslav went against the will of the Kievan *boyars*.

The rule of Izyaslav was filled with struggle against the Olgovichi and Yuri Dolgoruky who succeeded in twice occupying Kiev for short periods of time.

It was in the course of this struggle that Izyaslav's prisoner, Prince Igor Olgovich, was killed in Kiev according to a sentence passed by the popular assembly (in 1147).

Yuri Dolgoruky died in Kiev in 1157. It is supposed that the Suzdal prince whom Kievans disliked was poisoned.

The future heroes of *The Lay of Igor's Host*—Svyatoslav Vsevolodich and his cousin Igor Svyatoslavich—were repeatedly mentioned during these feuds of the mid-12th century. They were third-rate young princes taking part in battle in vanguard forces, ruling small towns and "pledging full submission on the cross" to the senior princes. Somewhat later they settled in larger cities: Svyatoslav in Chernigov in 1164 and Igor in Novgorod-Seversky. In 1180, not long before the events described in *The Lay* Svyatoslav had become the Kiev Grand Prince.

In view of the fact that Kiev was often the apple of discord among the princes, the Kievan *boyars* concluded a "contract" with the princes and introduced a peculiar system of duumvirate sustained through the entire second half of the 12th century. Izyaslav Mstislavich and his uncle Vyacheslav Vladimirovich, Svyatoslav Vsevolodich and Rurik Rostislavich were the duumirs, or co-rulers. According to this original system members of two hostile dynastic branches were simultaneously invited to Kiev and this served to some extent to avoid quarrels and establish a relative balance. One prince, considered to be the senior, lived in Kiev, while the other in Vyshgorod or Belgorod (he had the land at his disposal). They took part in expeditions jointly and carried on a coordinated diplomatic correspondence.

The foreign policy of the Kievan principality was occasionally determined by the interests of some prince but, in addition, there were two permanent fields of struggle requiring daily preparedness. The first and most important, of course, was the Polovtsi steppe where feudal khanates were formed in the second half of the 12th century, uniting individual tribes. Usually Kiev coordinated its defensive actions with Pereyaslavl (owned by the Rostov-Suzdal princes), and thereby a more or less single defence line was created along the Ros and the Sula. In view of this, the headquarters of the common defence passed from Belgorod to Kanev. The southern border outposts of the Kievan land, located in the 10th century along the Stugna and the

Sula, now moved down the Dnepr to the Orela and Sneporod-Samara.

The Vladimir-Suzdal principality was the second field of struggle. From the time of Yuri Dolgoruky the northeastern princes, who had not to wage a continual struggle against the Polovtsi due to their geographical position, directed their military forces to conquer Kiev using the border Pereyaslavl principality for the purpose. The haughty tone of the Vladimir chroniclers has sometimes deceived historians, and the latter thought that Kiev was in a state of complete decline at the time. Particular importance was attached to the expedition by Andrei Bogolyubsky, Yuri Dolgoruky's son, against Kiev in 1169.

Having witnessed the three-day plundering of the town by the victors, the Kievan chronicler described the events so colourfully that the impression of a terrible catastrophe was created. Actually Kiev continued to live the full-blooded life of the capital of a rich principality even after 1169. Churches were built in the town, the Russian-wide chronicle was written and *The Lay of Igor's Host* created, something quite incompatible with the idea of decline.

The Lay describes the Kiev Prince Svyatoslav Vsevolodich (1180-1194) as a talented military leader. His cousins, Igor and Vsevolod unleashed the evil which not long before Svyatoslav, their feudal suzerain, had managed to cope with:

> *The great, the terrible*
> *Svyatoslav of Kiev*
> *Like a thunderstorm,*
> *He struck men with awe,*
> *With his mighty hosts*
> *And his swords of steel*
> *He invaded the Polovets land,*
> *Trampled land lill and gully,*
> *Muddied lake and river,*
> *Scorched up stream and swamp.*
> *He swept from the sea-coast*
> *The pagan Kobyak,*
> *Like a whirlwind, he snatched him*
> *From the thick of the mighty iron Polovets host,*

*And Kobyak fell prostrate
In the city of Kiev,
In Svyatoslav's hall.
Now Germans, Venetians,
Now Greeks and Moravians
Sing the praises
Of Svyatoslav;
They blame Prince Igor...*

The poet was referring to the victorious expedition by joint Russian forces against Khan Kobyak in 1183.

As we said, Rurik Rostislavich was Svyatoslav's co-ruler; the former reigned in the Russian land from 1180 to 1202, and then became the Kiev Grand Prince for a certain time.

The Lay of Igor's Host is completely on the side of Svyatoslav Vsevolodich and says very little about Rurik. The chronicle, on the contrary, was in the sphere of Rurik's influence. That is why the activities of the duumvirs are presented by the sources in a biassed light. We know about conflicts and differences between them, but it is also known that at the end of the 12th century Kiev flourished and even attempted to play the part of a Russian-wide cultural centre. This is indicated by the 1198 chronicle of Father-Superior Moses, included together with the Galich 13th-century chronicle, in what is known as the Ipaty chronicle.

The Kievan collection of chronicles offers a broad picture of various Russian lands in the 12th century drawing on chronicles of individual principalities. It opens with *The Tale of Bygone Years* telling about the early history of Rus and ends with a rendering of the grandiloquent speech delivered by Moses on the occasion of a wall reinforcing the banks of the Dnepr being built at the expense of Prince Rurik. Having prepared his speech for collective performance in "one voice" (cantata?) the orator calls the Grand Prince tsar and his principality—"an autocratic power ... known not only in Russian parts, but also in distant lands overseas to the end of the Universe".

Following Svyatoslav's death, when Rurik began to rule in Kiev, his son-in-law Roman Mstislavich of Volyn (great-great-grandson of Monomakh) became his co-ruler of the Russian land, i. e. the southern Kievan lands, for a short while. The latter received the best lands with the towns Tripolye, Torchesk, Kanev and others, making up half the principality.

However, this "handsome district" aroused envy on the part of Vsevolod the Big Nest, the prince of the Suzdal land who wanted to be co-ruler of the Kievan area in some form. A long struggle ensued between Rurik, supporting Vsevolod, and the offended Roman of Volyn. As always, the Olgovichi, Poland and Galich were quickly involved in the quarrel. In the end Roman was supported by many towns and the Chernye Klobuki, and finally, in 1202, "the Kievans opened the gates for him".

In his first year as the Grand Prince Roman organised an expedition deep into the Polovtsi steppe, "captured Polovtsi *yurtas*, brought many prisoners and freed many Russian people from captivity. And there was great rejoicing in the Russian land".

Rurik was not long in reciprocating and on January 2, 1203, allied to the Olgovichi and "the whole Polovtsi land", and captured Kiev. "There was great misfortune in the Russian land; such evil had not befallen Kiev since the Baptism (988)... The lower town was taken and burned, the Hill was taken and the Cathedral of the Russian metropolitans—St Sophia; the Church of the Tithe was plundered ... the monasteries were robbed and the precious settings torn from all the icons..." Further on it is described how Rurik's allies, the Polovtsi, hacked to death all the elder monks, priests and nuns, and drove away to their camps the younger nuns, wives and daughters of the Kievans.

Obviously, Rurik did not hope to stay in Kiev since he laid waste to the town and departed for his own castle in Ovruch.

In the same year, after the joint expedition against the Polovtsi in Tripolye, Roman seized Rurik and forced all the members of his family into a monastery (including his own wife, Rurik's daughter). But Roman did not rule Kiev for long: in 1205 he was killed by the Poles when he rode too far from his men on a hunt in his western possessions.

Roman Mstislavich is described in poetical lines of

the chronicle which, unfortunately, have come down to us only in part. The author calls him the autocrat of all Rus, praises his wit and valour, particularly pointing out his struggle against the Polovtsi: "He attacked the Polovtsi like a lion; was mean as a lynx, annihilated them like a crocodile and crossed their land like an eagle, was brave as a wild ox." In connection with Roman's Polovtsi expeditions the chronicler recalls Vladimir Monomakh and his victorious struggle against the Polovtsi. There are *bylinas* mentioning Roman's name, too.

A chronicle drawn upon by V. N. Tatishchev which has not reached us reports extremely interesting things about Roman Mstislavich. Allegedly after Rurik and his family were forced into a monastery Roman proclaimed to all the Russian princes that he had dethroned his father-in-law for violating the treaty.

There follows an account of Roman's views concerning the political order of Rus in the 13th century: the Kiev prince had to "defend the Russian land from everywhere and keep good order in the brotherhood of Russian princes, so that they would not offend each other or ride into other lands and lay waste to them". Roman accused the junior princes attempting to capture Kiev without having the forces for its defence, and those princes who "bring the pagan Polovtsi".

Then comes a plan to elect the Kiev prince in case his predecessor has died. Six princes must vote: Suzdal, Chernigov, Galich, Smolensk, Polotsk and Ryazan; "the junior princes should not be involved in the elections". These six principalities must be passed down to the elder son and not divided into parts "so the Russian land not diminish in strength". Roman proposed that a council of princes be convened to introduce the new system.

It is difficult to say whether this is all true, but in 1203 such a system would have been a positive phenomenon were it possible to implement it. However, suffice it to recall the good intentions on the eve of the Lubech assembly in 1097, the commendable decisions adopted and the ensuing tragic events.

V. N. Tatishchev has retained descriptions of Roman and his rival Rurik:

"That Roman Mstislavich, Izyaslav's grandson, was not very tall but stout and of immense strength; he had a handsome face, dark eyes, long aquiline nose, dark short hair; he was wild in anger; when in a rage, he could not say a word for a long time; he revelled much with the lords, but was never drunk. He loved many wives, but not one possessed him. He was a brave warrior, cunning in leading troops... He spent his whole life in wars, scored many victories and was defeated only once".

Rurik Rostislavich was described in different terms. It is pointed out that he was Grand Prince for 37 years, but was expelled six times and "suffered much, finding peace nowhere. He relied on many and was possessed by wives, gave little attention to governing and his safety. His judges and rulers in towns caused the people much misfortune, and for that reason he was not loved by the people or honoured by princes."

It is obvious that these descriptions filled with medieval colour were written down by a Galich-Volyn or Kievan chronicler sympathising with Roman.

It is interesting to note that Roman was the last of the Russian princes sung by the *bylinas*; the written and the folk traditions coincided here, which happened very rarely; the people were very careful in choosing the heroes for their *bylinas*.

Roman Mstislavich and the lover of wisdom Rurik Rostislavich were the last outstanding figures in the list of 12th- and 13th-century Russian princes. They were followed by weak rulers who left no memories either in the chronicles or in folklore.

Internecine strife continued around Kiev even in the years when a new unprecedented danger—the Tatar-Mongol invasion—threatened Rus. In the time from the Battle on the Kalka in 1223 to Batu's arrival at the walls of Kiev in 1240, many princes were replaced and numerous battles fought for Kiev. In 1238, Kiev Prince Mikhail fled fearing the Tatars to Hungary, and in the fatal year of Batu's arrival he was collecting the tribute—wheat, honey, cattle and sheep—sacrificed to him in the principality of Daniil of Galich.

Kiev, the Mother of Russian cities, had an eventful history over several centuries, but in the last thirty years of its pre-Mongolian history the negative traits of feudal disunity became acutely pronounced, and the Kievan principality in effect fell apart into a number of lands.

The poet of *The Lay of Igor's Host* was unable to stop the historical process with his inspired verses.

Chernigov and Seversky Principalities

These two lands, just as the Kievan and Pereyaslavl principalities, constituted parts of the initial Rus which emerged in the 6th and 7th centuries but retained its name for much longer.

The Seversky land with Novgorod-on-the-Desna, Putivl, Rylsk, Kursk-on-the-Sejm and Donets (near the modern Kharkov) did not break away from the Chernigov land right away: this only happened in the 1140s and 1150s, but relations between them were felt subsequently as well. Both principalities were in the hands of the Olgovichi. Possibly Svyatoslav Vsevolodich of Kiev was regarded in *The Lay of Igor's Host* as the suzerain of both the Chernigov and the Seversky princes because he was grandson of Oleg Svyatoslavich, i. e. a direct Olgovich and the eldest among them. Before coming to Kiev, he was the Grand Prince of Chernigov and upon becoming the Kiev Prince frequently travelled to Chernigov, Lubech and the distant Karachev.

The lands of the Radimichians and the Vyatichians belonged to the Chernigov principality; the principality's northeastern frontier nearly reached Moscow. Even far-off Ryazan gravitated towards Chernigov in the dynastic and clerical respects.

Chernigov's southern links with the Polovtsi steppe and the coastal town of Tmutarakan were particularly important. The Chernigov-Seversky lands were open to the steppe along a large area; frontier defence lines were built there, and the nomads expelled by the new masters of the steppe, the Polovtsi, from good pasturelands, settled there.

The frontier principality of Kursk, having experienced numerous Polovtsi raids, became something like the later Cossack areas where constant dangers made the local people brave and experienced warriors. Vsevolod the Furious Bull tells Igor:

> *My men of Kursk*
> *Are all tried warriors,*
> *Born to the blare of bugles,*
> *Rocked beneath helmets,*
> *Nurtured at the point of the spear!*
> *The paths are known to them.*
> *The gullies are known to them.*
> *Their bows are taut,*
> *The quivers open,*
> *Their swords whetted,*
> *They scour the field*
> *Like hoary grey wolves,*
> *For themselves seeking honour,*
> *And for their prince—glory!*

Beginning with, "...the valiant Mstislav who slew Rededya before the Kassog host..." and up to the early 12th century, the Chernigov princes owned Tmutarakan (modern Taman), an ancient town at the Kerch Strait, then a major international port in which Greeks, Russians, Khazars, Armenians, Jews, and Adyge lived. Medieval geographers calculating the length of Black Sea routes frequently took Tmutarakan as one of the basic reference-points.

In the mid-12th century links between Tmutarakan and Chernigov were ruptured, and the sea port passed into the hands of the Polovtsi which explains Igor's desire

> *To seed the city of Tmutarakan,*
> *Or to drink a helmetful of Don water,*

i. e. revive the old routes to the Black Sea, the Caucasus, the Crimea and Byzantium. If Kiev held the road from the Greeks to the Varangians, Chernigov possessed its own ways to the Black Sea; only these ways were firmly closed by the nomad settlements of several Polovtsi tribes.

If the Kiev princes widely used the Chernye Klobuki

as a defence against the Polovtsi, the Chernigov Olgovichi had their own "pagans".

In the *Golden Word* Svyatoslav reproaches his brother Yaroslav of Chernigov for shunning the common expedition against the Polovtsi and defending only his own land:

> *No more do I see the power*
> *Of my mighty and wealthy brother,*
> *Yaroslav, lord of many hosts.*

It is possible that Svyatoslav refers to Turkic warriors who came to the Chernigov area long before, in the times of the great-grandfathers; or perhaps they were Turks-Bulgars or tribes brought from the Caucasus by Mstislav in the early 11th century.

The Chernigov principality in effect broke away from Kievan Rus back in the second half of the 11th century and was in vassal dependence on the Kiev prince only for a while under Monomakh. Unexpected proof of the fact that the Chernigov princes regarded themselves as equals of the Kiev princes was provided by excavations in the capital of the Golden Horde, Sarai, where archaeologists found an enormous silver toasting cup with the inscription: "This cup belongs to Grand Prince Volodimir Davydovich". Vladimir ruled in Chernigov together with his younger brother Izyaslav (died in 1161) in 1140-1151.

Its geographical position, the princes' relations of kinship and an old tradition of friendship with the nomads made the Chernigov principality a kind of wedge in the other Russian lands; Polovtsi invited by the Olgovichi often were in charge of affairs in the principality. This was the reason why Oleg Svyatoslavich, his sons Vsevolod and Svyatoslav were disliked; that was why his third son Igor Olgovich was killed in Kiev. Oleg's grandson, the hero of *The Lay of Igor's Host* was linked by friendship to none other than Konchak.

Igor was born in 1151 (during the famous expedition he was only 35) and became prince of Novgorod-Seversky in 1180. The same year, among the other Olgovichi and together with the Polovtsi, he marched deep into the Smolensk principality and fought against Davyd Rostislavich at Drutsk. Then, with Konchak and

White stone carved capitals (Boris and Gleb Cathedral, 12th century)

Kobyak, Igor moved against Kiev, and they made Svyatoslav Vsevolodich Grand Prince. At the head of the Polovtsi force Igor guarded the Dnepr, but Rurik Rostislavich, expelled by them from Kiev, defeated the Polovtsi. "Seeing that the Polovtsi [his allies] had been routed, Igor together with Konchak got on a ship and sailed to Gorodets at Chernigov".

Three years later Igor was fighting the Polovtsi, the same Konchak who had attacked Rus. During that expedition Igor quarrelled with Vladimir of Pereyaslavl about who should ride in the vanguard. It was not a matter of honour, just the vanguard seized more booty. In a fit of anger Vladimir turned his forces and laid waste to Igor's Seversky principality.

In 1183, Igor had an idea of undertaking separate

expeditions against the Polovtsi. The forces from Kiev, Pereyaslavl, Volyn and Galich defeated Kobyak and many other khans on the Orela River near the Dnepr rapids. The Olgovichi refused to take part in the expedition, but upon learning that the main Polovtsi forces had been defeated far from his principality Igor undertook an expedition together with his brother Vsevolod against the Polovtsi camps along the Merl River in the vicinity of the town of Donets. The expedition was successful.

The year 1185 set in: it was destined to be filled with major events. In early spring the "accursed and execrable" Konchak marched against Rus. The Chernigov princes maintained a policy of friendly neutrality and sent their *boyar* to Konchak.

Svyatoslav and Rurik defeated the Polovtsi on March 1 on the Khorol, seizing large amounts of arms and horses.

Igor Svyatoslavich of Seversk did not take part in the expedition, but the chronicler attempts to exonerate him by reporting that the messenger from Kiev was late in arriving and the warriors in the *boyar* duma dissuaded the prince from taking part in it.

In April, Svyatoslav won another victory over the Polovtsi: he captured some of their lands, many prisoners and horses.

Having learned about this, Igor allegedly told his vassals: "Are we not princes too? Let us set out on an expedition and win glory!" The expedition began on April 23. When the troops reached the Russian frontier on May 1, 1185, there was an eclipse of the sun, a fact widely used in *The Lay of Igor's Host* as a poetical image:

> *The sun then crossed*
> *His path with darkness.*
> *Night awakened the birds*
> *With its stormy moaning,*
> *The whistling of marmots arose.*

Igor ignored the warning sign of nature and moved into the steppe south of the Seversky Donets towards the Sea of Azov. On Friday May 10, the troops encountered the first Polovtsi nomad camp, the male population of which from the youngest to the oldest defended their carts but were defeated.

> *Early on a Friday* morn*
> *They trampled underfoot*
> *The pagan Polovets host,*
> *And scattering like arrows*
> *Over the field,*
> *They whirled away*
> *The fair Polovets maidens*
> *And with them gold and satin,*
> *And precious samite.*

On the next day Konchak arrived on the scene with the joint Polovtsi forces and surrounded "the brave nest of the Olgovichi". The terrible, three-day hand-to-hand fighting on the banks of the Kayala ended in the annihilation of the Russian forces: Igor and part of the princes and *boyars* were taken prisoner (it was hoped to obtain an enormous ransom for them), 15 men slipped out of the encirclement, and all the rest died

> *In that strange field*
> *In the heart of the Polovets land.*

> *Of gory wine they had scarce enough.*
> *There the brave Russians ended their feast.*
> *They made their kinsmen** drunken,*
> *And were laid low themselves*
> *For the Russian land.*

Following the victory, the Polovtsi forces marched against Rus in three directions: on the now defenceless principality of Igor and Vsevolod the Furious Bull, on Pereyaslavl and on Kiev itself where Konchak was drawn by recollections of Khan Bonyak who beat the Golden Gates of Kiev with his sabre.

At the time of Igor's expedition the Kiev prince Svyatoslav was peacefully making the rounds of his old Chernigov domain, and only when his boats reached Chernigov did Belovolod Prosovich, a participant in

---

* 10 May 1185.

** This refers to the fact that the children of Igor and Konchak had intermarried.

Igor's expedition who had slipped out of the encirclement, arrive there. The latter told the prince about the tragedy on the banks of the Kayala and that Igor's defeat had "opened the gates to the Russian land".

It is to be assumed that after the Grand Prince received the news from Chernigov, he did not continue his sailing down the winding Desna but, recalling the fast riding of Monomakh, rushed on horseback to Kiev, riding "from the morning to the evening service".

Then Prince Svyatoslav "sent messengers to his sons and all the princes, and they gathered in Kiev, and from there marched towards Kanev (on the Dnepr south of Kiev.— *B. R.*)."

The defence strategy was as follows: Svyatoslav's son Oleg with military chief Tudor were immediately dispatched to repulse the Polovtsi on the banks of the Sejm (in the principality of the imprisoned Igor), Dolgoruky's grandson Vladimir Glebovich was already fighting them in Pereyaslavl, while the main forces undertook to defend the Russian land on the Dnepr at Kanev, guarding the Ros and the strategically important Zarubintsy Ford linking Pereyaslavl with the Dnepr's left bank.

The entire summer of 1185 was spent in holding back the Polovtsi; the chronicle reports the arrival of troops from Smolensk, exchange of messengers with Pereyaslavl and Tripolye, and concealed manoeuvres by the Polovtsi attempting to find weak spots in the 600-kilometre Russian defence hastily organised under the worst of circumstances.

The need for fresh forces and participation by the distant principalities was pressing all summer. But perhaps even greater was the need for all Russian forces to unite, even if only those which were already under the banners of the Kiev prince.

The princes were reluctant to march against the Polovtsi. Yaroslav of Chernigov gathered his forces but failed to move in order to join Svyatoslav, for which he was denounced in *The Golden Word*. Davyd Rostislavich of Smolensk brought his troops to the Kiev land but deployed them in the rear of the Kievan forces at Tripolye, in the mouth of the Stugna, and refused to move any further.

At this time Konchak laid siege to Pereyaslavl; Vladimir barely managed to save himself during the battle, wounded by three spears. He sent Svyatoslav a message: "The Polovtsi have attacked me, help me!"

Svyatoslav and his co-ruler Rurik Rostislavich could not set out immediately because Davyd of Smolensk was preparing to return home. The Smolensk troops held a *veche* and declared that they had agreed to go only to Kiev, that there was no battle now, and they couldn't go any further: "We are tired".

While this disgraceful haggling was taking place with Davyd, Konchak attacked Rimov on the Sula and the Polovtsi killed or took captive all its inhabitants.

Svyatoslav and Rurik who were coming to the rescue of Pereyaslavl and Rimov were delayed due to the treachery of Davyd. The chronicle directly links the destruction of Rimov to the delay of the Russian forces "waiting for David and his Smolensk troops".

When the joint forces of Svyatoslav and Rurik crossed the Dnepr to repel Konchak, Davyd left Tripolye and turned his Smolensk troops back.

The author of *The Lay of Igor's Host* wrote about that with great bitterness. He recalled the princes of old, regretted the fact that old Vladimir (Svyatoslavich) could not be left here, on the Kievan hills, for ever, and described how Rus was moaning, because now there were "the banners of Rurik and next to them of his brother Davyd, but their *bunchuks** swayed differently and their spears sang differently".

The poet's recalling of the old Vladimir was not accidental: it was here, on the banks of the Stugna, where the Smolensk prince betrayed his own people, that two centuries earlier Vladimir Svyatoslavich set up a chain of his warriors' strongholds. The author's thoughts return insistently to this river: when he describes Igor's flight and recalls the death of the brother of Monomakh in 1093 in the waters of the Stugna, he juxtaposes that river to the Donets which "has gently rocked a prince upon its waves".

It is quite possible that the author of *The Lay of*

---

* A short shaft with a horsetail fastened to it, a symbol of authority.— *Tr.*

Igor's Host was with his prince Svyatoslav and spent the grim summer of 1185 in the Russian camp between Kanev and Tripolye, between the Ros and the Stugna and witnessed the arrival of messengers from besieged towns, the sending of messengers for fresh assistance, and the cowardly betrayal of his own people by Davyd at Tripolye on the Stugna.

Was it not in these months of confrontation, when it was necessary to find particularly inspired words to unite the Russian forces, to involve the princes of distant lands in the defence, that the remarkable *Golden Word* was written? This part of *The Lay of Igor's Host* ending with the words about Davyd's betrayal does not contain a single fact going chronologically beyond those few months when Svyatoslav and Rurik defended the Dnepr from the Vitichev to the Zarubintsy Ford, from Tripolye to Kanev. Was it not from the unassailable Kanev heights filled with the pagan spirit of olden times that the author of *The Lay of Igor's Host* observed Rus and the steppe at the time?

He deeply deplored the death of Russians and could not refrain from bitter reproaches against Igor. The latter was not the hero of the work, but only a pretext to write a patriotic appeal whose importance was not exhausted by the events of 1185.

In the spring of 1186, Igor fled from captivity: he wandered through the undergrowth of small streams for 11 days and finally appeared at home.

In 1199, following Yaroslav's death, Igor Svyatoslavich became the Grand Prince of Chernigov and in his last years instituted his own chronicle which was included in the Kievan collection. In it Igor was shown as a very noble prince, always thinking about the well-being of the Russian land. Igor died in 1202. Finding themselves in the Galich land, his sons pursued a harsh anti-*boyar* policy, killed about 500 noble *boyars* and were finally hanged in Galich in 1208.

The subsequent history of the Chernigov-Seversky land is of little interest. Increased in number, the Olgovichi continued to participate eagerly in quarrels and gradually divided the land into several small estates. In 1234, Chernigov underwent a gruelling siege by the forces of Daniil of Galich: "There was a fierce battle at Chernigov. The Tatars set up battering rams and also catapulted enormous stones into the town. Each stone could be lifted only by four men."

In 1239, together with all of the left Dnepr bank Chernigov was taken by the Tatar forces.

Galich-Volyn Lands

The author of *The Lay of Igor's Host* addresses the Galich prince Yaroslav Vladimirovich with the most solemn appeal, describing with his usual brilliance, in a few lines, the importance of the rich and flourishing Galich principality:

> *O Osmomysl-Yaroslav of Galich!*
> *You are seated high*
> *On your throne of gold,*
> *Pressing back the Hungarian hills*
> *With your iron hosts,*
> *Barring the way to the king,*
> *Making fast the gates to the Danube,*
> *Casting hosts over the clouds,*
> *Sitting in judgement*
> *Even as far as the Danube!*
> *Your thunder spreads*
> *Through many a land;*
> *You unlock the gates of Kiev,*
> *You shoot at sultans*
> *Beyond your domains*
> *From your father's golden throne.*
> *Shoot, o lord, at Konchak,*
> *The pagan slave,*
> *Stand up for the Russian land,*
> *Avenge the wounds of Igor,*
> *Svyatoslav's bold son!*

The reader or the listener of the poem could clearly imagine the powerful West Russian state stretching from the Carpathians and the Danube to Kiev and the Polovtsi "sultans". The lines correctly reflected the rapid rise of the Galich principality which emerged from the estates of exiled or fugitive minor princes of the 11th and early 12th centuries.

It was less pompously but also respectfully that the author of *The Lay* hailed the princes of Volyn and particularly the famous Roman Mstislavich who soars

> *High, in your daring,*
> *To valiant deeds,*
> *As falcons hovering*
> *Upon the winds...*

He and his vassals wear "iron breastplates and Latin helmets", and his troops in armour defeat both Polovtsi and Lithuanians. The poem also mentions second-rate princes of the small Lutsk principality, Ingvar and Vsevolod Yaroslavich. The poet calls on all the Volyn princes, the great-great-grandsons of Monomakh:

> *You shoot at sultans*
> *Beyond your domains...*
> *Stand up for the Russian land,*
> *Avenge the wounds of Igor...*

In the history of the Galich-Volyn lands the historical centre shifted: in ancient times the Dulebs union of tribes was in the first place; it was located between the East and the West Slav tribes in the foothills of the Carpathians and the Volyn area. In the 6th century that union of tribes was destroyed by the Avars, the old tribal centre of Volyn deteriorated, and the centre of these lands shifted to Vladimir Volynsky named after Vladimir Svyatoslavich who paid much attention to the Russian western lands.

Fertile soil, a moderate climate and relative security from the nomads made the abundant land of Volyn one of the richest in Rus. Feudal relations developed intensely here and a strong *boyar* section emerged. Such towns as Peremyshl, Lutsk, Terebovl, Cherven, Kholm, Berestye, Drogichin appeared here. But in the 12th century Galich developed from a small provincial town belonging to a minor prince into the capital of a major principality which arose on the lands of Slav tribes such as the White Croatians, Tivertsi and Ulichians. At the turn of the 13th century Roman Mstislavich of Volyn united the Galich land and Volyn into one large state which survived the Tatar-Mongol invasion and existed until the 14th century. Such, in outline, is the history of Western Rus.

The West Russian princes, for example, Vasilko Rostislavich of Terebovl blinded after the Lubech assembly, his brother Volodar, Prince of Peremyshl, and their enemy Davyd Igorevich of Volyn, and then of Dorogobuzh attempted to pursue an independent policy in respect to Kiev back in the 11th century.

The last minor *izgoi* prince was Ivan Rostislavich Berladnik, Volodar's grandson, whose biography was filled with various adventures. In 1144 he was prince of the small Zvenigorod (north of Galich), and the inhabitants of Galich, taking advantage of the fact that their prince Vladimir Volodarevich was far away on a hunting expedition, invited Ivan and "brought him into Galich as their prince". When Vladimir besieged Galich, the whole town sided with Ivan, but finally the latter was forced to flee to the Danube, while Vladimir "killed many people" after entering the town. It was on the Danube that Ivan Rostislavich received the nickname of Berladnik after the Berlad area.

In 1156, we see Berladnik in the Vyatichian forests where he served the unfortunate ally of Yuri Dolgoruky Svyatoslav Olgovich for 12 grivnas of gold and 200 grivnas of silver. Then he passed to the other camp, and an interest was shown to him both by Yuri Dolgoruky who managed to seize and imprison him in Suzdal and, on the other end of Rus, in Galich, by Yaroslav Osmomysl who remembered Berladnik's quarrel with his father. Yaroslav sent a force to Yuri in order to deliver Berladnik to Galich and execute him. But along the way the warriors of Chernigov Prince Izyaslav Davydovich unexpectedly recaptured Berladnik from the Suzdal troops, and he was saved from a cruel death.

In 1158, he left the hospitable Izyaslav who had become the Grand Prince of Kiev, because the diplomatic conflict concerning him had assumed a European scale: envoys arrived in Kiev from Galich, Chernigov, Hungary and Poland demanding that Izyaslav surrender Ivan Berladnik to them. Berladnik returned to the Danube again, and at the head of a 6,000-strong force set out from there against the Galich principality. The *smerds* openly sided with him, but his Polovtsi allies abandoned him because he refused to allow them to lay waste to the Russian towns. Izyaslav and the Olgovichi supported Berladnik and undertook an expedition against Galich, but Yaroslav's Galich troops acted more quickly, appeared at Kiev and soon captured the capital. Yaroslav opened the gates of Kiev and Izyaslav and Berladnik fled to Vyr and Vshchizh.

Three years later, in 1161, Ivan Berladnik turned up in Byzantium and died in Salonika; the princes who hated him reached him even there: "Others say he died of poison." The prince for whom the townsfolk of Galich fought to the last during a whole month, who did not permit the Polovtsi to plunder Rus, and to whom "the *smerds* came running despite all obstacles" was, of course, an interesting figure for the 12th century but he was dealt with in the chronicle which was hostile to him in a much too biassed way.

From 1118 on, the Volyn principality was retained by the descendents of Monomakh and his son Mstislav. It was from here that Izyaslav Mstislavich marched at lightning speed, covering 100 kilometres a day, and burst into feasting Belgorod and into Kiev, and it was here that he returned (to his Vladimir Volynsky) after being defeated in battle, when the Kievans and the Chernye Klobuki told him: "You are our prince only when you are strong, but now it is not your time. Go hence!" The grandchildren of Izyaslav Mstislavich divided the land into five portions, and at the time of *The Lay of Igor's Host* they had not united yet.

The Galich principality arose next to the Volyn principality in the mid-12th century, and immediately became a rival of its neighbour and even of Kiev. The first Galich prince, Vladimir Volodarevich (1141-1153), as we just saw, had to overcome the resistance of the minor princes such as Ivan Berladnik and also the townsfolk and local *boyars* who had become firmly entrenched here during the time of the existence of small estates.

The entire subsequent history of the Galich-Volyn lands constitutes a struggle between centripetal and

Decorative tiles (12th and 13th centuries). Galich

centrifugal trends. The former trend was represented by the princes of Vladimir Volynsky and Galich, the latter by the minor princes and rich *boyars* accustomed to independence.

The flourishing of the Galich principality was connected with Yaroslav Osmomysl (1153-1187), son of Vladimir Volodarevich, Ivan Berladnik's cousin, praised in *The Lay of Igor's Host*.

We come upon him in the chronicle under the following circumstances: the Kievan prince Izyaslav Mstislavich, who fought a great deal against Vladimir Volodarevich and defeated him in 1152 with the help of the Hungarian king, sent his *boyar* Pyotr Borislavich (apparently the author of the prince's chronicle) to Galich in early 1153. The envoy reminded prince Vladimir of some promises he made kissing a cross. Poking fun at the envoy, the prince of Galich asked: "Did I kiss this little cross?" and finally he drove out the Kievan *boyar* and his retinue: "You've talked your fill, now get thee hence!"

The envoy left the prince the deeds concerning the kissing of the cross and departed from the town on unfed horses. A new war was declared. Once again it was necessary for the royal troops from the west, the Kiev troops from the east and the Volynian troops from the north to ride towards Galich, once again the prince of Galich had to send messengers to the other end of Rus requesting assistance from Yuri Dolgoruky, a relative and erstwhile ally. But a messenger rode along the Kievan road and returned Pyotr Borislavich. In Galich the envoy saw servants in black apparel descending from the palace; the young prince Yaroslav in a black mantle and black monk's headdress was seated on the golden throne, and a guard of knights stood over the coffin of the old prince Vladimir Volodarevich.

Yaroslav hurried to smooth over the imprudent arrogance of his father and showed complete submission to the grand prince: "Accept me like your son Mstislav. Let Mstislav ride at your stirrup on one side, and I with my warriors at your other stirrup." With this vivid acknowledgement of feudal dependence Yaroslav let the envoy go, "but in his heart he had quite different intentions," adds the chronicler. And the war broke out in the same year.

Prince Yaroslav did not take part in battle, the *boyars* told him: "You are still young, O Prince, return to the town." Apparently the *boyars* simply did not trust the prince who had only recently pledged allegiance to Kiev. Yaroslav Osmomysl was not really that young: three years before the battle he married Olga, the daughter of Yuri Dolgoruky.

The *boyars* subsequently continued to interfere energetically in the prince's affairs. In 1159, when the conflict because of Ivan Berladnik had not ended yet, the inhabitants of Galich persistently showed their sympathy for the Danubian gallant and turned to his patron, the prince of Kiev Izyaslav Davydovich, with the proposal for him to march against their own town: "As soon as your banners will appear, we will abandon Yaroslav!"

A new conflict between Yaroslav and the *boyars* occurred in 1173. Princess Olga with her son Vladimir fled from her husband together with prominent *boyars* of Galich to Poland. Vladimir Yaroslavich cadged the town of Cherven from his father's rival; the town was strategically convenient both for relations with Poland and for attacking his father. It was the Vladimir of Galich, the drunkard and carouser, so colourfully presented in Borodin's opera *Prince Igor*. Igor Svyatoslavich was married to Vladimir's sister Yefrosinia, daughter of Yaroslav Osmomysl (Yaroslavna). The quarrel with his father was due to the fact that Yaroslav had a mistress named Nastasia and her son Oleg was given preference by Yaroslav over his legitimate son Vladimir.

For eight months Olga Yuryevna and Vladimir remained abroad, but finally received a letter from the *boyars* of Galich, requesting them to return to Galich and promising to take into custody her husband. The promise was kept with a vengeance: Yaroslav Osmomysl was arrested, his friends and allies the Polovtsi were hacked to death, and his mistress Nastasya burned at the stake. "Having kindled a big bonfire, the Galicians burned her and threw her son into prison. The prince was forced to pledge that he would live with the legitimate princess. It was left at that." The seemingly familial conflict was settled for the time being in this peculiar medieval manner.

Next year Vladimir escaped to Volyn, but having hired Poles for 3,000 grivnas, Yaroslav Osmomysl burned down two Volyn towns and demanded that his insurgent son be turned over to him; Vladimir fled to the Ros area and hoped to hide in Suzdal. Seeking refuge, Vladimir of Galich visited many towns and finally came to his sister in Putivl where he lived for several years until Igor reconciled him with his father.

Yaroslav Osmomysl died in autumn 1187, leaving as his heir not Vladimir but Oleg, son of Nastasya. Immediately "there was a great insurgency in the Galich land". The *boyars* drove out Oleg and gave the throne to Vladimir, but that prince also failed to satisfy them. "Vladimir was prince in the Galich land. He was much taken to drinking and did not seek the advice of his *boyars*." The latter fact was decisive: if the prince ignored the *boyar duma*, if he failed to listen to the noblemen, he was a bad prince and all sorts of negative traits were ascribed to him in the chronicle: that he drank a lot, that he "abducted a priest's wife and made her his wife", and that in the town, "taking a fancy to someone's wife or daughter, he would take her by force".

Knowing that the *boyars* of Galich were displeased with Vladimir, Roman Mstislavich of Volyn suggested that they drive out Vladimir and accept him, Roman. The *boyars* repeated what they had done with their prince's father: they threatened to kill Vladimir's mistress: "We don't want to bow to a priest's wife; we seek to kill her!" Having taken his gold, silver, the "priest's wife" and her two sons, Vladimir of Galich fled to Hungary.

Roman Mstislavich did not rule in Galich for long: he was driven out by the Hungarian king who, taking advantage of superior forces, put not Vladimir who sought his assistance on the throne in Galich but his son Andrei. Vladimir was imprisoned in the tower of a Hungarian castle.

The *boyars* of Galich continued to look for a prince to their liking: Roman was reported to say that "the Galicians want to make me their prince", but *boyar* envoys invited Rostislav Ivanovich, Berladnik's son. Pinning his hopes on the Galician *boyars*, Rostislav appeared at the wall of Galich with a small force in 1188. "The *boyars* of Galich were not of one mind", and Rostislav's force was surrounded by the Hungarians and part of the Galicians; the prince himself was thrown off his horse.

When Hungarians carried the badly wounded prince to Galich, the townsfolk "were outraged and sought to recapture him from the Hungarians and restore him as prince. The Hungarians learned of this, and applied a poison to his wounds".

In 1189, Vladimir of Galich escaped from prison. He cut up a tent which was on the top of his tower, twisted ropes and climbed down; two supporters helped him reach Germany. The Emperor Friederich Barbarossa agreed (provided he received 2,000 grivnas a year) to help the fugitive to regain Galich. With the support of Germany and Poland, Vladimir began to rule in his "fatherland and grandfatherland".

Roman Mstislavich became the prince of Galich after Vladimir's death in 1199; Volyn and Galich were united under one prince, forming a large and strong state equal to the major European kingdoms. When Roman also seized Kiev, he ruled an enormous and compact piece of Russian lands equal to The Holy Roman Empire of Friederich Barbarossa. Forced to pledge allegiance to the *boyars* of Galich when he ascended the throne, Roman subsequently acted harshly, provoking the displeasure of the *boyars*.

We may conclude from hints in the chronicle that Roman was concerned with enriching his prince's domain and settled war prisoners on his land. It was with Roman that refuge was sought by the Byzantine Emperor Alexius III Angelus driven out of Constantinople in 1204 by the crusaders who in Christian Byzantine found a better place to loot than the distant Holy Land.

The short rule of the victorious Roman in Galich, Kiev and Vladimir Volynsky, when he was called the autocrat of All Rus, strengthened the position of the West Russian lands and laid the ground for their further rise.

In addition to the colourful and dramatic external history of principalities and princes described above, this age is of great interest to us for the aggravated relations between princes and *boyars*, clearly evident from the time of Yaroslav Osmomysl. If we disregard the element of personal gain and interest which undoubtedly determined many actions of the princes, it is to be acknowledged that the policy they pursued of concentrating land, weakening the estates of minor princes and consolidating the central power was certainly progressive, because it coincided with popular interests. In implementing this policy, the princes relied on broad sections of townsfolk and the petty feudal lords they had bred themselves, who depended completely on the prince.

The actions of the *boyars* aimed against the princes resulted in a struggle between *boyar* parties and in further quarrels, and made the state helpless in the face of external dangers. In view of the intertwining of princes' interests and the relative balance of power in the larger principalities, particular importance was attached to the question of succession to the throne.

Many princes' marriages were concluded then with political aims between children of from five to eight years old. When the young prince grew up and entered into a marriage, he obtained not the kin he would have chosen for himself in his own interest but that which was in the interests of his parents decades earlier. The *boyars* could take advantage of these contradictions, and the prince had the only option of passing the throne to his illegitimate son. This, perhaps, explains the persistence with which Svyatopolk Izyaslavich, Yaroslav Osmomysl and his son Vladimir clung to their mistresses and illegitimate sons.

Yaroslav's father-in-law was the powerful and audacious Yuri Dolgoruky who sought to interfere in the affairs of other lands. Vladimir's father-in-law was the "great and harsh" Svyatoslav Vsevolodich of Kiev. While Vladimir and his mistress and children were in Hungary imprisoned in a tower, his father-in-law decided to take Galich, the home of his son-in-law, for himself personally (1189). Such actions could easily be presented as defence of the lawful rights of his daughter and grandchildren who were already supported by the *boyars* of Galich.

When the *boyars* burned Nastasia, drove out her son Oleg or rebelled against the priest's wife of Vladimir, it was not because of the prince's moral behaviour but because they did not want to permit the prince to be the autocratic ruler under the circumstances, so the *boyars* would not lose their allies within the prince's family and the strong support of the crowned parents of the princess.

A similar struggle between the prince's and the king's power and the feudal lords who sought to isolate themselves in their estates was carried on at the time in Western Europe, in the Georgian Kingdom, in the Orient and in a number of Russian principalities.

It should not be concluded that all the *boyars* without exception fought against the prince. Considerable and influential *boyar* circles actively contributed to strengthening the prince's power and making it more effective.

In Galich-Volyn Rus the struggle between various feudal elements reached its peak during the rule of Roman's son who was as famous as his father, Daniil of Galich (circa 1201-circa 1264). Daniil was orphaned at the age of four, and his whole childhood and younger years passed against a backdrop of quarrels and fierce feudal struggle. The *boyars* of Vladimir Volynsky wanted Roman's widow princess and children to remain on the throne, while the *boyars* of Galich invited the sons of Igor Svyatoslavich of Chernigov. The princess was forced to flee; servant Miroslav carried Daniil in his arms through an underground passage out of the town. The refugees found asylum in Poland.

The Galich-Volyn principality broke up into several allotments enabling Hungary to conquer it. The Igorevich princes lacking any support in these lands attempted to hold on to them by means of repressions: they killed about five hundred *boyars* but only strengthened the followers of the exiled widow princess. In 1211 the *boyars* pompously crowned the boy Daniil in the cathedral of Galich. As to the Igorevichi, they were hanged "for the sake of vengeance".

The *boyars* of Galich very soon decided to get rid of the princess who had powerful intercessors in Poland. The court chronicler of Daniil of Galich who wrote much later recalled the following: the *boyars* drove the princess out of the town; Daniil wept as he accompannied her, refusing to part. An official grabbed the reins of Daniil's horse; Daniil whipped out his sword and began to swing it, until his mother took the weapon away from him.

It is possible that the chronicler deliberately described the event as an epigraph to Daniil's subsequent actions aimed against the *boyars*. *Boyar* Vladislav began to rule Galich, provoking the indignation of the feudal elite: "It is not proper for a *boyar* to rule Galich." After this the Galich land underwent foreign intervention again.

It was only in 1221, with the support of his father-in-law, Mstislav the Bold, that Daniil managed to become prince of Vladimir, and he finally gained power over Galich only in 1234.

The major landowners of Galich behaved like princes: "Althought the *boyars* of Galich called Daniil their prince, they ruled all the lands themselves." Such was *boyar* Dobroslav who even ran the prince's domain; such was Sudislav whose castle was a stronghold filled with supplies and arms and capable of fighting the prince.

The *boyars* first invited Daniil, then conspired against him. Thus, in 1230, "there was treason among the godless *boyars* of Galich". The *boyars* decided to set fire to the palace during a session of the *boyar duma* and to kill the prince. Daniil's brother Vasilko managed to prevent the conspiracy. Then one of the *boyars* invited the princes to dinner in the Vyshensky castle; Daniil's friend, the head of a Thousand, warned him: "The feast is being prepared for sinister purpose: you will be killed." Daniil arrested 28 *boyars* but did not dare execute them. Some time later, when Daniil "was making merry at a feast, one of the godless *boyars* splashed wine from his cup in his face. And the prince tolerated it."

It was necessary to find a new, more reliable basis for support. And Daniil convened a *veche* of "servicemen", junior members of the prince's troops who were prototypes of the later *dvoryane*. The warriors supported their prince: "We are loyal to God and you, our master!" and head of a Hundred Mikula offered Daniil advice which determined the prince's subsequent policy: "O master! Without swatting bees, you can't eat honey!"

Following the battle on the Kalka (before which Daniil went to look at the "unheard-of host", and after which, wounded, he "turned back his mount"), feudal quarrels and strife continued to sap the strength of the rich Russian lands, while the centripetal forces represented here by Daniil were insufficiently strong and unable to resist both internal and external enemies. Continually relying on either Poland or Hungary, the *boyar* opposition failed to turn the Galich-Volyn land into a *boyar* republic but considerably weakened the principality. No wonder that in passing to this pre-Tatar period in the life of one of the most developed and cultured Russian principalities, the chronicler noted bitterly: "Let us begin the story of innumerable wars and harsh expeditions, many quarrels and frequent uprisings and many insurgencies..."

The towns of the Galich-Volyn land—Galich, Vladimir, Peremyshl, Lutsk, Lvov, Danilov, Berestye (Brest) and others—were rich, populous and beautiful. The local craftsmen and architects worked there, surrounding the towns with strong walls and building elegant houses. They liked stone-carving here, also popular in Vladimir-Suzdal Rus; we know about a "cunning" Avdei skilled in stone-carving. We also know about the wise scholar Timofei who denounced the cruelty of the conquerors with his allegories and about the proud singer Mitus. We have at our disposal the exceptionally detailed and beautiful 13th-century Galich chronicle which is an historical biography of Prince Daniil.

Trade routes of European importance leading to Crakow, Prague, Regensburg and Gdansk passed through the Galich-Volyn land. Drogichin on the Bug was a kind of Russian-wide customs house: we have found there many thousands of trade seals dating back to the 11th-13th centuries belonging to many Russian princes. The well-known medieval map of the world compiled by the *Arabian* geographer Idrisi in Palermo in about 1154 shows such towns as Galich, Belgorod Dneprovsky, Lutsk and Peremyshl. The outlet to the Danube and the Black Sea linked the land to the Byzantine world. No wonder at different times emperors who suffered defeat in the empire sought refuge in Galich and were granted towns here "in consolation" (Andronicus, Alexius III).

Archaeological excavations in the Galich-Volyn towns give us a fair idea of the life of the simple townsfolk and the generally high cultural level in this southwestern Russian land. Not only neighbouring lands but also Germany, Rome, France and Byzantium displayed an interest in the affairs of Galich-Volyn Rus.

North-Russian Principalities in the 12th and Early 13th Centuries

Polotsk Principality

The Polotsk land was situated in the northwest of Rus; a most important route to Western Europe along the Western Dvina, a shorter way than the one through Novgorod, passed through the Polotsk land. The Lithuanian-Lettish tribes were the neighbours of Polotsk along a large stretch; when tribal warrior parties began to grow in the lands of Lithuania, Latgale and Zemgale, they occasionally raided the Russian areas along the Dvina. However, these expeditions bore no comparison to the devastating raids by the Polovtsi against the southern lands. Relations with neighbours were mostly peaceful.

An avid admirer of Vseslav of Polotsk, one of the leading participants in the Kiev uprising of 1068, the author of *The Lay of Igor's Host* speaks a lot about the Polotsk land and its princes, and even somewhat idealises them. He divided all the Russian princes into two unequal parts: Yaroslav's grandsons and Vseslav's grandsons; if in dynastic terms the Polotsk princes indeed constituted a separate branch, in size of possessions these two parts were very unequal.

The Polotsk land had all the conditions for gaining independence; in this respect it resembled Novgorod. It also had a strong local *boyar* section; a rich trade centre Polotsk had a town *veche* and, in addition, a sort of brotherhoods which fought against the prince (these were merchant unions of the guild type similar to that at the church of St John the Baptist at Opoki in Novgorod).

The power of the prince was not particularly strong here, and the Polotsk land broke up into several more or less independent apanages: Minsk, Vitebsk, Drutsk, Izyaslavl, Strezhev and others.

The long rule of Prince Vseslav Bryachislavich (1044-1101) was a brilliant age in the life of the Polotsk land. That energetic prince waged war against

Novgorod, Pskov, and the Yaroslavichi. Vladimir Monomakh who undertook expeditions against the Polotsk land from 1084 to 1119, was one of Vseslav's enemies. The princes of Kiev managed to establish their control over the land, which lived its isolated life, only for a short while.

The last decisive attempt to subordinate it was made by Mstislav the Great in 1127; he sent troops from all parts of Rus—from Volyn, Kursk, Novgorod and the Torkic area along the Ros. Each force had a specified itinerary, and all of them were told to invade the Polotsk principality on one and the same day. Seeing himself surrounded, the prince of Polotsk Bryachislav "was frightened and did not know whether to flee here or there". Two years later some princes of Polotsk were exiled to Byzantium where they stayed for ten years.

In 1132, Polotsk chose a prince independently and, simultaneously with the other lands of Rus, broke free of the authority of Kiev. But as opposed to neighbouring principalities, the Polotsk land immediately split into small parts; Minsk (Menesk) was the first to be ruled by its own, independent prince. The townsfolk of Polotsk and Drutsk took an active part in the struggle between Rogvolod Borisovich of Polotsk and Rostislav Glebovich of Minsk in 1158.

Vseslav's grandson Rogvolod turned out to be a prince without a principality; his kin "took away his possessions and estate". The people of Drutsk invited him: when he was near Drutsk with his warriors, 300 people of Drutsk and Polotsk went on boats to welcome the prince solemnly. Then there was "an enormous rebellion" in Polotsk. The townsfolk and *boyars* of Polotsk invited Rogvolod to be grand prince, and they wanted to lure Rostislav, instigator of the quarrels, to a feast on June 29, but the cautious prince wore chain mail under his clothes "and they did not dare attack him". On the next day an uprising against Rostislav's *boyars* began; it ended in Rogvolod becoming prince. But the attempts of the new prince of Polotsk to unite all the apanages failed. After one of the unsuccessful expeditions during which many men of Polotsk died, Rogvolod did not return to his capital, and the people of Polotsk once again had their way, like the people of Kiev or Novgorod: they invited Prince Vseslav Vasilkovich (1161-1186) from Vitebsk in 1162.

The Lay of Igor's Host refers to the brother of that Vseslav, Prince Izyaslav Vasilkovich who fought against the Lithuanian feudal lords.

Attacks by Lithuanian warriors had become possible as a result of the weakening of the Polotsk land and its splitting into numerous parts.

The author of *The Lay* reproaches all the princes both descendents of Yaroslav and of Vseslav:

> *O you, offspring of Yaroslav,*
> *And you, grandsons of Vseslav!*
> *Lower your banners, and sheathe*
> *Your blunted swords!*
> *Far, far have you fled*
> *From your forefathers' fame!*
> *For your brawls have brought the pagans*
> *Into the Russian land,*
> *Into Vseslav's realm!*
> *For your feuds have brought violence*
> *From the Polovets land!*

The poet compares the threat of Lithuanian raids (which naturally increased in connection with feudalisation) to the Polovtsi danger, and believes that Russians should submit to the existing order, because the cause of their defeats lay in their own quarrels and alliances with pagans.

The author ends the sad story of Polotsk quarrels, as a result of which warriors were left lying in the field and "birds have clothed ... warriors with their wings, the beasts have licked up their blood", with historical recollections, rapturously praising Vseslav the Oracle.

The history of the Polotsk land in the late 12th and early 13th centuries is not very well known to us. Unfortunately, the Polotsk chronicle belonging at the beginning of the 18th century to architect P. M. Yeropkin was destroyed. Tatishchev copied from it the most interesting description of 1217 events in Polotsk.

The wife of Prince Boris Davydovich Svyatokhna pursued complicated intrigues against stepsons Vasilko and Vyachko; she attempted to poison them, sent forged letters, had them sent away, and finally, with the help of her retinue, began to destroy Polotsk *boyars* hostile to her. The head of a Thousand, town elder and housekeeper were murdered. The *veche* bell rang, and the inhabitants of Polotsk, enraged because the princess's followers "were ruining the town and robbing the folk", came out against the plotter Svyatokhna Kazimirovna, and she was put under guard.

Tatishchev held the chronicle in his hands for a short time only. He noted that it had a lot written "about Polotsk, Vitebsk and other ... princes; only I had no time to copy it all and later could no longer get it".

Prince Vyachko subsequently fell in battle against the German knights, defending the Russian and Estonian lands.

The Polotsk-Vitebsk-Minsk land, which later, in the 14th century, became the basis of the Byelorussian people, possessed a peculiar culture and interesting history, but feudal disunity, at an advanced stage at that time, prevented it from retaining its unity and political independence; in the 13th century the Polotsk, Vitebsk, Drutsk and Minsk principalities were absorbed by a new feudal aggregation—the Lithuanian Grand Principality in which, however, Russian laws were in force and the Russian language prevailed.

Smolensk Principality

Addressing all the Russian princes in turn, the author of *The Lay of Igor's Host* expresses his appeal to the Smolensk princes, the two Rostislavich brothers, with great reserve and rather mysteriously:

> *O you furious Rurik,*
> *And you, o David!*
> *Were not those warriors yours*
> *Whose gilded helmets*

Sailed a sea of blood?
Are those brave men-at-arms not yours
That roar like wild bulls
Wounded with swords of tempered steel
In the unknown plains?
O lords, step into
Your golden stirrups,
Avenge the wrong of these days,
Stand up for the Russian land,
Avenge the wounds of Igor,
Svyatoslav's bold son!

As we know, Rurik was co-ruler and potential rival of the prince of Kiev. The poet failed to mention either of these facts, he merely put Rurik on a par with the Smolensk prince, the treacherous and egoistic Davyd. Without considering all the finer points of hostility between the princes which either spilled over in boundless ferocity as it happened in 1180 or was concealed as in 1185, the author of *The Lay of Igor's Host* reminded the princes of Smolensk that both of them had suffered sorely from the Polovtsi steel sabres.

In 1177, during "mermaid week", i. e. in June, the Polovtsi descended upon Rus; Rurik and Davyd were sent against them, but "Davyd did not arrive in time, and the brothers quarrelled badly": this was when their spears began "to sing differently". The Polovtsi inflicted a crushing defeat on all the Russian forces. Svyatoslav Vsevolodich demanded a trial over Davyd and to deprive him of his principality. Those were the long-past and rather unpleasant events which the author of *The Lay* was reminding Davyd of, and also Rurik, as if making him responsible for his brother.

The ten-year-long conflict between Svyatoslav and Davyd made the lines of the poem devoted to the prince of Smolensk quite inadequate and courteously unfriendly. It is very difficult to determine what Smolensk was like at the time.

The Smolensk principality was the ancient land of the Krivichians, in the middle of the Slav area, surrounded on all sides by Russian regions. Important highways to Western Europe and Byzantium passed through Smolensk: the route up the Dnepr ended at

Smolensk; it led further through a system of portages to the Western Dvina (to Polotsk and the Baltic Sea) and the Lovat and then to Novgorod.

The importance of Smolensk for trade was reflected in a treaty concluded in 1229 between Smolensk, on the one hand, and Riga and Gotland, on the other.

Emerging as a separate land from time to time in the 11th century, the Smolensk principality broke away from Rus under Rostislav Mstislavich (1127-1159), grandson of Monomakh and father of the above-mentioned Rurik and Davyd.

Smolensk was very conveniently linked to Kiev: a fleet of any size could be sent down the Dnepr, and only eight days later it would be at the walls of the capital. The only obstacle along the way was Lubech which belonged to the Chernigov princes, but it was eliminated. Taking advantage of the absence of the Chernigov forces in 1147, Rostislav burned Lubech and, as he wrote to his brother, "did much evil to the Olgovichi". After that only "dog-breeders and Polovtsi" lived in Lubech, and the Smolensk boats could sail to Kiev unhindered.

It may be that the important strategic proximity to Kiev, combined with the safety of the Smolensk principality from the Polovtsi, was the reason why nearly all the princes of Smolensk—Rostislav Mstislavich and his sons Roman and Rurik, grandson Mstislav Romanovich and Mstislav's son Roman—reigned in Kiev at some point.

We have a most interesting document from the time of Rostislav which describes in great detail the prince's and the feudal owner's domains. It is a deed from Rostislav Mstislavich to Bishop Manuil on the occasion of the founding of the Smolensk diocese in about 1137. The deed lists the prince's sources of revenue from various towns of the Smolensk principality, a tenth of which (tithe) was transferred to the church. The 36 items included taxes totalling 4,000 grivnas; these were tribute, sales, *polyudye*, trade tax, customs duties, visitor's payments and others. The bishop also received land with feudally dependent population (*izgois, bortniks* and others) and revenues from church courts considering particular crimes.

At the time all the established principalities founded independent dioceses and introduced bishops' ownership rights. This occurred on the initiative of the princes who ruled certain lands and sought to strengthen their position by means of the church's support.

The growth of the church's wealth and estates in the 1130s provoked sharp criticism. A well-known author of the mid-12th century, who was made Metropolitan by the will of a Kiev prince Kliment Smolyatich, wrote that he did not belong to those "who acquire a house to a house, a village to another village, attract all sorts of people, seize beehives, ploughed land and plots of land cleared of forest". It is possible that in answering a Smolensk priest, Kliment was hinting at the bishop of Smolensk, his political adversary Manuil. Kliment himself was accused, curiously, of being too interested, as a Christian, in "heathen philosophers" such as Homer, Aristotle and Plato.

In the rule of Davyd Rostislavich (1180-1197), already known to us for his unfamous deeds in the south, there were conflicts between the prince and the townsfolk of Smolensk. Prince Davyd had had numerous troubles with the Novgorod people in his youth, and they had "shown him the road" on many occasions. In 1186, soon after he returned from near Tripolye, "a conflict arose in Smolensk between Prince Davyd and the townsfolk. Many heads of the Smolensk *boyars* rolled". The chronicle does not report what the contradictions between the prince and the *boyars* were about.

The Smolensk principality was no exception from the rule: the struggle between the *boyars* and the princes was carried on in a very acute form in other lands as well.

In the early 13th century, highly interesting events occurred in Smolensk, partly revealing the internal social and ideological life of the Russian medieval town: abbots and priests held a public trial over a certain priest Abraham. Some wanted to imprison him, others "to nail him to the wall and burn him", still others to drown him. The abbots and priests "roared like bulls" and wanted, "were it possible, to eat him alive".

What had Abraham done to infuriate the clergy of

Smolensk to such an extent? It turns out that at one of the fringe monasteries in Smolensk, Abraham read books to the inhabitants and "explained" them to everyone—"common folk and noblemen, slaves and free men and craftsmen". It was said everywhere in Smolensk that "he had drawn the whole town to his side". He was accused of reading "deepgoing books" of which one is mentioned in his life story. It is what is known as *The Golden Chain*, collected sayings and words aimed occasionally against the "bad pastors", priests and monks. Anti-clerical ideas appeared in these collections, similar to the teaching of the West European Waldenses persecuted by the Catholic Church. Similar conditions in Rus gave rise to similar ideas.

The open preaching of ideas dangerous to the church, the preaching addressed to slaves and craftsmen provoked the hatred of the clergy. The prince saved Abraham from execution, but the church attached such importance to the heretic prophet that warriors (apparently the bishop's) were posted on the roads leading to Smolensk to stop Abraham's followers; they acted with such vigour that some people coming to see Abraham "were robbed".

Hidden from all external enemies inside the Russian lands, the Smolensk principality retained its independence for a long time, until the beginning of the 15th century. During the campaign of 1237-1238, Batu headed for Smolensk but then bypassed it. Apparently, a rich trading town, with dozens of supurb buildings and surrounded by strong walls, proved to be an impregnable obstacle for troops exhausted by the resistance of the Russian towns, so the bloodthirsty conqueror did not dare appear at its walls.

Novgorod the Great

The history of Novgorod is, first, the history of one of the largest cities in medieval Europe, and second, the history of a boundless country stretching from the Baltic to the Arctic Ocean and the Urals. When much

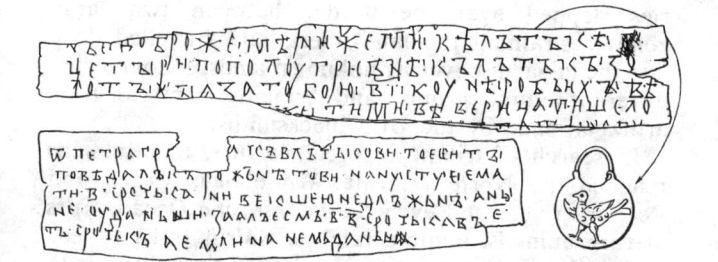

Birch-bark letters (12th century)

later, under Ivan III, the Novgorod lands were annexed by the centralised Moscow state, the latter's area was doubled.

The origins of Novgorod take us back to the distant time of Slav colonisation of the north when the Slav land-tillers settled little by little the entire zone of deciduous forests in Eastern Europe.

For a long time the Slavs did not settle beyond the large area suitable for land cultivation, which reached the lakes Chudskoye and Ilmen and the Kostroma lands along the Volga River. Further north lay the endless coniferous taiga sparcely settled by the local non-Slav population, which lived here from neolithic times and mostly engaged in hunting and fishing. The tribal settlements of the Slavs did not reach this harsh zone.

It was here, on the border between two large areas, where for hundreds of kilometres Slav and Finno-Ugric tribes—the ancestors of the Estonians, Karelians, Veps, Komi, and Udmurts—came into contact, that a chain of ancient towns emerged along the edge of the most northern lands to be reached by the Slavs during the tribal age. Such were Pskov and Izborsk near Lake Chudskoye, Novgorod on Lake Ilmen, Beloozero and Rostov. Some appeared in the pre-state period and were centres of tribal alliances, others were founded as "new towns", northern factories of Kievan Rus. It is probable that Novgorod, founded in the 9th century, was among the latter. The rise of the state in the south changed the fate of these frontier towns. The Russian warriors in the 9th and 10th centu-

303

ries stepped over the border between two large zones restraining the land-tillers, and travelled deep into the taiga, discovering unknown lands, encountering different ethnic groups and bringing back to Kiev artifacts made by the Ural blacksmiths.

In search of tribute in precious furs, the Russians reached the Nortern Dvina, White Sea, Mezen and Pechora rivers and even the very Arctic Ocean. Furs of rare animals, hunting falcons, walrus tusks ("dear fish tooth") was what attracted the Russian pioneers to the taiga and Polar tundra where the "going was extremely hard" and where "they travelled through impassable places. And there were no days or nights, but always darkness [Polar night]".

The chronicle contains a long list of tribes and peoples paying tribute to Rus from olden times; more than half were linked to Novgorod or subsequently were included among its possessions: Chud, Noroma, Yam, Chud Zavolochskaya, Perm, Pechora, and Yugra. As was the case in colonisation of the Rostov-Suzdal land, relations with these tribes were relatively peaceful. Conflicts occasionally arising between the Novgorod people and local population were of a local nature and never ended in cruel mass-scale killings and annihilation of the people as was the case in the early and late Middle Ages in other countries (from Europe to America inclusively). The local nobility gradually intermingled with the Russian *boyars* (for example, Chudin and his brother Tuky).

The far-off northern dealings of Novgorod were described in an interesting account to the chronicler by *boyar* Gyuryata Rogovich at the end of the 11th century:

"I sent my warrior to Pechora—these are people paying tribute to Novgorod—and from there he went to Yugra neighbouring in the north with the Samoyeds. The Yugra people told my warrior that three years earlier they discovered a miracle on the shore of the Ocean: in the place where huge mountains rising to the sky approach the ocean bay, they heard many people talking and shouting... Their language was not known to us, but pointing at our iron weapons, they gestured for us to give them the weapons. And if someone gave them a knife or an axe, in exchange they would offer furs. The route to these mountains lies through impassable abysses, snow and forest; that is why we did not always reach the place; besides we know there are people even further north..."

If we take a look at the map of the coast of the Arctic Ocean, it is easy to find the place about which Gyuryata talked with the chronicler: high mountains approach a bay only in one place, at Yugorsky Shar Bay and not far from it at Cape Russky Zavorot where a spur of the Urals—the Pai-Khoi Range—comes to the shore of the bay. The land situated directly north of this set of Russo-Yugorian geographical names is Novaya Zemlya. Thus, it is thanks to the people of old Novgorod that we learn about the neolithic way of life still existing far beyond the Polar Circle, on Novaya Zemlya at the end of the 11th century, and it was the Novgorod men who introduced a new culture to these distant tribes.

The numerous *pogosts* founded by the Novgorod people to collect tribute constitute traces of overland routes to the northeastern lands; a list of these *pogosts* was drawn up back in 1137. *Pogosts* existed along the Northern Dvina (Rakun, Ust-Yemets, Ust-Vaga and Toima) and along the Vaga, its tributary (Vel, Puita), and still further east (Pinega, Pomozdin on the Vychegda near the Izhma) where descendents of the ancient Novgorod people still live retaining Russian dress and customs, but as a result of the many-century-long isolation from their homeland, they have lost their native language and now speak Komi. The Vyatka land was Novgorod's furthermost colony.

The Novgorod people brought land cultivation to the north, and later many *boyar* estates and monasteries appeared on the Dvina and the Vaga coming in the wake of the peasant colonisation from the Novgorod and the Rostov lands. Travelling thousands of kilometres, the men of Novgorod often came in boats along rivers and by the sea. They probably sailed to Yugorsky Shar and Russky Zavorot, covering a total of 5,000 kilometres which is equal to the trip from Novgorod to London and back in distance. The chronicle refers to a sea journey around Europe via Kiev and Novgorod, the English Channel and Gibraltar, calling the Baltic-Atlantic part of the route "from the Varangians to the Greeks".

Novgorod itself was built at a most advantageous crossroads of trade routes which were important both for Kievan Rus and for all of Northern Europe. The town served as a "window into Europe" for Rus for nearly half a thousand years.

It was easy to travel to Sweden, to Gotland or the lands of the Baltic Slavs from Novgorod down the Volkhov River, through Lake Ladoga and the Neva River. From Novgorod one could go through Lake Ilmen and along the Msta River to the Volga and then to Bulgaria, Khazaria and the distant lands of the Orient. A third route—from the Greeks to the Varangians—went from Byzantium and Kiev up the Dnepr, by means of portages, then along the Lovat to Lake Ilmen and inevitably via Novgorod to the Volkhov River.

In Novgorod's favourable location at the source of the Volkhov lay its future contradictions: on the one hand, Kiev, "the mother of Russian cities", always carefully watched the new town, and the princes of Kiev sent their elder sons to rule Novgorod so as to have a stronger hold over this international port. On the other hand, the large distance to Kiev, the broadest relations with dozens of rich and powerful countries and the wealth of its own lands provided Novgorod with opportunities for growth, enhancement and, therefore, independence.

The early period when the settlement on the Volkhov River was a far-off factory belonging to Kiev was partly reflected in the feudal administrative divisions of the Novgorod land. Usually each Russian principality constituted a *tma*, i. e.,. ten Thousand, ten military and financial districts; and each Thousand was subdivided into Hundreds. But the Novgorod land had only one Thousand subdivided into Hundreds situated like a fan around Novgorod within a radius of 200 to 300 kilometres. This meant that Kiev refused to accept Novgorod as an equal to other parts of Rus (such as Volyn or Smolensk) and regarded it as a tenth of some whole (perhaps the Kievan ten Thousand?). The town itself, however, constituted another ten

Hundreds, i. e. another Thousand, but it was still far from a full ten-Thousand set.

Novgorod is located on the banks of the Volkhov, not far from the source of that river which flows from Lake Ilmen. Its most ancient site was, apparently, on the left bank where the Kremlin stands and where the memory of the pagan god of cattle and wealth Volos (Veles) is retained in the name of Volosov street. An idol of Perun set up on the order by the Kiev prince at the end of the 10th century stood almost at the very lake, outside the town. As an old legend goes, an inextinguishable fire burned around Perun; excavations found eight fire sites around the idol. Even as recently as the early 20th century, the inhabitants of Novgorod retained the custom of tossing a coin in the water when sailing past Perun as if offering sacrifice to the ancient god.

The left-bank ancient complex was, apparently, linked to the Rusins from Kiev who constituted the garrison of the frontier fort. Slaven Hill connected to a greater extent with the local tribe of Slovenians is situated on the right bank.

Rapid growth of the town resulted in a dense settlement of both banks linked by the famous Great Bridge across the Volkhov which played a major part in the town's history: hostile sides would come together to fight here following a boisterous *veche*, Vaska Buslayev of the Russian *bylinas* of the Novgorod epic committed his outrages, and death sentences were implemented here: the condemned were thrown off the bridge into the depths of the Volkhov River.

In the 11th-13th centuries Novgorod was a large and well-appointed city. The Kremlin, doubled in size, was fortified by a stone wall and held the St Sophia Cathedral (which also stored state documents) and the bishop's court. Another hero of Novgorod *bylinas*, the wealthy merchant Sadko Satinich, built the large Boris and Gleb Church in the southern part of the Kremlin.

Opposite the Kremlin there were the marketplace, the *veche* square, Yaroslav's court, the houses of foreign merchants and churches of merchant corporations (St John the Baptist at Opoki, Our Lady on the Marketplace, and the Varangian sanctuary). The banks of the Volkhov were divided into piers and were overcrowded with ships and boats from different countries and towns. There were so many vessels that if a fire started, it spread over all of them and reached to the other bank.

The monasteries were situated on the fringe of the town. The Yuryev Monastery built by Mstislav rose like a tower in the way of those who entered the city from the south, and from the direction of Lake Ilmen, and the Antoniev Cloister served as the gates to the city for those sailing from the north.

The streets were covered with wooden planking about which special rules existed.

The chroniclers of Novgorod were more attentive to their native town than their Kiev counterparts and continually reported news on life in the town. We know about city fires, tremendous floods when the waters of the Volkhov River engulfed the town and all the inhabitants climbed on house roofs; we know about years of drought and crop failures when grain had to be purchased in the Suzdal land.

A great deal for the understanding of the history of Novgorod, its culture and daily life was done by many years of excavations carried out by the expedition under A. V. Artsikhovsky.* The archaeologists have discovered households, homes, craft shops, *boyar* chambers. Many items have been found, from craftsmen's tools to golden seals and the finest decorations.

Of particular interest are the widely known birchbark scrolls—letters written by ordinary townsfolk on the most different occasions. They contain a request to lend a grivna, an invitation to a funeral, a note to a wife to send clean linen, a money receipt, an official request, a will, love letters, verses or just one name on a sheet for drawing lots. No other medieval European town can boast of such a variety of epistles written by craftsmen and merchants, housewives and *boyars*.

In the 12th and 13th centuries Novgorod the Great was a huge city; the largest part of its population consisted of craftsmen of different occupations—black-

---

* A. V. Artsikhovsky (1902-1978), a well-known Soviet archaeologist.— *Ed.*

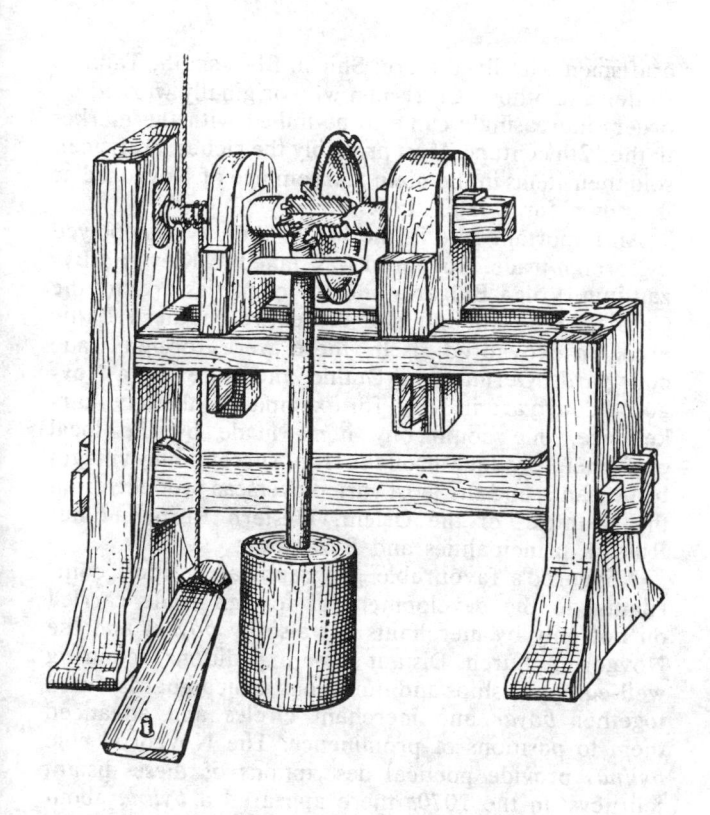

Novgorod lathe. Reconstruction by B. A. Kolchin

smiths, potters, gold- and silver-smiths and also craftsmen who specialised in making a single product—shields, bows, saddles, combs, nails and so on. Occasionally, the names of craftsmen appeared in chronicles; in other instances we learn about them from inscriptions on their own artifacts. We know two exquisite silver vessels possibly made for inhabitants of the *posad*; it is written on them: "Made by Bratilo" and "Made by Kosta".

The people of Novgorod were famed for being skilled carpenters, and many remains of wooden houses and carved ornaments were found at the excavation sites. A whole section of Novgorod was called Carpenter End, and many streets retained the memory of the craftsmen who lived there: Shield, Blacksmith, Tanner, Potter and others. Craftsmen who originally worked on orders increasingly came to be linked with the market in the 12th century. Most probably the richest craftsmen sold their items in the main marketplace of Novgorod as is known for a later time.

An important role in the life of the city was played by foreign trade. Novgorod was linked to Kiev and Byzantium, Volga Bulgaria and the countries around the Caspian Sea, Gotland and the entire southern Baltic area. In Novgorod itself, there were foreign trade courtyards, German and Gothic, and there was a Novgorod courtyard in Kiev, for example. At the city marketplace, one could buy items made by the local craftsmen, produce brought from surrounding villages by peasants, and the most varied overseas products from the countries of the Orient, Western Europe, other Russian principalities and Byzantium.

Novgorod's favourable geographical position contributed to the development of foreign trade carried on not only by merchants but also by *boyars* and the Novgorod church. Distant trade expeditions, requiring well-equipped ships and numerous armed guards, fused together *boyar* and merchant circles and advanced them to positions of prominence. The Novgorod epic *bylinas* provide poetical descriptions of these distant journeys: in the 1070s there appeared a *bylina* about an expedition to Korsun (Khersones) in the Crimea, the *bylina* about Sadko the rich merchant which draws a vivid picture of daily life in the 12th-century Novgorod the Great and 30 ships sailing on the blue sea.

Despite the fact that most of the population had to do with the crafts and trade, real power in Novgorod belonged to the land-owning *boyars* whose estates were both within the Novgorod Hundreds and in far-off colonies—in Zavolochye, on the Dvina and the Vaga. In view of the specifics of the Novgorod land, the *boyars* were firmly linked with foreign trade in furs, and this made them economically powerful and corporately united.

Until the beginning of the 13th century, when the German knightly orders appeared on the frontier of the Novgorod land, Novgorod knew no permanent fo-

Wooden dishes shaped on a lathe from the excavations in Novgorod

reign threat, and the military forces of the *boyars* provided defence to trade caravans, thousand-kilometre routes and far-off factories, the *pogosts*. Pskov and Ladoga were important foreposts of Novgorod; the *boyars* of these towns occasionally took part in the political life of their "elder brother", and in some instances even displayed an independent spirit.

Novgorod the Great was the scene of a continuous class struggle waged by the "black people" against the *boyars*, money-lenders and monasteries and a struggle between different groups of *boyars*; the resistance against Kiev's power also increased all the time. The desire to break free of Kiev was particularly evident at the early stages. It developed into a city-wide struggle waged by all sections and groups united together by common tasks. The existence of such common aims moved the class struggle to the background to some extent, because the *boyars* took advantage of the *veche* meetings demagogically, accusing unliked princes that they "did not look after the *smerds*", and represented their own struggle for power as a common fight for Novgorod's liberties.

During the 11th century the *boyars* of Novgorod many times imposed their will on grand princes and prince's vicegerents sent by Kiev to Novgorod. We recall how proud the Novgorod *boyars* were of victorious expeditions against Kiev under Yaroslav the Wise and of the deeds which asserted Novgorod liberties in 1015.

In the last twenty-five years of the 11th century there was a change in the formula adopted in the chronicle to report the beginning of the reign of a new prince: earlier it said that the Grand Prince of Kiev "put a prince on the throne in Novgorod". Now the formula was that the Novgorod folk "invited" a prince. The chronicle now abounded in the following phrases: "the prince fled", the Novgorod folk "expelled the prince", "showed the road to the prince". The first prince to be driven out was Gleb Svyatoslavich who opposed the whole city and defended the bishop and had, as we remember, personally hacked a wizard to death. The Novgorod folk "expelled him from the city and the prince fled beyond the portage (the watershed between the Ilmen and the Northern Dvina) and there he was killed by the Komi-Zyryanians". This occurred in 1078.

A new system of "rearing" the prince appeared. Novgorod invited a young prince to the city and made him learn the *boyar* order from early years. And if the Grand Prince attempted to replace the candidate with his elder son according to a long-standing tradition, the *boyars* stood up for their "rearing" prince firmly. This was what happened with Mstislav Vladimirovich, Monomakh's son who reigned in Novgorod from the age of 12. Some 14 years later, in 1102, Svyatopolk of Kiev attempted to replace him with his own son, but the Novgorod envoys engaged the Grand Prince in a "great argument" and stated rather impudently: "If your son has two heads, send him to us!"

Mstislav remained in Novgorod and even married for the second time to a daughter of the Novgorod town elder.

Fresh importance was attached at the time to the post of the town elder, a kind of "prime minister" in the *boyar* republic. Earlier the *posadnik* was a trusted agent of the Grand Prince sent from Kiev. In the 12th century, the Novgorod people elected the town elders from among the most noble *boyars*, and in the 13th century

Silver vessel (12th century). Made by craftsman Konstantin on the order from Novgorod *boyar* Petrila

it was maintained that "the Novgorod folk are free to choose their princes and town elders".

The last attempt to deal harshly with the Novgorod *boyars* was made under Vladimir Monomakh. When Mstislav was called back to the south by his father, and only his son Vsevolod remained in Novgorod, the *boyars* apparently behaved too independently. Vladimir and Mstislav jointly summoned all the Novgorod boyars to Kiev in 1118, made them pledge allegiance, and some of them, guilty of illegal confiscations, were detained in the capital and imprisoned. *Boyar* Stavr, head of a Novgorod Hundred, was among those imprisoned. His carefree life in Novgorod was described in a novella written in the *bylina* style, which said that he was his own master and ruler, and his trunks contained immense treasures. Summoned by Prince Vladimir, *boyar* Stavr arrived in Kiev, as the chronicle confirms, and ridiculed the Kievan *boyars* and even the Grand Prince himself. In those years a new wall was being built in Novgorod, started by Mstislav back in 1116;

313

it was "greater than the previous wall", and the Novgorod *boyar* commented ironically on Kiev's fortifications claiming that his own courtyard was better fortified than Kiev. Then, the *bylina* goes on, Vladimir was furious at the swaggering *boyar* from Novgorod and locked Stavr in "a deep dungeon".

The chronicle tells us nothing about his subsequent fate, but the novella is devoted to the cunning and daring actions undertaken by Stavr's young wife who deceived the prince and managed to have her husband freed.

However, reprisals against the Novgorod *boyars* undertaken to maintain the prestige of the young prince Vsevolod Mstislavich did not put an end to Novgorod's separatist strivings. Vsevolod (1118—1136) was the last prince under whom Kiev interfered in Novgorod's domestic affairs.

Vsevolod Mstislavich carried out Novgorod's various military missions for a long time. In 1132, however, following Mstislav's death and lured by the prospect of acquiring a large domain in the south, he rode to Pereyaslavl and occupied it, but managed to retain the town only for a few hours—by dinner-time he was driven out by Yuri Dolgoruky, his uncle.

Prince Vsevolod returned to Novgorod, apparently counting on the support of town elder Petrila Mikulchich and Archbishop Nifont. But here he found extraordinary unrest both in the city and the whole of Novgorod land: in their time the *boyars* had, apparently, concluded an agreement with him for his life-long reign as prince in order not to suffer from the heavy hand of Monomakh again as it had happened in the second year (1118) of the reign of the young Vsevolod. Now the people of Novgorod, Pskov and Ladoga assembled and reminded the prince of his promise ("I wish to die in your land") and as punishment for the thoughtless trip to Pereyaslavl "drove Vsevolod out of the city". But he was called back half-way.

A new conflict gathered head two years later, when Vsevolod attempted to interfere in southern affairs again. There were heated debates at the *veche* concerning the expedition against Suzdal. "The people of

Novgorod began to argue about the Suzdal war and killed someone (a *boyar* or a warrior?) throwing him off the bridge."

In the course of the expedition the town elder was replaced, and Vsevolod's man Petrila was dismissed. The defeat suffered by the Novgorod forces in the battle on Zhdan Hill in 1135 further increased Novgorodians' dissatisfaction with Vsevolod who had involved Novgorod in the disastrous war.

Two highly important documents devoted to the affairs of the merchant corporations date back to the stormy events of 1135-1136 which were sometimes even called the Novgorod Revolution. Considered together with the chronicle they may to a degree help us determine the prince's policy in the last critical years of the prince's rule in Novgorod.

Both documents were revised in the 13th-14th centuries, but their original text may be tentatively singled out.

In 1135, under town elder Miroslav, Prince Vsevolod compiled the *Manuscript* devoted to the benefits and privileges of the merchant brotherhood at the Church of St John the Baptist at Opoki built at the Novgorod marketplace in 1127-1130. In issuing the document the prince, obviosly, counted on the support of the merchants.

The *Manuscript* clearly asserts and defends the rights of the wealthy merchants. A council consisting of three elders was set up at the Church of St John the Baptist at Opoki. The merchants elected two elders, while there was only one from the well-to-do townsfolk and the mob, and he was not elected, it was an official, standing at the head of a *boyar* Thousand. The merchant brotherhood was granted self-rule and could administer justice in trade matters independently of the town elder. Only a rich merchant, or the son of a rich merchant could become a member of the guild after contributing 50 grivnas. The St John brotherhood received all the customs duties from wax brought to Novgorod from all parts of Rus.

The guild had its own community holiday on September 11 when 25 silver grivnas were spent from the common treasury, apparently to hold a feast,

70 candles were lighted in the church and the archbishop was invited to hold the service; he received one grivna in silver and woollen cloth. The holiday of the brotherhood of St John the Baptist lasted for three days. Such joint holidays of members of merchant or craftsmen guilds were typical of all medieval towns in Europe and the Orient.

Meanwhile, Novgorod attempted to say its word in Russian-wide politics in the context of the developing feudal disunity and conflicts between princes. Town elder Miroslav Gyuryatinich travelled to South Rus to reconcile Kiev and Chernigov. Remaining in Novgorod Prince Vsevolod offered contradictory advice as to which of the rivals Novgorod should be allied to.

Dissatisfaction of the Novgorod *boyars* with the prince grew simultaneously with their awareness of their own power. Apart from the *boyars* and the merchants there were two other forces in Novgorod on whom the prince could rely in search of support for his foundering throne—the church and the mob.

Vsevolod was hostile to the mob, a fact he was reproached for subsequently. There remained the church which constituted a considerable economic and political power in Novgorod. At this point the second document of Vsevolod Mstislavich was drawn up in which he partly annulled the privileges just granted to the merchants. It was the Rules on Church Courts and trade measures.

The Rules were made public in the following way; ten heads of Hundreds, a *biryuch* and two elders—one of them was the elder Vasyata of the St John the Baptist at Opoki — were invited to the session of the prince's council in the presence of *boyars*, the princess and the archbishop. The Rules outlined the range of persons within the authority of the church, the crimes tried by church courts (divorce, abduction, sorcery, wizardry, witchcraft, quarrels between relatives, robbing of the dead, pagan rituals, murder of illegitimate children and others).

However, the Rules begin with the prince determining to whom he entrusts justice and trade measures: the first place goes to the Church of Our Lady on the Marketplace, then the St Sophia Cathedral and bishop and the St John elder comes only in third place. After specifying certain economic details such as what rent payments were received by the St John priest and watchman, it is pointed out that the elders and merchants were to rule "the house of St John", "reporting to the bishop", in other words, the affairs of the merchant corporation were put under the control of the Novgorod archbishop.

The Church of Our Lady on the Marketplace was founded by Prince Vsevolod jointly with archbishop Nifont in 1135. In winter Nifont went to Kiev—it is, perhaps, more correct to date Vsevolod's Rules by the beginning of 1136 when the church on the marketplace was already built, and the archbishop had returned from his diplomatic trip. The new document, provided we have understood it correctly, strengthened the prince's link with the church and its influential head, the archbishop, but must have provoked dissatisfaction of the Novgorod merchants whose church, St John at Opoki, proved to be in the background, while the newly built Church of Our Lady occupied the first place.

Subsequent events showed that the prince had miscalculated: on May 28, 1136, in accord with the verdict by the *veche* in which people from Pskov and Ladoga participated, Vsevolod was arrested and placed in the bishop's palace together with his wife, children and mother-in-law where 30 armed warriors guarded him, and perhaps also the bishop, for two months. In July Vsevolod was let out of the city having been accused of: 1) not looking after the *smerds*; 2) having tried to capture Pereyaslavl in 1132; 3) having been the first to flee from the battlefield in 1135; 4) having sought an alliance with Chernigov and then ordered the alliance to be dissolved.

Since then freedom-loving Novgorod the Great had finally become a *boyar* feudal republic. The colourful notes of 1136 supposedly made in the chronicle by a mathematician Kirik show the events of 1136 in particularly bold relief, but in effect, as we have seen, the *boyars* of Novgorod came to power much earlier.

Vsevolod found refuge in Pskov and after his

expulsion Svyatoslav Olgovich from Chernigov was invited to Novgorod. Passions continued to run high in Novgorod; the local people threw some *boyar* off the bridge, the archbishop refused to marry the new prince and prohibited the clergy from attending the wedding, some well-wisher of the expelled Vsevolod shot an arrow at Svyatoslav, and certain men of Novgorod secretly invited Vsevolod to return.

When the secret proposal came to light, "there was a great rebellion in Novgorod: the people did not want Vsevolod". The *boyar* friends of Vsevolod either fled to him in Pskov and their property was confiscated, or paid enormous tribute. It is important to note that the 1,500 grivnas collected from Vsevolod's "companions" were distributed amongst the merchants to equip them for the war against Vsevolod.

The last princes of Novgorod were, in effect, hired military commanders. Ruled by the *boyars*, Novgorod the Great was the scene of a tense class struggle in the 12th and 13th centuries. The town's independence of the power of the Kiev prince was reflected in the fact that the *boyar* government took increasingly greater part in internal conflicts in other lands; this dramatically worsened the position of peasants and common townsfolk on whose shoulders fell the full burden of internecine strife which devastated the country and hindered the delivery of grain from the more fertile lands.

The uprising of 1136 was far from the only one. An uprising against town elder Dmitr Miroshkinich broke out in 1209. His treasures were distributed amongst the insurgents, and "each townsman received three grivnas".

In 1229 the "common folk" of Novgorod rose against archbishop Arseny and head of a Thousand Vyacheslav. "The whole town was in turmoil", writes the chronicler, and further describes how the armed people moved straight from the *veche* to smash the *boyars*' and archbishop's courts. Another archbishop was appointed, and his assistants included armourer Mikifor Shchitnik.

In the 12th and early 13th centuries Novgorod was a rich town of merchants and craftsmen, the capital of an enormous land whose frontiers almost reached the shores of the Arctic Ocean. It grew rapidly, developed, expanded its trade links and created a unique culture.

The city most similar to Novgorod in Western Europe was Florence, a wealthy commercial and aristocratic republic whose internal history was also filled with struggles between feudal parties and the conflicts between poor townsfolk and moneylenders and patricians.

The history of Novgorod was not interrupted as tragically as that of Kiev, Chernigov and other towns by the Tatar invasion. Novgorod successfully repelled the German knights and survived the establishment of Tatar domination easier than other lands, but still, the first decades of Tatar domination affected it strongly.

Novgorod the Great played a major part in the history of Rus, Western Europe and the distant Northeast where Russian crafts and methods of land cultivation reached in the course of peaceful Novgorod colonisation. This paved the way for the subsequent advance into Siberia.

Vladimir-Suzdal Principality

As if in anticipation of the fact that Northeastern Rus would serve as the link between the pre-Mongolian period in Russian history and the entire subsequent history of Muscovite Rus, the author of *The Lay of Igor's Host* speaks with admiration and inspiration about the mighty prince of Suzdal Vsevolod the Big Nest (1176-1212):

> *O great Prince Vsevolod!*
> *Is it not in your thoughts*
> *To come flying from far off*
> *To guard your father's golden throne?*
> *For you are able*
> *To splash away the Volga*
> *With your oars,*

*To scoop up the Don
With your warriors' helmets.
If you were here—
Slave-girls would be
A* nogata *each,
Bondmen—but a* riezana...*

His large principality included the ancient lands of the Krivichians, partly the Vyatichians and the areas where Slav colonisation had advanced from time immemorial: the lands of the Merya, Muroma and Ves, i. e. the area between the Volga and the Oka rivers with the fertile Suzdal fields and the area of Beloozero. With time the Rostov-Suzdal land expanded further into the taiga forest, to the Northern Dvina, Ustyug Veliki and even to the White Sea, reaching the borders of the Novgorod colonies.

The relations between the Slavs who had come here and the local Finno-Ugric population were undoubtedly peaceful on the whole. Both peoples gradually merged enriching each other with elements of their culture.

The geographical position of the Rostov-Suzdal land had its advantages: it was not threatened by Polovtsi raids because the steppe was far away, and here, beyond the impassable forests of the Vyatichians, the Kiev princes and their officials could not behave as brazenly as they did near Kiev. The Varangian forces could get here only through a system of portages in the Valdai forests, and not along water routes as they did to Ladoga or Novgorod. All this made Northeastern Rus relatively safer.

On the other hand, the Suzdal princes had such a route as the Volga River which led "through seventy channels upon the Khorezm (Caspian) Sea", along the shores of which lay the fabulously wealthy countries of the Orient which were eager to purchase fur and Slav wax. All the Novgorod routes to the Orient passed through the Suzdal land, and this was widely taken advantage of by the local princes.

In the 11th century, when the Volga and the Oka

---

* *Nogata* and *riezana*—small coins.—*Ed.*

were part of Kievan Rus, uprisings took place there: in the Suzdal land in 1024; and in about 1071 on the Volga and Sheksna rivers and at Beloozero; the latter was suppressed by Jan Vyshatich.

The towns of Rostov, Suzdal, Murom, Ryazan, Yaroslavl and others already existed at the time. In the black-earth parts of the Suzdal land the local *boyars* grew rich by supplying grain even to Novgorod.

The actual establishment of the prince's rule in these parts began with Vladimir Monomakh who, since his childhood days, had to ride "through the Vyatichians" to reach distant Rostov. The long years when Monomakh as the prince of Pereyaslavl also owned the Rostov domain affected the life of the northeast lands. It was in the northeast that such towns appeared as Vladimir-on-the-Klyazma, and Pereyaslavl called Zalessky (beyond the forests) as distinct from the southern Pereyaslavl; and even the names of southern rivers were transferred to these parts. It was here that Vladimir built towns, it was here that he waged a war against Oleg Svyatoslavich, and it was here, somewhere on the Volga, that he wrote his *Sermon* "riding in a sled"*. The relations between Suzdal country and Pereyaslavl Russky (the modern Pereyaslav-Khmelnitsky) continued during the entire 12th century.

The Rostov-Suzdal land broke away from Kiev at the same time as the other Russian lands—in 1132-1135. The land was ruled by one of the younger sons of Monomakh, Yuri called Dolgoruky (the Long-Armed), evidently for his unrestrained desire to seize distant foreign possessions. His foreign policy had three basic directions: wars against Volga Bulgaria, a trade rival of Rus; diplomatic and military pressure against Novgorod, and the exhausting and useless wars for Kiev which filled the last nine years of his reign.

Yuri Dolgoruky became involved in his southern adventures gradually. It all began when, having been driven out of Kiev in 1146, Svyatoslav Olgovich,

---

* The actual meaning of the expression is "On the threshold of death" (the dead were driven on sleds to be buried, even in summer).— Tr.

his neighbour, turned to Yuri for help. Having sent his ally troops from the far-off Beloozero Yuri Vladimirovich first of all started wars against his neighbours: he himself fought successfully against Novgorod, and sent Svyatoslav against the Smolensk land. When Svyatoslav Olgovich began successful actions in the upper reaches of the Protva, a messenger arrived from Yuri inviting him to the frontier Suzdal town, apparently to celebrate the victories: "Come to me, brother, in Moscow". No one thought at the time that this small town in the Vyatichian forests was destined to become one of the largest cities in the world.

First Svyatoslav's son arrived in Moscow from the banks of the Protva, bringing Dolgoruky a present of a hunting cheetah, a swift animal no reindeer could escape. Then on April 4, 1147, Svyatoslav arrived in Moscow with his son Vladimir and his retinue which included a ninety-year-old *boyar* who had served even Svyatoslav's father Oleg. On the next day "Yuri ordered an enormous feast to be held and received Svyatoslav with great pomp, giving him many gifts". This was how Moscow was first mentioned; originally it was the castle of *boyar* Kuchka, in 1156 a frontier fortress, in the 13th century a prince's apanage town, and in the 15th century the capital of the enormous Russian state which foreigners called Muscovy.

Besides Moscow Yuri Dolgoruky either built or fortified the towns of Yuryev-Polskoi, Dmitrov, Kosnyatin, Kideksha, Zvenigorod, Pereyaslavl and others.

In his southern affairs, fighting for Kiev against his nephew Izyaslav Mstislavich or his elder brother Vyacheslav, Yuri first won battles almost reaching the Carpathians with his troops, then fled hastily from Kiev in a boat leaving behind his warriors and even his secret diplomatic correspondence.

V. N. Tatishchev has the following description of Yuri Dolgoruky, apparently derived from Kievan sources hostile to him: "That Grand Prince was of considerable height, stout, white-faced; his eyes were not very large, he had a long and crooked nose, small beard; and he loved women, sweet victuals and drink; he was more concerned with merry-making than with quarrels and warriors, and the latter were in the charge and supervision of his lords and favourites."

Yuri died in Kiev in 1157.

Dolgoruky's son, the harsh, power-seeking and energetic Andrei Yuryevich Bogolyubsky became the real master of Northeastern Rus in 1157-1174.

While his father was still alive and ruled firmly in Kiev, Andrei, violating his father's instructions, went to the Suzdal land in 1155, evidently invited by the local *boyars*. Following the death of Yuri Dolgoruky, Andrei was elected prince. The people of Rostov and Suzdal "after deliberating, invited Andrei".

Rostov and Suzdal, ancient *boyar* centres influencing the entire course of events, sought to have their own prince and dynastic branch on a par with other lands, so as to put an end to the endless change of princes who were not connected with the interests of the locality they ruled over. Having won fame by his knightly deeds in the south as a young man, Andrei seemed to be a suitable candidate. As to Andrei, he probably was happy to exchange his unreliable fortune of vassal warrior receiving first one then another town in reward for his services for the firm possession of an enormous land in which order had already been established under his father and grandfather.

The new prince, however, immediately and firmly placed himself not next to the *boyars* but above them. He made Vladimir, a relatively new town, his capital, and the superb white-stone castle in Bogolyubovo near Vladimir built by his craftsmen—his residence. The prince's first act was to drive out his younger brothers who might have become rivals with time and the father's warriors who always interfered in affairs of state under such circumstances. "He did so in order to be the autocrat in the Suzdal land." Since then Andrei had to beware of the *boyars*; according to some sources he even prohibited the *boyars* from taking part in the prince's hunting expeditions—we know instances when princes did not return from a hunt.

In his struggle for power Andrei sought to rely on the church too, using the bishop's office. He wanted Fyodor, who supported the prince unequivocally, to be the bishop of Rostov, but the church powers in Kiev and Constantinople strongly objected, and in 1168 "the false bishop" Fyodor was executed as a heretic.

In foreign policy Andrei continued to act in the same three directions outlined by Yuri Dolgoruky: expeditions against Volga Bulgars, and expeditions against Novgorod and Kiev. Novgorod successfully repulsed the Suzdal forces, but Andrei's troops managed to capture Kiev and plunder it in 1169.

It is to be repeated that the plundering of Kiev so colourfully described by a contemporary Kievan did not lead to economic or political decline of the former capital where lineages of princes independent of the Northeastern prince became firmly established soon afterwards. When the conqueror of Kiev Andrei "overflowing with arrogance, attempted to give orders to the South-Russian princes in 1174, his envoy swordsman Mikhna had his head and beard shaved and sent back in this unbefitting state. When Andrei Bogolyubsky saw the shaved *boyar* and heard from him that the princes had firmly refused to submit, "his face changed" and "his reason was dimmed by anger and intemperance".

In the second expedition against Kiev undertaken by Andrei an unprecedented number of princes and warriors took part, but it ended in a futile two-months siege of Vyshgorod. "And thus returned all the troops of the prince of Suzdal Andrei... They had gone proud and arrogant but came back to their homes humbled."

The too extensive military designs of Prince Andrei which were not related to the needs of defence or the interests of the *boyars* were bound to exacerbate contradictions within the principality. It is probable that conflicts with the *boyars* were also caused by Andrei Bogolyubsky's internal policy by which he attempted to take the *boyars* in hand. It was here, in Northeast Rus, that author Daniil the Exile advised the *boyar* to set up his court and villages

Prince Andrei Yuryevich Bogolyubsky. Reconstruction by M. M. Gerasimov on the basis of Bogolyubsky's skull

at a distance from the prince's residence so as not to be ruined by the latter.

Legends about the early Moscow describing how the prince took away the castle from *boyar* Stepan Ivanovich Kuchka refer us to Andrei. Although the chronicle links the building of the prince's fortress in 1156 to the name of Yuri, we know that in that year Yuri was in Kiev, made peace with the Polovtsi at the Zarubintsy Ford, welcomed the Metropolitan from Constantinople and was preparing an expedition against Volyn.

The prince who built a fortress in place of Kuchka's court was obviously Andrei Bogolyubsky. The *boyars* would not watch calmly how their castles were taken away to become part of the prince's domain.

In 1173 Andrei planned a new expedition against

Volga Bulgars; in addition to the main Vladimir forces, the Murom and Ryazan troops took part. All the hosts were to gather at Gorodets on the Volga in the mouth of the Oka (Nizhny Novgorod, the modern Gorky). For two weeks the princes waited for their *boyars* in vain: the *boyars* "were loathe to go" and, without disobeying the prince directly, they found a clever way of avoiding the undesirable expedition— "going they did not go"—pretending to go they actually did not.

All these events point to the extreme tension in relations between the "autocratic" prince and the *boyars*. Equally sharp conflicts flared up at the same time on the opposite end of Rus in Galich. In the same 1173 the Galich *boyars* burned alive the prince's mistress, the mother of the heir to the throne, while the Suzdal *boyars* freed themselves from military service by pretending that they were coming.

The year 1174 of the unsuccessful and inglorious expedition against the Kiev land brought the tragic end closer. A group of *boyars* headed by the sons of Kuchka formed a conspiracy in 1174 (according to other chronicles in 1175) against Andrei. Twenty of the conspirators, including Yakim Kuchkovich, Pyotr, Kuchka's son-in-law, and housekeeper Anbal were feasting at Pyotr's court in Bogolyubovo near the prince's palace. The event did not provoke suspicion, because it was June 29, the name-day of *boyar* Pyotr. Yakim Kuchkovich, having received news that the prince intended to execute his brother, made a speech: "Today he executes one, tomorrow it will be us. Let us give thought to this prince!"

In the night, the armed conspirators, having drunk wine, went up to the prince's bedchamber and broke open the door. Andrei groped for the sword usually hanging in the bedchamber, but the conspirators had removed the sword; physically very strong, the prince fought the crowd of drunken *boyars* armed with swords and spears for a long time in the dark. Finally the murderers left, but the prince they believed to be dead managed to come down the stairs. Hearing his groans, the *boyars* returned, lit candles, found Andrei and finished him off. The part of the palace where this bloody tragedy occurred still exists in Bogolyubovo.

Anthropological study of the skeleton of Andrei Bogolyubsky confirmed the words in the chronicle about the prince's physical strength and the wounds inflicted on him. Using Andrei's skull the prominent anthropologist M. M. Gerasimov recreated the appearance of this outstanding ruler who was a military leader and an author, and on whose orders excellent architectural monuments were built.

Tatishchev's notes describe Andrei as follows: first, like Solomon, he built a remarkable temple, the Cathedral of the Assumption in Vladimir, second, he "expanded Vladimir and increased the number of various inhabitants in it such as merchants, and settled different artisans and craftsmen there. He was brave in war, and few princes equalled him, but he loved peace more than war and loved truth more than great gains. He was not of great stature, but broad and very strong, had black curly hair, a high forehead, large and radiant eyes. He lived for 63 years."

The next day after the prince's murder the townsfolk of Bogolyubovo, the artisans from the palace workshops and even the peasants from the surrounding villages rebelled against the prince's administration: they laid waste to the houses of the town elders and officials, and the prince's stewards and junior warriors were killed. The uprising spread to Vladimir.

What were the pros and cons of the rule of Yuri Dolgoruky and Andrei Bogolyubsky?

Undoubtedly positive was the extensive building of towns which were not only fortresses but also hubs of crafts and trade, major economic and cultural centres of the feudal state. A prince ruling a land temporarily and ready to set out for another principality at any moment would not bother about building towns. Yuri and Andrei, continuing the policy of Monomakh, linked their principal interests with the Rostov-Suzdal land, and this was objectively a positive trend.

As some sources indicate, an influx of colonists to new towns and newly-settled lands began at that time, and the *boyars* approved of Yuri's policy in the

1140s, a period of relative harmony between the prince's and the *boyars'* interests.

The building of towns was promoted by the development of productive forces, on the one hand, and on the other, these new towns provided a more extensive basis for the productive forces' further growth.

It immediately affected cultural development. The edifices that have come down to us from the age of Andrei Bogolyubsky reveal Russian architects' profound understanding of their tasks in art. A subtle and profound mathematical analysis of proportions, carefully considered details emphasising the harmony of the whole—these qualities of Andrei's architects were the result of a generally high level of culture. The Church of the Intercession on the Nerl, the complex of the Bogolyubovo castle restored by the Soviet scholar N. N. Voronin, and Vladimir's Golden Gates are all unfading works of art which enabled the chronicler to compare Andrei to the Biblical King Solomon and allowed us to perceive the remarkable beauty of Russian architecture at the time of the writing of *The Lay of Igor's Host*. Literary activities were also flourishing at the court of Andrei Bogolyubsky; the prince himself was a writer. Fragments of the chronicle of Andrei's reign have survived.

The centralisation of power which infringed upon the interests of related princes and *boyars* should also be regarded as a positive aspect in the activities of Yuri and Andrei. In peacetime, centralisation could exist within reasonable bounds, with the power of the Grand Prince restraining centrifugal forces and directing them into a single channel.

The negative aspects of autocracy in the principality-kingdom were the conflicts arising from the inclusion of the *boyars'* estates into the prince's domain, and the splitting up of the principality into apanages belonging to the prince's sons. This led to the division of such long-established bodies as the 12th-century "land" or "principality", which, as we have seen, went back to the ancient tribal alliances of the 6th-8th centuries. It was quite irrational to destroy, to cut up what had been achieved by tribal society.

However, this reproach does not apply to Andrei.

He did not divide his principality amongst his children; two of his sons died in his lifetime, and the only son who survived his father, Georgi Andreyevich who later became the King of Georgia, was not taken into account in dynastic partitions of the Vladimir (Rostov-Suzdal in the old *boyar* terminology) principality. The danger of such divisions was felt later when the "Big Nest" of Prince Vsevolod sought to spread to all the towns of Northeastern Rus.

A negative aspect in the activities of Andrei Bogolyubsky was, of course, his drive to rule Kiev, the Russian land, i. e. the partly wooded steppe along the Dnepr. These efforts were in no way connected with the everyday interests of Suzdal *boyars*; these were the personal ambitions of Andrei, grandson of Monomakh.

During the 200-year-long struggle against the Pechenegs and the Polovtsi the economy of the South Russian *boyars* and princes adapted to the needs of constant defence and constant readiness to withstand a siege or undertake an expedition. This was possibly why *zakups* became widespread (they were kept within fortified *boyars*' courts); hence an increase in the use of *kholop* labour in the 12th century, which allowed necessary stores of food to be quickly accumulated, and the rise of "peasant towns", prototypes of military settlements such as the frontier town of Izyaslavl on the Goryn. The main burden of constant military service in the south had been transferred by that time to the many-thousand-strong Berendei horsemen along the Ros.

There was nothing of the kind in the Vladimir land, fenced off by the Bryn, Moscow and Meshchera forests from the Polovtsi steppe. Each expedition disrupted the feudal economy, to say nothing of its devastating effect upon the people. In the five years before the conspiracy of Kuchka's sons Andrei Bogolyubsky undertook five distant expeditions: against Novgorod, to the Northern Dvina, against the Bulgars and two times against Kiev. According to the most modest estimates the troops marched about 8,000 kilometres under Andrei's banners through forests, swamps and watersheds, i. e. spent a whole year only to reach their destination, to say nothing of long sieges and manoeuvres. It is to be added that three expeditions ended unsuccessfully. No wonder Andrei's reign ended in armed action by the *boyar* elite and in an outburst of popular anger against the prince's administration.

The uprising of 1174 in Bogolyubovo and Vladimir resembles the Kievan uprising of 1113 which also broke out following the death of a prince who overtaxed popular patience.

After Andrei's death, Rostov and Suzdal, the centres of the old local *boyars*, applied the duumvirate system invented by the *boyars* of Kiev: they invited two of Andrei's nephews, minor princes, who were not dangerous for the local nobility.

However, at this point, a new town entered the scene: it was Vladimir which had grown into a large centre of the chafts and trade under Andrei. The Vladimir folk accepted Mikhail Yuryevich, Andrei's brother. A war began between Rostov and Vladimir: angered by Vladimir's rise the Rostov people threatened: "Let us burn the town! Or send our town elder there again: those people are our *kholops*, stone masons!"

The above phrase is filled with aristocrats' disdain for democratic sections of the town—craftsmen, stone masons and artisans who only a short while before had done away with the prince's swordsmen and junior warriors and now wanted to have their own prince who was not to the liking of Rostov and Suzdal.

Rostov won a temporary victory: Mikhail left Vladimir, and the *boyars'* chosen men began to rule the town, "heeding the advice of the *boyars*, and the *boyars* taught them to gain more property". The junior warriors "greatly burdened the people by various fines in the name of the prince".

Finally, the townsfolk of Vladimir, "new minor people", invited Mikhail again and decided to stand firm for him. Mikhail defeated the forces of Andrei's nephews and became the prince of Vladimir. He was accompanied by his brother Vsevolod Yuryevich. The victory of Vladimir's townsfolk had major consequences — a social rift occurred in old Suzdal as well.

The townsfolk of Suzdal also invited Mikhail (1176) saying that they, common Suzdal people, had not fought against him, that only the *boyars* had supported his enemies, "do not be angry with us, come to us!"

In these years the sources frequently mention Moscow (Moskov, Kuchkovo) as a town standing at the crossing of the most frequently used road from Chernigov to Vladimir at the border of the Vladimir land.

In 1177 Mikhail Yuryevich died after a long illness. The *boyars* of Rostov once again began the struggle for political hegemony, supporting their former candidate Mstislav Rostislavich Bezoky against Vsevolod Yuryevich who was supported by such towns as Vladimir, Pereyaslavl Zalessky and Suzdal. The arrogant *boyars* of Rostov interfered impertinently in the prince's affairs; when Mstislav was about to make up with his uncle, the *boyars* said: "If you give him peace, we won't!"

The conflict was settled by the battle at Yuryev on June 27, 1177, which brought victory to Vsevolod. The Rostov *boyars*' villages and herds were taken by the victors. Then Vsevolod laid waste to Ryazan where his enemies had hidden. The Prince of Ryazan Gleb (of the Olgovichi) and Mstislav Bezoky with his brother Yaropolk were taken prisoners.

The *boyars* and merchants of Vladimir favoured resolute action, they came to the prince's court, "a great multitude with arms", and insisted that the imprisoned princes were executed. Svyatoslav of Chernigov, Vsevolod's friend, intervened on their behalf, but it did not help and the captured rivals were blinded, and Gleb died in prison.

Thus the reign of the "Great Vsevolod" began. The strength of the new prince lay in his alliance with the broad sections of the town population.

In addition, another force was created at the time supporting the prince's power, the *dvoryane* (noblemen), i. e. a section depending personally on the princes and receiving for military or government service either land in temporary ownership or rewards in money or in kind, or the right to collect some of the prince's revenues part of which went to the collectors.

There was no single term yet, but we must include in this category of junior warriors and the prince's ministers *detskies, otroks, grids, pasynkis, milostniks, mechniks, virniks, birichs, tiuns* and others. Some of them were almost slaves, others reached the rank of *boyars* by selfless service; it was a numerous and varied section.

A great deal in the fate of these people depended on their personal abilities, on chance and on the generosity or stinginess of the prince. They knew the prince's life, carried out their duties in the palace, took part in wars, administered justice, rode as messengers to distant lands, accompanied envoys, made the rounds of far-off *pogosts*, secretly murdered the prince's rivals, shackled them, attended tourneys, organised riding to hounds and falconry, kept accounts of the prince's household, and perhaps, even wrote chronicles. In peacetime all of them had something to do in the large principality where state interests merged with the prince's personal ones, while in war they could now make up the basis of the prince's troops, the junior cavalry.

We learn about one of those who regarded the prince as their only patron, from his own petition written in an elaborate style but with great skill and erudition. He is Daniil the Exile (Pseudo-Daniil, circa 1230) who wrote a petition letter to the prince of Pereyaslavl Yaroslav Vsevolodich in the 13th century. Daniil was of *kholop* origin but was brilliantly educated and well-read, and in his own words, was not so much brave in battle as rather sharp-witted. He condemns the wealthy *boyars* and asks the prince to enroll him in his service:

> My Prince, Sir! As an oak is held by many roots, so our town is supported by your power...
> On the ship the helmsman is the most important person, and you, O Prince, are the most important man for your subjects...
> Spring adorns the land with flowers, and you, O Prince, bedeck us with your favours...
> I would rather drink water in your house than honey in the court of a *boyar*...

Intelligent but poor, educated but of humble origin, young but not fit for military service which would immediately give him a lot of opportunities, he sought to find a place in life near the prince. He did not intend to become rich by marrying a wealthy bride, neither did he want to go to a monastery, and he had no hope for help from friends; all his thoughts were directed towards the prince who did not store up treasures but showered "favours" not only on members of his household but also on people "from other countries ... coming to him".

Daniil expressed the interests of the section of "government service" men which grew during the 12th century; these were mostly people who entered military service as the prince's junior warriors, but as an exception, sought service which required "sharp wit". Their anti-*boyar* bias enabled the prince to rely on them in his struggle against the proud and independent *boyars*.

Under Vsevolod the Big Nest the principality of Vladimir grew stronger and larger due to the support of the towns and *dvoryane*; it became one of the major feudal states in Europe widely known beyond the frontiers of Rus. Vsevolod could influence the policy of Novgorod, obtained a prosperous domain in the Kiev land, occasionally interfered in South Russian affairs but did it without the costly expenditures his brother Andrei had been forced to make.

Vsevolod was almost totally in control of the Ryazan principalities; the latter were ruled by six Glebovichi brothers who were continually quarreling with each other. In *The Lay of Igor's Host* the author says about Vsevolod that he could throw "the dashing sons of Gleb" like incendiary shells with "Greek fire". The reference is to the victorious campaign against Volga Bulgaria in 1183 in which the four Glebovichi took part on Vsevolod's orders. In 1185 the Glebovichi rebelled, but the author of the poem did not know this when he was writing the relevant part of his poem.

The Vladimir principality was also linked with the principality of Pereyaslavl Russky. Vsevolod assigned his sons to rule the latter.

Vsevolod died in 1212. In the last year of his life a conflict broke out in connection with the succession to the throne: the Grand Prince sought to leave the principality under the rule of the town of Vladimir, the new capital, as it had been before, but his elder son

Konstantin, a scholar and friend of the Rostov *boyars*, wanted to return to the old times of Rostov's supremacy.

Then Vsevolod convened something similar to a council of the land: "Grand Prince Vsevolod assembled all his *boyars* from the towns and *volosts*, Bishop Ioann, the Fathers-Superior, priests, merchants, *dvoryane* and all men." The assembly pledged allegiance to his second son, Yuri. But the latter managed to become prince after his father's death only in 1218. Yuri Vsevolodich was killed in 1238 in the battle against the Tatars on the Sit River.

At the beginning of the 13th century Vladimir-Suzdal Rus split up into several parts ruled by the numerous sons of Vsevolod the Big Nest.

The history of the Vladimir-Suzdal principality was a brilliant page in the whole of Russian history, and it is no wonder that *The Lay of Igor's Host* dedicates solemn lines to it.

The rich and varied culture of Northeastern Rus found an adequate reflection in that brilliant poem; the white-stone architecture, the sculpture imbued with medieval philosophy, chronicles, a polemical literature, painting and the intricate patterns created by gold- and silver-smiths, popular *bylinas* about local and Russian *bogatyrs*, the colourful folk art—all the above fully bears out the poetic words of the great author addressed to Prince Vsevolod the Big Nest, who ruled over the enormous expanses in the Northeast which subsequently became the core of the Moscow state which, once again, forged Rus into a single power.

THE CULTURE OF RUS
IN THE 9TH-13TH CENTURIES

The culture of Kievan Rus became the starting point and primary foundation of the culture of Russians, Ukrainians, and Byelorussians. Kievan Rus created a single Russian literary language; the East Slavs became literate in this period; the epics about Kievan *bogatyrs* of the 10th and 11th centuries survived until the 20th century in the Russian North. Nestor's Kievan chronicle about the early centuries of Russian history (1113) was copied under Alexander Nevsky and Ivan the Terrible, continuing the manuscript tradition into the 18th century.

The single ancient Russian nationality formed in the age of Kievan Rus, from which the Byelorussians and the Ukrainians gradually branched off only in the 14th and 15th centuries. Many of our modern cities arose in the united Kievan Rus of the 9th-12th centuries, and the townsfolk learned many trades and arts. In our day cultured people all over the world admire the harmony of Ancient Rus architecture, the sublime art of the icon painters and refined craftsmanship of ancient Russian goldsmiths who produced delicate lacework out of gold, enamel, silver and niello.

It can be said without any exaggeration that the culture of the first Eastern Slav state, Kievan Rus, has become part of our modern Soviet culture. Ancient Rus did not receive such a rich legacy from the past as did Greece, Italy, France or Spain. However, the culture of Rus did not arise from nowhere, and its origins go back to distant proto-Slav or even earlier Indo-European times when land cultivation was first introduced, ideas on the structure of the world were created, as yet very distant from scientific knowledge,

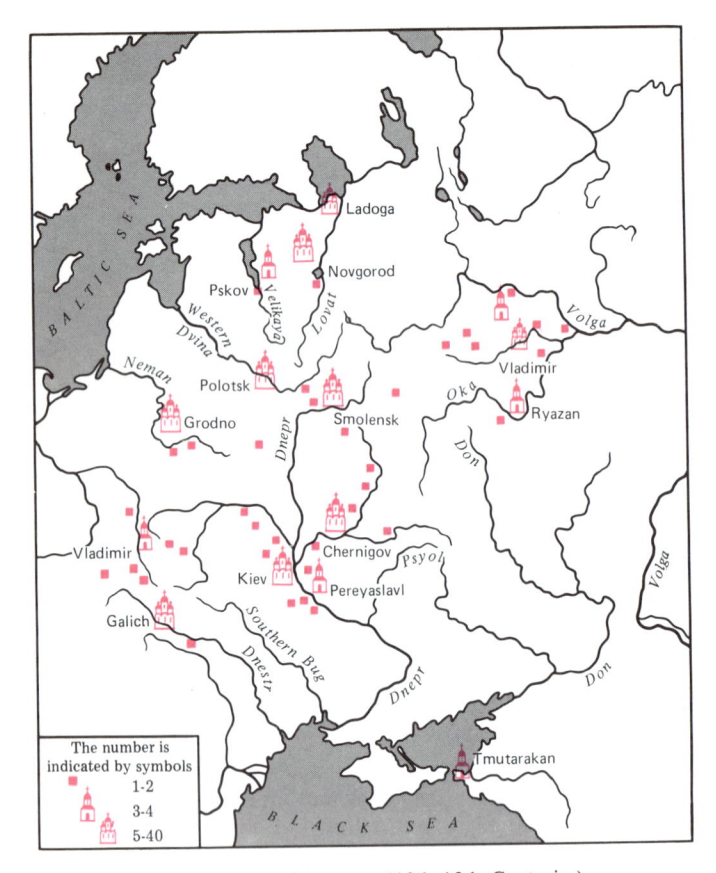

Monuments of Russian Architecture (10th-13th Centuries)

a large vocabulary evolved making it easier for separate tribes to communicate with each other, three metals were discovered one after another—copper, bronze alloys and iron, and the routes were laid for primitive trade in salt, ore and different items.

The degree of knowledge about nature and the world on the whole may be judged quite precisely from data concerning proto-Slavonic language: many names of trees, weeds, animals, birds, fish, elements of the landscape and stars go back to the distant proto-Slav period, which means that a continuous process of learning went on among the people over many hundreds of years—older generations passed down to younger ones all the accumulated and classified knowledge of nature, taught them to know the world, and acquainted them with the large oral vocabulary of concepts elaborated by distant ancestors.

A historical understanding of the culture of medieval Rus (historical in the full sense of the word) must take into account both the legacy Rus received from preceding ages and the contribution Kievan Rus made to the entire Russian culture, including the culture of the 20th century.

In the second millennium B. C., when the proto-Slav tribes were consolidated for the first time breaking away from the general Indo-European population, they already had an extensive vocabulary reflecting various aspects of their life, different work skills (building of houses, land cultivation, animal husbandry, making of tools of labour and metal decorations), and a complicated system of religious beliefs. The lingual and cultural ancestors of the proto-Slavs included tribes belonging to the so-called Tripolye culture which reached the high level of the art of land cultivation.

A new stage in the proto-Slav's cultural development came with the discovery of iron, which could be found in large quantities in the lakes and swamps of the Slav proto-homeland.

A considerable cultural legacy was received by a group of Eastern Slavs which in the first millennium B. C. constituted a part of the conglomerate of tribes tentatively known as Scythia. The tribes of the proto-Slav part of Scythia called themselves *Scoloti*. The

A church item

Scoloti Kingdom was situated in the partly wooded steppe zone of the Middle Dnepr. It was here that in the 5th century B. C. the Father of History Herodotus wrote down a number of historical tales belonging to the proto-Slavs-Scoloti which can be clearly traced in Russian and Ukrainian folk stories. These are the stories of three kingdoms, about the king of the Golden Kingdom, and the hero who vanquished the serpent and who bore the radiant name of Svetozar similar to the Sun Tsar of Herodotus. The hero of 10th-century Kievan epic Prince Vladimir called Red Sun in the folk *bylinas* was the intermediary link between Herodotus' epic hero and the later folk-tale hero.

The Slav nobility living along the Dnepr in the times of Herodotus had already had a firmly established route to the Greek towns on the Black Sea; they brought grain there, to the "marketplace of the Dneprians", and purchased there, in Olviopol, items of luxury made by the Greeks.

Of course, the Slavs were still a long way from adopting Greco-Roman culture, but they already saw parts of that culture while they walked through the streets of a wealthy Greek town, spoke with merchants, went on board the ships, bought articles made by Greek workshops, and attended public celebrations.

Such contacts with the Greco-Roman world continued with interruptions for about a thousand years. In the 6th century A. D., when the great migration of the Slavs began in Europe, the Slav tribes settled nearly on the whole of Balkan Peninsula, in dozens of towns beyond the Danube. This was another step towards mastering elements of Greco-Roman culture. The settlers probably maintained ties with their native land.

Slavs' relations with the external world and the centres of medieval world culture were greatly extended when the Kievan state was founded. Selling the tribute collected in the course of *polyudye* on world markets, the large fleets of Russian merchant warriors entered the Black Sea or the Caspian. The fleets sailed to Constantinople or along the Caspian Sea to its southern shores from where the merchants travelled in caravans, on camels, to Baghdad in Iraq or Balkh in

Afghanistan. The Rus saw ships from different seas and with various riggings, and dozens of ports, and traded for half a year on end in such large cities as Constantinople, Rey, Itil and Baghdad.

The Russian language borrowed many Greek and Persian words used in trading practices. Many Russian merchants knew Greek. This is attested to by a rather curious fact: in the 19th century, Russian peddlers who went from village to village carrying haberdashery in hampers sometimes used a secret language which turned out to be Greek, strongly distorted over a thousand years.

By the time of the long-distance overseas travels and caravan trips, i. e. the 9th and 10th centuries, Rus was at a much higher level than in the times of the great Slav migration. There were already towns with developed artisan production. Carpenters and architects built strongholds, blacksmiths made weapons and tools of labour, goldsmiths produced intricate decorations for ladies, potters shaped all sorts of vessels, bone cutters made all kinds of articles ranging from combs and plates for quivers and saddles to the finest needles for sewing.

Naturally not all of the things the Russian travellers saw during their visits to foreign lands could be immediately reproduced by Russian craftsmen, but now foreign articles were not only miracles but also models to be copied.

The historical achievement of Kievan Rus was not only in that a new social and economic formation appeared and hundreds of primitive tribes (Slav, Finno-Ugric, Lettish-Lithuanian) formed a united state, the largest in Europe. In the period of its state unity Kievan Rus managed to produce a single nationality. We tentatively call it the ancient Russian nationality, a parent nationality in respect to the Ukrainians, Russians and Byelorussians who emerged in the 14th and 15th centuries.

The unity of the ancient Russian nationality was manifest in the appearance of a common literary language which engulfed the local tribal dialects, in the rise of a common culture, and in the national awareness of unity.

The feudal culture was most fully displayed in the

St Sophia Cathedral. Kiev

St Sophia Cathedral. Novgorod

St George Cathedral at the Yuryev Monastery near Novgorod. Early 13th century

Church of the Intercession on the Nerl near Vladimir

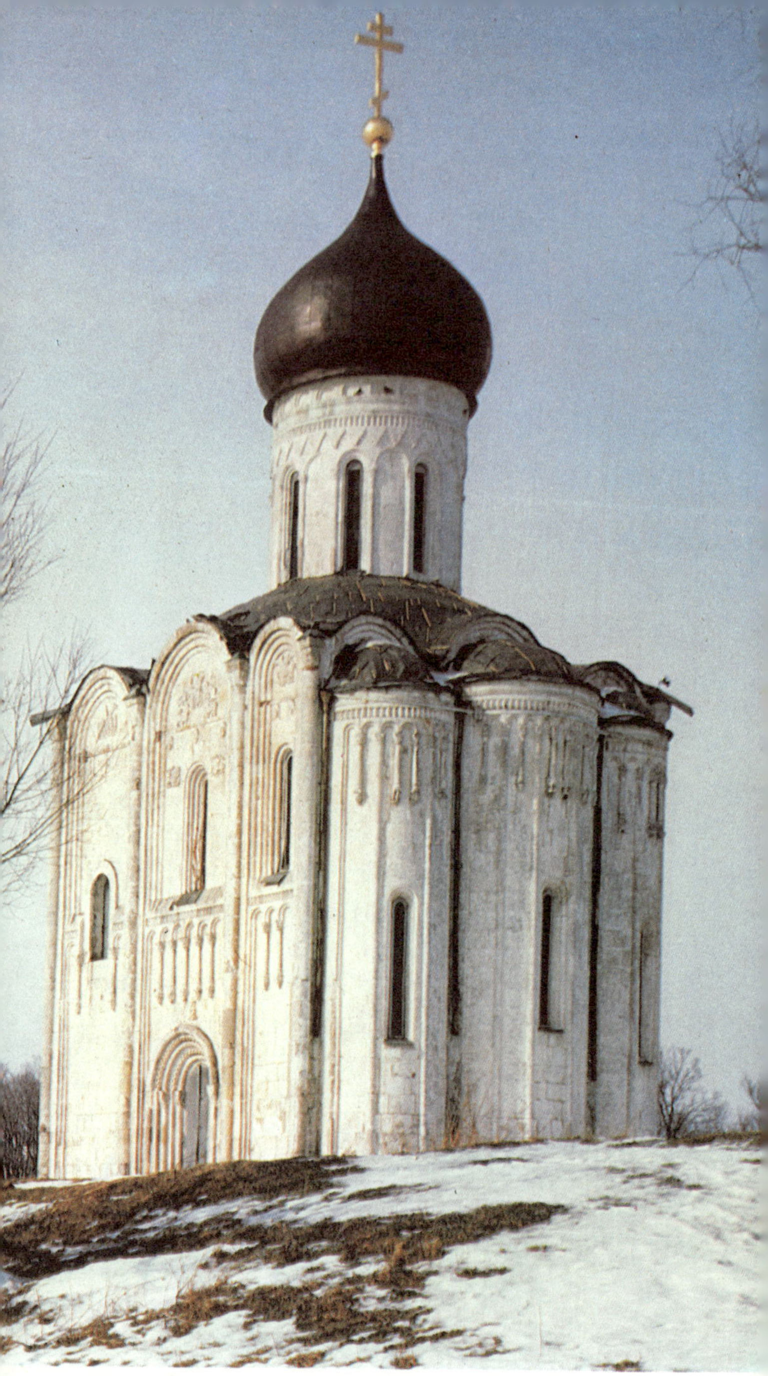

St Demetrius Cathedral. Late 12th century. Vladimir

Church of the Nativity of Our Lady at the Peryn Monastery near Novgorod. Early 13th century

St George Cathedral in Yuryev-Polskoi near Vladimir. Early 13th century

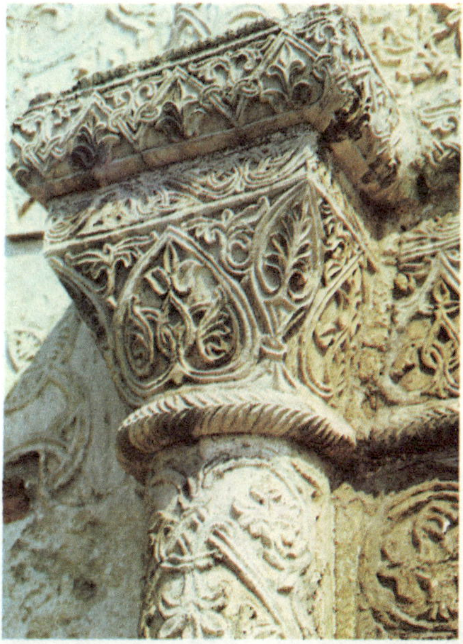

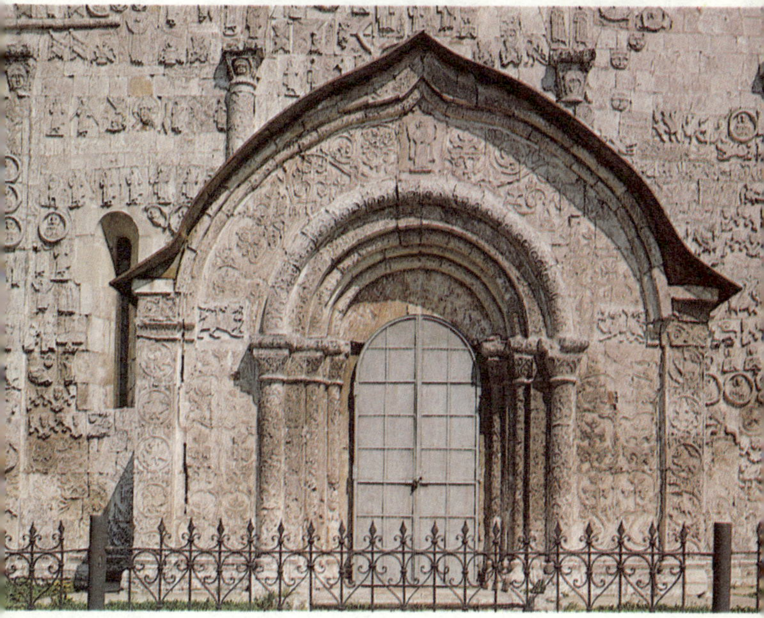

Pskov Kremlin

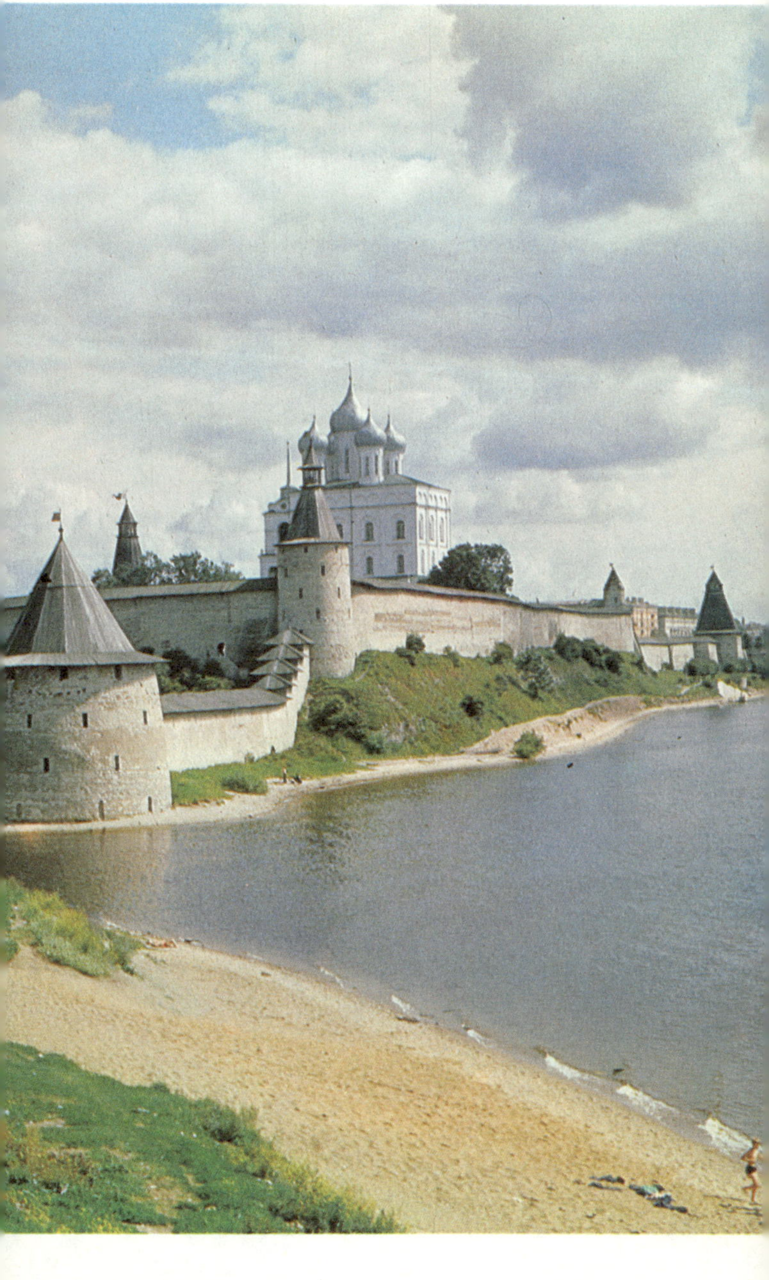

Pskov Kremlin

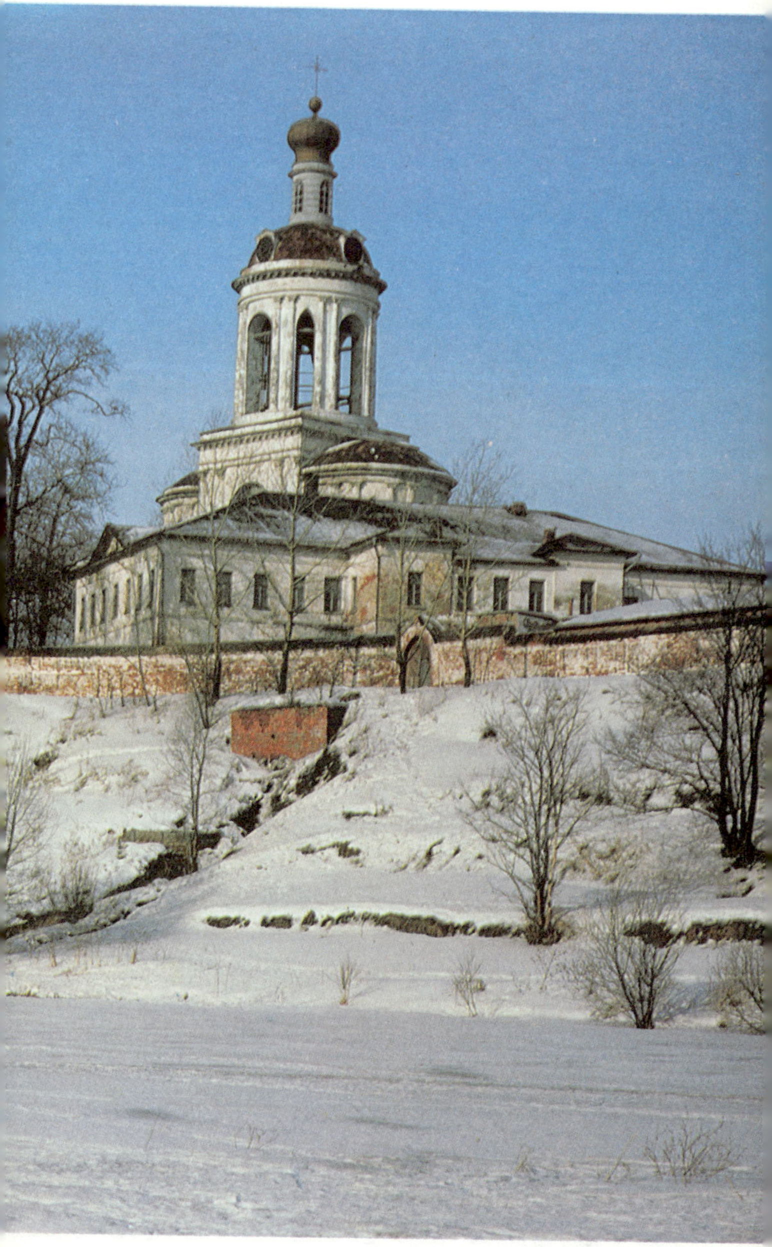

The general view of Novgorod

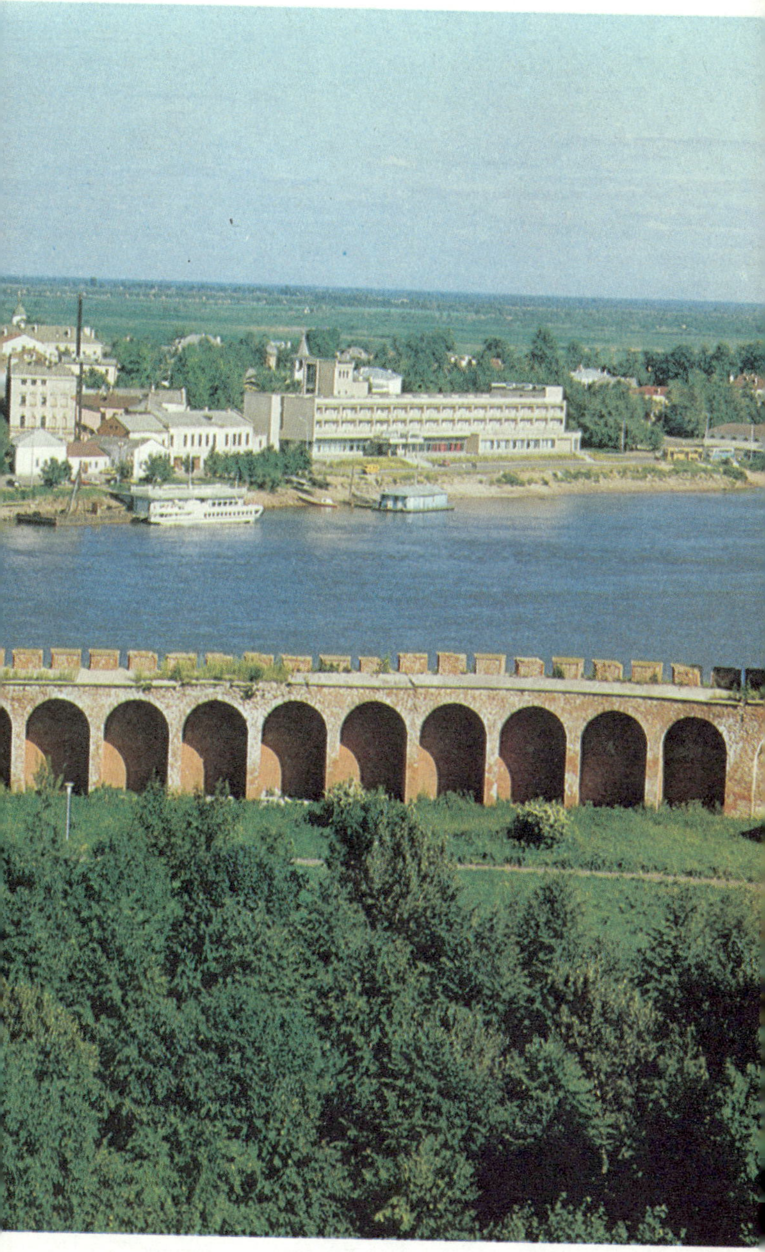

Church of the Saviour-on-the-Nereditsa. 12th century

towns. But it should be kept in mind that the medieval town was not uniform: its population consisted of feudal lords, rich merchants and the clergy on the one hand, and common townsfolk—craftsmen, vendors, captains and sailors in the ports, and workingmen, on the other.

The townsfolk were the advanced part of the population; it was the hands, mind and artistic taste of the people that produced the everyday part of feudal culture—the strongholds and palaces, the white-stone carving on the churches, the many-coloured enamelling on crowns and shoulder ornaments, ships with bows shaped like the head of some beast and silver bracelets depicting mermaid games. The craftsmen were proud of their works and inscribed their names on them.

Townsfolk's view of the world was incomparably broader than that of the rural land-tillers who were tied to their narrow world of a few villages. The town people had relations with foreign merchants, went to other lands, were literate and knew how to count. It was the townsfolk—craftsmen, merchants, warriors and sailors—who changed the ancient notion of the tiny rural world (one day of travel!), enlarging it to include the concept of "the whole wide world".

It was in the towns that the inhabitants played merry pagan games, encouraged wandering musicians, and broke all the taboos of the church. In the towns poets wrote satirical verses, a sharp weapon in the social struggle, the heretics put forward their humanistic ideas raising their voices against the clergy, the church and occasionally even God. It was the common townsfolk who wrote witticisms on the walls of the churches in Kiev and Novgorod in the 11th and 12th centuries destroying the legend of universal religiousness in the Middle Ages.

The discovery in Novgorod of the birch-bark letters dating back to the 11th-15th centuries is of exceptional importance. These remarkable documents once again confirm the fact of widespread literacy among Russian townsfolk.

The Russian countryside remained illiterate for a long time, but in the towns there was widespread literacy, something attested to by numerous inscriptions

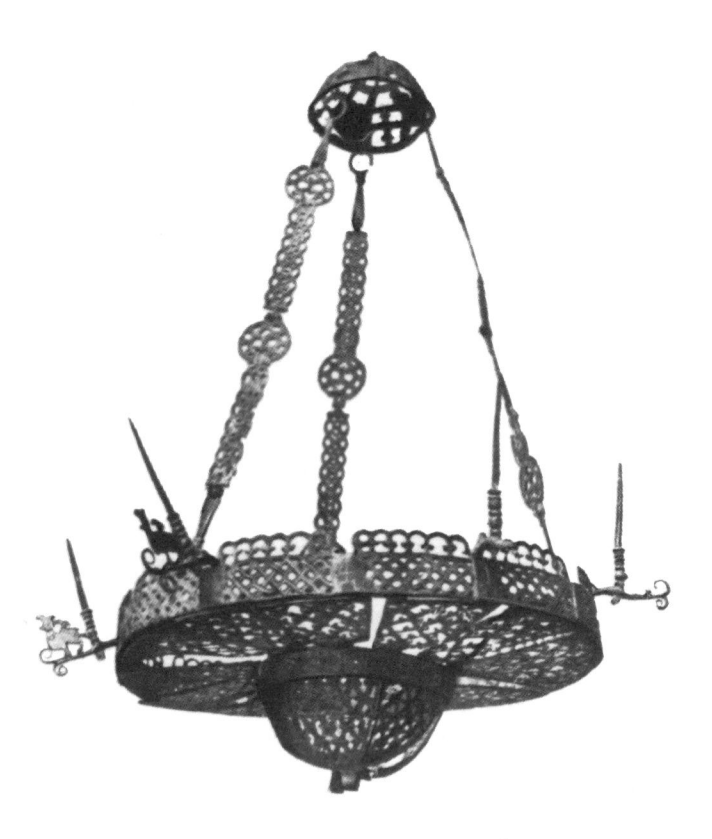

Censer-khoros (12th century). Kiev

on household articles and on church walls in addition to the birch-bark letters. A prince's man noted on a clay amphora: "Bogunka sent the prince fine wine"; stone cutter of Lubech Ivan made a tiny, almost toy whorl and wrote on it: "Ivanko has made this for you, my only daughter"; on another whorl a wench who was learning to read scratched the Russian alphabet to have it handy at all times.

There are several indications of the existence of schools for the young; in 1086 Monomakh's sister set up a school for girls in Kiev at one of the convents.

Members of the lower clergy, deacons and psalm readers frequently fulfilled the role of teachers. Archaeologists have found interesting note-books by two schoolchildren of Novgorod dated 1263. They help us gain an idea of teaching in the Middle Ages: the 13th century pupils studied commercial correspondence, figures, and the principal prayers.

To some extent the Kiev-Pechersky Monastery was a college of the medieval type. It produced high-ranking clergymen (heads of monasteries, bishops and metropolitans) who completed a course in theology, Greek, church literature and rhetoric.

An example of such church rhetoric is the grandiloquent cantata in honour of the Grand Prince composed by a Father-Superior in 1198. A series of sermons against paganism is considered to be a summary of lectures read at the Kiev-Pechersky Monastery.

An idea of the level of knowledge is given by a peculiar kind of 11th-century encyclopedia — the *izborniks* of 1073 and 1076 with entries on grammar, philosophy and other subjects. The Russian people of the time were well aware of the fact that "books are rivers filling the Universe with wisdom". Learned books were sometimes called "deepgoing books".

It is possible that some Russian people studied at foreign universities: one author of the late 12th century, seeking to show how plain his education was, wrote to the prince: "I, O Prince, did not go overseas and did not learn from the philosophers (professors), but, like a bee gathering nectar from flowers and filling combs with honey, I was looking for sweet words and wisdom in many books" (Daniil the Exile).

Russian social thinking of the time was reflected in such remarkable monuments of literature as the *bylinas* and chronicles. Both genres narrate important events of their time, both are intended for their contemporaries and descendants, and often for posterity. We, distant descendants, are thankful to the ancient storytellers and chroniclers for the precious glimpses of information about the fate of Rus, the struggle against the nomads, various affairs of towns and princes which have come down to us in the oral tradition of the *bylinas* and on the parchment of book chronicles.

The value of the epics about the *bogatyrs* lies in their popular origin which links them closely to the *smerds*—warriors who tilled the land and fought against the Pechenegs and the Polovtsi under the Kievan banners.

The heroic epics are probably rooted in the thousand-year-old history of the primitive tribal society. Only a small fraction of the *bylinas* have reached us; they were created in the early centuries of the Russian state and survived only due to the specific historical conditions of the Russian North.

The *bylinas* were created and renewed up to the Tatar-Mongolian invasion of Rus; crushing defeats at the hands of the nomads and the establishment of foreign rule could not contribute to the appearance of many new heroic *bylinas* but, no doubt, it did not kill Russian people's desire to preserve their old fund of epics as a memory of the glory of Kievan Rus, of the rise of their state and popular defence of their country. The *bylinas* raised the fighting spirit and called people for the struggle against the Tatars; no wonder the Pechenegs and the Polovtsi, the real enemies of Rus in the age when the *bylinas* were created, were later almost completely replaced by the Tatars.

The people elaborated and carefully preserved the epic verse in the course of the entire millennium; it served as a kind of an oral textbook of native history passed down from one generation to the next. Instances were recorded by 19th-century ethnographers when the performance of *bylinas* became an obligatory part of New Year's celebration in villages, when not only the future was exhorted ritually but also the past summed up. *Bylinas* were sung at feasts, "in the course of peaceful conversations, drinking honey and wine".

We find traces of epic poetry in the written sources of Kievan Rus as early as the 997 chronicles praising the rule of Vladimir Svyatoslavich. The chronicler acted on a par with the authors of the *bylinas* which were focussed on the same Prince Vladimir the Red Sun.

The *bylinas* contain the following names of persons who can, in varying degrees, be compared to real historical figures known to us from the chronicles:

Kievan Prince Vladimir the Red Sun (it is assumed that this hero combines Vladimir Svyatoslavich (980-1015) and Vladimir Monomakh (died in 1125), Volga (Oleg) Svyatoslavich (975-977), Dobrynya (the 980s), Gleb (died in 1078), Wizard Vseslavich (Vseslav of Polotsk, died in 1101), Apraksa *korolevishna* (Empress Yevpraksia, Monomakh's sister), Kozarin (1106), *boyar* Stavr (1118), pilgrim *bogatyr* Daniil (1107), boyar Putyata (1113), Sadko (1167), Prince Roman (died in 1205). Also mentioned are the Polovtsi khans Sharukan (Shark the Giant, Kudrevan), his son Otrak and his grandson Konchak (Konshak), Khan Sugra (1107), Tugortkan (Tugarin the Serpent, 1096) and the Tatar khans Batu and Kalin Tsar (possibly Mengu-Kaan, 1239).

Of the towns the following are frequently mentioned: Kiev, Chernigov, Novgorod, Murom (possibly, initially Moroviisk on the Desna). Certain *bylinas* mention other towns whose names are considerably distorted. The rivers in *bylinas* are chiefly South Russian: the Dnepr, Puchai-river (Pochaina in Kiev), the Smorodina (Sneporod, a left tributary of the Dnepr) and others.

The geography of all the heroic *bylinas* and most of the stories are linked to Kiev and the pre-steppe Russian belt in the South; part of the stories are related to Novgorod. Occasionally the *bylinas* mentioned some sea and different overseas lands, Constantinople and Jerusalem (probably the influence of religious verses).

The names of historical figures yield the following earliest and latest dates: 975 and 1240 (except a few individual later *bylinas*). Within this time interval many *bylinas* are grouped according to historical names into two chronological sections: a) 980-1015 and b) 1096-1118, i. e. around two Vladimirs famous in Russian history—Vladimir I Svyatoslavich, "the Holy", and Vladimir II Monomakh, a fact already pointed out by the earliest scholars who studied the *bylinas*. This provides us with some not very reliable guidelines, because, according to the law of epic unity, the *bylinas* identified the two Vladimirs to such an extent that they completely lost their individuality and, besides, absorbed the names of other princes of the 11th and 12th centuries into the archetypal epic Vla-

Ancient Russian musical notation

dimir. Kiev was always the capital of Rus in the *bylinas*, and the "gentle Prince Vladimir" was always the Grand Prince of Kiev which makes dating *bylina* events difficult but not hopeless.

Additional details may help specify date of the event described, but a complex of indications confirming each other is necessary for a conjecture to become the basis for a precise date. Let us consider just one example concerning the above-mentioned *boyar* Stavr Gordyatinich of Novgorod.

The rare name of the *boyar* in the *bylina* about Stavr and his wife Vassilisa has long ago enabled scholars to identify him with *boyar* Stavr mentioned in the chronicle under 1118. The situation described in the chronicle is fully reflected in the first part of the *bylina*: in 1118 Vladimir Monomakh summoned all the *boyars* from Novgorod to Kiev and forced them to pledge allegiance to him; the Grand Prince ordered several *boyars* including Hundred head Stavr, to be imprisoned. According to the *bylina* Stavr is an old and wealthy Novgorod *boyar*. As in the chronicle, Stavr is also imprisoned by Vladimir, but the main action in the *bylina* begins with Stavr's young wife winning Stavr's freedom in a game of chess with Vladimir; the short note in the chronicle does not feature the latter detail, but all the circumstances having to do with Stavr's arrest coincide fully in the chronicle and the *bylina*.

Stavr (Stavko) Gordyatich is first mentioned in the chronicle in 1069-1070; in 1118 he must have been about 70, and the Stavr Godinovich of the *bylina* is correctly called an "old *boyar*".

The coincidence of all the particularities convinces us that the *bylina* about Stavr and Vassilisa was based on a real event of 1118.

The ancient epics of the tribal age were, no doubt, widespread in Kievan Rus. But it is very difficult for us to say something definite about their content. They probably had a strong archaic mythological element, and the constant danger of raids by steppe nomads was represented in the form of a huge serpent overwhelmed by the Slav *bogatyrs*. These tales are echoed in the Ukrainian legends about the blacksmith brothers who defeated the serpent, harnessed it to a huge plough and made an enormous furrow which became the Serpent Wall, Slav frontier fortifications facing the steppe. The harnessed serpent is apparently a symbol of the captive nomads forced after being defeated to dig deep pits and raise high ramparts which have survived to our day.

The story about the prince of the Polyanian land Kii, the founder of Kiev, should also be attributed to the heroic epics. Chronicler Nestor supplies the tale of the three brothers building a town with an additional episode about expeditions (apparently the 6th century A. D.) by Slav warriors commanded by Kii to the Danube and Byzantium. The author of *The Lay of Igor's Host* still knew songs about expeditions through the steppe to the Balkans ("riding to Trajan's monument [at the village of Adamklisi in Dobruja — *B. R.*] through the steppe to the mountain ranges") which might have reflected 6th-century events when large masses of Slavs fought victoriously against Byzantium. He also remembered even earlier laments on the tragic fate of the Slav prince of the 4th century Bous taken prisoner in a battle against the Goths and tortured to death by them.

The excerpts from ancient epics going back to the age of military democracy indicate that these epics were heroic and popular in nature: they described joint expeditions by many tribes against the mighty Byzantium, mourned the death of the seventy Slav chieftains killed together with Bous, and sung praise to the victory over the steppe people which ended with the building of fortifications which protected the lands of several Slav tribes (Polyanians, Rus, Severyanians and Ulichians). Some subjects featured in later epic *bylinas* may also be attributed to these distant times or perhaps even to an earlier period of Slav contacts with the Scythians: such, for example, is the story of a fight between father and unrecognised son *(Ilya and the Falconer*; the Iranian parallel is *Rustam and Sohrab)* and other themes with universal human implications not connected with specific events.

The Kievan cycle of *bylinas* about Prince Vladimir the Red Sun, Dobrynya (brother of Vladimir's mother) and Ilya of Murom was formed at a point when the Kievan state abruptly changed its policy: from distant expeditions to foreign, unknown lands, in which, perhaps, hired Varangian seafarers also participated, it passed to planned defence of Rus from the Pechenegs and the expulsion of the arrogant Varangian mercenaries. Judging by numerous individual signs, the first *bylina* in the cycle, "Volga Svyatoslavich and Mikula Selyaninovich", must be connected with the events of 975-977 when Prince Oleg Svyatoslavich of the Drevlyanians began a struggle against the Varangian Sveneld and had to resort to a peasant militia in order to reinforce his warriors. *Bogatyr* ploughman Mikula whose rural origin is attested to by his symbolic patronymic Selyaninovich takes the central place in the *bylina*, personifying not only the freedom-loving Drevlyanians who had come out against the unjust tribute levied on them by the prince as far back as 945 but also the entire Russian people who were building their new state at the time in a struggle against the Varangians and the nomads.

The *bylina* about Volga and Mikula who joins the prince's warriors may be regarded as an epigraph to the entire body of epic *bylinas* which reflects events of popular importance, and in which the people are presented as the chief force either under the name of Drevlyanian land-tiller Mikula or town craftsman Nikita Kozhemyaka, or peasant son Ilya of Murom. Popular judgement lies at the basis of the choice of figures to be praised in *bylinas*. The epics do not feature the names of Svyatoslav who neglected his native land, or Yaroslav (the Wise according to church terminology) who surrounded himself with Varangians. But there is in every *bylina* "the gentle prince of the capital Kiev, Volodimer", whose image combines Vladimir I (the Holy) who fought against the Pechenegs, set up a line of strongholds to protect Rus and persecuted robbers, and Vladimir II Monomakh who also organised resistance against the nomads and issued legal Rules easing the position of the lower sections of the population.

The folk *bylinas* about *bogatyrs* were complemented by court *bylina* tales imitating the folk stories in form. These include the songs of the wooing by the Norwegian King, the poet Harald, of the daughter of Yaroslav the Wise (Solovei Budimirovich), the story of the wife of *boyar* Stavr who saved her husband by beating Monomakh at chess (Stavr Godinovich), the ironic tale of Prince Vsevolod Olgovich, dandy and rake who caused much harm to the Kievans (Churila).

The chroniclers hardly dealt with the life of the people. They took part in and recorded the affairs of the princes, cloisters and occasionally the towns. However, the many details written down in the chronicles and the existence of chronicles in different towns

(Kiev, Chernigov, Novgorod, Galich, Vladimir, Pskov, Ryazan and others) makes them an invaluable source for the study of native history and the native language as distinct from many European countries where the chronicles were written in Latin, a language alien to the people.

The Kievan Nestor (early 12th century) stands out in particular among the chroniclers. He wrote a thorough historical introduction to the chronicle of events *The Tale of Bygone Years*. The introduction spans a period from the 5th-6th centuries A. D. to 860 when the Rus first emerged as a force equal to the Byzantine Empire.

Nestor's historical and geographical introduction to the history of the Kievan Rus, written with great breadth of vision and authenticity, deserves our full confidence.

It outlines the nature of the country and those elements of nature which influenced the historical development of the nation: mighty rivers linking Rus to North Europe, Asia and South Europe, the large unpopulated forests on the watersheds such as the Okovsky woods, the troublesome steppe expanses of Great Scythia from where the hordes of nomad horsemen appeared.

Nestor, one of the most brilliantly educated persons of his time and owner of a huge library of Russian, Greek, West Slavic and Bulgarian books, painted a picture of the life of all Slav peoples and compared their daily life and mores with those of the people of the whole Old World. Nestor leads the reader to the most different places: to the forest tribes of the Drevlyanians, Radimichians and Vyatichians, to the steppe Polovtsi, to misty Britain, to India and the Brahmans or even further to the islands of Indonesia, and to the very edge of the then known world, to China.

Nestor wrote the truth about the primitive customs of the Drevlyanians and the Radimichians (approximately at the time of the Zarubintsy culture) juxtaposing them to the "wise and reasonable" Polyanians (tribes of the Chernyakhovo culture). As if anticipating the biased interpretations originating from the Normanists, he sought to show that many peoples of

Temple rings (12th century)

the world had strange customs: some of them "kill people", "are irritable beyond all measure", others fornicate with their own mothers and nieces, still others have women who behave like dumb beasts, and finally there are those who eat human flesh.

Paying tribute to the biblical legends inevitable for the medieval monk historian, Nestor quickly passes to a description of the Slav world in its totality. He does not list the legendary Czech, Lech and Rus usual in West European chronicles, but indicates all the really existing large alliances of tribes in the area of the Slav's original settlement in Europe.

The territory on which the Slavs (West and East) lived at the turn of the first millennium A. D. is quite precisely outlined and coincide with our contemporary view, formed on the basis of linguistic, anthropological and archaeological data.

The keen insight of a historian prompts Nestor to select faultlessly the basic, key elements in the life of the Slavs: first, there is the 6th century, the time of the Slav expeditions against Byzantium, the time of the rise of powerful and stable tribal alliances ruled by princes, the time when Kii travelled to Constantinople, and Kiev was founded as the capital of the tribal "principality" of the Polyanians.

In the periods adopted in contemporary scholarship we also single out the 6th century as a turning point

Golden diadems (12th and 13th centuries) from the treasures buried during Batu's invasion in 1240

very important in the history of Slav prefeudal formations.

The second age Nestor singles out is the 9th century, a time when Slav feudal states were formed such as Kievan Rus, the Great Moravian State, the Bulgarian Kingdom; it was the time when Slav written language appeared, and Christianity penetrated the Slav world.

As we have seen, the periods Nestor chose coincide with ours; he singled out the same points in the history of Slavs as we do today.

In the 12th century chronicles began to be kept in nearly every large town expressing the independence of individual principalities. We are familiar with the chronicle of Novgorod's "younger brother" Pskov; we know the chronicles of Vladimir and Rostov. Chronicles were also written in the southwestern part—in Galich, Vladimir-Volynsky and in Pinsk.

The Smolensk chronicle and the extremely interesting Polotsk chronicle were known to V. N. Tatishchev who had them only for a short time and only managed to make a few notes.

We are much better acquainted with the chronicles of Vladimir and Rostov.

Fragments of chronicles from Ryazan, Pereyaslavl Russky and Chernigov have also survived.

It is most probable that the fragments of various principalities' chronicles which survived as parts of the later collected chronicles hardly reflect the actual situation in chronicle-writing in the 12th and early 13th centuries. There were many more chronicles, but a considerable part of them perished during Polovtsi raids, princes' internal wars and particularly when Russian towns were burned during the Tatar invasion. We know instances when in the 14th and 15th centuries Moscow stone cellars were filled with books up to the ceiling in order to preserve them, but they were consumed by fire anyway.

Of all the chronicle collections dating back to the time we are concerned with, the most interesting in terms of history and culture is perhaps the Kievan collected chronicle of 1198 (it is sometimes dated 1199 or 1200) compiled by the Father-Superior of the Vydubitsky Cloister Moses under Prince Rurik Rostislavich. The editor and also the author of a few entries concerning the 1190s ended his work with the text of a pompous cantata sung "in chorus" by the monks of his cloister in honour of the Grand Prince.

The rich Vydubitsky Cloister near Kiev apparently had a large historical library consisting of chronicle manuscripts which helped the Father-Superior to compile an interesting work on Russian history of the entire 12th century. Moses had at his disposal chronicles of different princes from different principalities. That was why the historian of the end of the century could depict, say, some war from different vantage points: both from the viewpoint of the attackers and from that of the defenders or the besieged, which made it possible to achieve a more objective view of the event. The Kievan collection of 1198 reflects not only Kievan events but also the affairs of Chernigov, Galich, Novgorod, Vladimir on the Klyazma, Pereyaslavl Russky, Ryazan and a number of other Russian towns, and sometimes even foreign events such as Friederich Barbarossa's Fourth Crusade. It is possible to single out several chronicles used by Moses.

We can single out separate chronicles on the basis

of various features, such as the dialectal specifics of the language, differences in the cliches of the princes' titles, ways of writing the dates, presence or absence of church phraseology, literary style, manner of describing events, breadth of outlook, and, most important, the attitude of the chronicler to one or another prince.

On the basis of the sum of features it is possible to single out about ten historical manuscripts used by the Kievan Father-Superior Moses in compiling his chronicle of 1198. The first half of the collection is taken by Nestor's *The Tale of Bygone Years* and further down excerpts are used from the chronicles of Vladimir Monomakh and his sons ("Volodimer's tribe"). Then come fragments from the chronicle of Yuri Dolgoruky and his son Andrei Bogolyubsky who ruled Kiev for a very short time but left a "regal" chronicle praising the monarch. There are traces of the Galich chronicle (or a work by someone from Galich written in Kiev in the 1170s and the 1180s). The collection also includes a special account of the murder of Andrei Bogolyubsky probably written by Andrei's favourite Kuzmishcha Kiyanin who left notes concerning 1174-1177. Some of the notes in the chronicle, chiefly about court affairs, belong to Moses himself.

It is particularly interesting to compare two authors: one of them is the clergyman Polikarp (all attributions of specific texts to historical persons are tentative including Nestor) who ended his life as Archimandrite of the Kiev-Pechersky Monastery, the other is a noble *boyar*, Kievan Thousand head Pyotr Borislavich, known for his diplomatic deeds.

Polikarp was an advocate of the Chernigov-Seversky princes who were often hostile to Kiev. He particularly actively defended the interests of Prince Svyatoslav, son of Oleg (and father of Igor, the hero of *The Lay of Igor's Host*). Parts of Polikarp's chronicle found in different places of Moses' collection show Polikarp as a mediocre writer registering events with great bias. His vocabulary is overburdened with church rhetoric; his outlook is narrow.

A curious individual feature of this chronicler is his tendency to list the sums of money and items of the prince's household. He is a type of a chronicler bookkeeper, drawing up a detailed list of property captured by the enemy—from a church Gospel to haystacks and "mares of the herd"; he knows precisely what values were presented to the cloister by the aging princess and how much money was paid to a landless prince for taking part in an internecine conflict.

Father-Superior Moses abridged Polikarp's manuscript, throwing out much of the rhetorical praising of Prince Svyatoslav Olgovich. Muscovite historians of the 16th century made fuller use of Polikarp's work in compiling the Nikon chronicle, and the praise has been retained.

This chronicler book-keeper stands in complete contrast to the Kievan chronicler of the middle and second half of the 12th century who may with a large degree of certainty be identified with Pyotr Borislavich mentioned in the chronicle in the 1150s and the 1160s. The latter's highly interesting work was also abridged by Father-Superior Moses who left out many political judgements. We know this because in the 1730s V. N. Tatishchev had an ancient manuscript on parchment (known as the *raskolnik* manuscript) which constituted the complete text of the *boyar*-chronicler's historical work, judging by the notes made by Tatishchev.

Pyotr Borislavich wrote the chronicle of one branch of princes, "Mstislav's tribe", descendants of the elder son of Monomakh, Grand Princes of Kiev—Izyaslav Mstislavich (1146-1154), his son Mstislav Izyaslavich (1167-1170) and his nephew Rurik Rostislavich who reigned with interruptions from 1173 to 1201. The chronicle reaches 1196.

Pyotr Borislavich knew how to take a broad look of events, and he began each entry in the chronicle with a general review of relations between princes, alliances, quarrels, treaties or violations of oaths. The reviews included both neighbouring principalities and distant lands—Novgorod, Karela, Bohemia, Poland, Polotsk and others.

In each complicated situation Pyotr Borislavich sought to exonerate his prince, showing him in the most favourable light, but he did it much more skilfully than his political opponent Polikarp: instead of exclamations he offered proof in the shape of authentic documents from the prince's archives. Pyotr Borislavich introduced into the chronicle treaties with princes, letters of princes and kings, documents from the archives of Yuri Dolgoruky captured from the enemy, and so on.

It is to be noted, however, that having taken up the pen, the Kiev Thousand head did not become a humble servant of the princes. In his writings he preserved his position of a feudal vassal who retained the "right of departure". In those instances when the Grand Prince ignored the advice of the *boyar duma* the chronicler quoted the *boyars*' documents at length and, not without malice, put down on his pages both a description of the prince's defeat and the unfavourable decision of the *boyar duma*: "O Prince! Get thee gone; we don't need you."

The chronicle of Pyotr Borislavich abounds in "speeches made by wise *boyars*". Most probably, this was only a literary device by means of which the shrewd author expounds the *boyar* programme. The political programme of the 12th-century Russian *boyars* consisted of the following: the prince should rule the principality jointly with the largest land-owning *boyars* living near him in the capital; the prince would have to decide all questions of war and peace with the *boyars*.

The prince should think about justice and the "land order". Distant expeditions were of no interest to the *boyars*, and they regarded conflicts between princes as extremely harmful and sought to restrain the prince from undertaking reckless actions. The only reason for which "horses might be saddled" was to defend Rus from foreign enemies. As we can see, the programme is largely quite progressive which can be explained by the fact that the *boyars* were the carriers of the newly established and still far from declining feudal mode of production, a progressive phenomenon compared to the primitive tribal order.

It is interesting to point out that this author has no church rhetoric or interest for church events, but everything having to do with military matters, diplomatic negotiations or the prince's assemblies is presented in great detail and with the knowledge of the subject.

In its original form retained in Tatishchev's notes the chronicle of Pyotr Borislavich contained extremely interesting political portraits of the Grand Princes of Kiev during the entire 12th century. The author described the princes, most of whom were his contemporaries, according to a definite pattern: appearance, temper, attitude to ruling the land and justice, military talents, concern for his warriors, relation to palace etiquette and individual traits. His judgements are subjective but by all means interesting, because we are presented with a gallery of monarchs described by one person.

We learn from these verbal portraits, for example, that Izyaslav Mstislavich was handsome, that he richly awarded loyal vassals and valued his honour, and that his son Mstislav was so strong that "hardly anyone could bend his bow". The latter prince was so brave that "all princes feared and esteemed him. Although he often made merry with damsels and warriors, neither damsels nor wine possessed him..., [the prince] read many books and in ruling sought the advice of the lords..."

It turns out that Igor Olgovich (killed by the Kievans in 1147) was fond of hunting and bird catching "and well trained in church singing. I have often sung in church with him" (the chronicler writes about himself—*B. R.*).

On the whole the *boyar* chronicle of Pyotr Borislavich in which he wrote about the events he witnessed from 1146 to 1196, with its deeds from the princes' archives, diaries of campaigns, minutes of sessions of the *boyar duma* and important princes' assemblies, its literary devices and most striking portraits of the grand princes is of undoubtable historical interest.

Russian literature of the 11th-13th centuries was not limited to chronicles; it was quite varied and, most probably, very extensive, but only a small part has survived due to the numerous Tatar destructions of Russian towns in the 13th-16th centuries.

In addition to the historical works showing that despite the youth of the Russian state and its culture Russian writers have attained the level of the Greeks, we have at our disposal works of other genres. Nearly everything that was created in the 10th-12th centuries was rewritten and copied in subsequent times. Readers continued to be interested in many things. A revealing work was *The Travels* of Father-Superior Daniil to the Middle East (about 1107). Daniil went to Jerusalem, the centre of the Christian tradition, and provided a detailed account of the trip, and of the countries and towns he saw. He arrived in Jerusalem during the First Crusade and became a friend of the leader of the crusaders King Baldwin. Daniil gave a very precise description of Jerusalem and its environs, pointing out the distance and the size of architectural monuments. *The Travels* served for a long time as a reliable Russian guidebook to the Holy Places which also attracted thousands of pilgrims from all parts of Europe.

Another interesting genre was the "lives of saints" which served as a strong tool of church propaganda where we clearly perceive real life through the sentimental praising of the persons exemplary from the viewpoint of the church—the holy, the righteous, and the blessed—all those canonised by the church; the "lives" gave the notion of the class structure of the cloisters, monks' greed, some princes' cruelty and love of money, and the use by the church of mentally retarded persons, and a lot more.

Of particular interest is the *Kiev-Pechersky paterik* which is a collection of tales of different times about the monks of the Pechersky Monastery. It is supplemented by an exceptionally revealing correspondence between Bishop Simon and a church careerist Polikarp seeking to obtain a high clerical office for a bribe (the money was provided by the daughter of Vsevolod the Big Nest).

One more genre also connected with the church was the admonitions against paganism; they condemned the folk religion and merrymaking and festivities. They also describe many curious everyday details.

Extremely popular in the Middle Ages were the collections of maxims, sayings and proverbs (*Pchela*).

Of immense interest are two literary works, *A Word of Daniil the Exile* and *A Supplication of Daniil the*

Exile sometimes incorrectly attributed to one person.

A Word of Daniil is a request sent by a certain Daniil exiled to Lake Lacha, to Prince Yaroslav Vladimirovich in about 1197. This is a brilliant work describing various aspects of Russian life of the late 12th century in the form of aphorisms, of which medieval authors were so fond. Daniil exposes the prince's *tiuns* and *ryadoviches* oppressing small feudal owners, expresses a dislike of rich but foolish people heeded only because of their position, and pokes fun at messengers and envoys who spend their time in "feasting houses" instead of fulfilling their duties.

The author, a well-read and intelligent person persecuted in the past for his literary work, offers his services to the prince, because he is "poor in dress but rich in mind". Apparently he is not only a writer but also an eloquent speaker. "My tongue is like the pen of a scrivener, and my lips are gracious like the murmur of a stream". It is possible that Daniil was writing the chronicle at the court of Vsevolod the Big Nest for some time. Under 1192 the chronicle presents a didactic homily concerning the fire in Vladimir; it condemns the wealthy who reduced to slavery the helpless victims of the fire "by unfair duties".

A Word of Daniil the Exile was very popular; it was copied and read for many centuries. Thirty years later it was imitated by an anonymous author who signed it with the name of Daniil, but also wrote frankly that he himself "was no sage, but wore the dress of the wise and the boots of the sharp-witted". This pseudo-Daniil called his work (circa 1229) *A Supplication* including nearly the entire *Word of Daniil* in it and adding several new and revealing aphorisms. The *Supplication* is addressed to the prince of Pereyaslavl, Yaroslav, a son of Vsevolod the Big Nest. The author was the son of a bondswoman, he was abandoned in childhood by his parents, experienced the "working yoke" and received no schooling.

Pseudo-Daniil is an advocate of the prince's power (the prince is the helmsman of his land); the *boyars* are regarded as an intelligent milieu of the prince. It is interesting that the author has a sharply negative attitude to the monks and the "obscene customs" of

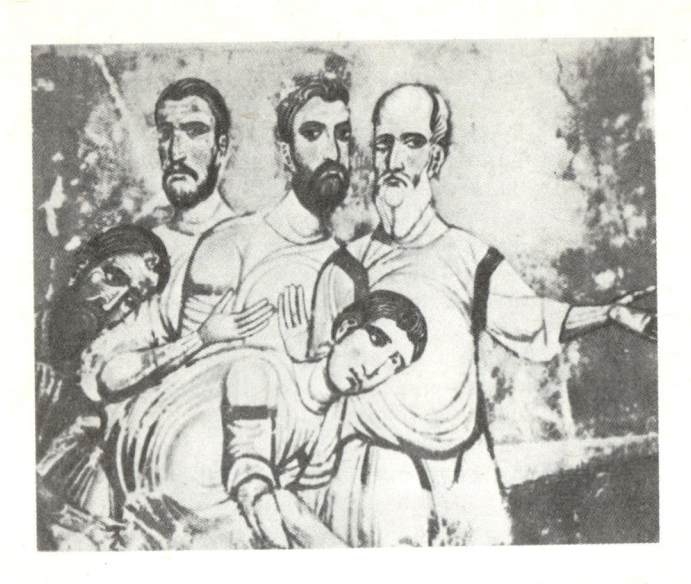

Fresco in the Spas-Mirozhsky Cloister in Pskov (12th century). *The Miracle on Lake Tiveriadskoye*

the "fawning dogs", the monks. Both works, the *Word* and the *Supplication*, acquaint us with the social thinking of the lower sections of Russian feudal society at the turn of the 13th century.

The most important and world-famous work of ancient Russian literature is *The Lay of Igor's Host* written in 1185 in Kiev. The poem was emulated by contemporaries and authors of the early 13th century, it was quoted by Pskov writers at the beginning of the 14th century, and following the Battle of Kulikovo, a poem on the victory over Mamai, *Zadonshchina*, was written in Moscow in imitation of *The Lay of Igor's Host*.

The Lay of Igor's Host might be called a political treatise, so great is the insight and the breadth with which important historical questions are considered. The author delves into the antiquity of Trajan's Age (2nd to 4th centuries A.D.), and the time of Bous (375), so unhappy for the Slavs, but his principal attention is focussed on revealing the roots of the internal strife which helped the Polovtsi lay waste to the Russian land. One of the first princes to blame for the situation was Oleg Svyatoslavich (died in 1115), grandfather of the vanquished Igor. Oleg is juxtaposed to the poetic image of the sorcerer prince Vseslav of Polotsk, the hero of the Kievan popular rebellion of 1068, and Vladimir Monomakh. The historical concept of the author is remarkably clear-cut and deep.

The main part of the poem-treatise is the *Golden Word* addressed to all princes with an ardent patriotic appeal to "jump in the stirrup for the Russian land", to rescue the unfortunate Igor. The superb poetical skill has made the poem immortal. The poet's favourite image is that of the falcon soaring high up in the sky and peering sharply into the faraway distances. The author seems to be lifting the reader high up above the ground and everything you can see on it— warriors on horseback, trees, lands, boundless steppe, swans, wolves, foxes and towns with palaces—in order to show to him all of Rus from the Carpathians to the Volga River, from Novgorod and Polotsk to far-off Tmutarakan on the Black Sea.

The poetical images are derived primarily from nature: disturbed animals and flocks of birds, leaves falling from the trees at the wrong time, the blue mist and the silver river waters. The verbal ornamentation of this knightly poem contains much gold, mother-of-pearl, silver, all kinds of weapons, silk and brocade.

Similarly to the future poets of the Renaissance who revived ancient mythology, the author of *The Lay of Igor's Host* widely resorts to images of Slav paganism: Stribog, the ruler of the winds, Veles, the patron of poets, the mysterious Div, and the Sun Khoros. It should be noted that the author almost completely avoids church language, while paganism occupies a prominent place which, perhaps, was the reason why the clergy took part in destroying manuscripts of the poem in the 14th-17th centuries.

Although Russian literature is highly patriotic we do not find a trace of advocacy of aggressive actions in it. The struggle against the Polovtsi was regarded only as Russian people's defence from unexpected destructive raids. A typical feature is the absence of any chauvinism and a humane attitude to people of different nationalities: "Have a kind attitude not only to people of your faith, but to followers of other religions ... whether Hebrews or Moslems, or heretics or Catholics or one of the pagans—have mercy on each and rescue him from misfortune."

An interesting manifestation of Russian culture is the Vladimir collection of chronicles of 1206 compiled, perhaps, with the participation of the elder son of Vsevolod, Konstantin the Wise about whom contemporaries said that he was "very fond of reading books and was taught in many sciences, ... he collected many of the ancient princes' deeds and wrote himself, and many others laboured with him".

The original manuscript has not reached us, but we have copies made in the 15th century in Smolensk which had been first introduced into the scientific world by Peter the Great (the Radziville, or Königsberg chronicle). The collection describes "the deeds of ancient princes" from Kii to Vsevolod the Big Nest.

Of special value in the Radziville chronicle are the 618 colour miniatures aptly called "windows opening on an extinct world".

A. Shakhmatov and A. Artsikhovsky established that the drawings and the text reproduce the original chronicle of 1206. Further analysis revealed that the authors and artists of the Vladimir collection were only copyists: they had at their disposal a whole library of illustrated chronicles including the collection of 997, Nikon's chronicle of 1076, Nestor's *Tale of Bygone Years*, the Kievan chronicles of the age of Monomakh and his sons, and various chronicles dating back to the second half of the 12th century. They even had such illustrated chronicles from which they took mostly pictures but not the text. It is possible to assume that the Kievan chronicle of Pyotr Borislavich was illustrated, because the Radziville Copy has miniatures showing events not described in this chronicle and only present in the Kievan collection of 1198 (Ipatyevsky chronicle), such as a council of Izyaslav Mstislavich with the Hungarian king, the delegation of a *boyar* Pyotr Borislavich sent to Vladimir of Galich (1152) and others. Nowhere in the text of the Radziville chronicle is it indicated that the princess took part in the murder of Andrei Bogolyubsky, while in the picture we see, in addition to the *boyar* murderers, the princess carrying her husband's cut-off hand. Other sources confirm the princess' part in the conspiracy.

The existence of illustrations in the 997 chronicle is proved by the shape of the swords typical of the mid-10th century and the shape of vessels also of the 10th century. It was retained when the illustrations were copied.

Of major interest are the drawings which show the original appearance of the ancient architecture of Kiev, Pereyaslavl and Vladimir. The Church of the Tithe in Kiev (996) destroyed by Batu in 1240 was unknown to the copyists of the 15th century, but on the miniature it is depicted in a form which was restored only on the basis of the 20th-century excavations.

The original illustrative material of the 1206 collection related to different 11th- and 12th-century chronicles introduces us to the literary and political struggles of the time perhaps even in a greater degree than the text, because the choice of subjects for illustrations reflected particularly clearly the bias of the illustrator. The miniatures of Nikon of Tmutarakan (1076) clearly indicate his sympathy for Mstislav of Tmutarakan and hostility for Yaroslav the Wise and his elder son Izyaslav. In his turn, the artist who drew the miniatures for Izyaslav's chronicle displayed unheard-of impudence: he took revenge on Nikon depicting him as an ass (!) on the seat of the Father-Superior in the church.

The editing of Nestor's work by Prince Mstislav consisted of the introduction of numerous illustrations concerning all, even minor, events of Mstislav's own youth. Of interest in the art school of the age of Monomakh and Mstislav were the ironic additional drawings on the margins: a serpent (victory over the Polovtsi), a dog (princes' quarrels), cat and mouse (successful expedition of 1227), monkey (frightened

Torks), a lion beaten with a cudgel (defeat of Yuri Dolgoruky who had a lion in his coat-of-arms), and so on. One such picture is of particular interest: when in 1136 the Olgovichis of Chernigov started one of those gory conflicts about which people said: "Wherefore do we ruin ourselves?" the Kievan artist drew a symbolic picture of a warrior stabbing himself with a knife. This was like an epigraph to the story of the splitting up of Kievan Rus.

The Vladimir chronicle of 1206 was not only an example of a sumptuous state chronicle of one principality: it reflected several centuries of Russian artistic culture.

Architecture is an important indicator of culture. In towns, the majority of residential buildings, fortifications, palaces and even churches were made of wood. Archaeological excavations showed the variety of wooden structures and the existence in the 11th-13th centuries of three and four-storeyed buildings (dungeons and chamber palaces). Many wooden designs—towers, gabled roof—subsequently influenced stone architecture.

Ecclesiastical buildings were the quintessence of medieval architectural ideas both in the Christian West and in the Moslem Orient. This was also the case in Rus. The church building was intended both to strike the imagination of the believers and make the church the venue of theatricalised religious service; it was a school for learning the new religion and a long-lasting monument linking the builders with posterity.

Scholars have called the medieval cathedral a "chronicle" of the age; the architect organises the architectural form which must blend with the town landscape, while the interior must conform to the tasks of church service; the artists painted frescoes in several rows on all the walls and vaults; gold- and silver-smiths forged, cast and chased the censers and church utensils; artists painted icons; the embroiderers ornamented the curtains, and the scribes and miniature artists produced a library of needed books.

That is why each such church complex reflected the level of intelligence and craftsmanship in a town.

It was believed for a long time that the ancients built their edifices without any calculations and very roughly. The latest research has shown that architects of ancient Rus knew very well the proportions (the golden section, ratios of the $a:a\sqrt{2}$ and others) and also the Archimedes' formula $\pi = 66/22$. To make architectural calculations easier a complicated system of four kinds of *sazhen* (measure of length) was invented. Calculations were helped by "Babylonian" graphs containing a complicated system of mathematical relations. Each edifice was based on a mathematical system which determined the size of the bricks, thickness of the walls, radius of the arches, and, of course, the overall size of the building.

The single-cupola cube-shaped church building with smoothly rounded tops on each façade became the typical design in the 12th century. In view of the appearance of tall three- and four-storeyed houses in towns at the turn of the 13th century a new style of church architecture was born: the temples rose up higher in order not to be lost in the variety of town buildings.

The walls of churches were lavishly painted with frescoes depicting biblical and Evangelical subjects. In the cupola above the row of windows an enormous picture of Christ Pantocrator was invariably painted as if he were looking down upon the preying people in the church from the sky.

Russian artists attained great skill both in icon painting and in the frescoes. They had superb mastery of the composition and colour scheme and also were able to convey a complex range of human emotions. Soviet restorers have done extensive work to restore the original appearance of the ancient Russian painting, and at the present time the whole world admires works by Russian masters of the 11th-13th centuries.

The age of feudal disunity was a time of the flourishing of culture in general and architecture in particular in all the newly emerged sovereign principalities.

Many excellent edifices were built in the second

half of the 12th century and the early 13th century; the number of churches in the capital towns reached many dozens. Rus became an equal participant in creating a Europe-wide Romanesque style, elaborating its own local versions in each principality. A brilliant specimen of Russian-type Romanesque (Russian overall design and Romanesque details) is the whitestone Cathedral of St Demetrius in Vladimir built by Vsevolod the Big Nest at the end of the 12th century.

The abundant ornamentation in the St Demetrius Cathedral does not interfere with its harmonious wellbalanced proportions. No wonder this cathedral is often compared to *The Lay of Igor's Host*—in both works the ornamentation is integrally linked to the overall idea and does not overshadow it. In both works the viewer or the reader is struck by the monumental qualities, elegance, pithiness and depth.

The Tatar invasion interrupted the development of Russian architecture for some 60 years. The St George Cathedral in Yuryev-Polskoi completely covered with stone carving from the ground to the cupola was the swan song of white-stone architecture. It was built in 1236, but the stone carving was not completed; the next year Batu's hordes swept through the Suzdal land. The cathedral was destroyed. At the end of the 15th century, lover of books, chronicles and antiquity V. D. Yermolin restored the building out of the stone fragments and thereby preserved it for us.

Painting also achieved a high level in Rus. Artists painted icons and made frescoes on wet plaster in the churches, embellished theological books and chronicles with colour pictures (miniatures) and drew beautiful initials. There were many conventional medieval elements in the style of painting, but the art's impact upon viewers was great.

The applied arts of ancient Rus were very rich. Many workshops where gold- and silver-smiths produced masterpieces of jewelry have been found during excavation works in Kiev, Novgorod, Galich, Smolensk and other towns. Gold ornaments with unfading colour enamel, intricate works of silver with niello and gilt, elegant chasing and artistic embellishments on weapons—all this put Rus on an equal footing with the advanced countries of Europe. No wonder a German connoisseur of crafts Theophilus of Paderborn (11th century) in his *Schedula diversarum artium* put Rus in an honorary place among the countries distinguished in some craft, since its masters were known in foreign countries for their articles of gold with enamel and silver with niello.

During Batu's invasion the townsfolk hid their precious things in the ground. Even today these treasures are still being found during excavation works in Kiev and other towns, and on their basis experts restore the level of the applied arts of the 10th-13th centuries.

In the course of several centuries the culture of Rus developed and was enriched by new relations. By the end of the 11th century it attained the level of the advanced European countries and continued to progress all through the 12th century. The rise of feudal principalities in the first thirty years of the 12th century did not stop cultural development but even contributed to its further flourishing. All the most important and genuinely excellent monuments of art and literature were created in the age of feudal disunity when its negative aspects had not yet come to the fore to a full extent. The Tatar invasion interrupted this development and held it back for one and a half or two centuries.

On the eve of this calamity an anonymous author of the early 13th century wrote *The Lay of the Ruin of the Russian Land*, a work of superb form, where ruin refers not to total destruction but to the affliction of feudal strife. Having witnessed the bloody battle between the sons of Vsevolod the Big Nest in the course of which thousands died (contemporaries kept account of the casualties), the author recalls the flourishing of Kievan Rus under Monomakh and blames princes who were ruining a wonderful land. His brilliant lines about the native land are filled with profound and sincere patriotism:

O radiant light and ornately ornamented Russian land!
You are filled with exquisite beauty...
You are filled with all, O Russian land!

Chronological Table

Circa 15th century B.C.	Separation of the proto-Slav tribes from the Indo-European massif.
8th-3rd centuries B.C.	Scythians in the Black Sea area.
6th century B.C.	Founding of Greek colonies on the Black Sea (Olviopol, Panticapaeum and others).
6th-4th centuries B.C.	The formation of proto-Slav (Scoloti) tribal alliances (kingdoms) along the Middle Dnepr, in the eastern part of the Slav proto-homeland.
512 B.C.	War between the Scythian (and neighbouring) tribes and the Persian King Darius Hystaspes.
5th century B.C.	Herodotus travels to the Scythians and their neighbours. The beginning of a lively trade between the Middle Dnepr and Greece.
3rd century B.C.	Advance of the Sarmatian tribes to the Dnepr. Founding of Scythian Naples in the Crimea.
109 A.D.	The end of the conquest of Dacia by Rome. The setting up of the victory monument to the Emperor Trajan (Trajan's path in *The Lay of Igor's Host*). Resumption of trade relations between the Slavs and the Greco-Roman towns.
4th century A.D.	Invasion of Eastern Europe by the Huns.
375.	Wars between the Slavs and the Goths. Goths' retreat to the Balkans under Hun pressure.
5th century A.D.	Tribal alliance of Huns under Attila.
6th century.	Great migration of the Slavs. The Slavs (Ants and Slavins) advance to the Balkans. The appearance of the Avars in Eastern Europe. The first mention of the people Ros.
7th century.	Transcaucasia and Central Asia conquered by the Arabs. The founding of the Khazar kaganate.
737.	Expedition by Arab military leader Marwan against Khazaria.

Early 9th century.	The forming of the core of Kievan Rus.
9th century.	Invasion of the South Russian steppe by the Magyars and their advance beyond the Danube.
860.	First expedition by the Rus against Constantinople.
860s.	Adoption of Christianity by a part of the Rus.
Late 9th century.	Appearance of Scandinavian groups (Varangians) in Kievan Rus.
911.	Oleg's expedition against Constantinople.
915.	Pecheneg expedition against Rus.
920.	Igor's expedition against the Pechenegs.
921.	Ibn Fadlan travels to the Volga River.
945.	Igor's death.
945-969.	Olga's reign.
965.	Khazaria routed by Svyatoslav.
969-972.	Svyatoslav Igorevich rules in Kiev.
980-1015.	The reign of Vladimir Svyatoslavich.
988.	Adoption of Christianity by Rus.
1019-1054.	The reign of Yaroslav the Wise.
1015.	Uprising against the Varangians in Novgorod. *The Rules* of Yaroslav the Wise.
1015-1024.	Strife between the sons of Vladimir I.
1036.	Building of the Our Saviour Cathedral in Chernigov.
1037.	Building of the St Sophia Cathedral in Kiev.
1060s-1070s.	Peasant uprisings in the North of Rus.
1068.	Polovtsi attack Rus. Uprising in Kiev.
1078-1093.	Reign of Vsevolod Yaroslavich.
1095.	Defeat of Polovtsi Khan Tugortkan.
1103.	Dolob assembly of princes.
1111.	Expedition by Russian princes against the Polovtsi on the Donets.
Early 12th century.	Long Russkaya Pravda.
Circa 1113.	Nestor's chronicle.
1113.	Uprising in Kiev.
1113-1125.	Reign of Vladimir Monomakh in Kiev.
1125-1132.	Reign of Mstislav Vladimirovich in Kiev.

1136.	Uprising in Novgorod. The emergence of individual Russian principalities.
1146-1154.	Reign of Izyaslav Mstislavich in Kiev.
1147.	First mention of Moscow.
1152-1187.	Reign of Yaroslav Osmomysl in Galich.
1156-1174.	Reign of Andrei Bogolyubsky in Vladimir of Suzdal principality.
1157.	Death of Yuri Dolgoruky.
1170s-1180s.	New Polovtsi onslaught upon Rus.
1177-1212.	Reign of Vsevolod the Big Nest.
1180-1194.	Reign of Svyatoslav Vsevolodich in Kiev.
1183.	Joint expedition by Russian princes against Khan Kobyak.
1185.	Expediton by Igor Svyatoslavich against the Polovtsi, expedition by Konchak and Gzak against Rus.
1185.	The writing of *The Lay of Igor's Host*
1209.	Uprising in Novgorod.
1216.	Battle of Lipitsk.
1219-1221.	Conquest of Central Asia by the Tatar-Mongols.
1223.	Battle of the Russians against the Tatar-Mongols on the Kalka River.
1237-1241.	Batu's invasion of Rus.

PROGRESS PUBLISHERS

Will soon publish

NEMIROVSKY, A. *Tales of the Ancient World*

Anyone interested in the history of antiquity will find entertaining things in this book of stories from the history of the Ancient Orient, Greece, and Rome. The author's aim is to take readers back into the ancient world and make them witnesses of the events of remote times.

PROGRESS PUBLISHERS

Will soon publish

Modern History (1640-1870)

This is a study aid for college students on the main events in the history of the countries of Europe and Latin America, and the USA from 1640 to 1870.

PROGRESS PUBLISHERS

Will soon publish

GUMILEV, L. *Ethnogenesis and the Biosphere*

Glasnost made this book available. The author, a geographer and historian, is the son of the Russian poets Nikolai Gumilev and Anna Akhmatova. In the 30s he was repressed for the "sins" of his late father, in the 50s for those of his mother. After rehabilitation he worked in Leningrad University.

The book offered here is his *magnum opus* on the way a country's environment moulds and affects its national character. It, too, has had its vicissitude. It was completed in 1975 but was not printed. In 1978, however, the university authorities ordered one copy to be printed which was deposited with the Institute of Scientific Information. Demand for the work was such that a thousand copies were made from this original one. Now perestroika has rescued it for the general reader in the Soviet Union and the English-speaking world.

PROGRESS PUBLISHERS

Will soon publish

Tales from the Middle Ages

This Reader for students and teachers contains stories about the life and history of countries in Western, Central, and Eastern Europe, and partly the Orient, in the millennium of the Middle Ages (5th to 15th century), the time when most of the modern states of Europe and Asia arose. It was a period of important inventions, and the beginning of printing and of great works of literature and art, of the European discovery of America and the first round-the-world voyages.

The stories in this Reader will help teachers and students to broaden their ideas about the mediaeval world.

REQUEST TO READERS

Progress Publishers would be glad to have your opinion of this book, its translation and design and any suggestions you may have for future publications.

Please send all your comments to 17, Zubovsky Boulevard, Moscow, USSR.